AF777442

Emerging Distributed/Parallel Computing Systems

Emerging Distributed/Parallel Computing Systems

Guest Editors

Yawen Chen
Fei (Travis) Dai

MDPI

Basel • Beijing • Wuhan • Barcelona • Belgrade • Novi Sad • Cluj • Manchester

Guest Editors

Yawen Chen
School of Systems and Computing
University of New South Wales
Canberra
Australia

Fei (Travis) Dai
School of Computing
Eastern Institute of Technology
Napier
New Zealand

Editorial Office
MDPI AG
Grosspeteranlage 5
4052 Basel, Switzerland

This is a reprint of the Special Issue, published open access by the journal *Electronics* (ISSN 2079-9292), freely accessible at: https://www.mdpi.com/journal/electronics/special_issues/Distributed_Parallel_Computing.

For citation purposes, cite each article independently as indicated on the article page online and as indicated below:

Lastname, A.A.; Lastname, B.B. Article Title. *Journal Name* **Year**, *Volume Number*, Page Range.

ISBN 978-3-7258-6858-2 (Hbk)
ISBN 978-3-7258-6859-9 (PDF)
https://doi.org/10.3390/books978-3-7258-6859-9

© 2026 by the authors. Articles in this reprint are Open Access and distributed under the Creative Commons Attribution (CC BY) license. The reprint as a whole is distributed by MDPI under the terms and conditions of the Creative Commons Attribution-NonCommercial-NoDerivs (CC BY-NC-ND) license (https://creativecommons.org/licenses/by-nc-nd/4.0/).

Contents

About the Editors . . . . **vii**

Preface . . . . **ix**

Yawen Chen and Fei Dai
Emerging Distributed/Parallel Computing Systems
Reprinted from: *Electronics* **2026**, *15*, 438, https://doi.org/10.3390/electronics15020438 . . . . . . **1**

Chunle Fu, Bailing Wang and Wei Wang
Software-Defined Wide Area Networks (SD-WANs): A Survey
Reprinted from: *Electronics* **2024**, *13*, 3011, https://doi.org/10.3390/electronics13153011 . . . . . **4**

Guoheng Wei, Yanlin Qin, Guangyue Kou and Zhihong Sun
Lightweight Certificate-Less Anonymous Authentication Key Negotiation Scheme in the 5G Internet of Vehicles
Reprinted from: *Electronics* **2024**, *13*, 3288, https://doi.org/10.3390/electronics13163288 . . . . . **16**

Jiuxing Zhou, Wei Fu, Wei Hu, Zhihong Sun, Tao He and Zhihong Zhang
Challenges and Advances in Analyzing TLS 1.3-Encrypted Traffic: A Comprehensive Survey
Reprinted from: *Electronics* **2024**, *13*, 4000, https://doi.org/10.3390/electronics13204000 . . . . . **36**

Jongwook Kim
DistOD: A Hybrid Privacy-Preserving and Distributed Framework for Origin–Destination Matrix Computation
Reprinted from: *Electronics* **2024**, *13*, 4545, https://doi.org/10.3390/electronics13224545 . . . . . **67**

Gaopeng Wang, Jingyi Ding and Fanlin Hu
Deep Reinforcement Learning Recommendation System Algorithm Based on Multi-Level Attention Mechanisms
Reprinted from: *Electronics* **2024**, *13*, 4625, https://doi.org/10.3390/electronics13234625 . . . . . **88**

Jiaqing Mo, Zhihua Zhang and Yuhua Lin
A Practically Secure Two-Factor and Mutual Authentication Protocol for Distributed Wireless Sensor Networks Using PUF
Reprinted from: *Electronics* **2025**, *14*, 10, https://doi.org/10.3390/electronics14010010 . . . . . . **108**

Fei Dai, Md Akbar Hossain and Yi Wang
State of the Art in Parallel and Distributed Systems: Emerging Trends and Challenges
Reprinted from: *Electronics* **2025**, *14*, 677, https://doi.org/10.3390/electronics14040677 . . . . . . **129**

Linlin Ma, Haomin Li, Wenke Zang, Xincheng Liu and Minghe Sun
Tensor-Based Uniform and Discrete Multi-View Projection Clustering
Reprinted from: *Electronics* **2025**, *14*, 817, https://doi.org/10.3390/electronics14040817 . . . . . . **168**

About the Editors

Yawen Chen

Yawen Chen works at the School of Systems and Computing, UNSW Canberra, University of New South Wales, Australia. Her research interests include computer networks and systems, parallel and distributed computing, artificial intelligence acceleration, and photonic computing and communication, with additional interests in wired and wireless networking and graph theory. Her work advances scalable and efficient system and network design, spanning topics such as optical networks on chip interconnects, resource optimisation, and energy-aware computing. She served as a Guest Editor of the Special Issue "Emerging Distributed and Parallel Computing Systems", which is republished in this Reprint.

Fei (Travis) Dai

Fei (Travis) Dai works at the School of Computing, Eastern Institute of Technology, Napier, New Zealand. His research focuses on optical interconnect systems, parallel and distributed training for deep neural networks, optical deep learning accelerators, communication optimisation, embedded systems, and the Internet of Things. He contributed to this Special Issue through a review on emerging trends and challenges in parallel and distributed systems, and serves as a Guest Editor of the Special Issue "Emerging Distributed and Parallel Computing Systems", which is republished in this Reprint.

Preface

This Reprint brings together eight published papers from the Special Issue "Emerging Distributed and Parallel Computing Systems". Our motivation for producing this Reprint was simple: progress in modern computing is increasingly driven by systems that must scale across nodes, protect data in motion, and support intelligent, data driven workloads under tight efficiency constraints. The selected contributions reflect this reality across a range of complementary perspectives.

Several papers focus on trust and privacy for distributed environments, including authentication and key agreement for wireless sensor networks and for the 5G Internet of Vehicles, as well as a hybrid privacy-preserving distributed framework for origin–destination matrix computation. Other contributions highlight the growing role of machine learning methods and data representation, including deep reinforcement learning-based recommendation and tensor-based multi-view projection clustering. Three review articles consolidate current knowledge and point to open research directions, covering trends in parallel and distributed systems, analysis of TLS 1.3-encrypted traffic, and software-defined wide-area networks.

This Reprint is intended for researchers, practitioners, and postgraduate students who want a concise snapshot of current methods, challenges, and research opportunities in distributed and parallel computing.

Yawen Chen and Fei (Travis) Dai
Guest Editors

electronics

MDPI

Editorial

Emerging Distributed/Parallel Computing Systems

Yawen Chen [1,*] and Fei Dai [2,*]

[1] School of Systems and Computing, University of New South Wales, Canberra, ACT 2600, Australia
[2] School of Computing, Eastern Institute of Technology, Napier 4112, New Zealand
* Correspondence: wendy.chen1@unsw.edu.au (Y.C.); tdai@eit.ac.nz (F.D.)

1. Introduction

Computing continues to evolve rapidly, driven by data-intensive applications, AI workloads, and increasingly heterogeneous, interconnected infrastructures. Distributed and parallel computing systems are foundational to this evolution, enabling scalable performance, resilience, and efficient resource utilization across cloud, edge, and cyber–physical deployments. This Special Issue, titled "Emerging Distributed/Parallel Computing Systems", will highlight cutting-edge advances, emerging trends, and key challenges spanning architectures, algorithms, systems, and applications in distributed and parallel computing.

The Special Issue is now closed (deadline: 15 November 2025) and includes eight peer-reviewed papers—five research articles and three review papers—covering surveys of timely subfields, as well as research contributions to security, privacy, and learning-enabled data processing.

2. Overview of Published Contributions

A helpful way to understand the collection is through dividing its papers into four themes.

Theme A—Foundations and surveys: trends, programmability, and encrypted visibility

"State of the Art in Parallel and Distributed Systems: Emerging Trends and Challenges" surveys key trends across parallel computing and modern distributed paradigms, and it clarifies how the two areas are related. It also summarizes open challenges and future opportunities, providing a concise roadmap for researchers and practitioners. Two additional surveys provide deep dives into important enabling layers of modern distributed systems. The survey on Transport Layer Security (TLS) 1.3 encrypted traffic analysis [1] reviews how new protocol features change what can (and cannot) be inferred from encrypted traffic and organizes state-of-the-art techniques and limitations. The software-defined wide area network (SD-WAN) survey [2] synthesizes architectures and research directions, including traffic engineering, orchestration, and security considerations in programmable wide-area networking.

Theme B—Lightweight security and authentication in distributed environments

Two papers address authentication and key agreement in settings characterized by openness, mobility, and constrained endpoints. One proposes a practical two-factor mutual authentication protocol for distributed wireless sensor networks using physical unclonable functions (PUFs), strengthening resistance to impersonation and node capture while supporting efficient session key negotiation. Another introduces a lightweight certificateless anonymous authentication and key negotiation scheme for the 5G Internet of Vehicles, targeting the security–latency requirements of high-mobility vehicular scenarios.

 https://doi.org/10.3390/electronics15020438

Theme C—Privacy-preserving distributed computation

DistOD presents a hybrid privacy-preserving distributed framework for origin–destination matrix computation, reflecting the growing need for distributed analytics tools that protect sensitive information while still supporting practical deployment and scalability.

Theme D—Learning-enabled methods for modern data processing pipelines

Two papers explore learning-driven approaches relevant to scalable decision-making and analytics workflows. One proposes a deep reinforcement learning recommendation approach based on multi-level attention mechanisms. The other presents a tensor-based method for uniform and discrete multi-view projection clustering, contributing to efficient optimization under multi-view settings.

3. Research Outlook

Across these contributions, two issues stand out. First, trustworthiness, including authentication, privacy, and operating under encrypted visibility, is increasingly central to distributed/parallel system design. Second, intelligence as an optimization tool (e.g., learning-based methods) is becoming more common across system and data pipeline contexts.

Motivated by the topics represented in this Special Issue, promising future directions include the following:

- Security and privacy by design for distributed endpoints (sensors, vehicles, Internet of Things), supported by strong threat models and practical efficiency constraints;
- Measurement and control under encryption, balancing operational needs with privacy expectations;
- Programmable wide-area infrastructures and orchestration mechanisms that enforce performance and security policies end-to-end;
- Scalable privacy-preserving analytics, especially for mobility, smart cities, and cross-organization data collaboration;
- Bridging systems and machine learning (ML), including federated and distributed learning, with methods that are reproducible, interpretable, and deployment-ready [3].

4. Conclusions

This Special Issue brings together eight papers that reflect the continued evolution of distributed and parallel computing systems to become more secure, more privacy-aware, and increasingly data- and learning-driven. We hope that this collection serves as a useful reference for the community and helps to shape future research and developments in emerging distributed/parallel computing systems.

Acknowledgments: We thank all authors for their valuable contributions and all reviewers for their time and constructive feedback. We also thank the *Electronics* Editorial Office for their professional support throughout the Special Issue process.

Conflicts of Interest: The authors declare no conflicts of interest.

List of Contributions:

1. Fu, C.; Wang, B.; Wang, W. Software-Defined Wide Area Networks (SD-WANs): A Survey. *Electronics* **2024**, *13*, 3011. https://doi.org/10.3390/electronics13153011.
2. Wei, G.; Qin, Y.; Kou, G.; Sun, Z. Lightweight Certificate-Less Anonymous Authentication Key Negotiation Scheme in the 5G Internet of Vehicles. *Electronics* **2024**, *13*, 3288. https://doi.org/10.3390/electronics13163288.

3. Zhou, J.; Fu, W.; Hu, W.; Sun, Z.; He, T.; Zhang, Z. Challenges and Advances in Analyzing TLS 1.3-Encrypted Traffic: A Comprehensive Survey. *Electronics* **2024**, *13*, 4000. https://doi.org/10.3390/electronics13204000.
4. Kim, J. DistOD: A Hybrid Privacy-Preserving and Distributed Framework for Origin–Destination Matrix Computation. *Electronics* **2024**, *13*, 4545. https://doi.org/10.3390/electronics13224545.
5. Wang, G.; Ding, J.; Hu, F. Deep Reinforcement Learning Recommendation System Algorithm Based on Multi-Level Attention Mechanisms. *Electronics* **2024**, *13*, 4625. https://doi.org/10.3390/electronics13234625.
6. Mo, J.; Zhang, Z.; Lin, Y. A Practically Secure Two-Factor and Mutual Authentication Protocol for Distributed Wireless Sensor Networks Using PUF. *Electronics* **2025**, *14*, 10. https://doi.org/10.3390/electronics14010010.
7. Dai, F.; Hossain, M.; Wang, Y. State of the Art in Parallel and Distributed Systems: Emerging Trends and Challenges. *Electronics* **2025**, *14*, 677. https://doi.org/10.3390/electronics14040677.
8. Ma, L.; Li, H.; Zang, W.; Liu, X.; Sun, M. Tensor-Based Uniform and Discrete Multi-View Projection Clustering. *Electronics* **2025**, *14*, 817. https://doi.org/10.3390/electronics14040817.

References

1. Rescorla, E. *The Transport Layer Security (TLS) Protocol Version 1.3*; Internet Engineering Task Force: Fremont, CA, USA, 2018. [CrossRef]
2. Ouamri, M.A.; Alharbi, T.E.A.; Singh, D.; Zenadji, S. A comprehensive survey on software-defined wide area network (SD-WAN): Principles, opportunities and future challenges. *J. Supercomput.* **2025**, *81*, 291. [CrossRef]
3. Li, T.; Sahu, A.K.; Talwalkar, A.; Smith, V. Federated learning: Challenges, methods, and future directions. *IEEE Signal Process. Mag.* **2020**, *37*, 50–60. [CrossRef]

Disclaimer/Publisher's Note: The statements, opinions and data contained in all publications are solely those of the individual author(s) and contributor(s) and not of MDPI and/or the editor(s). MDPI and/or the editor(s) disclaim responsibility for any injury to people or property resulting from any ideas, methods, instructions or products referred to in the content.

electronics

MDPI

Review

Software-Defined Wide Area Networks (SD-WANs): A Survey

Chunle Fu, Bailing Wang * and Wei Wang

School of Computer Science and Technology, Harbin Institute of Technology, Weihai 264200, China; 16b903044@stu.hit.edu.cn (C.F.); wwhit@hit.edu.cn (W.W.)
* Correspondence: wbl@hit.edu.cn

Abstract: SD-WANs are an innovative software-defined network (SDN) technology used to reinvent networks, services, and applications in wide area network (WANs). The development of SD-WANs ranges from network optimization in the past to service provision platforms at present and distributed computing systems in the future. The existing surveys on SD-WANs are fragmented, covering specific problems only, and are not comprehensive with detailed research directions. This paper seeks to provide a systematic survey on SD-WANs by introducing major research directions and stating specific problems. Therefore, four major research directions related to traffic engineering, network optimization and systems, service orchestration, and the security issues of SD-WANs are sequentially introduced, along with detailed statements relating to specific problems and the classification of state-of-the-art research. Finally, the trends and challenges regarding SD-WANs are summarized and our future work is described.

Keywords: SD-WAN; SDN; traffic engineering; network optimization and systems; service orchestration; security issues

1. Introduction

SD-WANs were first proposed in Google's B4 data centers to achieve high utilization, load balancing, and elastic computing of valuable interconnected links between geographically distributed clouds [1]. Over the last decade, SD-WANs have always been recognized as an innovative SDN technology that can be used to reinvent networks, services, and applications in WANs, ranging from remodeling the architecture of internet service provider (ISP) [2] to facilitating the ubiquitous connectivity of smart cities [3], enabling the heterogeneous interconnection in fog computing [4], and establishing the Internet of Everything in Internet of Things (IoT) [5].

The development of SD-WANs can be divided into three stages, namely SD-WAN 1.0, SD-WAN 2.0, and SD-WAN 3.0, representing the past, present, and future of SD-WAN, respectively. SD-WAN 1.0 provided low-cost deployment, high-efficiency management, and a high utilization bandwidth of network optimization, while SD-WAN 2.0 has evolved into an abundant service provision platform, providing services such as network interconnection, secure remote access, quality of service (QoS) strategies, cybersecurity policies, and other advanced on-demand services. SD-WAN 3.0 is considered as a promising distributed computing system combined with cutting-edge technologies of artificial intelligence, fog computing, edge computing, network security, and IoT.

To further investigate research directions related to SD-WANs, seven surveys on SD-WANs [6–12] can be found, although six of them are conference papers or short papers. The other study [6], presented a review on a specific control failure problem in SD-WANs, and does not comprehensively cover the vast majority of SD-WAN research directions. Therefore, this paper seeks to provide a systematic survey on SD-WANs by introducing major research directions, specific problems, and the classification of state-of-the-art research.

This paper reviews 79 studies on SD-WANs, and then provides a systematic and comprehensive survey by revisiting 7 existing surveys, introducing 4 research directions and classifying the state-of-the-art research according to specific research problems. As shown in Figure 1, the structure and content of this survey can be divided into five parts: surveys, traffic engineering, network optimization and systems, service orchestration, and the security issues of SD-WANs.

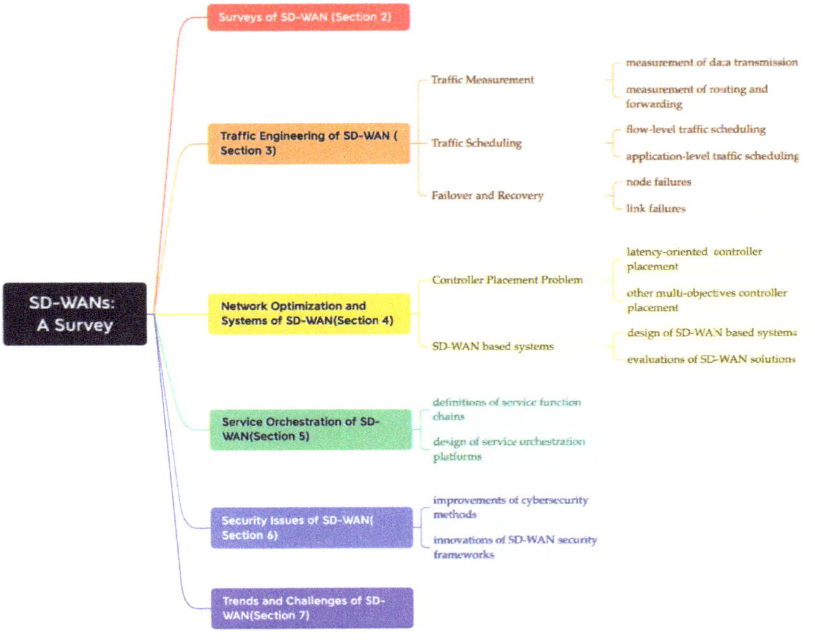

Figure 1. Structure and content of this survey.

The rest of this paper is organized as follows. Section 2 provides the related work. Section 3 to Section 6 introduce traffic engineering, network optimization and systems, service orchestration, and the security issues of SD-WANs, respectively. Section 7 discusses the trends and challenges relating to SD-WANs. Section 8 concludes this paper.

2. Related Work

Seven surveys on SD-WANs can be found, although six of them are conference papers or short papers. Dou and Guo [6] presented a review of a specific control failure problem by stating its impacts on path programmability and network performance, classifying solutions of state-of-the-art network recovery under controller failures, evaluating limitations of the existing technologies, and pointing out future challenges and potential directions. Yalda et al. [7] reviewed SD-WANs from both physical and logical perspectives to clarify differences and provided a comparison and classification of existing technologies, ranging from definitions, fundamentals, capabilities, and advantages to architectures of the state-of-the-art SD-WANs. Rose Varuna and Vadivel [8] conducted a survey to discuss characteristics of SD-WANs in orchestration and automation, the capabilities of self-learning and failover, the applications for end-to-end secure communication and cloud environments, and solutions for network attacks and security issues. Ujan et al. [9] reviewed the latency-oriented controller placement problem for SD-WANs to prove that other functional objectives should be complemented for multi-objective optimization so that the placement of the controller can achieve a well-rounded outcome for various scenarios. Rajagopalan [10] carried out a brief overview for SD-WANs and solutions of load balancing through SD-WANs. Yang et al. [11] revisited the status and challenges of legacy WANs, then introduced the architecture of an SD-WAN and its representative advances, finally an SD-WAN-based multi-objective network and its applications were mentioned. Michel and Keller [12] provided an overview of SDNs in WANs, focusing on the evolution of SDNs, along with research and future directions relating to SD-WANs.

To summarize, the existing surveys on SD-WANs are fragmented, covering specific problems only, and are not comprehensive with detailed research directions. This paper seeks to provide a systematic survey on SD-WANs by introducing major research directions and stating specific problems.

3. Traffic Engineering of SD-WAN

The traffic engineering of SD-WANs was first mentioned in [1,13] for network deployment, traffic management, and edge controllability of interconnected data centers to achieve the high utilization and elastic provision of cloud-based services. As SD-WANs are gradually applied in the interconnection of enterprise branches, fog computing, edge computing and IoT, subsequent research was conducted on traffic measurement [14–20], traffic scheduling [1,13,21–32], and failover and recovery [33–43], as classified in Table 1.

Table 1. Research contents, specific problems, and work related to SD-WAN traffic engineering.

Research Contents	Specific Problems	Related Work
Traffic measurement	Measurement of data transmission	[14–17]
	Measurement of routing and forwarding	[18–20]
Traffic scheduling	Flow-level traffic scheduling	[1,13,21–26]
	Application-level traffic scheduling	[27–32]
Failover and recovery	Node failures and recovery	[33–37]
	Link failures and recovery	[38–43]

3.1. Traffic Measurement

Research on traffic measurement is mainly based on testbeds or commercial platforms to evaluate the performance of data transmission [14–17] and routing and forwarding [18–20] in the SD-WAN data plane. Details of the research on traffic measurement are shown in Table 2.

Table 2. Details of the research on traffic measurement.

Paper	Measurement Objects	Measurement Tools	Measurement Environment	
			Testbeds	Real Network
[14]	Overlay	Open source tools	√	
[15]	Overlay	Open source tools	√	
[16]	Overlay	Commercial platform		√
[17]	Overlay	Commercial platform	√	√
[18]	Overlay	Open source tools	√	
[19]	Overlay	Open source tools	√	
[20]	Underlay/overlay	Open source tools	√	

In relation to the measurement of data transmission, Scarpitta et al. [14] realized a high-performance user-space solution to monitor transmission delay for segment routing with IPv6(SRv6)-based SD-WAN services and integrated and evaluated this solution in an open source SD-WAN prototype called EveryWAN. Iddalagi and Mishra [15] analyzed the impacts of a bidirectional forwarding detection (BFD) protocol on the performance of data transmission, established an SD-WAN testbed based on open source tools, and proved that BFD traffic introduces additional delay and jittering and forms an overhead in the uplink streams, affecting mainstream traffic as well. Manova et al. [16] carried out a case study on an active WAN of an Indonesian company, which has three connections, namely an SD-WAN, traditional Multiprotocol Label Switching (MPLS), and an Ethernet over Internet Protocol (EoIP), respectively. Performance tests relating to QoS and data transmission on

SD-WAN systems were conducted to measure network delay and the change in delay in different time periods. Troia et al. [17] built two SD-WAN testbeds with the open source software ONOS for a municipal network of Italian cities and simulation platforms in their laboratory. Then, a ONOS-based traffic measurement plugin was developed and the open source tool eBPF was used to monitor real-time network traffic. Finally, the SD-WAN was proved to be capable of network recovery and service failover.

Regarding the measurement of routing and forwarding, Emmanuel et al. [18] built an SD-WAN testbed with the open source project GNS3 to capture real-time data packets for traffic classification so that the results of classification were further utilized as guidelines for controllers to improve network performance and resource utilization. Fares et al. [19] studied the routing optimization problem in SD-WAN autonomous network systems and built an SD-WAN experimental platform based on open source projects including ONOS, Mininet, and Quagga for obtaining the statistics of network traffic, the construction of SD-WAN topologies, and the selection of routing algorithms. The experimental results showed that the increase in topology complexity and node size leads to poor routing performance. Zhao et al. [20] provided an accurate queueing system of packet forwarding in an SD-WAN and measured the average packet delay through an OpenFlow switch to achieve an optimization model of controller cluster deployments in WANs.

3.2. Traffic Scheduling

Considering the granularity of traffic scheduling, related work can be divided into flow-level traffic scheduling [21–26] and application-level traffic scheduling [27–32]. Detailed optimization objectives of the research on traffic scheduling are shown in Table 3.

Table 3. Detailed optimization objectives of the research on traffic scheduling.

Paper	Optimization Objectives							
	Latency	Bandwidth	Utilization Rate	Load Balancing	Resilience	System Overhead	Network Overhead	Time Overhead
[1]		√	√	√	√	√	√	
[13]		√	√		√	√	√	
[21]				√		√	√	
[22]		√	√				√	
[23]	√				√	√		
[24]	√	√		√				
[25]	√				√			
[26]	√							√
[27]	√					√	√	
[28]	√						√	
[29]	√				√	√	√	
[30]		√	√	√				
[31]	√			√				
[32]	√					√		√

In terms of flow-level traffic scheduling, Guo et al. [21] proposed a threshold-based critical flow routing method to maintain SD-WAN load balancing with less controller synchronization. Ma et al. [22] proposed a distributed storage mechanism of two-dimensional routing in combination with SRv6 and a corresponding SRv6 header compression method to realize the lightweight deployment of SD-WAN multipath routing. Borgianni et al. [23] explored using reinforcement learning algorithms to predict network performance degradation and to change routing information proactively for improving SD-WANs' overall network performance. Xin and Wang [24] presented a load balancing method by partitioning traffic demands into multiple groups within a scalable SD-WAN framework and defined a link-based optimization formulation under constraints of both bandwidth and latency. Ouamri et al. [25] formulated a QoS-oriented problem of joint optimization for SD-WAN average request delay and survivability, and then proposed a multi-agent deep

Q-Network algorithm to redefine its reward function with the optimization objectives. Ghaderi et al. [26] redefined a neural network-based traffic encoding matrix and designed a deep-reinforcement-learning-based traffic engineering framework for SD-WANs.

In terms of application-level traffic scheduling, Fan et al. [27] proposed a relay node selection and routing approach to minimize the number of relay nodes under transmission latency constraints in a cloud-native SD-WAN and solved this combinatorial optimization problem based on constraint programming. Botta et al. [28,29] proposed a control and orchestration plane for SD-WANs based on a cooperative version of multi-agent reinforcement learning for dynamic overlay selection and accommodating diverse network policies with varying QoS and cost objectives. Quang et al. [30] proposed a global QoS policy optimization model to dynamically adjust the rate limits of applications based on their requirements according to the evolution of network conditions. Ouamri et al. [31] studied component migration to balance load between headquarters and branch sites by proposing an MPLS-based SD-WAN and formulating a non-linear binary program to jointly optimize load balancing and running costs. Du et al. [32] proposed a federated learning method to minimize the total time of routing and forwarding through well-designed client selection and scheduling in an SD-WAN, which significantly reduced the upload time of each iteration, with slight impacts on the number of iterations.

3.3. Failover and Recovery

Network failures in SD-WANs can be classified as node failures and link failures, with the corresponding studies being [33–37] and [38–43], respectively. Details of the research on failover and recovery are shown in Table 4.

Table 4. Details of the research on failover and recovery.

Paper	Optimization Objective	Method	Algorithm	Evaluation
[33,34]	Robustness and availability	Switch-controller mapping	/	Simulation
[35–37]	Programmability recovery	Flow-controller mapping	Heuristic	Simulation
[38]	Time overhead	Protocol optimization	/	Simulation
[39,40]	Availability and resilience	/	/	Testbed
[41]	Throughput and resilience	Protocol optimization	/	Simulation
[42]	System and network overhead	Multi-objective optimization	Heuristic	Testbed
[43]	QoS and time overhead	Routing optimization	Reinforcement learning	Testbed

To solve the controller failure problem in SD-WANs, Altheide et al. [33,34] proposed a fully distributed SD-WAN control plane and achieved a highly robust traffic engineering solution to implement fine-grained global policies while remaining responsive even in the event of device failures, network failures, or network partitioning. Guo et al. [35] proposed a switch-level programmability recovery scheme based on high-end commercial SDN switches. A mixed-integer programming of joint-flow-mode selection and switch mapping problem was defined and solved with an efficient heuristic algorithm, representing an improved method based on their previous research [36,37].

Botta et al. [38] studied the effectiveness of the BFD protocol to monitor SD-WAN links for rapid failure detection and seamless failover, and then proposed an automatic tuning mechanism for the parameters of the BFD protocol to enhance the accuracy of detection and reduce the time of failover across diverse WAN types. Troia et al. [39,40] established two SD-WAN testbeds in a municipal network and a campus network, respectively, to prove the ability of SD-WANs to guarantee service availability and resilience in cases of network failure. Zhang et al. [41] presented a WAN-aware MPTCP to aggregate multiple WAN links into a virtualized large pipe for better resilience, thus minimizing application performance degradation under WAN link failures. Shojaee et al. [42] formulated the SD-WAN failure recovery problem as a multi-objective MILP optimization problem for all possible single-link failures and designed a software-defined proactive recovery mechanism to improve bandwidth allocation and switch-memory usage. Golani et al. [43] proposed a fault-tolerant reactive routing system for SD-WANs to monitor various network parameters in real time and to recover failure links if necessary.

4. Network Optimization and Systems of SD-WAN

Research on the network optimization and systems of SD-WANs mainly includes the controller placement problem [44–51] and SD-WAN-based systems [52–61], which are introduced in Sections 4.1 and 4.2, respectively.

4.1. Controller Placement Problem

The controller placement problem was first proposed in [62] to determine the number of controllers and their locations in an SDN topology. The placement of controllers directly determines the overall network performance of software-defined networking architectures, especially for SDNs in WANs. Therefore, related controller placement in SD-WANs can be classified by optimization objectives.

The vast majority of related work focuses on the optimization of control latency. Dou et al. [44] defined a controller placement with a switch-controller mapping solution and developed a programmability explorer by calculating the programmability of critical flows at switches to optimize the control latency of SD-WANs. Adebayo et al. [45] addressed a switch-to-controller allocation problem that considered switch-to-controller latency and heterogeneity of controller capacities and proposed two neighborhood centrality-based algorithms to implement ideal allocation and placement. Qi et al. [46] optimized SD-WAN control latency by rationally placing controllers, establishing switch-controller mapping and developing a heuristic algorithm to achieve the trade-off between network performance and time complexity. Adekoya and Aneiba [47] applied and improved an evolutionary algorithm called Non-Dominated Sorting Genetic Algorithm III of Mechanical Engineering to achieve high convergence and the diversification of controller placement. Chakraborty et al. [48] designed a distributed scheme on coalition formation game and social choice theory which is able to optimally place controllers and periodically assess the placement of controllers based on real-time network traffic. Sminesh et al. [49] proposed a modified-density peak clustering algorithm to determine multi-controller placement and proved its effectiveness by comparing it to the hierarchical k-means, modified affinity propagation, and basic DP clustering algorithms in selected networks from the Internet Topology Zoo.

Other complementary optimization objectives of the controller placement problem in SD-WANs include the capacity of controllers [45,50], the failure of nodes [51], and the transmission latency of the data plane [27].

4.2. SD-WAN Based Systems

Research on SD-WAN-based systems can be divided into the design of SD-WAN-based systems [52–56] and evaluations of SD-WAN solutions [57–61].

In terms of the design of SD-WAN-based systems, Menoni et al. [52] proposed an SD-WAN embedded white-label solution with low cost and low energy consumption which is suitable for commercial and academic use. Borgianni et al. [53] proposed an innovative architecture by integrating an SD-WAN and Satellite 6G to support applications in remote areas or in high-latency environments. Elizabeth et al. [54] established a dynamic multipoint VPN solution for SD-WANs by applying open source protocols, namely multipoint generic routing encapsulation, IPsec (Internet Protocol Security) encryption, and the next hop resolution protocol. Ushakov et al. [55] proposed an SD-WAN-based solution for the Internet of Vehicles by integrating an SD-WAN API controller with the edge points of overlay networks and solving the problem of bandwidth overload of overlay networks with encrypted traffic. Scarpitta et al. [56] introduced SD-WAN scenarios, illustrated the principles of SDNs and NFV, and designed an open source implementation called EveryWAN.

In terms of the evaluation of SD-WAN solutions, Tiana et al. [57] tested an SD-WAN platform of a telecommunications company in Indonesia and proved that the SD-WAN offers significant improvements over traditional WANs, including increased network efficiency, better management and control, flexibility in deployment and scalability, increased security, and lower operating costs. Troia et al. [58] presented the performance evaluation results measured in an SD-WAN testbed deployed in the municipal network to prove the capabilities of service availability and network protection of an SD-WAN. Hussain et al. [59] presented their case studies on Google's deployment of SD-WANs in data center networks and TMNA's deployment of SD-WANs and provided suggestions and best practices for deploying and managing SD-WANs. Soejantono et al. [60] carried out failover and recovery tests on an IPsec-based SD-WAN instance deployed in Indonesia and obtained results indicating that an SD-WAN works appropriately when one of the multiple links is down. Hong et al. [61] presented the five-year evolution of B4, Google's private software-defined WAN from the perspectives of hierarchical network topologies, traffic engineering, and solutions to network failures.

5. Service Orchestration of SD-WAN

Research on SD-WAN service orchestration mainly focuses on service function chaining (SFC) [63–65] and service orchestration platforms [28,66–68].

Regarding research on SFC, Jiang et al. [63] formulated an SFC problem considering the heterogeneity of geographically distributed SD-WANs and designed heuristic algorithms to deploy SFC requests in batches. Leivadeas et al. [64] established collaboration and information exchange between enterprise branches and networks by configuring security, data privacy, and routing services of Amazon SD-WAN services, examining and evaluating the overall performance. Zhang et al. [65] proposed a service offloading method for jointly allocating communication and computation resources based on cloud-edge collaboration in SD-WANs.

Regarding research on service orchestration platforms, Botta et al. [28] designed an SD-WAN control and orchestration plane for network policy orchestration in order to implement dynamic overlay selection and to guarantee on-demand network performance. Perez et al. [66] set up a flexible, resilient and cloud-native SD-WAN orchestration solution for enterprise and academic networks purely based on open source tools. Kone and Kora [67] put forward a practical approach for management and orchestration based on open source platforms and evaluated their proposed testbed by orchestrating services of the Voice over Internet Protocol. Balachandran et al. [68] proposed a blockchain-based orchestration framework to allow the SDN clients and vendors to create, manage, and execute services through an auditable and zero-trust based solution.

6. Security Issues of SD-WAN

Research on security issues includes improvements to cybersecurity methods for SD-WANs [69–73] and innovations relating to SD-WAN security frameworks [68,74–77].

In terms of improvements to cybersecurity methods for SD-WANs, Ergawy et al. [69] introduced a game-based theoretic approach to model potential attack scenarios and to drive a proactive moving target defense method to prevent the potential exploitation of SD-WANs. Zhang et al. [70] proposed a machine learning-based anomalous traffic detection framework to extract representative features directly from the raw traffic and to make real-time adjustments based on an evolving isolation forest in complex environments. Lembke et al. [71] proposed a secure network update protocol for SD-WANs to preserve security by authenticating network events, to provide reliability by replicating the control plane, and to maintain resilience by using a distributed ledger for failure detection. Satheesh et al. [72] applied a machine learning framework to detect Distributed Denial of Service (DDoS) attacks in SD-WAN environments and improved the random forest algorithm to obtain better performance in traffic classification. Fan et al. [73] built blockchain-coordinating controllers (BCCs) to secure the control channel of SD-WANs formed by the distributed controllers spread across multiple domains, providing resilience against security threats in the control plane and guaranteeing secure control communications, even when the credentials of n controllers are compromised.

In terms of innovations relating to SD-WAN security frameworks, Yiliyaer and Kim [74] studied a secure access service edge (SASE) framework via the comparison of an MPLS VPN and an SD-WAN, the introduction of a zero-trust architecture, and the detailed implementation of secure web gateways and a cloud access security broker. Szymanski et al. [75] presented a cybersecurity via determinism paradigm for IoT by designing a forwarding sublayer for deterministic SD-WANs, along with services of access control, rate control, and isolation control for improvements to cybersecurity. Bustamante and Avila-Pesantez [76] compared the cybersecurity of SD-WANs in commercial mechanisms versus an open source solution. It was found that the commercial solution provides better security mechanisms regarding confidentiality, integrity, and availability, while the open source solution offers tools for adaptability to future threats thanks to the efforts of the community. Balachandran et al. [68] presented a blockchain-based authentication and access control framework for a multi-stakeholder SD-WAN infrastructure that adheres to the zero-trust security model. Lopez-Millan et al. [77] proposed a solution to manage IPsec SAs with SD-WAN architectures to avoid manual configuration in the network resources and to enable the reduced involvement of network administrators.

7. Trends and Challenges of SD-WAN

SD-WANs were born as a combinatorial technique of WANs, SDNs, and network function virtualization (NFV) to reinvent networks, services, and applications in WANs. To leverage the controllability and programmability of SDNs, SD-WANs were originally used in data center networks and ISP networks to achieve high-efficiency management and a high utilization bandwidth. Therefore, SD-WAN 1.0 was considered as a network optimization technology to enhance the efficiency of network management, operations, and utilization.

Due to automatability and extensibility of NFV, SD-WANs are now applied to establish ubiquitous interconnections [78] in cloud computing, edge computing, and the Internet of Everything by constructing overlay networks, orchestrating user-defined services, and scheduling system-defined resources. As a result, SD-WAN 2.0 has evolved into a network service provision platform, providing services such as network interconnections, network acceleration, remote access, and cybersecurity solutions. Compared to the traditional WANs, SD-WAN 2.0 is superior in its zero-touch network deployment, high-performance service provision, and auto-constructed security solutions.

SD-WAN 3.0 is considered as a promising distributed computing system combined with cutting-edge technologies of artificial intelligence, fog computing, edge computing, network security, and IoT. Therefore, the challenges relating to SD-WANs can be divided into three aspects. First, the optimization of distributed resource management and scheduling is compulsory to guarantee the QoS of services and applications. Second, improvements to parallel service orchestration, placement, and deployment are challenging due to complex network structures, multi-dimensional network elements, and abundant network services. Last but not least, cybersecurity issues of SD-WAN are vital to consider, meaning that software-defined security and software-defined perimeters for hierarchical topologies and heterogeneous devices are worthy of further investigation.

8. Conclusions

The existing surveys on SD-WANs are fragmented, covering specific problems only, and are not comprehensive with detailed research directions. This paper seeks to provide a systematic survey on SD-WANs by introducing the major research directions, presenting the research contents, and stating specific problems. Traffic engineering, network optimization and systems, service orchestration, and security issues are sequentially introduced as the four major research directions in SD-WANs. Specific research contents or problems relating to traffic measurement, traffic scheduling, failover and recovery, and the placement of controllers are illustrated and classified according to the corresponding state-of-the-art research.

It is found that studies in the past decade have mainly focused on traffic engineering, network optimization, and SD-WAN systems. However, more attention has been paid toward service orchestration and security issues in the last 5 years. The trends in the research indicate the development of SD-WANs that migrate from network optimization to service provision, revealing that SD-WANs are far more than software-defined networking. Therefore, SD-WANs are regarded as a variety of software-defined features in wide area networks, including their services relating to network interconnections, network acceleration, remote access, and cybersecurity solutions. In the near future, SD-WANs can be considered as promising distributed computing systems combined with cutting-edge technologies of artificial intelligence, fog computing, edge computing, network security, and IoT. Therefore, challenges in the related research include distributed resource management, parallel service orchestration, software-defined security issues, and software-defined perimeter problems.

Funding: This research was funded by the National Key R&D Program of China (2021YFB2012400), National Natural Science Foundation of China (62272129) and Key Research and Development Program of Shandong Province (No. 2023CXPT065).

Data Availability Statement: Data are contained within this article.

Conflicts of Interest: The authors declare no conflicts of interest.

References

1. Jain, S.; Kumar, A.; Mandal, S.; Ong, J.; Poutievski, L.; Singh, A.; Venkata, S.; Wanderer, J.; Zhou, J.; Zhu, M.; et al. B4: Experience with a globally-deployed software defined WAN. *ACM SIGCOMM Comput. Commun. Rev.* **2013**, *43*, 3–14. [CrossRef]
2. Iskandar, D.; Farisyihab, J.R.; Bahari, M.H.T.; Nurfaishal, M.D.; Khairullah, M.D. Application of the SD-WAN Load Balancing Method in Managing Internet Bandwidth at IDN Bogor Vocational School. *Int. J. Softw. Eng. Comput. Sci. (IJSECS)* **2024**, *4*, 24–39. [CrossRef]
3. Asif, R.; Ghanem, K. AI secured SD-WAN architecture as a latency critical IoT enabler for 5G and beyond communications. In Proceedings of the 2021 IEEE 18th Annual Consumer Communications & Networking Conference (CCNC), Las Vegas, NV, USA, 9–12 January 2021; pp. 1–6.
4. Rzepka, M.; Boryło, P.; Assuncao, M.D.; Lasoń, A.; Lefèvre, L. SDN-based fog and cloud interplay for stream processing. *Future Gener. Comput. Syst.* **2022**, *131*, 1–17. [CrossRef]
5. Pamplin, S. SD-WAN revolutionises IoT and edge security. *Netw. Secur.* **2021**, *2021*, 14–15. [CrossRef]
6. Dou, S.; Guo, Z. Path Programmability Recovery under Controller Failures for SD-WANs: Recent Advances and Future Research Challenges. *IEEE Commun. Mag.* **2024**, 1–7. [CrossRef]
7. Yalda, K.G.; Hamad, D.J.; Ţăpuş, N. A survey on Software-defined Wide Area Network (SD-WAN) architectures. In Proceedings of the 2022 International Congress on Human-Computer Interaction, Optimization and Robotic Applications (HORA), Ankara, Turkey, 9–11 June 2022; pp. 1–5.
8. Rose Varuna, W.; Vadivel, R. Recent Trends in Potential Security Solutions for SD-WAN: A Systematic Review. *Intell. Comput. Innov. Data Sci. Proc. ICTIDS* **2021**, *2021*, 1–9.
9. Ujan, C.; Mohamad, M.M.; Kasim, A. A Review of the Role of Latency in Multi-controller Placement in Software-Defined-Wide Area Networks. In Proceedings of the International Conference of Reliable Information and Communication Technology, Online. 22–23 December 2021; Springer: Cham, Switzerland, 2021; pp. 435–445.
10. Rajagopalan, S. An overview of sd-wan load balancing for wan connections. In Proceedings of the 2020 4th International Conference on Electronics, Communication and Aerospace Technology (ICECA), Coimbatore, India, 5–7 November 2020; pp. 1–4.
11. Yang, Z.; Cui, Y.; Li, B.; Liu, Y.; Xu, Y. Software-defined wide area network (SD-WAN): Architecture, advances and opportunities. In Proceedings of the 2019 28th International Conference on Computer Communication and Networks (ICCCN), Valencia, Spain, 29 July–1 August 2019; pp. 1–9.
12. Michel, O.; Keller, E. SDN in wide-area networks: A survey. In Proceedings of the 2017 Fourth International Conference on Software Defined Systems (SDS), Valencia, Spain, 8–11 May 2017; pp. 37–42.
13. Hong, C.Y.; Kandula, S.; Mahajan, R.; Zhang, M.; Gill, V.; Nanduri, M.; Wattenhofer, R. Achieving high utilization with software-driven WAN. In Proceedings of the ACM SIGCOMM 2013 Conference on SIGCOMM, Hong Kong, 12–16 August 2013; pp. 15–26.
14. Scarpitta, C.; Sidoretti, G.; Mayer, A.; Salsano, S.; Abdelsalam, A.; Filsfils, C. High performance delay monitoring for SRv6 based SD-WANs. *IEEE Trans. Netw. Serv. Manag.* **2023**, *21*, 1067–1081. [CrossRef]

15. Iddalagi, P.; Mishra, A. Impact Analysis of Tunnel Probing Protocol on SD-WAN's Mainstream Traffic. In Proceedings of the 2023 15th International Conference on COMmunication Systems & NETworkS (COMSNETS), Bangalore, India, 3–8 January 2023; pp. 252–259.
16. Manova, R.Y.; Sukmadirana, E.; Nurmanah, N.S. Comparative Analysis of Quality of Service and Performance of MPLS, EoIP and SD-WAN. In Proceedings of the 2022 1st International Conference on Information System & Information Technology (ICISIT), Yogyakarta, Indonesia, 27–28 July 2022; pp. 403–408.
17. Troia, S.; Mazzara, M.; Zorello, L.M.M.; Maier, G. Performance Evaluation of Overlay Networking for delay-sensitive services in SD-WAN. In Proceedings of the 2021 IEEE International Mediterranean Conference on Communications and Networking (MeditCom), Athens, Greece, 7–10 September 2021; pp. 150–155.
18. Emmanuel, I.D.; Linge, N.; Hill, S. Analysis of SD-WAN Packets using Machine Learning Algorithm. In Proceedings of the 2023 Conference on Information Communications Technology and Society (ICTAS), Durban, South Africa, 8–9 March 2023; pp. 1–6.
19. Fares, O.; Dandoush, A.; Aitsaadi, N. Sdn-based platform enabling intelligent routing within transit autonomous system networks. In Proceedings of the 2022 IEEE 19th Annual Consumer Communications & Networking Conference (CCNC), Las Vegas, NV, USA, 8–11 January 2022; pp. 909–912.
20. Zhao, J.; Hu, Z.; Xiong, B.; Yang, L.; Li, K. Modeling and optimization of packet forwarding performance in software-defined WAN. *Future Gener. Comput. Syst.* **2020**, *106*, 412–425. [CrossRef]
21. Guo, Z.; Li, C.; Li, Y.; Dou, S.; Zhang, B.; Wu, W. Maintaining the Network Performance of Software-Defined WANs With Efficient Critical Routing. *IEEE Trans. Netw. Serv. Manag.* **2023**, *21*, 2240–2252. [CrossRef]
22. Ma, D.; Wang, P.; Song, L.; Chen, W.; Ma, L.; Xu, M.; Cui, L. A lightweight deployment of TD routing based on SD-WANs. *Comput. Netw.* **2023**, *220*, 109486. [CrossRef]
23. Borgianni, L.; Troia, S.; Adami, D.; Maier, G.; Giordano, S. Assessing the Efficacy of Reinforcement Learning in Enhancing Quality of Service in SD-WANs. In Proceedings of the GLOBECOM 2023–2023 IEEE Global Communications Conference, Kuala Lumpur, Malaysia, 4–8 December 2023; pp. 1765–1770.
24. Xin, Y.; Wang, Y. Partitioning Traffic Engineering in Software Defined Wide Area Networks. In Proceedings of the 2023 14th International Conference on Information and Communication Technology Convergence (ICTC), Jeju Island, Republic of Korea, 11–13 October 2023; pp. 596–601.
25. Ouamri, M.A.; Azni, M.; Singh, D.; Almughalles, W.; Muthanna, M.S.A. Request delay and survivability optimization for software defined-wide area networking (SD-WAN) using multi-agent deep reinforcement learning. *Trans. Emerg. Telecommun. Technol.* **2023**, *34*, e4776. [CrossRef]
26. Ghaderi, M.; Liu, W.; Xiao, S.; Li, F. Learning traffic encoding matrices for delay-aware traffic engineering in SD-WANs. In Proceedings of the NOMS 2022–2022 IEEE/IFIP Network Operations and Management Symposium, Budapest, Hungary, 25–29 April 2022; pp. 1–9.
27. Fan, C.; Zhang, X.; Zhao, Y.; He, Y.; Yang, Y. Dynamic relay node selection and routing for cloud-native Software Defined WANs. *Comput. Netw.* **2024**, *241*, 110219. [CrossRef]
28. Botta, A.; Canonico, R.; Navarro, A.; Stanco, G.; Ventre, G. Adaptive overlay selection at the SD-WAN edges: A reinforcement learning approach with networked agents. *Comput. Netw.* **2024**, *243*, 110310. [CrossRef]
29. Botta, A.; Canonico, R.; Navarro, A.; Stanco, G.; Ventre, G. Scalable reinforcement learning for dynamic overlay selection in SD-WANs. In Proceedings of the 2023 IFIP Networking Conference (IFIP Networking), Barcelona, Spain, 12–15 June 2023; pp. 1–9.
30. Quang, P.T.A.; Leguay, J.; Gong, X.; Huiying, X. Global QoS Policy Optimization in SD-WAN. In Proceedings of the 2023 IEEE 9th International Conference on Network Softwarization (NetSoft), Madrid, Spain, 19–23 June 2023; pp. 202–206.
31. Ouamri, M.A.; Barb, G.; Singh, D.; Alexa, F. Load balancing optimization in software-defined wide area networking (SD-WAN) using deep reinforcement learning. In Proceedings of the 2022 International Symposium on Electronics and Telecommunications (ISETC), Timisoara, Romania, 10–11 November 2022; pp. 1–6.
32. Du, C.; Xiao, J.; Guo, W. Bandwidth constrained client selection and scheduling for federated learning over SD-WAN. *IET Commun.* **2022**, *16*, 187–194. [CrossRef]
33. Altheide, F.; Buttgereit, S.; Rossberg, M. Increasing Resilience of SD-WAN by Distributing the Control Plane [Extended Version]. *IEEE Trans. Netw. Serv. Manag.* **2024**, *21*, 2569–2581. [CrossRef]
34. Altheide, F.; Buttgereit, S.; Rossberg, M.; Schaefer, G. Increasing resilience of SD-WAN by distributing the control plane. In Proceedings of the 2023 14th International Conference on Network of the Future (NoF), Izmir, Turkiye, 4–6 October 2023; pp. 10–18.
35. Guo, Z.; Dou, S.; Wu, W.; Xia, Y. Toward flexible and predictable path programmability recovery under multiple controller failures in software-defined WANs. *IEEE/ACM Trans. Netw.* **2023**, *31*, 1965–1980. [CrossRef]
36. Dou, S.; Guo, Z.; Xia, Y. ProgrammabilityMedic: Predictable path programmability recovery under multiple controller failures in SD-WANs. In Proceedings of the 2021 IEEE 41st International Conference on Distributed Computing Systems (ICDCS), Washington, DC, USA, 7–10 July 2021; pp. 461–471.
37. Guo, Z.; Dou, S.; Jiang, W. Improving the path programmability for software-defined WANs under multiple controller failures. In Proceedings of the 2020 IEEE/ACM 28th International Symposium on Quality of Service (IWQoS), Hang Zhou, China, 15–17 June 2020; pp. 1–10.

38. Botta, A.; Canonico, R.; Navarro, A.; Stanco, G.; Ventre, G. Towards a Highly-Available SD-WAN: Rapid Failover based on BFD Protocol. In Proceedings of the 2023 IEEE Conference on Network Function Virtualization and Software Defined Networks (NFV-SDN), Dresden, Germany, 7–9 November 2023; pp. 153–158.
39. Troia, S.; Mazzara, M.; Zorello, L.M.M.; Pattavina, A. Resilience in SD-WAN with eBPF monitoring: Municipal network and video streaming use cases. In Proceedings of the 2021 17th international conference on the design of reliable communication networks (DRCN), Milano, Italy, 19–22 April 2021; pp. 1–3.
40. Troia, S.; Mazzara, M.; Savi, M.; Zorello, L.M.M.; Maier, G. Resilience of Delay-sensitive Services with Transport-layer Monitoring in SD-WAN. *IEEE Trans. Netw. Serv. Manag.* **2022**, *19*, 2652–2663. [CrossRef]
41. Zhang, Y.; Tourrilhes, J.; Zhang, Z.L.; Sharma, P. Improving SD-WAN resilience: From vertical handoff to WAN-aware MPTCP. *IEEE Trans. Netw. Serv. Manag.* **2021**, *18*, 347–361. [CrossRef]
42. Shojaee, M.; Neves, M.; Haque, I. SafeGuard: Congestion and memory-aware failure recovery in SD-WAN. In Proceedings of the 2020 16th International Conference on Network and Service Management (CNSM), Izmir, Turkey, 2–6 November 2020; pp. 1–7.
43. Golani, K.; Goswami, K.; Bhatt, K.; Park, Y. Fault tolerant traffic engineering in software-defined WAN. In Proceedings of the 2018 IEEE Symposium on Computers and Communications (ISCC), Natal, Brazil, 25–28 June 2018; pp. 01205–01210.
44. Dou, S.; Qi, L.; Yao, C.; Guo, Z. Exploring the impact of critical programmability on controller placement for software-defined wide area networks. *IEEE/ACM Trans. Netw.* **2023**, *31*, 2575–2588. [CrossRef]
45. Adebayo, I.O.; Adigun, M.O.; Mudali, P. Neighbourhood Centality Based Algorithms for Switch-to-Controller Allocation in SD-WANs. In Proceedings of the 2023 International Conference on Artificial Intelligence, Big Data, Computing and Data Communication Systems (icABCD), Durban, South Africa, 3–4 August 2023; pp. 1–6.
46. Qi, L.; Dou, S.; Guo, Z.; Li, C.; Li, Y.; Zhu, T. Low control latency SD-WANs for metaverse. In Proceedings of the 2022 IEEE 42nd International Conference on Distributed Computing Systems Workshops (ICDCSW), Bologna, Italy, 10 July 2022; pp. 266–271.
47. Adekoya, O.; Aneiba, A. An adapted nondominated sorting genetic algorithm iii (nsga-iii) with repair-based operator for solving controller placement problem in software-defined wide area networks. *IEEE Open J. Commun. Soc.* **2022**, *3*, 888–901. [CrossRef]
48. Chakraborty, A.; Misra, S.; Maiti, J. Mobility-Aware Controller Orchestration in Multi-Tier Service-Oriented Architecture for IoT. *IEEE Trans. Veh. Technol.* **2021**, *71*, 1820–1831. [CrossRef]
49. Sminesh, C.N.; Kanaga, E.G.M.; Roy, A. Optimal multi-controller placement strategy in SD-WAN using modified density peak clustering. *IET Commun.* **2019**, *13*, 3509–3518. [CrossRef]
50. Cai, N.; Han, Y.; Ben, Y.; An, W.; Xu, Z. An effective load balanced controller placement approach in software-defined WANs. In Proceedings of the MILCOM 2019–2019 IEEE Military Communications Conference (MILCOM), Norfolk, VA, USA, 12–14 November 2019; pp. 361–366.
51. Mojez, H.; Bidgoli, A.M.; Javadi, H.H.S. Star capacity-aware latency-based next controller placement problem with considering single controller failure in software-defined wide-area networks. *J. Supercomput.* **2022**, *78*, 13205–13244. [CrossRef]
52. Menoni, P.; Palma, J.M.; Morais, C.F. Assessing the Feasibility of Developing a White Label SD-WAN Solution for Smart Cities. In Proceedings of the 2023 IEEE CHILEAN Conference on Electrical, Electronics Engineering, Information and Communication Technologies (CHILECON), Valdivia, Chile, 5–7 December 2023; pp. 1–6.
53. Borgianni, L.; Adami, D.; Giordano, S. Optimizing Network Performance and Reliability with an Integrated SD-WAN and Satellite 6G Architecture. In Proceedings of the 2023 2nd International Conference on 6G Networking (6GNet), Paris, France, 18–20 October 2023; pp. 1–4.
54. Elizabeth, S.J.M.; Xavier, J.P.F.; Rubén, P.C.M. SD-WAN Software defined networking using DMVPN for corporate enterprises. In Proceedings of the 2023 18th Iberian Conference on Information Systems and Technologies (CISTI), Aveiro, Portugal, 20–23 June 2023; pp. 1–6.
55. Ushakov, Y.; Ushakova, M.; Legashev, L. Problems of Building Infrastructure Vehicular Ad Hoc Networks Based on SD-WAN Technologies. In Proceedings of the 2022 International Siberian Conference on Control and Communications (SIBCON), Tomsk, Russian Federation, 17–19 November 2022; pp. 1–4.
56. Scarpitta, C.; Ventre, P.L.; Lombardo, F.; Salsano, S.; Blefari-Melazzi, N. EveryWAN-an open source SD-WAN solution. In Proceedings of the 2021 International Conference on Electrical, Computer, Communications and Mechatronics Engineering (ICECCME), Mauritius, Mauritius, 7–8 October 2021; pp. 1–7.
57. Tiana, D.G.; Permana, W.A.; Gutandjala, I.I.; Ramadhan, A. Evaluation of Software-Defined Wide Area Network Architecture Adoption Based on The Open Group Architecture Framework (TOGAF). In Proceedings of the 2023 3rd International Conference on Intelligent Cybernetics Technology & Applications (ICICyTA), Denpasar, Bali, Indonesia, 13–15 December 2023; pp. 278–283.
58. Troia, S.; Maier, G.; Bregni, S. Experimental Evaluation of SD-WAN Performance in a Municipal Network Test Bed. In Proceedings of the 2023 IEEE Latin-American Conference on Communications (LATINCOM), Panama City, Panama, 15–17 November 2023; pp. 1–5.
59. Hussain, S.I.; Yuvanesh, S.; Yokesh, S. Revolutionizing Networking: An Exploration of Software-Defined Networking. In Proceedings of the 2023 2nd International Conference on Automation, Computing and Renewable Systems (ICACRS), Pudukkottai, India, 11–13 December 2023; pp. 1020–1026.
60. Soejantono, G.K.; Nashiruddin, M.I.; Hertiana, S.N.; Nugraha, M.A. Performance Evaluation of SD-WAN Deployment for XYZ Enterprise Company in Indonesia. In Proceedings of the 2021 IEEE 12th Annual Information Technology, Electronics and Mobile Communication Conference (IEMCON), Vancouver, BC, Canada, 27–30 October 2021; pp. 0311–0316.

61. Hong, C.Y.; Mandal, S.; Al-Fares, M.; Zhu, M.; Alimi, R.; Bhagat, C.; Jain, S.; Kaimal, J.; Liang, S.; Mendelev, K.; et al. B4 and after: Managing hierarchy, partitioning, and asymmetry for availability and scale in google's software-defined WAN. In Proceedings of the 2018 Conference of the ACM Special Interest Group on Data Communication, New York, NY, USA, 20–25 August 2018; pp. 74–87.
62. Heller, B.; Sherwood, R.; McKeown, N. The controller placement problem. *ACM SIGCOMM Comput. Commun. Rev.* **2012**, *42*, 473–478. [CrossRef]
63. Jiang, Y.; Su, L.; Feng, W.; Ge, N. Congestion-Aware Algorithms for Service Function Chaining in Software-Defined Wide Area Networks. In Proceedings of the ICC 2023-IEEE International Conference on Communications 2023, Rome, Italy, 28 May–1 June 2023; pp. 1086–1092.
64. Leivadeas, A.; Pitaev, N.; Falkner, M. Analyzing the performance of SD-WAN enabled service function chains across the globe with AWS. In Proceedings of the 2023 ACM/SPEC International Conference on Performance Engineering, Coimbra, Portugal, 15–19 April 2023; pp. 125–135.
65. Zhang, Y.; Xu, C.; Muntean, G.M. Revenue-Oriented Service Offloading through Fog-Cloud Collaboration in SD-WAN. In Proceedings of the GLOBECOM 2022–2022 IEEE Global Communications Conference 2022, Rio de Janeiro, Brazil, 4–8 December 2022; pp. 5753–5758.
66. Perez, R.; Zabala, A.; Banchs, A. Alviu: An intent-based SD-WAN orchestrator of network slices for enterprise networks. In Proceedings of the 2021 IEEE 7th international conference on network softwarization (NetSoft), Tokyo, Japan, 28 June–2 July 2021; pp. 211–215.
67. Koné, B.; Kora, A.D. Management and orchestration for network function virtualization in a VoIP testbed: A multi-domain case. In Proceedings of the 2021 44th International Conference on Telecommunications and Signal Processing (TSP), Brno, Czech Republic, 26–28 July 2021; pp. 372–376.
68. Balachandran, C.; Ramachandran, G.; Krishnamachari, B. EDISON: A blockchain-based secure and auditable orchestration framework for multi-domain software defined networks. In Proceedings of the 2020 IEEE International Conference on Blockchain (Blockchain), Rhodes, Greece, 2–6 November 2020; pp. 144–153.
69. Ergawy, R.R.; Elkamchouchi, H.M.; Azab, M.; ELfahar, A. Open Source Intelligence Driven Moving Target Defense for Secure Software-defined WAN: A Game Theoretic Approach. In Proceedings of the 2023 IEEE Global Conference on Artificial Intelligence and Internet of Things (GCAIoT), Dubai, United Arab Emirates, 10–11 December 2023; pp. 134–141.
70. Zhang, P.; He, F.; Zhang, H.; Hu, J.; Huang, X.; Wang, J.; Yin, X.; Zhu, H.; Li, Y. Real-time malicious traffic detection with online isolation forest over sd-wan. *IEEE Trans. Inf. Forensics Secur.* **2023**, *18*, 2076–2090. [CrossRef]
71. Lembke, J.; Ravi, S.; Roman, P.L.; Eugster, P. Secure and reliable network updates. *ACM Trans. Priv. Secur.* **2022**, *26*, 1–41. [CrossRef]
72. Satheesh, K.K.; Janani, M.; Venkateswarlu, S.C.; Kumar, R.G.; Gupta, A.; Kotaiah, B. AI and Machine Learning Enabled Software Defined Networks. In *Data Engineering and Intelligent Computing: Proceedings of 5th ICICC 2021*; Springer: Singapore, 2022; Volume 1, pp. 131–144.
73. Fan, W.; Chang, S.Y.; Kumar, S.; Zhou, X.; Park, Y. Blockchain-based secure coordination for distributed sdn control plane. In Proceedings of the 2021 IEEE 7th International Conference on Network Softwarization (NetSoft), Tokyo, Japan, 28 June–2 July 2021; pp. 253–257.
74. Yiliyaer, S.; Kim, Y. Secure access service edge: A zero trust based framework for accessing data securely. In Proceedings of the 2022 IEEE 12th Annual Computing and Communication Workshop and Conference (CCWC), Las Vegas, NV, USA, 26–29 January 2022; pp. 0586–0591.
75. Szymanski, T.H. The "cyber security via determinism" paradigm for a quantum safe zero trust deterministic internet of things (IoT). *IEEE Access* **2022**, *10*, 45893–45930. [CrossRef]
76. Bustamante, J.R.; Avila-Pesantez, D. Comparative analysis of Cybersecurity mechanisms in SD-WAN architectures: A preliminary results. In Proceedings of the 2021 IEEE Engineering International Research Conference (EIRCON), Lima, Peru, 27–29 October 2021; pp. 1–4.
77. Lopez-Millan, G.; Marin-Lopez, R.; Pereniguez-Garcia, F. Towards a standard SDN-based IPsec management framework. *Comput. Stand. Interfaces* **2019**, *66*, 103357. [CrossRef]
78. Fu, C.; Wang, B.; Liu, H.; Wang, W. Software-Defined Virtual Private Network for SD-WAN. *Electronics* **2024**, *13*, 2674. [CrossRef]

Disclaimer/Publisher's Note: The statements, opinions and data contained in all publications are solely those of the individual author(s) and contributor(s) and not of MDPI and/or the editor(s). MDPI and/or the editor(s) disclaim responsibility for any injury to people or property resulting from any ideas, methods, instructions or products referred to in the content.

electronics

MDPI

Article

Lightweight Certificate-Less Anonymous Authentication Key Negotiation Scheme in the 5G Internet of Vehicles

Guoheng Wei, Yanlin Qin *, Guangyue Kou and Zhihong Sun

Department of Information Security, Naval University of Engineering, Wuhan 430030, China
* Correspondence: qinyanlincool@163.com

Abstract: In the current 5G vehicle network system, there are security issues such as wireless intrusion, privacy leakage, and remote control. To address these challenges, an improved lightweight anonymous authentication key negotiation scheme based on certificate-less aggregate signatures is proposed and its security and efficiency are analyzed. The result shows that the scheme can offer security attributes including anonymity, traceability, and revocability, as well as effective identity authentication, and it can resist forgery attacks, man-in-the-middle attacks, tampering attacks, and smart card loss attacks. Moreover, compared with similar schemes, it possesses superior security and more efficient computational efficiency and less communication overhead, thereby being more appropriate for high-speed, large-capacity, low-latency, and resource-constrained 5G vehicle network application scenarios.

Keywords: Internet of Vehicles; certificate-less aggregate signature; authentication key negotiation scheme; elliptic curve

1. Introduction

The 5G Internet of Vehicles regards vehicles as the fundamental unit and interacts with roadside infrastructure RSU (Road Side Unit), cloud servers, and humans. It depends on key technologies such as 5G communication technology, sensor technology, information security technology, vehicle autonomy [1], big data and cloud computing technology, and human–computer interaction technology to achieve the efficient unification and information interaction of "vehicle-person-road-cloud". In the current 5G Internet of Vehicles system, there are numerous nodes, complex channels, an open network, and substantial information interaction. Security issues such as wireless intrusion, privacy leakage, and remote control keep emerging during the application of the Internet of Vehicles, seriously threatening the communication security and data privacy of the Internet of Vehicles. A secure and efficient authentication key negotiation protocol is a crucial means to counter such security attacks. The focus of this paper is to meet the requirements of authentication key negotiation of users in the Internet of Vehicles with a large number of vehicles and reduce the calculation cost of the authentication key negotiation scheme in the meanwhile.

2. Related Work

Currently, the authentication key negotiation schemes are mainly based on public key infrastructure, identity-based, and certificate-less cryptography. The authentication scheme based on PKI is the most commonly used one [2–5]. However, the PKI-based authentication scheme struggles to deal with the application scenarios in the Internet of Vehicles, because there are a large number of on-board units (OBUs) in circulation, whose certificates need to be issued, updated, and revoked frequently. At the same time, digital certificates are often broadcast during the interaction process, resulting in a large communication overhead and affecting system efficiency. To address the issue of large public key certificate management overhead in the authentication scheme based on PKI,

Internet of Vehicles authentication key negotiation schemes based on identity have been proposed [6–9]. The identity-based authentication scheme utilizes known user information as the public key to avoid the use of digital certificates, such as identity ID, telephone number, etc. But in the identity-based authentication scheme, the public–private key pair is generated by the key generation center based on user information, thereby causing a key escrow problem. To avoid this problem, scholars have proposed a certificate-less cryptography-based [10] authentication key negotiation scheme [11–14]. In the certificate-less authentication key negotiation scheme, the user controls his own secret value and the partial private key allocated by the KGC together as the private key, thereby avoiding the key escrow problem and also reducing the certificate management overhead. In 2020, Zhang et al. [11] introduced a pre-signature mechanism to achieve the identity authentication of vehicle users and designed an anonymous authentication key negotiation protocol for cloud services in the Internet of Vehicles, but due to the use of relatively fixed temporary identity information, it does not have strong anonymity, and the scheme fails to meet security characteristics such as resistance to temporary key leakage attack, perfect forward security, and resistance to spoofing attack [12]. In 2021, Zhang [13] proposed an efficient anonymous identity authentication and key negotiation scheme based on certificate-less aggregate signatures, but this scheme employs computationally intensive bilinear pair operations, which is not suitable for Internet of Vehicles systems with low latency and low computational overhead requirements. Xiong [14] proposed a lightweight group-based 5G V2X anonymous access authentication and digital transmission scheme, leveraging the advantages of low latency and high reliability of the 5G network to form a temporary group for a certain range of OBUs, combining certificate-less aggregate signcryption technology and the Chinese remainder theorem to achieve efficient management of group keys. In 2022, Liu et al. [15] proposed an elliptic curve certificate-less anonymous authentication scheme without bilinear pairs that supports batch verification, reducing the computational load of RSUs. However, this scheme is prone to user identity leakage when the vehicle smart card is lost and struggles to withstand spoofing attacks. Wang et al. [16] proposed a certificate-less aggregate signature algorithm for vehicular Ad hoc Network, which lacks anonymity and is unable to resist replay attack and simulation attack. Xi et al. [17] proposed a data sharing and security authentication scheme in the Internet of Vehicles. Compared to the scheme in [16], it has been improved, featuring authenticated identity anonymity and the ability to resist simulation attack, but it still cannot counter replay attack. Ye et al. [18] proposed an aggregate signature algorithm that introduces a timestamp to resist replay attack but still has a key escrow problem. Bao et al. [19] proposed a certificate-less anonymous authentication scheme for VANETs, which utilizes ring signature to achieve strong anonymity. However, it involves bilinear operation with a high calculation cost, and thus, its scalability in large-scale deployments is weak. In 2023, Shahidinejad A et al. [20] proposed a self-certified key exchange protocol for hybrid electric vehicles based on Blockchain. And then, in 2024, Shahidinejad et al. [21] proposed an anonymous lattice-based authentication protocol for vehicular communications; it is a post-quantum scheme.

The key contributions of our work are as follows. To offer more secure and efficient authentication and key negotiation for the 5G Internet of Vehicles with a large number of vehicles, an improved anonymous authentication key negotiation scheme based on certificate-less aggregate signatures is proposed. The scheme adopts a certificate-less public key cryptosystem, and the KGC generates a partial private key of the vehicle user. This, along with a random number generated by the vehicle user itself, constitutes the user's private key, thereby resolving the key escrow issue in the identity-based authentication scheme as well as the large public key certificate management overhead in the authentication scheme based on PKI. To protect the privacy of users, this scheme introduces long-term pseudonyms and short-term pseudonyms. The long-term pseudonym is employed to conceal the real identity of the vehicle user and generate the user's private key, and then the short-term pseudonym is used to hide the vehicle's long-term pseudonym to safeguard the identity privacy of the vehicle user during each authentication process. In the process of signature authentication and key negotiation, to reduce the system's computational overhead and enhance the interaction efficiency between users, a lighter elliptic curve-based algorithm without the bilinear pair operation is adopted. Security analysis is provided to show that the proposed scheme meets the standard security objectives for the authentication key negotiation protocol. And a formal security proof is also provided to prove that it is secure under the random oracle security model and the assumption of ECDLP. Security and efficiency comparison analysis is provided to demonstrate the superiority of the proposed scheme against state-of-the-art methods.

3. Security Objectives and Models

3.1. Security Objectives

This section will define the security objectives that need to be fulfilled by the efficient anonymous identity authentication and key agreement scheme of the 5G vehicle network based on the certificate-less aggregate signature, including the anonymity of vehicles [22], traceability and revocability, effective identity authentication, unlinkability, forward security and backward security, and the ability to resist various attacks.

3.1.1. The Anonymity of Vehicles

The vehicle network system is required to encrypt or conceal the real identity information of vehicles to prevent attackers from obtaining the real identity information of vehicles by using the obtained messages when monitoring the communication channel. This anonymity of vehicles is conditional rather than absolute. Since the identity of vehicles cannot be derived from the exchanged messages, they can still be identified by the network activity.

3.1.2. Traceability and Revocability

The vehicle network system needs to possess the ability to trace false identities and false information and revoke the identities of illegal vehicles.

3.1.3. Effective Message Authentication

A secure vehicle network protocol needs to possess the ability to effectively authenticate information with a large amount of interaction, including the authentication of its timeliness and integrity, thereby ensuring the correctness and reliability of the source of the message.

3.1.4. Unlinkability

Due to the close association among each node in the vehicle network system, it is necessary to guarantee unlinkability to prevent attackers from attacking one attribute and associating it with other secret information.

3.1.5. Forward Security and Backward Security

In the large amount of data interaction in the vehicle network system, it is necessary to prevent attackers from analyzing the historical and future values of this secret information based on the obtained secret information, that is, it should have forward and backward security.

3.1.6. The Ability to Resist Various Attacks

A secure vehicle network authentication key agreement protocol should be able to deal with the primary attack modes, such as eavesdropping attack, tampering attack, replay attack, man-in-the-middle attack, and simulation attack [23].

3.2. Security Model

This section will elaborate on the security model of the proposed vehicle network authentication key agreement scheme [24] based on the certificate-less aggregate signature.

Firstly, we define two types of adversaries, namely A_{I} and A_{II}. Adversary A_{I} can query the private key of a legitimate vehicle and can also query and replace the public key of the legitimate vehicle with its own generated public key. Adversary A_{II} is an internal attacker, equivalent to a malicious but passive KGC, who can query the master key of the KGC and some private keys of the vehicle user, yet is unable to replace the public key.

The attack capabilities of these two types of adversaries are defined through the description of five random oracles:

Hash query, where the adversary queries this oracle and obtains the corresponding hash record on the vehicle list;

Partial private key extraction query, where the adversary makes this query to the oracle and acquires the partial private key on the record list;

Public key extraction query, where the adversary queries this oracle and retrieves the public key on the record list;

Secret value extraction query, where the adversary queries this oracle and obtains the private key of the user on the record list;

Signature query, where the adversary queries this oracle and obtains a legal signature of a message.

Next, we define two games, namely $Game_0$ and $Game_1$. Adversary A_{I} plays $Game_0$ with challenger C, and Adversary A_{II} plays $Game_1$ with challenger C.

$Game_0$: The system parameters p, adversary A_{I}, and challenger C are defined.

1. In the Initialization stage, the challenger C sends the system parameters, excluding the system master key after initialization, to the adversary A_{I}, and randomly selects an identity to await the start of the challenge.
2. In the Query stage, the adversary conducts hash queries, partial private key extraction queries, public key extraction queries, secret value extraction queries, signature queries, and other random oracle queries.
3. In the Forgery stage, adversary A_{I} generates a forged signature based on the information obtained from the query.

According to the forking lemma [25], if the adversary AI successfully outputs three sets of legal signatures using the above queries, then it is said that the adversary AI wins this game.

$Game_1$: The system parameters p, adversary A_{II}, and challenger C are defined.

1. In the Initialization stage, the challenger C sends the initialized system parameters to the adversary A_{II}, and randomly selects an identity to await the start of the challenge.
2. In the Query stage, the adversary conducts hash queries, partial private key extraction queries, public key extraction queries, secret value extraction queries, signature queries, and other random oracle queries.
3. In the Forgery stage, adversary A_{II} generates a forged signature based on the information obtained from the query.

According to the forking lemma [25], if the adversary A_{II} successfully outputs three sets of legal signatures using the above queries, then it is said that the adversary A_{II} wins this game.

4. Lightweight Certificate-Less Anonymous Authentication Key Negotiation Scheme

4.1. Design of the Scheme

The overall design diagram of the scheme is shown in Figure 1, including the key generation center (KGC), the trusted center (TA), the Road Side Unit (RSU), and the on-board unit (OBU). The brief description of the scheme is as follows.

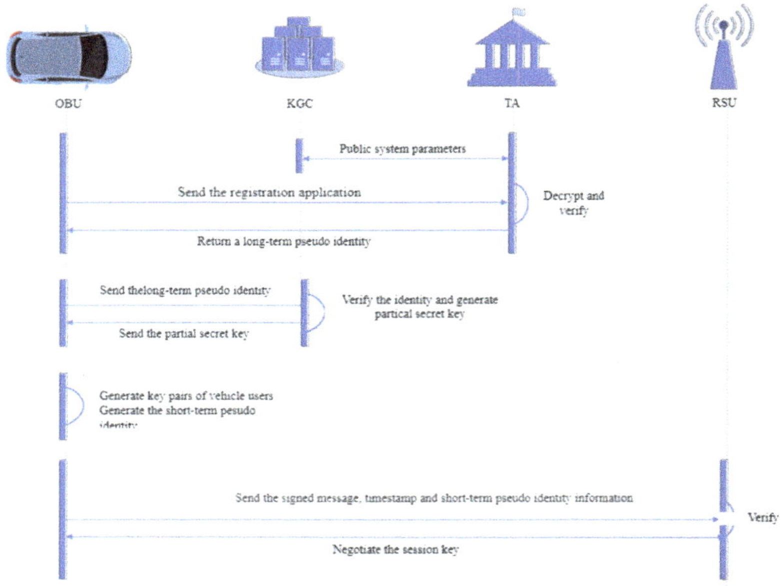

Figure 1. Design of the lightweight authentication key negotiation protocol based on certificate-less aggregate signature in 5G Internet of Vehicles.

System initialization: KGC and TA generate the public parameters and public–private key pairs of the system.

Generation of long-term pseudonym: The TA verifies the identity information of OBU_i and password PW_i in the system, and outputs the long-term pseudonym PID_i of the vehicle according to the identity information of the vehicle OBU_i, and sends it to the vehicle OBU_i through a secure channel, and the vehicle OBU_i stores the long-term pseudonym on the smart card.

Generation of partial private key: The vehicle OBU_i secretly sends the long-term pseudonym to the KGC, and the KGC generates the partial private key psk_i of the vehicle, and sends it to the TA and OBU_i through a secure channel.

Generation of the vehicle public–private key pair: After the vehicle successfully validates the partial private key, it combines this partial private key to generate the vehicle public–private key pair.

Generation of short-term pseudonym: The vehicle generates a short-term pseudonym LID_i based on the real identity OID_i and the long-term pseudonym PID_i.

Signature: OBU_i use the partial private key generated by the KGC and the secret value generated by itself to sign the message.

Single verification: The message recipient verifies the legitimacy of the signature on the message, and if it is legal, it outputs as true.

Key negotiation: The vehicle OBU_i negotiates a pair of safe and correct shared secret values K_{UR} and K_{RU} with RSU_i, and performs a calculation to obtain the shared session key SK.

Aggregate signature: Aggregate the message signatures of the vehicle OBU_i, OBU_i, ..., OBU_n and output the aggregate signature $\sigma = R_1, R_2, \ldots, R_n, \tau$.

Batch verification: Verify the legitimacy of the aggregate signature $\sigma = R_1, R_2, \ldots, R_n$, τ of the aggregated message $M_1, M_2, \ldots, M_n$ and if it is legal, it outputs as true.

A more detailed description will be given in Section 4.2.

4.2. Description of the Scheme

This section will give a detailed description of the scheme. The lightweight authentication key negotiation protocol based on certificate-less aggregate signature includes the Algorithms 1–9.

Algorithm 1. System initialization.

Both KGC and TA are the trusted third parties that generate the public parameters and the public–private key pairs of the system. The system initialization algorithm is as follows:

1. TA constructs the elliptic curve G and the generator P on the elliptic curve.
2. TA constructs a random number $\alpha \in Z_q^*$, calculates $T_p = \alpha \cdot P$, where TA secretly stores α as its own master key.
3. KGC constructs a random number $\beta \in Z_q^*$, calculates $P_p = \beta \cdot P$, where KGC secretly stores β as its own master key.
4. Use α and β jointly to form the master key of the Internet of Vehicles system.
5. KGC selects hash functions $H_1, H_2, H_3, , H_4$, where $H_1 : \{0,1\}^* \rightarrow Z_q^*$, $H_2 : \{0,1\}^* \times G \times G \rightarrow Z_q^*$, $H_3 : G \times \{0,1\}^* \rightarrow \{0,1\}^*$, $H_4 : G \times G \times \{0,1\}^* \times G \times G \times G \rightarrow Z_q^*$, and TA and KGC publish the public parameter $p = \{G, P, P_p, T_p, H_1, H_2, H_3, H_4\}$.

Algorithm 2. Long-term pseudonym generation.

The long-term pseudonym generation stage is divided into two parts; one part is for the TA to verify the real identity of the vehicle, and the other part is for the TA to generate a long-term pseudonym PID_i for the vehicle.

1. The vehicle inputs its real identity OID_i and password PWD_i, takes T_p as the public key of the encryption algorithm, and sends the encrypted identity information ID_i and PW_i to TA. Then, TA decrypts it to obtain the real identity information of the vehicle and compares it with the information in the vehicle list U_L to verify the legitimacy. If it exists in the list and the information is true, the vehicle can be regarded as a legitimate vehicle.
2. TA decrypts the information sent by vehicle OBU_i to obtain the real identity of the vehicle OID_i, selects a random number $t \in Z_q^*$, calculates the long-term pseudonym $PID_i = (t + \alpha H_1(OID_i)) mod\ q$, and stores it in the smart card, then distributes the smart card to the vehicle.

Algorithm 3. Key generation.

KGC and OBU_i perform the following operations to generate the public–private key pair of the vehicle.

1. OBU_i encrypts the long-term pseudonym with the public key P_p and transmits the encrypted message to KGC.
2. KGC decrypts the message to obtain the long-term pseudonym of the vehicle; it should verify whether the long-term pseudonym exists in the vehicle list U_L. If the verification is successful, KGC selects a random number $r_i \in Z_q^*$, calculates $R_i = r_i \cdot P$, $h_i = H_2(PID_i \| R_i \| P_p)$, $s_i = (r_i + h_i \cdot \beta)\ mod\ q$, and generates the partial private key $psk_i = (s_i, R_i)$ of the vehicle OBU_i.
3. KGC sends (OID_i, PID_i, psk_i) to TA through a secure channel, and TA stores it in the vehicle list U_L.
4. KGC sends the partial private key psk_i to the vehicle OBU_i through a secure channel.
5. After the vehicle OBU_i receives the partial private key, it first verifies whether $s_i \cdot P = R_i + h_i \cdot P_p$ is established, to obtain the legitimacy of psk_i. If it is established, psk_i can be regarded as the available partial private key.
6. OBU_i selects a random number $a_i \in Z_q^*$ as the other partial private key of the vehicle, so the public–private key pair of the vehicle is $pk_i = a_i \cdot P$, $sk_i = (a_i, psk_i)$.

Algorithm 4. Short-term pseudonym generation.

OBU_i generates the one-time short-term pseudonym LID_i using the real identity of the vehicle and the long-term pseudonym according to the following steps. The short-term pseudonym LID_i of the vehicle consists of two parts as follows.

1. The first part is LID_1^i. OBU_i randomly selects $\delta \in Z_q^*$, and calculates $LID_1^i = \delta \cdot P$.
2. The second part is composed of the real identity of the vehicle, the long-term pseudonym, the password, and the timestamp T_i. OBU_i is calculated.
3. $LID_2^i = OID_i \oplus H_3[(\delta \cdot T_p) \| PID_i \| T_i || H_1(PWD_i)]$.

Therefore, the short-term pseudonym LID_i of the vehicle is as follows:

$$LID_i = \left(LID_1^i, LID_2^i, T_i\right) = \begin{cases} LID_1^i = \delta \cdot P \\ LID_2^i = OID_i \oplus H_3[(\delta \cdot T_p) \| PID_i \| T_i || H_1(PWD_i)] \end{cases} \quad (1)$$

Algorithm 5. Signature generation.

OBU_i constructs the signature of the vehicle according to the following steps and broadcasts the signed message to all other members in the system.

1. OBU_i randomly selects $\gamma_i \in Z_q^*$, and calculates $D_i = \gamma_i \cdot P$.
2. OBU_i calculates $w_i = H_4\left(D_i, LID_1^i, LID_2^i, T_j, pk_i, R_i, P_p\right)$,
   $v_i = H_4\left(m_i, D_i, LID_1^i,\ LID_2^i, T_j, pk_i, R_i, P_p\right)$, $\tau_i = \gamma_i + v_i(w_i \cdot a_i + s_i) \bmod q$.
3. OBU_i constructs the signature of the vehicle, that is, the tuple $\sigma_i = (R_i, D_i, \tau_i)$.
4. OBU_i constructs the tuple $M_i = \left(LID_i, pk_i, m_i, h_i, \sigma_i, T_j\right)$, and broadcasts this tuple to all other members in the Internet of Vehicles system.

Algorithm 6. Single verification.

After the message recipient (taking RSU_i as an example) receives the signed message broadcasted by OBU_i, it verifies the signature. If the verification result is true, the identity of the message sender is authenticated as legal; otherwise, the message sender is an illegal user.

1. RSU_i verifies whether the timestamp T_i is valid, to ensure the freshness of the short-term pseudonym LID_i of the vehicle OBU_i.
2. RSU_i verifies whether the timestamp T_j is valid. If it is invalid, the information will be discarded directly. If it is valid, the subsequent steps will be carried out.
3. RSU_i calculates $w_i' = H_4\left(D_i, LID_1^i, LID_2^i, T_j, pk_i, R_i, P_p\right)$,
   $v_i' = H_4\left(m_i, D_i, LID_1^i,\ LID_2^i, T_j, pk_i, R_i, P_p\right)$.
4. RSU_i verifies whether the equation $\tau_i \cdot P = D_i + v_i'(w_i' \cdot pk_i + R_i + h_i \cdot P_p)$ is established. If it is established, it is considered that the output is true and the vehicle's identity is legal and trustworthy; otherwise, the vehicle's identity is illegal and untrustworthy. The correctness proof is as follows:

$$\begin{aligned} \tau_i \cdot P &= [\gamma_i + v_i(w_i \cdot a_i + s_i)] \cdot P \\ &= \gamma_i \cdot P + v_i(w_i \cdot a_i + s_i) \cdot P \\ &= D_i + v_i(w_i \cdot a_i \cdot P + s_i \cdot P) \\ &= D_i + v_i(w_i \cdot pk_i + s_i \cdot P) \\ &= D_i + v_i[w_i \cdot pk_i + (r_i + h_i \cdot \beta) \cdot P] \\ &= D_i + v_i[w_i \cdot pk_i + (r_i \cdot P + h_i \cdot \beta \cdot P)] \\ &= D_i + v_i(w_i \cdot pk_i + R_i + h_i \cdot P_p) \end{aligned} \quad (2)$$

If the information in the broadcast message $M_i = \left(LID_i, pk_i, m_i, h_i, \sigma_i, T_j\right)$ has not been modified, then $w_i' = w_i$, $v_i' = v_i$, which means

$$D_i + v_i'(w_i' \cdot pk_i + R_i + h_i \cdot P_p) = D_i + v_i(w_i \cdot pk_i + R_i + h_i \cdot P_p) = \tau_i \cdot P \quad (3)$$

Algorithm 7. Key negotiation.

In this section, the two communicating parties need to negotiate a same-session key (taking the communication between OBU_i and RSU_i as an example). After the signature authentication, the key negotiation scheme is designed, as shown in Figure 2.
As shown in Figure 2, OBU_i and RSU_i take the following steps to negotiate the same-session key:

1. OBU_i selects a random number $k_U \in Z_q^*$, calculates $h_U = H_2(LID_U \| R_U \| pk_U)$, $TU = (k_U \cdot (a_U + s_U h_U))P$.
2. OBU_i selects a random number $k_R \in Z_q^*$, calculates $h_R = H_2(ID_R \| R_R \| pk_R)$, $TR = (k_R \cdot (a_R + s_R h_R))P$.
3. OBU_i sends TU to RSU_i, and at the same time, RSU_i sends TR to OBU_i.
4. After receiving TR, OBU_i calculates the shared secret value $K_{UR} = (k_U \cdot (a_U + s_U h_U))TR$.
5. After receiving TU, RSU_i calculates the shared secret value $K_{RU} = (k_R \cdot (a_R + s_R h_R))TU$.

Then, the same-session key can be calculated, respectively, by OBU_i and RSU_i, as follows:

$$SK = H_4(LID_U, TU, TR, K_{UR}) = H_4(LID_U, TU, TR, K_{RU}) \tag{4}$$

The correctness analysis is as follows:

$$\begin{aligned} K_{UR} &= (k_U \cdot (a_U + s_U h_U))TR \\ &= (k_U \cdot (a_U + s_U h_U))(k_R \cdot (a_R + s_R h_R))P \\ &= (k_R \cdot (a_R + s_R h_R))(k_U \cdot (a_U + s_U h_U))P \\ &= (k_R \cdot (a_R + s_R h_R))TU \end{aligned} \tag{5}$$

Algorithm 8. Aggregate signature.

When there are n messages in the system that need to be signed, the n signatures for these n messages are aggregated by RSU_i. The messages and signatures are $M_1, \sigma_1 = (R_1, D_{n1}, \tau_1)$, $M_2, \sigma_2 = (R_2, D_2, \tau_2) \ldots, M_n, \sigma_n = (R_n, D_n, \tau_n)$, and the aggregated certificate-less signature is $\sigma = R_1, D_1, R_2, D_2, \ldots, R_n, D_n, \tau$, where $\tau = \sum_{i=1}^{n} \tau_i$.

Algorithm 9. Batch verification.

After the message recipient receives the aggregated certificate-less signature σ, it verifies the aggregated signature. If the verification is passed, the aggregated signature is considered legal; otherwise, it is not legal. The verification steps are as follows:

1. Calculate $\tau' = \sum_{i=1}^{n} \tau_i'$, and if $\tau' = \tau$, then the aggregated signature is considered valid; otherwise, the aggregated signature is invalid, and it will be discarded directly.
2. Calculate $w_i', v_i', i = 1, 2, \ldots, n$, by following the steps in Algorithm 6.
3. Verify the equation

$$\tau' \cdot P = \sum_{i=1}^{n} D_i + \sum_{i=1}^{n} v_i'(w_i' \cdot pk_i + R_i + h_i \cdot P_p) \tag{6}$$

If it is established, the aggregated certificate-less signature is considered legal.

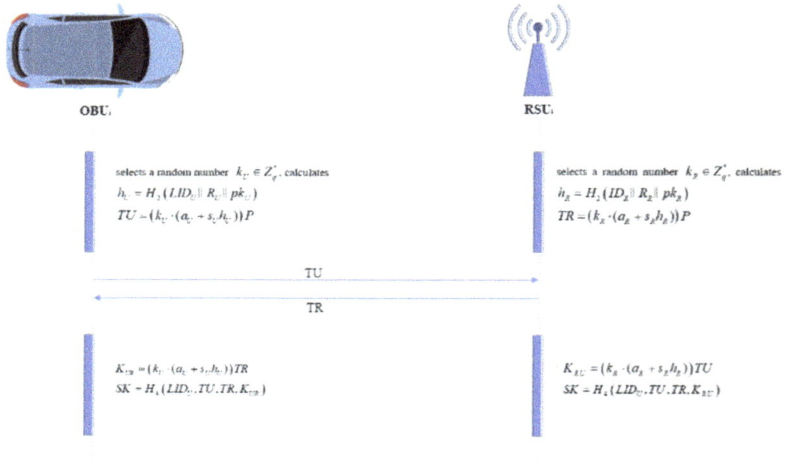

Figure 2. Key negotiation stage.

5. Security Analysis and Proof

5.1. Security Analysis

This section will analyze whether the protocol proposed in this paper meets the standard security objectives proposed in Section 3.1.

5.1.1. Anonymity of Vehicles

During communication, the vehicles need to conceal their initial real identities. When a vehicle applies to the TA for a long-term pseudonym, it uses an encryption algorithm to encrypt the real identity OID_i with the encryption key T_p. Therefore, the attacker cannot calculate the real identity of the vehicle without knowing the master key α of the TA; the TA calculates and distributes the long-term pseudonym $PID_i = (t + \alpha H_1(OID_i)) mod\ q$. Due to the one-way nature of the hash function and the fact that the attacker cannot obtain the random number t, the attacker cannot calculate the real identity OID_i of the vehicle through the long-term pseudonym PID_i, ensuring the anonymity of the real identity OID_i of the vehicle. To further ensure the security of the vehicle's identity, this paper introduces the concept of a vehicle's short-term pseudonym, so that the identity of the vehicle in the communication process is *sessionized*, like the session key. The short-term pseudonym consists of the real identity, long-term pseudonym and password of the vehicle, and a timestamp, which can be calculated as

$$LID_i = \left(LID_1^i, LID_2^i, T_i\right) = \begin{cases} LID_1^i = \delta \cdot P \\ LID_2^i = OID_i \oplus H_3\left[(\delta \cdot T_p) \| PID_i \| T_i \| H_1(PWD_i)\right] \end{cases} \quad (7)$$

If the attacker wants to obtain the real identity of the vehicle, he needs to calculate the equation $OID_i = LID_2^i \oplus H_3\left[(\delta \cdot T_p) \| PID_i \| T_i \| H_1(PWD_i)\right]$. However, the attacker cannot obtain δ; even if he obtains the smart card which stores the long-term pseudonym of the vehicle, he cannot obtain the password of the vehicle, so the attacker cannot calculate the result of this equation and thus cannot obtain the real identity OID_i, that is, the anonymity of the vehicle can be ensured.

5.1.2. Traceability and Revocability

TA usually stores and maintains the vehicle list U_L, so when a vehicle has a dispute or other untrusted behavior during the communication process, TA can compare the suspect identity information and long-term or short-term pseudonym with the vehicle list U_L, and then it can calculate $OID_i = LID_2^i \oplus H_3\left[(\alpha \cdot LID_1^i) \| PID_i \| T_i \| H_1(PWD_i)\right]$ to trace the real identity and legality of this disputed vehicle; thus, the user behavior can be traced and verified in the Internet of Vehicles system. And the illegal vehicles will be revoked from the vehicle list. Therefore, this protocol can guarantee the traceability and revocability of the Internet of Vehicles system.

5.1.3. Effective Message Authentication

All of the communication entities in the RSU_i or domain of RSU_i can verify the legitimacy of the message m_i by validating the pseudonym LID_i, signature σ_i, and other information of the vehicle OBU_i.

In the Internet of Vehicles system, if the vehicle OBU_i wants to communicate with other entities, it first needs to be verified by the TA. Then, the TA will distribute a long-term pseudonym PID_i to the vehicle OBU_i, and at the same time, the TA will also save the OBU_i to the vehicle list U_L. Therefore, it can ensure that the attacker cannot attack the real identity of the vehicle during the communication process. Then, the vehicle can use its short-term pseudonym LID_i, which is composed of the real identity OID_i, long-term pseudonym PID_i, timestamp, and password, to interact with other communication entities. After the message recipient receives the message, it should first check the timestamp. If the time has expired, the message will be discarded; otherwise, it then checks whether the equation $\tau_i \cdot P = D_i + v_i'(w_i' \cdot pk_i + R_i + h_i \cdot P_p)$ holds. If it holds, it can be considered that the signature is authenticated, and the message sender can be recognized as a legal user. If it does not hold, then it is considered that the message sender is illegal, and the message will be discarded. Therefore, the protocol designed in this paper can complete the authentication in terms of timeliness and integrity.

5.1.4. Unlinkability

In the certificate-less authentication scheme proposed in this paper, by constructing different random numbers t, δ, the real identity OID_i of the vehicle is hidden during the communication with the long-term pseudonym PID_i and the short-term pseudonym LID_i. The existence of the random numbers t, δ reduces the correlation between the long-term pseudonym PID_i and the short-term pseudonym LID_i, and the attacker cannot obtain one pseudonym through linking another pseudonym. Therefore, the protocol in this section can meet the unlinkability requirement of the Internet of Vehicles system.

5.1.5. Forward Security and Backward Security

The attacker may intercept the signature $\sigma_i = (R_i, D_i, \tau_i)$ of the vehicle OBU_i, where $\tau_i = \gamma_i + v_i(w_i \cdot a_i + s_i) \bmod q$, and γ_i is randomly selected, so the attacker cannot obtain the previous and future signatures through the signature currently obtained. In addition, for the session key $SK = H_4(LID_U, TU, TR, K_{UR}) = H_4(LID_U, TU, TR, K_{RU})$, due to the existence of the random numbers k_U, k_R and the one-way nature of the hash function, the attacker also cannot obtain the previous and future session keys by using the current session key. Therefore, the proposed authentication key agreement scheme in this section satisfies the requirements for forward security and backward security.

5.1.6. Ability to Resist Attacks

The following analysis shows the proposed scheme's ability to resist regular attacks against the authentication key negotiation protocol.

1. Replay attack: In the authentication key agreement scheme designed in this section, a timestamp is introduced. During each authentication, the validity of the timestamp is first checked, and if it is valid, the subsequent steps will be carried out; otherwise, this message will be discarded. In this scheme, two timestamps need to be added. The first timestamp is added when generating the short-term pseudonym of the vehicle OBU_i, to ensure the timeliness of the short-term pseudonym. The second timestamp is added when broadcasting the message $M_i = (LID_i, pk_i, m_i, h_i, \sigma_i, T_j)$, to ensure the timeliness of the broadcast message. The introduction of timestamps can effectively

prevent the attacker from repeatedly sending the messages of the two communication parties in the channel and prevent the attacker from obtaining the secret information he expected. Therefore, the authentication key agreement protocol in this article can effectively resist replay attacks.

2. Man-in-the-middle attack: This protocol adopts a certificate-less authentication method, relying on the difficult problem of ECDLP. The adversary cannot completely simulate a vehicle to generate message $\{LID_i, pk_i, m_i, h_i, \sigma_i, T_j\}$ as a middleman, and the vehicle uses the public parameters published by the trusted party in the communication process, so there is no opportunity for a middleman to deceive the communication participants. Therefore, this scheme can resist man-in-the-middle attacks.
3. Tampering attack: In this scheme, the message $\{LID_i, pk_i, m_i, h_i, \sigma_i, T_j\}$ broadcasted by OBU_i is signed, where σ_i is the digital signature, which can ensure the integrity of the message. At the same time, this scheme has a traceability mechanism for suspicious information and identities. When the attacker tampers with the message in the communication channel, the traceability of the user identity can help to discover whether the information has been tampered with by the attacker. Therefore, the authentication scheme proposed in this article can resist tampering attacks.
4. Simulation attack: In the simulation attack, the attacker may imitate the structure of the pseudonym to disguise himself as a legitimate vehicle. However, under the assumption of ECDLP, the attacker cannot obtain the master key, which is protected by the trusted part, so he cannot forge a standardized pseudonym. Therefore, this scheme has the ability to resist simulation attacks.
5. Eavesdropping attack: Though malicious eavesdropping attacks on the Internet of Vehicles system are continuous and the occurrence of the eavesdropping behavior cannot be prevented, the proposed authentication key agreement scheme uses a secure channel or encryption to protect the secret information, and the session key negotiated will play an encryption role when the communication entities conduct dialogue interaction. Therefore, this scheme can prevent malicious attackers from obtaining confidential information and user privacy through eavesdropping.

5.2. Security Proof

This section will formally prove that the proposed scheme is secure under the security model in Section 3.2 and the assumption that the Elliptic Curve Discrete Logarithm Problem (ECDLP) is difficult to resolve.

Definition 1. *If two types of adversaries A_I and A_{II} win the game with a non-negligible probability in polynomial time to solve the ECDLP, then this scheme satisfies nonforgeability in the random oracle model and is computationally secure.*

Theorem 1. *In a probabilistic polynomial time, assuming that the adversary A_I performs the game for time t, performs $Q(h)$ hash queries, $Q(sk)$ partial private key extraction queries, $Q(pk)$ partial private key extraction queries, and $Q(\sigma)$ signature queries, and finally forges a legal signature with an advantage as ε, then within time $t' \leq t + O(Q(1) + Q(3) + (Q(2) + Q(4) + Q(sk) + Q(pk) + Q(\sigma))t_s)$, the adversary needs to solve the difficult ECDLP problem with a probability not lower than $\frac{\varepsilon}{Q(sk)}\left(1 - \frac{1}{Q(sk)}\right)^{Q(sk)}$, where t_s represents the operation time of a scalar multiplication on the elliptic curve group G.*

Proof of Theorem 1. The outline of the proof is shown in Figure 3. The specific derivation process is as follows:

Figure 3. Outline of proof of Theorem 1.

Construct $P, Q = aP$, where a is a randomly selected number, $a \in Z_q^*$, and P is a generator on the elliptic curve G. According to the assumption of the ECDLP, the challenger C needs to find a in order to solve the ECDLP.

1. Initialization stage: The challenger C initializes the system parameters and sends them to the adversary, and the challenger C randomly selects an identity ID' as its challenge identity in this game, and the system parameters are $p = \{G, P, P_p = Q, T_p, H_1, H_2, H_3, H_4\}$.
2. Query stage: The adversary A_I will perform the following random oracle queries.
   - H_1 query: When the adversary A_I queries this oracle, the challenger records the interaction between the adversary A_I and the challenger C in the list $L_1 = (ID_i, H_1(ID_i))$. When the challenger C finds the corresponding record in the list L_1, it returns $H_1(ID_i)$ to the adversary A_I; otherwise, it randomly selects $H_1(ID_i) \in Z_q^*$ and gives it to the adversary A_I, and adds $(ID_i, H_1(ID_i))$ to the list L_1.
   - H_2 query: When the adversary L_1 queries this oracle, the challenger records the interaction between the adversary A_I and the challenger C in the list $L_2 = (PID_i||R_i||P_p, r_i)$. When the challenger C finds the corresponding record in the list L_2, it returns r_i to the adversary A_I; otherwise, it randomly selects $r_i \in Z_q^*$ and gives it to the adversary A_I, and adds $(PID_i||R_i||P_p, r_i)$ to the list L_2.
   - H_3 query: When the adversary A_I queries this oracle, the challenger records the interaction between the adversary A_I and the challenger C in the list $L_3 = ((\delta \cdot T_p)||PID_i||T_i||H_1(PWD_i), u_i)$. When the challenger C finds the corresponding record in the list L_3, it returns u_i to the adversary A_I; otherwise, it randomly selects $u_i \in Z_q^*$ and gives it to the adversary A_I, and adds $((\delta \cdot T_p)||PID_i||T_i||H_1(PWD_i), u_i)$ to the list L_3.
   - H_4 query: When the adversary A_I queries this oracle, the challenger records the interaction between the adversary A_I and the challenger C in the list $L_4 = (D_i|| LID_1^i|| LID_2^i||T_j||pk_i||R_i||P_p, l_i)$. When the challenger C finds the corresponding record in the list L_4, it returns l_i to the adversary A_I; otherwise, it randomly selects $l_i \in Z_q^*$ and gives it to the adversary A_I, and adds $(D_i|| LID_1^i|| LID_2^i||T_j||pk_i||R_i||P_p, l_i)$ to the list L_4.

- Partial private key extraction query: When the adversary A_I queries this oracle, the challenger records the interaction between the adversary A_I and the challenger C in the list $L_{sk} = (PID_i, psk_i)$. When the challenger C finds the corresponding record in the list L_{sk}, it returns l_i to the adversary A_I; otherwise, if $PID_i \neq PID_i'$, it randomly selects $psk_i \in Z_q^*$ and gives it to the adversary A_I, and adds (PID_i, psk_i) to the list L_{sk}, and if $PID_i = PID_i'$, the game ends.
- Public key extraction query: When the adversary A_I queries this oracle, the challenger records the interaction between the adversary A_I and the challenger C in the list $L_{pk} = (PID_i, a_i, pk_i)$. When the challenger C finds the corresponding record in the list L_{pk}, it returns pk_i to the adversary A_I; otherwise, if $PID_i \neq PID_i'$, it randomly selects $a_i \in Z_q^*$ and gives it to the adversary A_I, and adds $(D_i \| LID_1^i \| LID_2^i \| T_j \| pk_i \| R_i \| P_p)$ and (PID_i, a_i, pk_i) to L_{sk} and L_{pk}, respectively.
- Secret value extraction query: When the adversary A_I queries this oracle, if $PID_i = PID_i'$, the challenger C quits and ends the game; otherwise, if there is a record (PID_i, a_i, pk_i), the challenger C returns a_i to the adversary A_I, and otherwise, the challenger C adds the record (a_i, pk_i) to the list L_{pk} and returns a_i to the adversary A_I.
- Signature query: When the adversary A_I queries this oracle, the challenger C obtains $H_1(PID_i)$, $H_2(PID_i \| R_i \| P_p)$, $H_3((\delta \cdot T_p) \| PID_i \| T_i \| H_1(PWD_i))$, $H_4(D_i \| LID_1^i \| LID_2^i \| T_j \| pk_i \| R_i \| P_p)$ from the lists L_1, L_2, L_3, L_4, respectively. If $PID_i \neq PID_i'$, the challenger C outputs the signature σ_i corresponding to the message m_i and returns it to the adversary A_I; otherwise, it calculates $D_i = \gamma_i \cdot P$, $w_i = H_4(D_i, LID_1^i, LID_2^i, T_j, pk_i, R_i, P_p)$, $v_i = H_4(m_i, D_i, LID_1^i, LID_2^i, T_j, pk_i, R_i, P_p)$, $\tau_i = \gamma_i + v_i(w_i \cdot a_i + s_i) \bmod q$, and returns the correct signature $\sigma_i = (R_i, D_i, \tau_i)$ of the message m_i to the adversary A_I.

3. Forgery stage: After the adversary A_I completes the above queries, it outputs a forged signature. If $PID_i = PID_i'$, the challenger C ends the game; otherwise, if the adversary wants to win the game, it needs to find out the corresponding signature information from the information obtained from the queries, and it needs to make the equation $\tau_i \cdot P = D_i + v_i'(w_i' \cdot pk_i + R_i + h_i \cdot P_p)$ hold.

According to the forking lemma [25], the adversary A_I also needs to obtain two other valid signatures $\sigma_i^{(\lambda)}, (\lambda = 2, 3)$, and all three signatures need to make the equation $\tau_i \cdot P = D_i + v_i'(w_i' \cdot pk_i + R_i + h_i \cdot P_p)$ hold. Since there is $pk_i = a_i \cdot P$, $P_p = \beta \cdot P$, $D_i = \gamma_i \cdot P$, then $\tau_i^{\lambda} \cdot P = D_i + v_i'(w_i' \cdot pk_i^{\lambda} + R_i + h_i \cdot P_p), \lambda = 1, 2, 3$.

The challenger C needs to solve this linearly independent equation and output a as the solution to the ECDLP.

In the partial private key extraction stage, the challenger C has a probability of at least $\left(1 - \frac{1}{Q(sk)}\right)^{Q(sk)}$ to not abandon the operation, and in the forgery stage, the challenger C has a probability of at least $\frac{1}{Q(sk)}$ to not abandon the operation. Therefore, the challenger C successfully solves the ECDLP within time $t' \leq t + O(Q(1) + Q(3) + (Q(2) + Q(4) + Q(sk) + Q(pk) + Q(\sigma))t_s)$ with a probability of at least $\frac{\varepsilon}{Q(sk)}\left(1 - \frac{1}{Q(sk)}\right)^{Q(sk)}$. Since the adversary A_I cannot win the game with a negligible probability in polynomial time, then this scheme has nonforgeability security in the random oracle model. □

The proof is completed.

Theorem 2. *In a probabilistic polynomial time, assuming that the adversary A_{II} performs the game for time t, performs $Q(h)$ hash queries, $Q(x)$ secret value extraction queries, $Q(pk)$ partial private key extraction queries, and $Q(\sigma)$ signature queries, and finally forges a legal signature with an advantage as ε, then within time $t' \leq t + O(Q(1) + Q(3) + (Q(2) + Q(4) + Q(pk) + Q(\sigma))t_s)$,* *the adversary needs to solve the ECDLP with a probability not lower than* $\frac{\epsilon}{Q(pk)}\left(1-\frac{1}{Q(pk)}\right)^{Q(pk)+Q(x)}$, *where* t_s *represents the operation time of a scalar multiplication on the elliptic curve group G.*

Proof of Theorem 2. The proof process is similar to that of Theorem 1, but the adversary A_{II} does not have the ability to perform partial private key extraction queries, and this will not be elaborated here. □

6. Discussion of Performance

This section will conduct a performance comparison and analysis of the proposed authenticated key agreement scheme in this paper from the aspects of security, computational overhead, and communication overhead.

6.1. Security Comparison

The following part will compare the protocol in this paper with the protocols proposed in other studies from the perspective of security. Table 1 shows the comparison results of this scheme and other similar schemes [15–18] in terms of anonymity, traceability and revocability, identity privacy, message authenticity, unlinkability, resistance to man-in-the-middle attack, resistance to replay attack, resistance to simulation attack, key escrow resilience [26], and batch verification.

The security comparison is shown in Table 1. The aggregate signature scheme proposed in [16] does not have anonymity, for the real identity of the vehicle is used in the authentication process. And it is proved in [17] that the scheme in [16] cannot resist replay attack and simulation attack, with relatively low security. These drawbacks make it unsuitable for large-scale IoV networks with high complexity and uncertainty. The scheme in [17] has been greatly improved compared to [16]; it possesses higher security for its identity anonymity in the authentication and the ability to resist simulation attack, but it still cannot resist replay attack, for it does not include a timestamp in the signature message. The scheme in [18] introduces a timestamp to resist replay attack, but it is constructed by using identity-based cryptography, and all user keys are generated by a third party, which will lead to a key escrow problem; this drawback makes it unsuitable for large-scale 5G IoV networks. The scheme proposed in [15] stores the vehicle's real identity and password in an anti-tampering smart card, which is costly. Furthermore, once the smart card is lost, the user's identity will be exposed. At the same time, when the trusted authority calculates the user's long-term fake identity, it does not use its own master key, which means that the malicious user without the trusted authority's master key can simulate and forge the long-term fake identity of the vehicle. In addition, when the KGC generates a partial private key for the user, it does not use a one-time random number, so attackers can analyze the historical and future values of the partial private key for the vehicle based on the obtained partial private key value, that is, the scheme proposed in [15] does not meet the requirement of forward security and backward security. According to the security analysis and proof in Section 5, the authenticated key agreement scheme proposed in this paper can solve the security problems in [15–18] and can resist more types of attacks. Vehicle users also do not need to use expensive anti-tampering devices. Even if the smart card is lost, as previously analyzed, the attacker cannot calculate the vehicle's real identity OID_i through the long-term pseudonym PID_i stored in the smart card. Therefore, the scheme can ensure the anonymity of the vehicle's real identity OID_i and has stronger security.

Table 1. Security comparison.

Scheme	Anonymity	Traceability and Revocability	Identity Privacy	Message Authenticability	Unlinkability	Resistance to Man-in-the-Middle Attack	Resistance to Replay Attack	Resistance to Simulation Attack	Key Escrow Resilience	Batch Verification
Scheme in [15]	√	√	√	√	√	√	√	×	√	√
Scheme in [16]	×	√	√	√	√	√	×	×	√	√
Scheme in [17]	√	√	√	√	√	√	×	√	√	√
Scheme in [18]	√	√	√	√	√	√	√	√	×	√
This paper	√	√	√	√	√	√	√	√	√	√

6.2. Computational Overhead Comparison

To analyze the computational overhead of the scheme, we define T_{bp} as the execution time of a bilinear operation, T_{em} as the execution time of a point multiplication operation on ECC, and T_{ea} as the execution time of a point addition operation on ECC. For the simulations, a PC with Inter Core i7-10710CPU and 16 GB of DDR3 memory was employed, and algorithms were chosen from MIRACL cryptographic library. The simulation steps are as follows. Construct elliptic curve $\overline{E} : y^2 = x^3 + x(\mathrm{mod} p_1)$ and $\overline{E} : y^2 = x^3 + ax - b(\mathrm{mod} p)$, where the lengths of integers p_1 and p are 64 bytes and 20 bytes, respectively, G_1 is a cyclic subgroup of elliptic curve $\overline{E}$, and G is a cyclic subgroup of elliptic curve E. Perform the bilinear pair operation e: $G_1 \times G_1 \rightarrow G_T$, point multiplication operation, and point addition operation on the cyclic group G, with an average of 5000 executions for each operation. The simulation results show that T_{bp} is approximately equal to 9.15 ms, T_{em} is approximately equal to 5.69 ms, and T_{ea} is approximately equal to 0.01 ms. Since the time consumption of hash function operation and modular multiplication operation is significantly lower than that of bilinear operation and point multiplication operation on ECC, they are not discussed in the comparison range of the computational overhead of the scheme. The comparison of the computational overhead of this scheme and similar schemes is shown in Table 2.

Table 2. Computational overhead comparison.

Scheme	Sign/ms	Verify/ms	Total/ms
Scheme in [15]	T_{ea}	$4T_{em} + 2T_{ea}$	$5T_{em} + 2T_{ea}$
Scheme in [16]	$4T_{em} + 2T_{ea}$	$3T_{em} + T_{ea} + 3T_{bp}$	$7T_{em} + 3T_{ea} + 3T_{bp}$
Scheme in [17]	$3T_{em} + 2T_{ea}$	$3T_{em} + 2T_{ea}$	$6T_{em} + 4T_{ea}$
Scheme in [18]	$3T_{em} + T_{ea}$	$3T_{em} + 2T_{ea}$	$7T_{em} + 4T_{ea}$
This paper's scheme	T_{ea}	$4T_{em} + 3T_{ea}$	$5T_{em} + 3T_{ea}$

The calculation overhead of each scheme is presented in Table 2, covering the execution time in the signature stage and the verification stage, as well as the total execution time. The time unit is ms. As shown in Table 2, this scheme does not utilize the bilinear operation. Instead, it employs point multiplication and point addition operations on the elliptic curve, which have a smaller computational overhead. In the signature process, the vehicle only employs one elliptic curve point multiplication operation. This is highly suitable for the vehicle end with limited computing power to generate signatures, and this relatively low calculation cost enables the scheme to be applicable in large-scale deployment environments with numerous vehicles. In the verification stage, this scheme also has a relatively smaller computational overhead compared with [16–18]. Although it performs one more elliptic curve point addition operation in the verification stage compared with the scheme in [15], this scheme has better security than the scheme in [15], and the time consumption of one point addition operation is significantly lower than that of one point multiplication operation, so the impact on the operational efficiency of the scheme is minor. Meanwhile, the processes of aggregate signature and batch verification enhance the overall efficiency of the scheme. Therefore, this scheme is more appropriate for the large-scale 5G vehicle network than other similar schemes. Figure 4 shows the comparison of the operation time of this scheme and similar schemes.

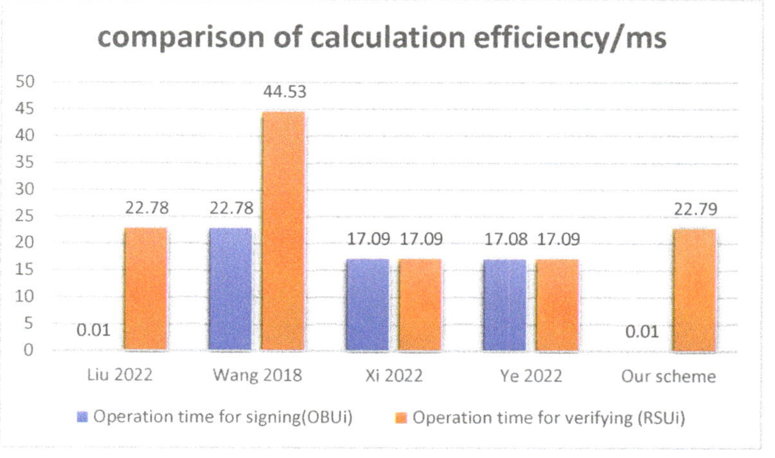

Figure 4. Operation time comparison [15–18].

6.3. Communication Overhead Comparison

This section will compare the scheme in this paper with other similar certificateless aggregation schemes [15–18] from the perspective of communication overhead. The comparison contents include the signature length of a single message and the length of the broadcast message M_i minus the message m_i. Elliptic curves $\overline{E}$ and E are constructed. The element $|G_1|$ in the bilinear mapping group $\overline{E}$ has a length of 128 bytes, and the integer has a length of 64 bytes. The element $|G|$ in the group E has a length of 40 bytes, and the integer has a length of 20 bytes. The comparison of communication overhead with other schemes is shown in Table 3.

Table 3. Communication overhead comparison.

Scheme	Length of Signature	Length of Broadcast Message
Scheme in [15]	60 Bytes	188 Bytes
Scheme in [16]	272 Bytes	272 Bytes
Scheme in [17]	120 Bytes	300 Bytes
Scheme in [18]	100 Bytes	248 Bytes
This paper's scheme	100 Bytes	228 Bytes

In the proposed scheme, the broadcast message $M_i = (FID_i, pk_i, m_i, h_i, \sigma_i, T_j)$, where the short-term pseudonym LID_i has a length of $|G| + \left|Z_q^*\right| + |T| = 64Bytes$, the public key pk_i has a length of $|G| = 40Bytes$, h_i has a length of $\left|Z_q^*\right| = 20Bytes$, the timestamp T_j has a length of $|T| = 4Bytes$, the signature σ_i has a length of $2|G| + \left|Z_q^*\right| = 100Bytes$, and the length of the broadcast message is $4|G| + 3\left|Z_q^*\right| + 2|T| = 228Bytes$.

Using the same method, we can calculate the communication overhead of the schemes in [15–18]:

In the scheme proposed in [15], the broadcast message $M_i = \left(m_i, \sigma_i, QID_i, FID^i, V_{pub_i}, T_j\right)$, where the long-term pseudonym QID_i has a length of $\left|Z_q^*\right| = 20Bytes$, the short-term pseudonym FID^i has a length of $|G| + \left|Z_q^*\right| + |T| = 64Bytes$, the public key V_{pub_i} has a length of $|G| = 40Bytes$, the timestamp T_j has a length of $|T| = 4Bytes$, the signature σ_i has a length of $|G| + \left|Z_q^*\right| = 60Bytes$, and the broadcast message length is $3|G| + 3\left|Z_q^*\right| + 2|T| = 188Bytes$.

For the broadcast message $M_i = (m_i, \sigma_i)$ in the scheme of [16], only the signature σ_i is included, and its length is $2|G| + |G_1| + \left|Z_q^*\right| = 272Bytes$, then the length of the broadcast message is also 272 bytes.

In the scheme of [17], the broadcast message M_i includes the pseudonym AID_i, the user's public key SPK_{AID_i}, the signature σ_i, where the pseudonym has a length of $|G| + \left|Z_q^*\right| = 60Bytes$, the user's public key has a length of $3|G| = 120Bytes$, the signature has a length of $|G| + 4\left|Z_q^*\right| = 120Bytes$, then the total length of the broadcast message is $5|G| + 5\left|Z_q^*\right| = 300Bytes$.

In the scheme of [18], the broadcast message M_i includes the signature σ_i, the timestamp TS, the fake identity PID, the secret value Q_i, the public key PK_{V_i}, where the signature σ_i has a length of $|G| + 3\left|Z_q^*\right| = 100Bytes$, the timestamp TS has a length of $|T| = 4Bytes$, the fake identity PID has a length of $|G| + \left|Z_q^*\right| + |T| = 64Bytes$, the secret value Q_i has a length of $|G| = 40Bytes$, the public key PK_{V_i} has a length of $|G| = 40Bytes$, so the total length of the broadcast message is $4|G| + 4\left|Z_q^*\right| + 2|T| = 248Bytes$.

Figure 5 shows the comparison of communication overhead. It can be observed that the proposed scheme has a lower communication overhead than the similar schemes in [16–18], and it is slightly higher than the scheme in [15], but it has higher security.

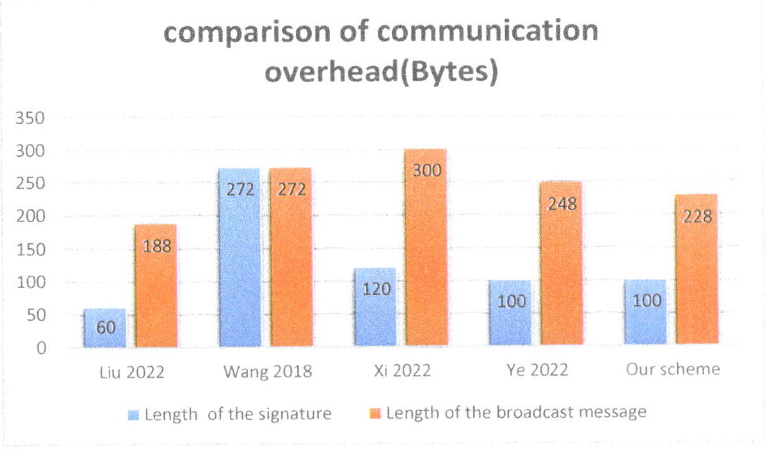

Figure 5. Communication overhead comparison [15–18].

7. Conclusions

In this paper, an anonymous authentication key negotiation scheme for 5G vehicle networks is proposed based on certificate-less aggregate signature. Two types of pseudonyms, namely long-term and short-term ones, are constructed to conceal the real identity of vehicles. Meanwhile, the partial private key of the vehicle is generated and distributed according to the long-term pseudonym to solve the problem of key escrow. Through security and performance analysis and verification, it is shown that the proposed scheme in this paper is provably secure under the random oracle model and meets the characteristics of anonymity, traceability and revocability, identity privacy, etc. Additionally, it can resist simulation attacks, man-in-the-middle attacks, and smart card loss attacks. Compared with similar schemes, it possesses stronger security and better computing efficiency and communication efficiency, making it more suitable for application in the 5G vehicle network. In future work, we will focus on potential extensions of the scheme, such as adaptations for different IoV environments, integration with emerging technologies like Blockchain, and further discuss the practical implementation challenges and potential deployment scenarios in real-world IoV systems.

Author Contributions: Conceptualization, G.W. and Y.Q.; methodology, Y.Q.; validation, G.W. and Y.Q.; formal analysis, G.W. and Y.Q.; writing—original draft preparation, G.W. and Y.Q.; writing—review and editing, G.W., Y.Q., G.K. and Z.S. All authors have read and agreed to the published version of the manuscript.

Funding: This research was funded by the National Natural Science Foundation of China, grant number (No. 62270273).

Data Availability Statement: The data presented in this study are also available upon request from the corresponding author.

Conflicts of Interest: The authors declare no conflict of interest.

References

1. Wiseman, Y. Autonomous Vehicles, Encyclopedia of Information Science and Technology. 2020, Volume 1, Chapter 1. pp. 1–11. Available online: https://u.cs.biu.ac.il/~wisemav/Autonomous-Vehicles-Encyclopedia.pdf (accessed on 20 July 2024).
2. Wei, Z.; Lu, X.; Shi, T. Cross-domain key agreement protocol based on PKI system. *Comput. Sci.* **2017**, *44*, 155–158+182.
3. Wang, Q.; Qiao, R.; Fan, N.; Duan, Z. An efficient conditional anonymo authentication scheme for VANETs. *J. Beijing Jiaotong Univ.* **2019**, *43*, 80–86.
4. Pu, W. A Lightweight Group-based Secure Authentication and Communication Scheme in VANETs. Master's Thesis, Wuhan University, Wuhan, China, 2019.
5. Huang, Y.; Wang, Y.; Chen, W.; Zhang, Z. PKI cross-domain authentication model based on alliance chain. *Comput. Eng. Des.* **2021**, *42*, 3043–3051.
6. Lv, L.; Zheng, D.; Zhang, Y.; Yan, M.; Su, H. Identity-based aggregated signature verification in vehicular ad hoc network. *Comput. Eng. Des.* **2018**, *39*, 1866–1871.
7. Yao, R. Research on Efficient Authentication Schemes with Conditional Privacy-Preserving for VANETs. Master's Thesis, Chongqing University, Chongqing, China, 2021.
8. Zhang, H.; Chen, Z.; Huang, H.; He, X. Intra-group mutual authentication key agreement protocol based on Chinese remainder theorem in VANET system. *J. Commun.* **2022**, *43*, 182–193.
9. Zhang, G. Research on Security and Privacy Traceability in Internet of Vehicle Based on 5G. Master's Thesis, Xidian University, Xi'an, China, 2021.
10. Al-Riyami, S.S.; Paterson, K.G. Certificate-less secure upload for drive-thru Internet. *Lect. Notes Comput. Sci.* **2003**, 452–473.
11. Zhang, W.; Lei, L.; Wang, X.; Wang, Y. Secure and Efficient Authentication and Key Agreement Protocol Using Certificateless Aggregate Signatu re for Cloud Service Oriented VANET. *Acta Electron. Sin.* **2020**, *48*, 1814–1823.
12. Wei, G.; Qin, Y.; Fu, W. Secure and efficient certificateless authentication key agreement protocol in VANET. In *Communications in computer and Information Science, CCIS, Proceedings of Emerging Information Security and Applications-3rd International Conference, EISA 2022*; Springer: Cham, Switzerland, 2022; Volume 1641, pp. 160–172.
13. Zhang, Z. Research on Certificateless Anonymous Authentication Scheme and Group Key Agreement Scheme in VANETs. Master's Thesis, Chongqing University, Chongqing, China, 2021.
14. Xiong, L. Research on Group-based Authentication and Key Management Mechanism in 5G V2X. Master's Thesis, Xidian University, Xi'an, China, 2021.
15. Liu, X.; Wang, L.; Huan, L.; Du, X.; Niu, S. Certificateless Anonymous Authentication Scheme for Internet of Vehicles. *J. Electron. Inf. Technol.* **2022**, *44*, 295–304.
16. Wang, D.; Teng, J. Probably Secure Cetificateless Aggregate Signature Algorithm for Vehicular Ad hoc Network. *J. Electron. Inf. Technol.* **2018**, *1*, 11–17.
17. Xi, W. Research on Data Sharing and Security Authentication Scheme in Internet of Vehicles Environment. Master's Thesis, Northwest Normal University, Lanzhou, China, 2022.
18. Ye, X. Research on Efficient Digital Signature Technology in Internet of Vehicles. Master's Thesis, University of Electronic Science and Technology of China, Chengdu, China, 2022.
19. Bao, J.; Luo, M.; Chen, Y.; Peng, C.; Bao, Z. A Certificateless Anonymous Authentication Scheme for VANETs Based on Ring Signature. *J. Circuits Syst. Comput.* **2024**, *33*, 245–253. [CrossRef]
20. Shahidinejad, A.; Abawajy, J. Blockchain-based self-certified key exchange protocol for hybrid electric vehicles. *IEEE Trans. Consum. Electron.* **2023**, *70*, 543–553. [CrossRef]
21. Shahidinejad, A.; Abawajy, J.; Huda, S. Anonymous Lattice-Based Authentication Protocol for Vehicular Communications. *Veh. Commun.* **2024**, *48*, 100803. [CrossRef]
22. Shahidinejad, A.; Abawajy, J. Anonymous blockchain-assisted authentication protocols for secure cross-domain IoD communications. *IEEE Trans. Netw. Sci. Eng.* **2023**, *11*, 2661–2674. [CrossRef]

23. Shahidinejad, A.; Abawajy, J. An all-inclusive taxonomy and critical review of blockchain-assisted authentication and session key generation protocols for IoT. *ACM Comput. Surv.* **2024**, *56*, 1–38. [CrossRef]
24. Shahidinejad, A.; Abawajy, J. Efficient provably-secure authentication protocol for multi-domain IoT using a combined off-chain and on-chain approach. *IEEE Internet Things J.* **2023**, *9*, 15241–15251.
25. Gope, P. PMAKE: Privacy-aware multi-factor authenticated key establishment scheme for advance metering infrastructure in smart grid. *Comput. Commun.* **2020**, *152*, 338–344. [CrossRef]
26. Wang, L. Research on Certificateless Anonymous Authentication and Conditional Privacy Preservation Scheme for Internet of Vehicles. Master's Thesis, Northwest Normal University, Lanzhou, China, 2022.

Disclaimer/Publisher's Note: The statements, opinions and data contained in all publications are solely those of the individual author(s) and contributor(s) and not of MDPI and/or the editor(s). MDPI and/or the editor(s) disclaim responsibility for any injury to people or property resulting from any ideas, methods, instructions or products referred to in the content.

electronics

MDPI

Review

Challenges and Advances in Analyzing TLS 1.3-Encrypted Traffic: A Comprehensive Survey

Jiuxing Zhou, Wei Fu, Wei Hu, Zhihong Sun *, Tao He and Zhihong Zhang

Department of Information Security, Naval University of Engineering, Wuhan 430030, China
* Correspondence: zhihong.sun@whu.edu.cn

Abstract: The widespread adoption of encrypted communication protocols has significantly enhanced network security and user privacy, simultaneously elevating the importance of encrypted traffic analysis across various domains, including network anomaly detection. The Transport Layer Security (TLS) 1.3 protocol, introduced in 2018, has gained rapid popularity due to its enhanced security features and improved performance. However, TLS 1.3's security enhancements, such as encrypting more of the handshake process, present unprecedented challenges for encrypted traffic analysis, rendering traditional methods designed for TLS 1.2 and earlier versions ineffective and necessitating the development of novel analytical techniques. This comprehensive survey provides a thorough review of the latest advancements in TLS 1.3 traffic analysis. First, we examine the impact of TLS 1.3's new features, including Encrypted ClientHello (ECH), 0-RTT session resumption, and Perfect Forward Secrecy (PFS), on existing traffic analysis techniques. We then present a systematic overview of state-of-the-art methods for analyzing TLS 1.3 traffic, encompassing middlebox-based interception, searchable encryption, and machine learning-based approaches. For each method, we provide a critical analysis of its advantages, limitations, and applicable scenarios. Furthermore, we compile and review key datasets utilized in machine learning-based TLS 1.3 traffic analysis research. Finally, we discuss the main challenges and potential future research directions for TLS 1.3 traffic analysis. Given that TLS 1.3 is still in the early stages of widespread deployment, research in this field remains nascent. This survey aims to provide researchers and practitioners with a comprehensive reference, facilitating the development of more effective TLS 1.3 traffic analysis techniques that balance network security requirements with user privacy protection.

Keywords: TLS 1.3; encrypted traffic analysis; machine learning; interception techniques; searchable encryption

1. Introduction

With the rapid development of the Internet, encrypted communication protocols have become crucial in safeguarding network communication security. According to Google's Transparency Report from April 2024 [1], 94% of traffic across all Google products and services, as well as web pages loaded via HTTPS in the Chrome browser (Windows system), is encrypted. Since its inception in 1999, the Transport Layer Security (TLS) protocol [2], the most widely used secure transmission protocol, has undergone multiple iterations and improvements. Notably, TLS 1.3, released in August 2018 [3], with enhanced security, higher performance, and greater flexibility, has garnered widespread attention and rapid adoption in both academia and the industry. According to the latest statistics from Qualys SSL Labs [4], as of May 2024, 70.1% of websites surveyed by SSL Labs support TLS 1.3, and this proportion is continuing to rise. It is foreseeable that TLS 1.3 will become the de facto standard for Internet communication encryption in the coming years.

However, the widespread adoption of TLS 1.3 presents new challenges for network traffic analysis. Compared to its predecessor, TLS 1.2 [5], TLS 1.3 introduces significant protocol design improvements and new features, making traditional traffic analysis methods based on TLS 1.2 and earlier versions difficult to apply directly. For instance, existing machine learning-based TLS 1.2 traffic classification methods primarily rely on plaintext features from the handshake phase, such as packet length and sequence patterns. Due to TLS 1.3's reduction in handshake round trips, the observed packet length sequences and traffic characteristics during the handshake phase have changed. This change leads to a decrease in the effectiveness of classification methods based on packet length sequences when distinguishing between different sessions or applications, necessitating adjustments to accommodate new patterns in TLS 1.3 traffic, as demonstrated by recent studies [6]. Additionally, TLS 1.3 enhances privacy protection by strengthening encryption during the handshake process, significantly reducing the plaintext information available during this phase. The Encrypted Server Name Indication (Encrypted SNI) extension further limits traffic analysis visibility, objectively restricting the effectiveness of traditional traffic analysis methods. Recent research [7] indicates that, to maintain high classification performance in TLS 1.3, existing models require corresponding adjustments. This includes re-selecting and extracting new features applicable to TLS 1.3, such as changes in traffic patterns caused by 0-RTT session resumption, and enhancing the feature extraction capabilities of models using time series analysis and deep learning techniques. Moreover, retraining models to encompass TLS 1.3-specific traffic characteristics is also a crucial step in improving classification performance.

In light of the pervasive adoption of TLS 1.3 and its significant impact on traffic characteristics, it is crucial to assess and improve the applicability of existing TLS 1.2 traffic analysis methods in the TLS 1.3 environment. On the one hand, security threats such as malware and botnets are actively utilizing TLS 1.3 to evade detection, making the analysis and identification of their traffic behavior urgent. On the other hand, network operators and service providers still need to legally and compliantly identify and manage TLS 1.3 traffic to achieve network optimization and anomaly diagnosis. Additionally, in specific fields such as cybercrime investigation and national security, there remains a need for the compliant analysis of TLS 1.3 traffic. Therefore, researching new traffic analysis methods and techniques for TLS 1.3 is not only a frontier topic in academic research but also has broad application prospects and practical relevance.

In response to the challenges posed by TLS 1.3, the academic community has conducted extensive and in-depth research. This paper not only deeply analyzes the new features introduced by TLS 1.3 and their impact on traffic analysis but also systematically reviews the latest achievements in TLS 1.3 traffic analysis to support future research.

1.1. Data Sources and Methodology of Study

In this survey, we systematically reviewed literature relevant to TLS 1.3 traffic analysis. We conducted comprehensive searches across major academic databases such as IEEE Xplore, ACM Digital Library, SpringerLink, ScienceDirect, and Google Scholar. Our search employed a range of keywords including "TLS", "TLS 1.3", "TLS-1.3", "network traffic", "encrypted traffic", "traffic analysis", "traffic classification", "machine learning", "middleboxes", and "searchable encryption". Although our primary focus was on publications from 2018 onwards—postdating the release of TLS 1.3—we also included seminal works from earlier years that remain relevant. Recognizing that some papers do not explicitly mention "TLS 1.3" but offer applicable methodologies (e.g., searchable encryption), we included these studies in our review. Additionally, we explored Internet standards repositories for relevant technical standards related to TLS.

In total, we collected 223 documents comprising papers, websites, technical standards, and other resources. After filtering out those not directly relevant to our study's focus, approximately 120 references were incorporated into our paper. For a detailed evaluation of TLS 1.3 traffic analysis techniques' progress, we prioritized high-impact papers published in leading conferences and journals, ultimately selecting 37 papers for in-depth assessment.

By detailing our data sources and methodology, we aim to provide transparency in our research process and facilitate reproducibility for future studies.

1.2. Differences from Existing Surveys

As early as 2015, Velan et al. [8] conducted a systematic review of methods for encrypted traffic analysis. Since then, extensive research has been conducted in this field by scholars. In this survey, we present existing research on encrypted traffic analysis, with a primary focus on TLS 1.3 traffic analysis techniques.

Table 1 compares this study with other surveys on encrypted traffic analysis. Recent studies have provided comprehensive surveys on encrypted traffic analysis [9–12], covering techniques and applications such as machine learning and deep learning. Some researchers have concentrated on the application of deep learning in anomaly detection [13] and network attack detection [14]. With the emergence of new network architectures and application scenarios, researchers have started investigating encrypted traffic analysis in fields such as mobile applications [15–17], the Internet of Things (IoT) [18], and Software-Defined Networking (SDN) [19]. Poh et al. [20] focused on privacy protection issues and surveyed techniques for privacy-preserving encrypted traffic inspection. In the field of TLS-encrypted traffic analysis, Oh et al. [21] investigated various techniques for detecting TLS 1.2-encrypted malicious traffic in Security Operations Center (SOC) scenarios. Although de Carnavalet et al. [22] studied TLS 1.3 and earlier versions, their work primarily focused on surveying and analyzing interception mechanisms and motivations, lacking investigation into other traffic analysis techniques. This paper aims to comprehensively review the research progress in TLS 1.3 traffic analysis techniques, discuss the applicability and limitations of existing methods, and explore future research directions.

Table 1. Differences between existing encrypted traffic analysis surveys and this survey.

Survey	Year	Encryption Protocol	Domain	Contributions
[8]	2015	Various	ETC	Summarized methods for ETC and analysis
[9]	2019	Various	ETC	Overviewed the application of DL in ETC tasks
[10]	2019	Various	NTC	Systematically reviewed the process of using ML techniques for TC
[13]	2019	Various	NAD1	Summarized various methods for NAD1 using DL techniques
[15]	2019	Various	Mobile	Extensively surveyed the application of DL techniques in Mobile
[16]	2019	Various	Mobile ETC	Evaluated the performance of DL in Mobile ETC tasks through experiments
[19]	2019	Various	SDN network intrusion detection	Investigated the current state of research on intrusion detection using ML methods in SDNs
[17]	2020	Various	Mobile ETC	Proposed a general framework for evaluating the effectiveness of DL in mobile ETC
[18]	2020	Various	IoT-TC	Reviewed various techniques and methods for IoT-TC
[11]	2021	Various	ETA	Comprehensive review of ETA research progress from application, technology, and countermeasure perspectives
[20]	2021	Various	Privacy protection	Investigated various privacy-preserving techniques for ETA over network middleboxes
[12]	2022	Various	ETA	Thoroughly reviewed various methods for ETA using ML techniques

Table 1. *Cont.*

Survey	Year	Encryption Protocol	Domain	Contributions
[21]	2022	TLS 1.2	Malicious ETA	Specifically surveyed various analysis techniques for detecting TLS malicious traffic in SOC scenarios
[14]	2023	Various	NAD2	Reviewed and analyzed DL-based NAD2 techniques
[22]	2023	TLS	Interception Technology	Discusses the implementation methods and underlying motivations of various TLS interception mechanisms
Ours	2024	TLS 1.3	ETA	Surveyed the latest advancements in ML-based TLS 1.3 traffic analysis techniques

Note 1: NTC denotes Network Traffic Classification. ETA denotes encrypted traffic analysis. ETC denotes encrypted traffic classification. NAD1 denotes network anomaly detection. NAD2 denotes network attack detection. Mobile denotes Mobile and Wireless Networks. TC represents traffic classification. ML represents machine learning and DL represents deep learning. Note 2: In this survey, we distinguish between ETA and ETC. ETA encompasses a wide range of techniques and applications for analyzing encrypted traffic, including traffic characterization, anomaly detection, and performance analysis. ETC, on the other hand, is a subset of ETA that specifically deals with categorizing encrypted traffic into predefined classes, such as application types or protocols.

1.3. Research Objectives and Contributions of This Paper

This paper aims to address the significant challenges posed by the adoption of TLS 1.3, focusing on several key research questions.

- What improvements does TLS 1.3 have compared to previous versions? What challenges do these changes pose to traditional traffic analysis methods?
  This question aims to identify specific features of TLS 1.3 that complicate existing analysis techniques and require new approaches.
- What are the main categories of current TLS 1.3 traffic analysis techniques? What are the latest advancements in these methods? How applicable and limited are these methods?
  By exploring this question, we aim to provide a comprehensive overview of current methodologies and their effectiveness in handling TLS 1.3 traffic.
- In studies using machine learning methods to analyze TLS 1.3 traffic, what TLS 1.3 datasets are currently available? What is the quality of these datasets?
  This question aims to summarize the main datasets used in the field of TLS 1.3 traffic analysis, analyze their importance in research, and point out the deficiencies of current datasets.
- What challenges do current TLS 1.3 traffic analysis techniques face? What are the future research directions?
  This question seeks to highlight gaps in current research and propose potential areas for future investigation.

By addressing these questions, this paper not only reviews existing literature but also provides a roadmap for future research in analyzing TLS 1.3-encrypted traffic.

The main contributions of this paper include the following:

- Firstly, this paper conducts a comprehensive survey of recent major techniques for TLS 1.3 traffic analysis, including middlebox-based interception techniques, searchable encryption techniques, machine learning-based traffic analysis methods, analyzing their advantages, disadvantages, and applicable scenarios. To our knowledge, this paper is the first study which specifically focuses on TLS 1.3 traffic analysis techniques.
- Secondly, this paper analyzes the impact of TLS 1.3 protocol changes on traffic analysis. We delve into the impact of new features in the TLS 1.3 protocol on traditional traffic analysis methods, such as encrypted ClientHello, 0-RTT session resumption, and PFS, highlighting the challenges posed by these changes.

- Moreover, we summarize the main datasets used in the field of TLS 1.3 traffic analysis, emphasize the importance of datasets in research and point out the current deficiencies in datasets.
- Finally, the existing issues and future directions of TLS 1.3 traffic analysis are analyzed in this survey.

1.4. Survey Organization

The organization of this paper is as follows. Section 1 outlines the research background, differences from existing surveys, and the main contributions of this study. Section 2 introduces the main application areas of TLS traffic analysis, including network security threat detection, network management and service quality assurance, user behavior analysis and privacy protection, and network censorship and forensics. Section 3 focuses on discussing the new features of TLS 1.3 and their impact on traffic analysis. We present the core part of this paper in Section 4, which comprehensively reviews the latest progress in TLS 1.3 traffic analysis techniques, including middlebox-based interception techniques, searchable encryption techniques, and machine learning-based analysis techniques. The key challenges in TLS 1.3 traffic analysis and explores future research directions are summarized in Section 5. Finally, a conclusion is drawn in Section 6. Through this organization, this paper aims to comprehensively and systematically introduce the latest research progress in the field of TLS 1.3 traffic analysis, analyze the advantages and disadvantages of existing methods, and identify directions for future research.

2. Applications of TLS Traffic Analysis

A significant portion of Internet traffic is now encrypted using the TLS protocol. Encrypted traffic analysis has broad applications in network security threat detection, network management and Quality of Service (QoS) assurance, user behavior analysis and privacy protection, and network censorship and forensics.

2.1. Network Security Threat Detection

Encrypted traffic analysis is widely used in network security threat detection. Many network attacks and malware utilize the TLS protocol to protect their communications, thereby concealing their malicious activities. However, detecting such attack traffic remains feasible, and machine learning methods have proven highly effective in identifying malicious TLS traffic. Researchers have proposed various methods for detecting malicious encrypted traffic [23–33], employing machine learning algorithms to analyze the behavior patterns of TLS-encrypted traffic and detect various security threats such as malware, botnets, and DDoS attacks. This is crucial for safeguarding critical information infrastructures in government, enterprises, and the financial sector. Additionally, using specific TLS configuration parameters to detect malware is a common method. For example, comparing the hash value of the ClientHello parameters during the TLS handshake (also known as TLS fingerprinting) with an internal database can detect malware [34].

2.2. Network Management and Quality of Service Assurance

With the widespread adoption of encryption protocols like TLS, the prevalence of encrypted traffic is increasing. Many studies analyze TLS-encrypted traffic to identify the applications or services to which the traffic belongs, such as distinguishing between video, gaming, and instant messaging applications. This helps Internet Service Providers (ISPs) or network managers understand the composition of traffic from different applications and services, facilitating tasks such as traffic engineering and bandwidth allocation to ensure the quality of critical services and improve user experience [35–39]. For instance, classification methods based on Server Name Indication (SNI) [40,41] are frequently used to provide QoS. Although encryption technologies like Encrypted Client Hello (ECH) may hinder SNI-based classification, research indicates that effective QoS-aware classification can still be achieved by analyzing the payload of the TLS handshake, even when SNI is hidden [42,43].

2.3. User Behavior Analysis and Privacy Protection

Although the TLS protocol aims to secure the content of data packets, encrypted traffic generated by different websites or applications still exhibits identifiable differences. These distinguishing features, such as packet length, direction, and sequence, can be used to infer the websites or applications a user is accessing, and even specific actions within an application. This analysis of user behavior and preferences is valuable for fields such as advertising and recommendation systems. However, excessive user behavior analysis can infringe on user privacy. Researchers have proposed privacy-preserving traffic analysis methods that focus on identifying potential information leaks from encrypted traffic, such as website fingerprinting [44–48], application fingerprinting [49–52], and user behavior identification [53–57]. These methods can detect and prevent behaviors that may infringe on user privacy, which is crucial for protecting user privacy. With the increasing number of privacy protection regulations, such as GDPR and CCPA, encrypted traffic analysis is also employed to ensure compliance with data processing activities.

2.4. Network Censorship and Forensics

As more Internet traffic is encrypted using protocols like TLS, various techniques are employed to censor TLS and extended HTTPS traffic, enabling censorship authorities to identify and filter illegal or inappropriate content in encrypted traffic, such as malware, spam, hate speech, terrorism-related content, and corporate policy compliance [58]. Since encryption limits the effectiveness of content-based filtering, many studies focus on identifying and intercepting traffic based on TLS handshake metadata [21,59–61]. For example, the SNI field can be used for censorship [62–66], and server certificates can be used to review HTTPS content [67]. Research on TLS interception techniques using middlebox network devices demonstrates that these devices can be used for detailed traffic analysis and monitoring within the network [68,69]. Machine learning algorithms are also commonly used in encrypted traffic censorship. By analyzing the TLS handshake process and traffic patterns, censorship authorities can identify specific services and applications and detect anomalies that may indicate security threats or prohibited content [11,21]. In the field of network forensics, censorship techniques can be used to extract evidence from TLS-encrypted traffic [70,71], investigate security incidents, data breaches, and cybercrimes, providing critical information for law enforcement.

In summary, these application areas illustrate the significant and multifaceted importance of TLS-encrypted traffic analysis in the contemporary network environment. Future research should prioritize the optimization of TLS-encrypted traffic while maintaining the confidentiality and security of the data.

3. New Features of TLS 1.3 and Their Impact on Traffic Analysis

3.1. Changes in TLS Protocol Versions

The Transport Layer Security (TLS) protocol is the cornerstone of secure Internet communication, evolving from the Secure Sockets Layer (SSL) protocol initially developed by Netscape. Its primary goal is to encrypt data transmitted over the Internet to prevent eavesdropping and tampering, thereby ensuring secure communication between web browsers and servers.

TLS 1.0, introduced in 1999 (RFC 2246 [2]), was an upgrade from SSL 3.0, addressing multiple security issues present in SSL 3.0. TLS 1.1, released in 2006, is documented in RFC 4346 [72]. TLS 1.2, published in 2008 (RFC 5246 [5]), introduced significant updates compared to TLS 1.1. As of today, TLS 1.2 remains the most widely used version, with 99.9% of surveyed websites supporting it [4]. Earlier versions, namely TLS 1.0 and TLS 1.1, were deprecated in March 2021 [73].

The latest version, TLS 1.3, released in 2018, is defined in RFC 8446 [3]. It represents a major overhaul of the TLS protocol, removing outdated encryption algorithms, shortening the handshake process to speed up connections, and implementing forward secrecy by default, thereby providing stronger security guarantees and better privacy. Unlike the slow adoption of previous TLS versions, TLS 1.3 has been rapidly deployed. Within 15 months of its standardization, approximately 20% of connections used TLS 1.3, and about 30% of popular domains had adopted it [74].

3.2. Impact of TLS 1.3 on Traffic Analysis

As the latest version of the secure transmission protocol, TLS 1.3 introduces several innovative features that enhance communication security and efficiency while presenting new challenges for traffic analysis. This section examines the main new features and their impacts.

(1) Simplified Handshake Process: In TLS 1.2 and earlier versions, completing a full handshake required two round-trip times (RTTs) (as shown in Figure 1). The first RTT involved negotiating encryption parameters through "ClientHello" and "ServerHello" messages, while the second RTT completed the key exchange. TLS 1.3 compresses the previous Hello negotiation process, reducing the handshake time to one RTT (as shown in Figure 2). The client includes all necessary key-sharing information (such as pre-shared keys or Elliptic Curve Diffie–Hellman key shares) along with a list of supported cipher suites in its initial ClientHello message. Upon receiving the ClientHello, the server selects a cipher suite and immediately sends the ServerHello, certificate, key exchange parameters, and all other messages in a single transmission. This design significantly reduces the number of round trips required for the handshake, thereby enhancing connection establishment speed [3,75]. This means that communication between the client and server is faster, especially when establishing new connections, thereby significantly enhancing performance and user experience. However, this simplified process also changes the observable characteristics of the TLS handshake, potentially complicating traffic classification methods that rely on analyzing handshake patterns.

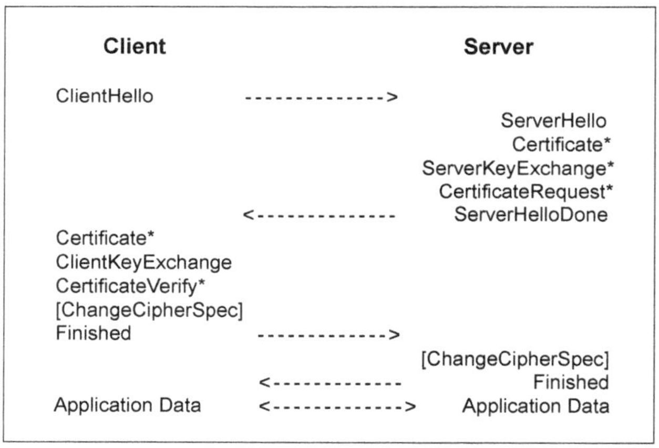

Figure 1. TLS 1.2 full handshake framework (from RFC 5246, * indicates a message that is optional).

Additionally, TLS 1.3 introduces the early_data extension, allowing for zero round-trip time (0-RTT) session resumption with previously visited websites. In TLS 1.3, if the client and server have previously established a connection and the server permits 0-RTT data, the client can send application data with the first handshake message. In contrast, TLS 1.2 and earlier versions required at least one full round-trip communication (1-RTT) to send application data. This necessitates redesigning session-based traffic classification methods, as the traffic characteristics under 0-RTT mode differ from those of traditional TLS handshake processes. Moreover, the 0-RTT mode introduces new scenarios for malicious traffic analysis, as attackers might exploit 0-RTT to conduct replay attacks.

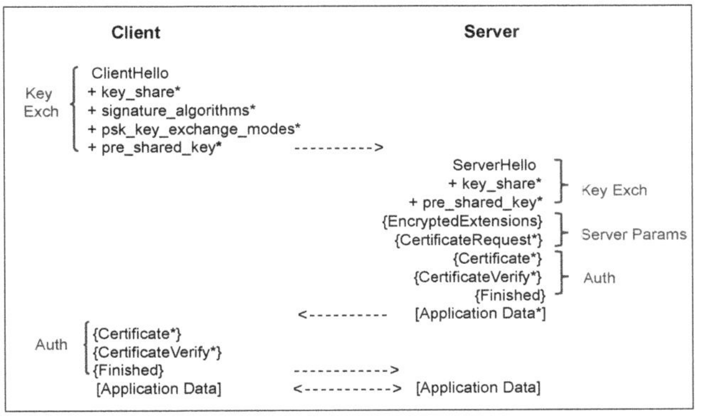

Figure 2. TLS 1.3 full handshake framework (from RFC 8446, + indicates noteworthy extensions sent in the previously noted message, * indicates a message that is optional).

(2) Enhanced Security: In TLS 1.2 and earlier versions, the RSA key exchange was a common method. In this mode, the client generates a pre-master secret (PMS), encrypts it with the server's RSA public key, and transmits it to the server. The server decrypts the PMS with its private key, and both parties derive session keys from the PMS for subsequent encryption of communication. Traditional TLS interception techniques could passively decrypt traffic if the middlebox possessed the server's RSA private key, thus enabling intrusion detection, content filtering, and other traffic analysis tasks [22]. However, TLS 1.3 makes significant changes by removing support for outdated and insecure encryption algorithms and mandating stronger encryption methods. It eliminates RSA-based key exchange, requiring all key exchanges to use forward-secure key agreement mechanisms such as Diffie–Hellman Ephemeral (DHE) or Elliptic Curve Diffie–Hellman Ephemeral (ECDHE). Perfect Forward Secrecy (PFS) ensures that, even if the server's key is compromised in the future, past communications cannot be decrypted, as each session utilizes independently generated ephemeral keys. These improvements in TLS 1.3 enhance security, particularly against key compromise and replay attacks. Even if a third party possesses the server's RSA private key or static DH private key, they are unable to decrypt TLS 1.3 communications. This means that traditional traffic analysis methods relying on passive decryption with the server's private key are no longer effective, posing challenges for middleboxes that need to perform specific network operations. Network operators, content providers, and security solution providers must reconsider their strategies and explore new methods to adapt to these changes.

(3) Encrypted ClientHello (ECH): TLS 1.3 introduces an extension called Encrypted ClientHello (ECH) [76], previously known as Encrypted Server Name Indication (ESNI). ECH is an extension to TLS 1.3 that is currently being standardized by the IETF TLS working group [77]. While not a standard component of TLS 1.3, and with a limited practical application in real-world networks at present, ECH represents a significant privacy-enhancing technology that warrants discussion due to its potential impact on traffic analysis. In traditional TLS handshakes, the client sends a ClientHello message to the server, which includes privacy-sensitive information such as Server Name Indication (SNI) and Application-Layer Protocol Negotiation (ALPN) in plaintext. Internet Service Providers (ISPs) often use SNI to identify specific applications and monitor network operations. ECH aims to encrypt most of the ClientHello content, including SNI, leaving only a minimal amount of necessary information in plaintext to facilitate the handshake. This enhancement, if widely adopted,

could significantly improve user privacy by preventing third parties from accessing the actual SNI information. However, it simultaneously poses challenges for traffic analysis based on service quality (QoS) classification and network monitoring. Many existing traffic classification methods, such as SNI-based classification [40,41], rely on unencrypted handshake metadata. The introduction of ECH represents a significant challenge in the field of network traffic analysis and management, requiring innovative approaches to maintain effective network monitoring and security in an increasingly privacy-focused Internet landscape.

In summary, TLS 1.3 introduces several new features, such as ECH, 0-RTT, and PFS, which enhance security and performance but present new challenges for traffic analysis. To address these challenges, researchers need to thoroughly analyze the TLS 1.3 protocol mechanisms, identify new traffic characteristics, and study new traffic analysis techniques.

4. TLS 1.3 Traffic Analysis Techniques

The new features of the TLS 1.3 protocol, such as the simplified handshake process and encrypted SNI, enhance communication security and efficiency, but they also present unprecedented challenges for traffic analysis. To address these challenges, researchers have devised various traffic analysis techniques. Generally, existing TLS 1.3 traffic analysis techniques can be categorized into two types: active detection and passive detection.

(1) Active Detection Techniques: These techniques primarily utilize middlebox devices to perform decryption or partial decryption of the original encrypted traffic, thereby making the payload information or keywords visible. This enables the use of deep packet inspection (DPI) or rule-based matching to identify malicious traffic. Common solutions encompass middlebox-based interception techniques, searchable encryption, and trusted execution environment (TEE) (e.g., SGX [78]).

(2) Passive Detection Techniques: These techniques do not alter the underlying protocol (i.e., TLS 1.3) nor decrypt the encrypted traffic for inspection. They primarily include machine learning-based analysis techniques and statistical analysis based on traffic characteristics. Passive detection techniques can analyze traffic without compromising the security of TLS 1.3, though their detection accuracy and granularity may not be as high as those of active detection techniques.

We introduce three primary types of TLS 1.3 traffic analysis techniques below: middlebox-based interception, searchable encryption-based analysis, and machine learning-based analysis. We discuss their fundamental principles, advantages, disadvantages, and challenges, with an emphasis on recent research progress. Middlebox-based interception techniques, despite facing certain challenges, remain the most widely used active detection methods. Searchable encryption-based analysis techniques achieve essential traffic detection functions while protecting privacy, thus becoming a new research direction. Machine learning-based analysis techniques have made significant progress in accuracy and efficiency with the development of deep learning, thereby becoming a research hotspot in passive detection techniques.

4.1. Middlebox-Based Interception Techniques

Middlebox-based interception techniques, such as SSL/TLS proxy servers, involve inserting an intermediary entity between the sender and receiver of encrypted traffic. This entity can decrypt and inspect the traffic, as shown in Figure 3. These techniques are mainly used for network security detection and censorship. Table 2 summarizes existing middlebox interception schemes that support TLS 1.3 traffic.

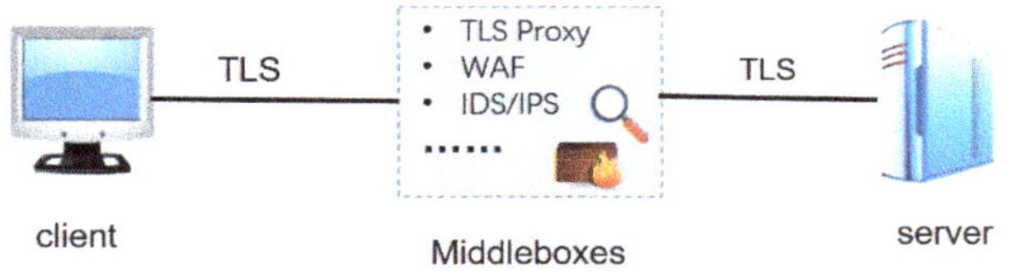

Figure 3. TLS traffic interception model based on middleboxes.

Table 2. Summary of middlebox solutions that support TLS 1.3.

Work	Year	Changes to TLS 1.3	Forward Secrecy	Privacy Protection	Performance			Deployment Complexity	Application Scenarios
					HL	CO	BO		
TLS_visibility [79]	2018	Yes	Partial	M	M	M	M	H	Enterprise server TLS inspection
ETS [80]	2022	No	No	M	M	L	L	M	Passive decryption of internal enterprise traffic
LURK [81]	2022	No	Yes	H	M	M	L	M	Centralized management of TLS certificates and keys in enterprise intranets, securityaudit systems for monitoring TLS traffic
RFC9345 [82]	2023	No	Yes	M	L	L	L	M	Content Delivery Networks, remote data centers
ACCE-AP [83]	2018	No	Yes	H	M	M	M	M	Content Delivery Networks, enterprise firewalls, and content filtering
MaTLS [84]	2019	Yes	Yes	H	M	M	L	H	Enterprise networks, Content Delivery Networks, Middlebox in cloud services
ME-TLS [85]	2019	No	Yes	M	M	L	L	M	Industrial IoT, smart homes
ZKMB [86]	2022	No	Yes	H	H	H	L	M	Encrypted DNS filtering, HTTP firewalls
Zombie [87]	2024	No	Yes	H	M	M	M	M	DNS filtering, keyword filtering for search engine queries, Data Loss Prevention (DLP)

Note: HL denotes the handshake latency. CO denotes the computational overhead. BO denotes the bandwidth overhead. H denotes high. M denotes medium. L denotes low.

4.1.1. Session Splitting and Key-Sharing Techniques

To inspect TLS-encrypted traffic, TLS sessions are typically split, or TLS keys/secrets are shared after session establishment to circumvent TLS. The primary method of session splitting involves inserting a middlebox into the TLS connection and dividing it into two or more sessions. The client establishes an end-to-end TLS session with a middlebox (usually a TLS proxy), which, in turn, acts as a client and communicates with the target server. At this point, the middlebox acts as both the client and server. This model requires proper configuration of the client to trust certificates issued by the middlebox.

When clients cannot accept split TLS sessions, some techniques inspect traffic by sharing TLS secrets provided by the client. Browsers like Firefox can log TLS encryption information [88] (such as handshake/application traffic encryption information for TLS 1.3) to passively decrypt corresponding TLS traffic, but support for this feature is limited to a few applications and is subject to restrictions, and it may be abused.

Sharing the server's certificate private key is another effective method for passively monitoring TLS traffic [79,89]. When systems like intrusion detection obtain the server's certificate private key, they can decrypt the TLS traffic. Although these practices compromise the end-to-end security of TLS and pose risks of man-in-the-middle attacks and privacy issues, they are still widely deployed in antivirus software and enterprise network devices [69,90,91]. Due to the enhanced security of TLS 1.3, particularly through the mandatory use of PFS and the removal of some outdated and insecure encryption suites, including RSA-based key exchange mechanisms, its suitability for passive monitoring has decreased. Possessing the server's private key is no longer sufficient to inspect TLS 1.3 traffic. These changes make traditional interception methods, such as man-in-the-middle attacks (MITM) and key sharing, more challenging or impossible.

To facilitate server-side traffic monitoring, a simple solution is to make the server's DH key share static [22] and then share the private part with the middlebox, which reconstructs the TLS session secrets similarly to the server. However, the resulting semi-static DH key exchange no longer provides forward secrecy, contradicting the original intent of TLS 1.3. ETS [80], standardized by ETSI (European Telecommunications Standards Institute), is a variant of TLS 1.3 with semi-static DH keys, primarily used for the passive decryption of internal enterprise traffic. In the scenarios described in the ETS standard, connections entering the public Internet are protected by regular TLS, and, once inside the enterprise or data center, the traffic is forwarded to the final server using ETS. ETS provides keys to enterprise servers and middleboxes through a key management server, which significantly increases deployment complexity and attack risk. Due to the lack of forward secrecy, ETS has been criticized by various organizations.

An Internet draft [79] suggests establishing a tls_visibility extension in TLS 1.3, allowing pre-approved third parties to inspect connections. Clients opt in by indicating their willingness in the ClientHello message. This proposal is suitable for inspecting TLS connections to internal enterprise servers. However, if malicious users control the client and choose not to disclose TLS keys and secrets, they can circumvent the IPS inspection of encrypted traffic.

4.1.2. Delegation Credential Mechanisms

Although session splitting and key-sharing techniques can enable the inspection of TLS traffic, these methods often reduce TLS security. To maintain TLS security while allowing limited access to encrypted traffic, some new mechanisms have been proposed that delegate certain operations to trusted third parties.

The Limited Usage of Remote Key (LURK) protocol [92,93] is an extension to the TLS protocol that outsources sensitive key material to a remote LURK server, allowing LURK clients to interact with it for cryptographic operations. This design allows TLS handshakes without directly exposing private keys, thereby increasing security, especially in distributed and multi-tenant environments. LURK has defined a specific extension for TLS 1.3 [81] to ensure secure and effective TLS delegation and key management when using TLS 1.3, but its security guarantees have yet to be formally verified.

Internet standard RFC 9345 [82] introduces the concept of delegation credentials to address some limitations between TLS endpoint operators and certificate authorities, such as certificate validity periods, usage modes, and supported algorithms. It designs a mechanism for using "delegation credentials" in the TLS 1.3 handshake protocol, compatible with TLS 1.3, but may face challenges in practical deployment and operation.

4.1.3. Multi-Party TLS Protocol Variants

While delegation credential mechanisms offer ways to securely delegate certain TLS operations to trusted third parties, they still maintain a relatively simple protocol structure. However, as TLS 1.3 becomes more widely adopted and security requirements continue to evolve, researchers have begun exploring more complex approaches that allow trusted middleboxes to participate in TLS sessions while maintaining end-to-end encryption. These approaches, often referred to as multi-party TLS protocol variants, attempt to strike a balance between security, functionality, and compatibility. Such protocols typically involve modifying the TLS handshake process, introducing new message types or extensions to enable middlebox awareness and control.

When simple TLS session splitting and key-sharing solutions are unsustainable, such as incompatibility with TLS 1.3, another approach is to involve middleboxes in the TLS handshake and assign them different permissions or selectively expose parts of the traffic. Naylor et al. [94] pioneered proxy accountability, proposing the mcTLS protocol, which provides fine-grained access control for all proxy TLS connections between clients and servers. However, mcTLS is designed based on TLS 1.2 and does not natively support TLS 1.3. Bhargavan et al. [83] proposed a provably secure alternative to mcTLS: a general TLS proxy protocol design whose security can be modularly proven based on the underlying TLS security. The study implemented a prototype system based on the miTLS library, demonstrating how to instantiate the proposed design with TLS 1.3. Due to the end-to-end encryption characteristics of TLS limiting the functionality of middleboxes, Lee et al. [84] proposed a modified TLS protocol called maTLS, designed to be middlebox-aware, allowing middleboxes to participate in TLS sessions in a controllable and auditable manner. In terms of TLS 1.3 compatibility, maTLS was specifically designed to support TLS 1.3 by adding an ExtendedFinished message after the server's Finished message in pure server authentication mode. Since maTLS requires additional processing to support middlebox functionality, it may impact some performance advantages of TLS 1.3.

Li et al. [85] designed and implemented the ME-TLS protocol based on TLS 1.3 to address some limitations of traditional TLS protocols in IoT environments, allowing endpoints to introduce middleboxes into sessions with mutual consent. In ME-TLS, middleboxes can participate in TLS sessions while maintaining communication security without modifying the TLS 1.3 handshake structure, ensuring compatibility with existing systems. In actual deployment and application, careful consideration of middlebox management, protocol implementation complexity, and security challenges is essential.

4.1.4. Zero-Knowledge Proof Schemes

Traditionally, middleboxes decrypt traffic for inspection to enforce network policies, which compromises user privacy. An alternative approach seeks to balance network policy enforcement with privacy preservation. Zero-knowledge proof schemes offer a promising direction by allowing middleboxes to verify compliance with network policies without decrypting the traffic.

Traditionally, middleboxes decrypt traffic for inspection to enforce network policies, but this compromises user privacy. Paul Grubbs et al. [86] proposed the concept of Zero-Knowledge Middleboxes (ZKMBs), which can verify whether traffic complies with specific network management policies without decrypting it. The paper demonstrated how to combine a ZKMB with unmodified TLS 1.3, designing optimized zero-knowledge proofs for TLS 1.3 session keys. However, its computational overhead is significant, adding several seconds of traffic delay even under optimistic assumptions and relatively simple policies. Subsequently, the authors proposed a novel system called Zombie [87] based on ZKMB, adopting three techniques to reduce end-to-end delay, capable of handling policies based on regular expression matching, specifically designed and implemented for TLS 1.3 to ensure policy enforcement on network traffic while maintaining TLS 1.3 security and privacy. Compared to previous work, Zombie can reduce client and middlebox overhead by about 3.5 times, but it is still far from deployment in real-world network environments.

In summary, TLS 1.3 presents new requirements and challenges for interception methods. While new interception schemes attempt to achieve lawful interception and analysis of traffic without compromising the security of TLS 1.3, the effectiveness, security, and feasibility of deployment of these schemes remain key issues to be addressed in both research and practice. For example, general solutions like maTLS require support from both parties, and, unless these new schemes are widely deployed, users can easily choose to use standard TLS. Additionally, formal verification and security analysis of TLS 1.3 interception schemes have not yet met the required standards and require further research. It is important to note that these interception techniques violate the end-to-end security characteristics, raising privacy and potential compliance issues, especially as user privacy awareness increases, often requiring a balance between security, privacy protection, and practicality.

4.2. Searchable Encryption Techniques

With the rapid development of the Internet and cloud computing, network security concerns have become increasingly prominent. Deep packet inspection (DPI) is an effective network security technology that can thoroughly analyze network traffic to detect and prevent malicious activities. However, traditional DPI techniques require decrypting traffic, which can lead to privacy violations and security risks. To address this issue, researchers have proposed searchable encryption (SE) [95], which can detect malicious traffic through token matching without decryption. The core idea of SE is to establish a mappable relationship between encrypted keywords (tokens) and encrypted rule sets via a searchable encryption scheme. This technology aims to protect data privacy while supporting the efficient search and processing of encrypted data.

Middlebox systems based on searchable encryption (as shown in Figure 4) typically cannot directly decrypt TLS session data. Instead, they deploy proxy modules on the client and server sides, maintaining a dedicated encrypted token transmission link for traffic detection. Specifically, endpoint proxies tokenize the original network traffic using TLS session keys, generating encrypted tokens. These tokens are then encrypted with keys derived from the TLS session key and transmitted through a dedicated link to the middlebox. The middlebox maintains a rule set encrypted with the same derived key, such as rules for malicious traffic, and performs rule matching on the received encrypted token data to identify potential threats. After detection, the endpoint proxy verifies the consistency between the TLS session data and the token transmission link data to prevent attackers from bypassing detection through forged token data.

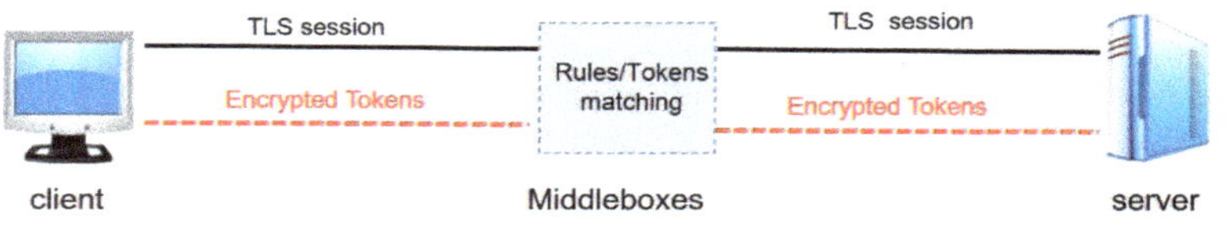

Figure 4. Middlebox model based on searchable encryption.

According to our literature search, no specific research on searchable encryption techniques for TLS 1.3 traffic exists. Theoretically, SE can handle any form of encrypted traffic without decrypting the content, as long as the traffic can be processed by the encryption/decryption and rule-matching mechanisms in the system. Since TLS 1.3 primarily enhances security and performance without changing the fundamental nature of encrypted traffic, SE techniques are applicable to both TLS 1.3 and other encrypted traffic types. We have reviewed relevant studies on encrypted traffic analysis using SE since 2018 (after the release of TLS 1.3), summarized in Table 3, and introduce them below.

Table 3. Summary of TLS traffic analysis techniques based on searchable encryption.

Work	Year	Changes to TLS 1.3	Cryptographic Techniques	Detection Functionality	Privacy Protection			Matching and Inspection	Deployment Complexity					Application Scenarios
					S	C	MB		S	C	MB	TTP	GW	
[96]	2015	Yes	AES	Full	H	H	M	Exact Matching, Regular Expression	✓	✓	-	-	-	DED, IDS, Parental filtering
[97]	2019	No	AES,DLP	Partial	H	H	H	Exact Matching	✓	✓	✓	-	-	ENS,ISP
[98]	2020	No	AES,PRF,DLP	Full	M	M	H	Exact Matching	✓	✓	✓	-	✓	ENS, CSSec
[99]	2020	No	AES, PRF, BF, Cuckoo Hashing	Partial	H	H	H	BF, Exact Matching	✓	-	✓	-	✓	Cloud-Assisted Middlebox
[100]	2020	No	Group Key Agreement, SymEnc	Full	H	H	M	Exact Matching	✓	✓	✓	✓	-	Encrypted Traffic Detection in IoT Scenarios
[101]	2021	No	AES, KH-PRF	Partial	H	H	H	Exact Matching	✓	✓	✓	-	-	IDS, IPS, DED
[102]	2021	No	PRF	Partial	H	H	H	Exact Matching	✓	✓	✓	-	-	ENS, CSSec
[103]	2022	No	SymEnc, Hash, PRF	Full	H	H	H	Exact Matching	✓	✓	✓	✓	-	Encrypted Traffic Detection in IoT Scenarios
[104]	2022	No	SMPC, SymEnc	Full	H	H	M	Exact Matching	✓	✓	✓	✓	-	IDS, DED
[105]	2023	No	AES, PRF, PRP, BF	Full	H	H	H	Exact Matching, TCK	-	-	✓	-	✓	ENS, IDS in Cloud Services
[106]	2023	No	HMAC ,CA	Full	H	H	H	Exact Matching	✓	-	-	✓	✓	IDS, WAF, DPI Services in the Cloud
[107]	2023	No	PRF, ECC, BF	Full	H	H	H	BF, Exact Matching	-	-	✓	✓	✓	Blockchain-based IIoT Environment

Note: S, C, and MB denote server, client, and middlebox. TTP and GW denote trusted third party and gateway. SymEnc denotes symmetric encryption, DLP denotes Discrete Logarithm Problem, PRF denotes Pseudorandom Function, KH-PRF denotes Key-Homomorphic Pseudo-Random Function, SMPC denotes secure multi-party computation, PRP denotes Pseudo-Random Permutation, HMAC denotes Hash-based Message Authentication Code, CA denotes Cryptographic Accumulator, BF denotes Bloom Filter, ECC denotes Elliptic Curve Cryptography, TCK denotes Token Continuity Check. Detection Functionality: Full means that all functions similar to plaintext detection can be realized, and Partial means restricted. Privacy Protection: indicates the degree of privacy protection of the client, server, and middleware. H means high, M means medium. Deployment Complexity: Whether or not clients, servers, middleware, trusted third parties, gateways, etc., need to be installed or configured. ✓ indicates that it is required and - indicates that it is not required. IDSs denotes intrusion detection systems, ISP denotes Internet Service Provider, ENS denotes Enterprise Network Security, CSSec denotes Cloud Service Security, DED denotes Data Exfiltration Detection, IPS denotes Intrusion Prevention System, IIoT denotes Industrial Internet of Things, WAF denotes Web Application Firewall.

4.2.1. Foundational Searchable Encryption Techniques

Sherry et al. [96] proposed BlindBox, the first DPI scheme based on searchable encryption, allowing middleboxes to match encrypted detection rules within encrypted packets without decryption, thus providing good user privacy protection. BlindBox establishes two connections between the client and server, one for the TLS session and another for token matching, thereby enabling the detection of encrypted traffic. Subsequently, several studies have utilized searchable encryption for encrypted traffic analysis (e.g., Embark [108], BlindIDS [109], SPABox [110], and Yuan et al. [111]). Generally, these studies incur high computational and communication overhead due to the use of encryption techniques.

4.2.2. Performance-Optimized Searchable Encryption Techniques

Building upon the foundational work in searchable encryption, researchers have focused on optimizing performance to address the high computational and communication overhead associated with earlier systems. These performance-oriented approaches aim to enhance encryption and detection speeds, improve rule processing efficiency, and reduce overall system latency.

Ning et al. [97] proposed the PrivDPI system, which significantly improved BlindBox's performance by introducing a reusable obfuscation-rule generation technique. Then, they further improved the performance of PrivDPI through the Pine scheme [98], which supports rule addition operations. Kim et al. [101] proposed the P2DPI system, which uses Key-Homomorphic Pseudo-Random Functions (KH-PRFs) to exchange encrypted detection rules, achieving the effective inspection of TLS-encrypted traffic without compromising user privacy. P2DPI shows significant improvements in connection setup and encryption speed, surpassing PrivDPI.

Canard et al. [102] proposed a symmetric encryption-based intrusion detection system, which demonstrates significant improvements in encryption and detection speed compared to BlindBox [96] and BlindIDS [109], showcasing better practicality.

These performance-optimized systems represent significant progress in making searchable encryption more viable for real-world applications. By addressing the challenges of speed and efficiency, these approaches have paved the way for more practical implementations of privacy-preserving deep packet inspection in encrypted networks.

4.2.3. Advanced Privacy and Security Mechanism

While performance optimization remains crucial, the evolving landscape of cyber threats and increasing privacy concerns have driven researchers to develop more sophisticated privacy and security mechanisms for searchable encryption. These advanced approaches aim to enhance the protection of both user data and detection rules, while maintaining the ability to effectively analyze encrypted traffic.

Ren et al. [99] proposed the EV-DPI system with a two-layer filtering architecture, ensuring the privacy of packet payloads and inspection rules while improving processing efficiency using fast symmetric encryption systems such as hash functions. EV-DPI supports deep packet inspection (DPI) in cloud environments, ensuring both privacy and efficiency. However, EV-DPI cannot dynamically add new rules and may fail when handling discontinuous tokens.

Jia et al. [104] proposed the OTEPI system, which uses Oblivious Transfer (OT) technology for rule encryption and natural language processing (NLP)-based tokenization to optimize text payload processing, thereby reducing the number of generated tokens to lower computational load. Results show that OTEPI can accurately detect rule matches in encrypted traffic while maintaining both traffic and rule privacy. Compared to previous methods, it achieves a better balance between communication traffic consumption and computational resource usage.

Deng et al. [105] proposed the DCDPI system for encrypted traffic detection, introducing the VBTree+ (an improved virtual binary tree structure) and token continuity check mechanism, supporting dynamic rule addition and efficient token continuity checks, enhancing system flexibility and robustness while ensuring forward privacy, i.e., not leaking the relationship between historical tokens and rules when updating rules.

Recently, Zhang et al. [106] proposed a privacy-preserving lightweight cloud-based DPI execution verification scheme, which protects the privacy of DPI rule sets. This scheme introduces a commitment-based delayed sampling mechanism and a trusted third party based on Intel SGX, thereby achieving efficient and secure verification.

These studies showcase innovative techniques that push the boundaries of privacy-preserving searchable encryption, introducing novel cryptographic methods, improved rule management, and robust verification mechanisms. These advancements not only address the limitations of earlier systems but also pave the way for more secure and flexible encrypted traffic analysis solutions.

4.2.4. Domain-Specific and Emerging Technology Solutions

As searchable encryption techniques continue to evolve, researchers are increasingly focusing on tailoring these solutions to specific domains and leveraging emerging technologies. This trend reflects the growing need for specialized approaches that can address the unique challenges posed by different environments, such as IoT ecosystems and industrial settings. Additionally, the integration of cutting-edge technologies like blockchain and trusted execution environments is opening up new possibilities for enhancing the security, efficiency, and functionality of searchable encryption systems.

In the cloud computing domain, the previously mentioned EV-DPI system by Ren et al. [99] stands out for its optimization for cloud environments. While its privacy-preserving aspects were discussed earlier, it is worth noting that EV-DPI's two-layer filtering architecture is particularly well suited for the distributed nature of cloud computing, offering a balance between privacy protection and efficient processing in large-scale cloud infrastructures.

Fan et al. [100] present GKA_DPI, an encrypted traffic detection scheme designed for IoT environments. This scheme addresses the limitations of existing schemes, such as PrivDPI, in the one/many-to-many communication model of IoT by using a dynamic group key agreement protocol to reduce power consumption. The scheme is particularly suitable for IoT environments using the MQTT protocol. Although GKA_DPI offers enhanced efficiency and security, it is more complex to deploy.

Chen et al. [103] proposed a novel scheme using symmetric encryption to extract tokens from traffic, combining hash functions and pseudo-random functions to obfuscate rules. This scheme is used to detect encrypted network traffic in IoT environments while protecting the privacy of transmitted data.

Zhang et al. [107] also proposed the BTDPI system, a blockchain-based privacy-preserving traceable encrypted traffic detection system designed for industrial IoT scenarios. BTDPI uses a two-layer filtering architecture and an online–offline certificate-free aggregate signature mechanism, enabling efficient detection and anomaly source tracing of encrypted traffic. Experimental results show that BTDPI is 26.7 times faster than existing systems when processing 3000 tokens and 3000 rules.

These domain-specific solutions demonstrate how searchable encryption techniques are being adapted to meet the diverse needs of modern network ecosystems. From IoT-specific protocols to cloud-optimized architectures and blockchain integration, these approaches showcase the versatility and potential of searchable encryption in various technological contexts.

Despite the progress made in using SE for encrypted traffic analysis, several challenges persist. First, these schemes typically require additional computational resources, which may increase performance overhead. Second, the limitations of regular expression detection prevent these schemes from fully replacing traditional DPI techniques. Although SE-based traffic analysis methods are theoretically applicable to TLS 1.3, practical deployment and application necessitate adapting and optimizing related systems to address the new security features and performance requirements of TLS 1.3. Future research should focus on proposing efficient and compatible SE schemes to support secure traffic analysis based on TLS 1.3, necessitating further exploration by academia and the industry.

4.3. *Machine Learning Methods for TLS 1.3 Traffic Analysis*

Machine learning has become a powerful tool for extracting information features without decrypting traffic, making it widely applicable to TLS-encrypted traffic analysis. Since the payload of TLS is encrypted, most machine learning methods utilize statistical or behavioral features of TLS-encrypted traffic, such as packet size, direction, and timing data, to train corresponding machine learning models.

The release of TLS 1.3 in 2018 brought significant security enhancements, including reduced handshake round trips and the removal of insecure encryption algorithms, altering the characteristics of TLS 1.3 traffic. For example, the TLS 1.2 handshake typically required the exchange of 5 to 7 packets, whereas the TLS 1.3 handshake can be completed with 0 to 3 packets. Therefore, the effectiveness of machine learning-based traffic analysis methods suitable for TLS 1.2 and earlier versions in the context of TLS 1.3 remains to be explored. In this section, we provide a comprehensive overview of the latest advancements in machine learning-based TLS 1.3-encrypted traffic analysis. As shown in Table 4, we summarize the relevant research on machine learning-based TLS 1.3 traffic analysis.

4.3.1. Feature Extraction and Representation Learning

The advent of TLS 1.3 has necessitated the development of new feature extraction and representation learning techniques. This is primarily because the TLS 1.3 protocol encrypts all information after the handshake, thereby significantly reducing plaintext information. This change renders many encrypted traffic analysis methods based on TLS 1.2 plaintext features ineffectual. Consequently, researchers have proposed various innovative approaches to address this challenge.

Akbari et al. [112] extracted features using flow statistics, traffic shape (size, time, and direction), and raw bytes of the TLS handshake, constructing a neural network architecture based on convolutional neural networks (CNNs) and stacked LSTM layers for encrypted web traffic classification. Although not specifically analyzed for TLS 1.3, this method reduces reliance on server identity exposure fields (such as SNI), making it adaptable to the TLS 1.3 environment.

Fu et al. [31] proposed an encrypted malicious traffic detection system called ST-Graph, which uses graph representation learning algorithms to analyze the spatial and temporal characteristics of network behavior by constructing interaction graphs between hosts and servers to reveal patterns of malicious activities. Experimental results show that even after removing features related to the TLS protocol, ST-Graph can still achieve 99.85% accuracy, demonstrating its potential for effective analysis and detection of malicious activities within the TLS 1.3 environment. Taking a novel approach to traffic representation, Chen et al. [123] proposed a novel traffic graph representation model called Weaved Flow Fragment (WFF) by deeply studying the transmission patterns and interaction characteristics of encrypted traffic, converting the packet sequence of encrypted traffic into a graph to better capture the intrinsic relationships between packet sequences. Based on this model, the authors proposed an integrated graph neural network (EGNN) architecture, significantly improving the accuracy of encrypted traffic classification through voting and stacking integration mechanisms. The dataset includes new protocols (TLS 1.3, QUIC, and DTLS) and applications, demonstrating EGNN's better applicability in open-world environments.

Table 4. Summary of machine learning-based TLS 1.3 traffic analysis research.

Work	Application Domain	Method	Granularity	Feature	Metrics	TLS 1.3	
						Theo	Data
[6]	Service Classification	LS-CapsNet	Packet-level	PDU length	P, R, F1	✓	✗
[112]	Service and Application Classification	CNN,LSTM	Flow-level	Flow statistics,TLS handshake packets	P, R, F1, Acc,Time	✓	—
[113]	Service Classification	LS-CapsNet, LSTM	Packet-level, Flow-level	multiPDU length sequence	P, R, F1	✓	✓
[114]	Cloud Platform Application Classification	NeuTic	Packet-level	Packet length,Packet window size, TCP flag	TP, FP, FN, P, R, F-m, Acc	✓	✓
[115]	Service Classification	AB-RF, RB-RF	Flow-level	TLS handshake packets	Acc, P, F1, Error Rate	✓	✓
[7]	Encrypted Application Classification	ET-BERT	Packet-level, Flow-level	Convert raw traffic data into a sequence of tokens	Acc,P, R, F1	✓	✓
[31]	Malicious Traffic Detection	ST-Graph	Packet-level, Flow-level	Flow statistics, TLS handshake packets	P, R, FP	✓	—
[116]	Application Layer Protocol Identification	GGFAS	Packet-level, Flow-level	Packet size, direction, and order	Acc, F1, Confusion Matrix	✓	✓
[117]	Malware Traffic Classification	R1DIT	Raw-level	The relative position of the original byte sequence of each packet	R, P, F1, TP, FAR	✓	✓
[118]	Webpage Fingerprinting	KNN	Trace-level	Distance between samples	Top-N Acc	✓	✓
[119]	Service Classification	LightGBM, CNN	Packet-level, Flow-level	Packet and flow statistics	Acc, F1, TP, FP, AUROC	✓	✓
[120]	Application Identification	PASS	Packet-level Raw-level	Packet length sequence Raw payload sequence	Acc, P, R, F1	✓	✓
[121]	Phishing Detection	LR, SVM, RF, XGBoost, LightGBM	Packet-level	12 characteristics such as SNI, selected Cipher Suite (SCS)	TP, FP, TN, FN, P,ACC	✓	✓
[122]	Traffic Classification	Rosetta	Flow-level	Packet length sequence	Acc, R, F1, FP	✓	—
[123]	Service Classification	WFF-EGNN	Flow-level	Packet length sequence	P, R, F1, Time	✓	✓
[124]	Application Classification	MISS	Packet-, Flow-, and Raw-level	Multiview sequence features such as packet length sequence, TLS header, and payload byte sequence	Acc, F1	✓	—

Note: Theo and Data represent theoretical and dataset, respectively. P and R denote Precision and Recall, respectively. F1 represents F1-Score. TP, FP, and FN denote True Positive, False Positive, and False Negative, respectively. Acc represents Accuracy. FAR denotes the false alarm rate. Top-N Acc denotes the attack success rate. ✓and ✗represent theoretical and dataset support, respectively. — denotes that the dataset does not specify TLS 1.3.

Yun et al. [114] proposed a new method called NeuTic, which is based on the packet sequence of each TLS flow. This method is designed to effectively classify raw TLS flows generated by multiple "cloud" applications. This method can automatically capture long-distance dependencies between elements in the packet sequence, achieving robust and accurate classification of encrypted TLS traffic. It should be noted that the dataset used in this study includes both TLS 1.2 and TLS 1.3 traffic, but the authors did not distinguish between these versions in subsequent experiments and analyses, treating them collectively.

Focusing on specific security threats, Kumar et al. [121] proposed a new machine learning model for detecting phishing URLs within encrypted traffic. For TLS 1.3 traffic, the authors extracted features from ClientHello and ServerHello messages for phishing detection, yielding significant results. However, these features mainly focus on visible information exchanged during the TLS handshake. Given the enhanced privacy protection in TLS 1.3, exploring deeper and more distinctive features from TLS 1.3 traffic remains a promising direction.

Addressing the challenge of web fingerprinting, Mavroudis et al. [118] proposed an adaptive method that learns low-dimensional representations (embedding models) of input data to achieve high-accuracy recognition of web pages in TLS 1.2- and TLS 1.3-encrypted traffic. To facilitate further research, the authors released the TLS 1.3 dataset, Github500. However, the single-source nature of this dataset and the lack of testing for scenarios with significant dynamic changes in web pages suggest that further validation and improvement of the model's adaptability is necessary.

Addressing the challenges of analyzing encrypted traffic across different TLS versions, Piet et al. [116] proposed an automated network traffic analysis framework called GGFAST, which searches for characteristic patterns in information length and provides corresponding packet length conversion functions for different encryption methods such as stream ciphers, block ciphers, and AEAD under different TLS versions. On a dataset collected from a large enterprise network, GGFAST was able to identify 95.1% of DNS-over-HTTPS (DoH) traffic within TLS traffic, partially overcoming the challenges of analyzing TLS 1.3-encrypted traffic.

Recently, Xie et al. [122] proposed a method called Rosetta, which uses TCP-aware traffic enhancement mechanisms and self-supervised learning to understand implicit TCP semantics, thereby extracting robust features of TLS traffic. Experiments show that Rosetta significantly improves the performance of existing deep learning models in classifying TLS traffic in diverse network environments. Although this study did not specifically analyze TLS 1.3 traffic, Rosetta's method is protocol-agnostic and applicable to TLS 1.3, aiding researchers and network administrators in better understanding and analyzing TLS 1.3-encrypted traffic. Li et al. [124] proposed an incremental learning framework called Multi-view Sequences Fusion (MISS), which improves the classification accuracy of encrypted traffic by extracting multi-view sequence features, generating cross-view information, and adaptively fusing multi-view data. The framework also mitigates the problem of knowledge forgetting during model evolution by designing plasticity and stability branches. Although the study did not specifically discuss the TLS 1.3 protocol, the methodology and techniques of the MISS framework provide a possible solution for classifying TLS 1.3-encrypted traffic.

These diverse approaches to feature extraction and representation learning demonstrate the ongoing efforts to adapt to the challenges posed by TLS 1.3, paving the way for more effective and robust encrypted traffic analysis techniques.

4.3.2. Deep Learning Models and Algorithms

While some researchers have focused on advancing feature extraction and representation learning techniques, others have concentrated on developing sophisticated deep learning models and algorithms to address the challenges posed by TLS 1.3-encrypted traffic analysis. The deep learning models and algorithms discussed in this section aim to improve classification accuracy, enhance generalization capabilities, and increase adaptability to new protocols and emerging threats.

Chen et al. [6] proposed a service classification method for encrypted traffic based on the length of multiple protocol data units (PDUs), utilizing the Markov properties between PDU length sequences and employing a length-sensitive capsule neural network (LS-CapsNet) model for traffic classification. Although this method is suitable for the TLS 1.3 environment, it has not been validated using a TLS 1.3 dataset. Subsequently, the authors proposed a length-sensitive composite deep learning (LSCDL) model to achieve encrypted traffic service classification [113], which showed good classification results on a proprietary dataset containing a significant amount of TLS 1.3 traffic.

Although ECH encrypts sensitive information (such as SNI) in the ClientHello message, posing challenges to existing algorithms that rely on this information for traffic classification, new algorithms can still effectively classify TLS-encrypted traffic. Shamsimukhametov et al. [115] proposed two new traffic classification algorithms (AB-RF and RB-RF) to address the challenges introduced by ECH. Even with ECH encryption in TLS 1.3, traffic classification based on the TLS handshake remains feasible.

Existing solutions heavily rely on deep features such as data size, making it difficult to generalize for unseen data. How to use open-domain unlabeled traffic data to learn representations with strong generalization capabilities remains a significant challenge.

Lin et al. [7] proposed a model called ET-BERT, which pre-trains deep datagram-level representations on large-scale unlabeled data and then fine-tunes on small-scale labeled data for specific tasks to achieve accurate classification of encrypted traffic. The authors collected a new dataset named CSTNET-TLS 1.3. ET-BERT significantly improved the F1 score of the encrypted application classification task by 10.0%, reaching an F1 score of 97.4%, significantly surpassing existing methods.

Barut et al. [117] proposed a residual one-dimensional image transformation model (R1DIT) based on raw data, using meta-learning methods (transfer learning and few-shot learning) to extend its classification accuracy to unseen malware categories, capable of identifying newly emerging TLS 1.3 malware traffic. Due to the very small size and highly imbalanced category distribution of the target dataset, further validation on larger and more comprehensive datasets is required to verify the proposed method's efficacy.

Luxemburk et al. [119] provided a robust framework and method set for analyzing TLS-encrypted traffic, creating and evaluating a large TLS dataset, and proposing effective methods for detecting unknown services. Although the dataset covers TLS 1.3 protocol traffic, the study did not specifically discuss TLS 1.3 traffic analysis separately.

Li et al. [120] proposed a new semi-supervised encrypted traffic classification framework called PASS, which improves the model's ability to learn features of minority class applications through contrastive pre-training and semi-supervised learning while reducing dependence on labeled training data. The study analyzed TLS 1.3 protocol traffic and validated the effectiveness of the PASS framework in handling the latest encrypted protocol traffic through experiments on the CSTNET-TLS 1.3 dataset.

4.3.3. Datasets

Table 5 lists the datasets used in the field of TLS 1.3 traffic analysis. It is important to note that many TLS datasets do not explicitly indicate whether they contain TLS 1.3 traffic, which can complicate the evaluation of machine learning models designed for this protocol version. Therefore, Table 5 only includes datasets that explicitly state that they contain TLS 1.3 traffic.

In the area of service classification, the study [115] used the WNL TLS dataset, which includes network traffic from 100 popular websites and background network traffic, covering 12 categories and 3547 flows, including TLS 1.3 traffic. The CSTNET-TLS 1.3 [7] is the first dataset for TLS 1.3, which was collected in 2021 and contains traffic from 120 applications deployed on Alexa Top-5000 websites using TLS 1.3.

We observed that, due to the scarcity of public datasets, most works in this section did not use public datasets to train models but instead used self-created datasets. For example, the dataset [113] collected in the CERNET environment includes traffic from seven services, with a significant amount of TLS 1.3-encrypted traffic. Another dataset [114] includes TLS traffic from 15 mobile applications from companies like Alibaba, Baidu, and ByteDance, as well as six video/short video mobile applications, covering both TLS 1.2 and TLS 1.3. The dataset used for encrypted application classification [116] consists of seven datasets, comprising 15 categories, including POP3-over-TLS, IMAP-over-TLS, SMTP-over-TLS, and HTTP-over-TLS.

The dataset [117] focuses on malware traffic classification, extracting TLS 1.3 traffic from the CICDDoS2019 dataset, covering five DDoS variants and 209 TLS 1.3 malware flows.

In addition to the aforementioned datasets, numerous other datasets have been released. However, a comprehensive statistical analysis of these datasets has not been conducted in this study, primarily because the majority of newly proposed datasets do not explicitly specify whether they include TLS 1.3 traffic, even when released during the period of widespread TLS 1.3 adoption. For instance, the Malicious_TLS dataset [125] serves as a valuable resource for studying encrypted malicious traffic. This dataset encompasses 22 categories of real-world encrypted malicious traffic generated by malware families active between 2018 and 2021, along with benign TLS traffic for comparative purposes. All samples were collected from actual networks and encrypted using TLS. However, the paper does not explicitly state whether the dataset contains TLS 1.3 traffic or specify the exact proportion of TLS 1.3 traffic within the dataset.

Although some public datasets are available for TLS 1.3 traffic analysis, the lack of publicly available, labeled datasets means that most research still relies on private datasets. This highlights the need for more comprehensive public datasets to support research and development in this domain. In addition, the lack of clear information on the distribution of TLS versions is also the reason for the current lack of TLS 1.3 datasets.

Machine learning techniques can be directly applied to existing TLS 1.3 traffic without any modifications to the protocol itself. This makes machine learning methods easy to deploy while preserving the end-to-end encryption security provided by the TLS 1.3 protocol. This contrasts with other technologies that require protocol modifications (such as access control technologies) or changes to client/server settings (such as middlebox, searchable encryption, and trusted hardware). However, machine learning struggles to achieve the fine-grained, rule-based detection capabilities of deep packet inspection. Current research mainly focuses on tasks such as traffic classification and anomaly detection, with limited capabilities for executing more complex security policies. Additionally, due to privacy and security concerns, publicly available TLS 1.3 traffic datasets are small and lack diversity. Most studies use privately collected datasets, which poses challenges for fair evaluation and comparison of algorithms and limits the reproducibility and generalization of research findings.

Table 5. Datasets used by works in TLS 1.3 traffic analysis.

Work	Analysis Objective	Name	Year	Available	Description
[113]	Service Classification	–	2020	Private	Including traffic from seven services, with a significant amount of TLS 1.3-encrypted traffic
[114]	Cloud Application Classification	–	–	Private	Generated by 15 mobile applications from three companies and six video mobile applications
[115]	Service Classification	WNL TLS	2021	Public	Includes web traffic from 100 popular websites and background web traffic
[7,120]	Application Classification	CSTNET-TLS 1.3	2021	Public	Including traffic from 120 applications deployed on Alexa Top-5000 websites using TLS 1.3
[116]	Protocol Identification	–	2022	Private	Composed of seven datasets, including 15 categories such as SMTP-over-TLS and HTTP-over-TLS
[117]	Malware Traffic Classification	–	2019	Private	Extracted from the CICDDoS2019 dataset, covering 5 DDoS variants and 209 TLS 1.3 malware flows
[118]	Web Fingerprinting	Github500	–	Private	Includes 500 TLS 1.3 categories generated by accessing the top 500 GitHub project pages
[119]	Service Classification	CESNET-TLS22	2021	Public	The dataset contains a total of 140 million flow records, covering 191 network services
[121]	Phishing Detection	–	–	Private	URLs collected from the Alexa database, phishing websites collected from Phishtank
[123]	Service Classification	CESNET-2022Service	2022	Public	Covering seven applications with TLS protocols, including TLS 1.2 and TLS 1.3

5. Challenges and Future Research Directions in TLS 1.3 Traffic Analysis

5.1. Challenges

(1) Technical Challenges Introduced by TLS 1.3: TLS 1.3 enhances security and efficiency through measures such as PFS, 0-RTT session resumption, and encryption of all handshake messages. While some new interception schemes for TLS 1.3 have been proposed, they often fall short in terms of security, performance, and deployment costs. For example, maTLS [84] and tls_visibility [79] lack sufficient security analysis and validation, and ETS [80] has been criticized for its lack of forward secrecy. Designing secure, efficient, and easily deployable interception schemes remains a significant challenge.

(2) Balancing Privacy and Security: TLS 1.3 further strengthens user privacy protection, but middlebox-based interception and searchable encryption technologies may pose information leakage risks. Users and privacy advocates typically aim to maximize the protection of communication content, while network operators need to inspect traffic for compliance or security reasons. Balancing user privacy protection with network security is a critical challenge in TLS traffic analysis.

(3) Comprehensive Detection Capabilities: Current technologies like searchable encryption and machine learning methods have limited detection capabilities compared to plaintext inspection. Searchable encryption primarily supports keyword matching and struggles with regular expression matching. While machine learning can perform traffic classification and anomaly detection, it falls short in executing complex security policies and rules. Expanding these technologies to cover more detection needs is an urgent challenge. Although trusted hardware solutions can achieve full functionality, their deployment flexibility is limited.

(4) Challenges for Machine Learning Techniques: Machine learning techniques can analyze traffic without changing existing network settings or decrypting network traffic, providing an optimal solution for passive detection. However, the standardization and widespread use of ECH pose significant challenges to these methods. With valuable feature information such as SNI becoming invisible, the statistical model of encrypted traffic changes dramatically. This shift increases the difficulty of traffic classification, demanding machine learning models with enhanced feature extraction and generalization capabilities to uncover patterns from limited metadata and temporal features of encrypted traffic. The impact of ECH on machine learning techniques extends beyond feature availability. It necessitates a fundamental rethinking of model architectures and training strategies to adapt to this new, more opaque traffic environment. Furthermore, the scarcity of publicly available TLS 1.3 traffic datasets hinders related research. Since TLS 1.3 is not yet widely deployed, most research is in the exploratory stage. To achieve the large-scale application of machine learning methods in TLS 1.3 traffic analysis, more work is needed in dataset construction, feature engineering, model performance optimization, and knowledge transfer.

(5) Incomplete Adoption and Complex Environment: The current limited adoption of ECH and the continued use of lower TLS versions for side channels create a complex environment [126] for traffic analysis. Researcher must now contend with a mix of fully encrypted, partially encrypted, and legacy traffic patterns. This diversity poses significant challenges for developing consistent and effective traffic analysis techniques. It requires adaptive methods capable of handling multiple protocol versions and encryption levels simultaneously, complicating both the design of analysis algorithms and their real-world deployment. Moreover, this transitional phase may persist for an extended period, necessitating flexible and scalable solutions that can evolve with the changing landscape of encrypted traffic.

5.2. Future Research Directions

Future research directions in TLS traffic analysis should include the following:

(1) Privacy-Preserving Traffic Detection Technologies: Research methods that combine various privacy-preserving technologies to allow authorized parties to perform limited detection on encrypted traffic without compromising forward secrecy. Implementing

privacy-preserving techniques can introduce significant computational overhead and complexity. Research should focus on optimizing cryptographic protocols to reduce overhead and improve efficiency, developing hybrid approaches that combine multiple privacy-preserving techniques. For example, exploring privacy-preserving traffic detection technologies based on searchable encryption, homomorphic encryption, secure multi-party computation, and trusted execution environments can meet network security and management needs while protecting user privacy. environments can meet network security and management needs while protecting user privacy.

(2) Machine Learning-Based Traffic Analysis Technologies: With the development of deep learning, graph neural networks, and multimodal learning, researchers are continuously exploring new methods to improve the accuracy and efficiency of encrypted traffic analysis. For example, using graph neural networks to model the spatiotemporal features of encrypted traffic and multimodal learning to integrate traffic metadata, external threat intelligence, and other heterogeneous information. The scarcity of labeled datasets and the need for robust feature extraction in the face of limited metadata visibility are significant hurdles. Active learning and federated learning can help address data scarcity by leveraging unlabeled data. Transfer learning and meta-learning can enhance model generalization, while graph neural networks and multimodal learning can improve feature extraction from encrypted traffic.

(3) System Verifiability and Transparency: Given the complexity of the TLS 1.3 protocol and the black-box nature of encryption, users find it difficult to verify whether the behavior of traffic analysis systems aligns with their claims. Some studies mention using trusted hardware and cryptographic proofs to provide partial transparency, but these face many challenges in actual deployment. Interdisciplinary research involving cryptography, formal verification, and secure hardware is needed to develop frameworks that ensure system trustworthiness. Combining formal verification with machine learning could automate verification processes, enhancing efficiency and coverage.

(4) Customized Interception Schemes: Security requirements, privacy protection needs, and performance optimization goals can vary significantly across different scenarios, complicating the design of interception schemes. This diversity necessitates the development of tailored interception approaches based on specific characteristics and requirements of each environment. To address this challenge, it is crucial to develop modular interception architectures customized for specific contexts, such as enterprise networks, cloud services, and IoT ecosystems. This approach will ensure robust security while optimizing performance for each unique setting. For example, enterprise networks may prioritize data leakage prevention and access control, cloud services may focus on multi-tenant isolation and virtualization security, and IoT may emphasize device authentication and lightweight encryption. Successful implementation of this strategy requires close collaboration with industry stakeholders to accurately identify and address their specific needs and concerns.

(5) Detection Function Expansion: Research technologies that can support multiple detection needs simultaneously to meet the requirements of various middlebox services, for example, developing technologies capable of regular expression matching and complex rule detection [20] to provide detection capabilities equivalent to plaintext analysis. Further exploration is needed of the application of machine learning in encrypted traffic analysis, expanding machine learning-based passive analysis techniques to cover more detection needs, for instance, using deep learning to automatically extract advanced features, unsupervised learning to discover unknown threats, and reinforcement learning to optimize detection strategies. Additionally, methods such as active learning and data synthesis can help generate high-fidelity labeled data for training models.

6. Discussion

Through a comprehensive review of the state-of-the-art research efforts in analyzing TLS 1.3-encrypted traffic, we have identified several key findings and lessons learned.

Middlebox interception techniques, such as TLS proxies and session splitting, have been widely used for network security and management. However, the enhanced security features of TLS 1.3, such as mandatory forward secrecy and the removal of insecure cryptographic algorithms, have rendered traditional interception methods less effective or even infeasible. While researchers have proposed various TLS 1.3-aware interception schemes, their security, performance, and deployability still require further investigation and improvement. This highlights the need for developing more secure, efficient, and easily deployable interception schemes that can adapt to the evolving TLS protocol.

Searchable encryption techniques enable encrypted traffic inspection without decrypting the content, providing a promising approach for privacy-preserving analysis. Although existing searchable encryption schemes are theoretically applicable to TLS 1.3 traffic, their practical deployment and adaptation to the new protocol features remain an open challenge. The limitations of existing schemes in terms of efficiency, functionality extension, and formal security analysis necessitate further research to make searchable encryption a viable solution for TLS 1.3 traffic analysis.

Machine learning has emerged as a powerful tool for encrypted traffic analysis, capable of extracting valuable information from encrypted traffic without decryption. Despite the challenges posed by TLS 1.3's enhanced encryption and reduced metadata visibility, researchers have developed innovative machine learning models that leverage various traffic features, such as packet lengths, timing, and flow patterns. However, the scarcity of publicly available TLS 1.3 datasets and the need for robust feature engineering and model optimization remain significant obstacles to the widespread adoption of machine learning techniques in this domain. Collaborative efforts in dataset creation and sharing, as well as advancements in feature extraction and model generalization, are crucial for the progress of machine learning-based TLS 1.3 traffic analysis.

Balancing privacy and security is a critical challenge in TLS traffic analysis. While TLS 1.3 strengthens user privacy protection, middlebox-based interception and searchable encryption technologies may pose information leakage risks. Finding solutions that protect user privacy while allowing necessary traffic inspection for security purposes requires a delicate balance and innovative approaches. Privacy-preserving traffic detection technologies that combine various techniques, such as searchable encryption, homomorphic encryption, secure multi-party computation, and trusted execution environments, hold promise for achieving this balance.

These findings underscore the importance of continued research and innovation in TLS 1.3 traffic analysis techniques. By addressing the identified challenges and exploring the proposed future research directions, we can develop more effective, secure, and privacy-preserving solutions for analyzing TLS 1.3-encrypted traffic.

7. Conclusions

The widespread adoption of TLS 1.3 has brought significant improvements in security and privacy for encrypted communication. However, this has also posed unprecedented challenges for encrypted traffic analysis. This survey provides a comprehensive overview of the state-of-the-art research efforts in analyzing TLS 1.3-encrypted traffic. We have systematically reviewed three major analysis approaches: middlebox interception techniques, searchable encryption methods, and machine learning-based techniques. For each approach, we have conducted a critical examination of its applicability, strengths, and limitations in the context of TLS 1.3.

TLS 1.3 traffic analysis is a dynamic and challenging field with significant implications for network security, management, and privacy. While existing techniques have made notable progress, there remain open problems and opportunities for future research. Several key research directions deserve further exploration, including the development of privacy-preserving traffic inspection techniques, advancements in machine learning techniques for encrypted traffic analysis, and the establishment of formal verification methods and security transparency frameworks. By addressing these challenges and exploring innovative solutions, we can fully realize the potential of encrypted traffic analysis in the context of TLS 1.3. This will enable effective network monitoring and protection while preserving user privacy.

Author Contributions: Conceptualization, J.Z. and Z.S.; methodology, J.Z.; formal analysis, J.Z. and Z.S.; investigation, J.Z.; resources, J.Z.; data curation, J.Z.; writing—original draft preparation, J.Z and Z.S.; writing—review and editing, W.F., W.H., T.H. and Z.Z.; visualization, J.Z. and Z.S.; supervision, Z.S.; project administration, J.Z.; funding acquisition, J.Z. All authors have read and agreed to the published version of the manuscript.

Funding: This study was funded by the University's Independent Research Project (Grant No. 2022508020).

Data Availability Statement: Data sharing is not applicable.

Conflicts of Interest: The authors declare no conflicts of interest.

References

1. Google. HTTPS Encryption on the Web. Available online: https://transparencyreport.google.com/https/overview (accessed on 18 April 2024).
2. Allen, C.; Dierks, T. The TLS Protocol Version 1.0. RFC 2246. 1999. Available online: https://www.rfc-editor.org/info/rfc2246 (accessed on 19 April 2024).
3. Rescorla, E. The Transport Layer Security (TLS) Protocol Version 1.3. RFC 8446. 2018. Available online: https://www.rfc-editor.org/info/rfc8446 (accessed on 19 April 2024).
4. Qualys. Qualys SSL Labs—SSL Pulse. Available online: https://www.ssllabs.com/ssl-pulse/ (accessed on 19 April 2024).
5. Rescorla, E.; Dierks, T. The Transport Layer Security (TLS) Protocol Version 1.2. RFC 5246. 2008. Available online: https://www.rfc-editor.org/info/rfc5246 (accessed on 19 April 2024).
6. Chen, Z.; Cheng, G.; Jiang, B.; Tang, S.; Guo, S.; Zhou, Y. Length matters: Fast internet encrypted traffic service classification based on multi-PDU lengths. In Proceedings of the 2020 16th International Conference on Mobility, Sensing and Networking (MSN), Tokyo, Japan, 17–19 December 2020; pp. 531–538.
7. Lin, X.; Xiong, G.; Gou, G.; Li, Z.; Shi, J.; Yu, J. Et-bert: A contextualized datagram representation with pre-training transformers for encrypted traffic classification. In Proceedings of the ACM Web Conference 2022, Lyon, France, 25–29 April 2022; pp. 633–642.
8. Velan, P.; Čermák, M.; Čeleda, P.; Drašar, M. A survey of methods for encrypted traffic classification and analysis. *Int. J. Netw. Manag.* **2015**, *25*, 355–374. [CrossRef]
9. Rezaei, S.; Liu, X. Deep learning for encrypted traffic classification: An overview. *IEEE Commun. Mag.* **2019**, *57*, 76–81. [CrossRef]
10. Pacheco, F.; Exposito, E.; Gineste, M.; Baudoin, C.; Aguilar, J. Towards the deployment of machine learning solutions in network traffic classification: A systematic survey. *IEEE Commun. Surv. Tutorials* **2018**, *21*, 1988–2014. [CrossRef]
11. Papadogiannaki, E.; Ioannidis, S. A survey on encrypted network traffic analysis applications, techniques, and countermeasures. *ACM Comput. Surv. (CSUR)* **2021**, *54*, 1–35. [CrossRef]
12. Shen, M.; Ye, K.; Liu, X.; Zhu, L.; Kang, J.; Yu, S.; Li, Q.; Xu, K. Machine learning-powered encrypted network traffic analysis: A comprehensive survey. *IEEE Commun. Surv. Tutorials* **2022**, *25*, 791–824. [CrossRef]
13. Kwon, D.; Kim, H.; Kim, J.; Suh, S.C.; Kim, I.; Kim, K.J. A survey of deep learning-based network anomaly detection. *Clust. Comput.* **2019**, *22*, 949–961. [CrossRef]
14. Yi, T.; Chen, X.; Zhu, Y.; Ge, W.; Han, Z. Review on the application of deep learning in network attack detection. *J. Netw. Comput. Appl.* **2023**, *212*, 103580. [CrossRef]
15. Aceto, G.; Ciuonzo, D.; Montieri, A.; Pescapé, A. Toward effective mobile encrypted traffic classification through deep learning. *Neurocomputing* **2020**, *409*, 306–315. [CrossRef]
16. Zhang, C.; Patras, P.; Haddadi, H. Deep learning in mobile and wireless networking: A survey. *IEEE Commun. Surv. Tutorials* **2019**, *21*, 2224–2287. [CrossRef]
17. Aceto, G.; Ciuonzo, D.; Montieri, A.; Pescapé, A. Mobile encrypted traffic classification using deep learning: Experimental evaluation, lessons learned, and challenges. *IEEE Trans. Netw. Serv. Manag.* **2019**, *16*, 445–458. [CrossRef]
18. Tahaei, H.; Afifi, F.; Asemi, A.; Zaki, F.; Anuar, N.B. The rise of traffic classification in IoT networks: A survey. *J. Netw. Comput. Appl.* **2020**, *154*, 102538. [CrossRef]
19. Sultana, N.; Chilamkurti, N.; Peng, W.; Alhadad, R. Survey on SDN based network intrusion detection system using machine learning approaches. *Peer Netw. Appl.* **2019**, *12*, 493–501. [CrossRef]
20. Poh, G.S.; Divakaran, D.M.; Lim, H.W.; Ning, J.; Desai, A. A survey of privacy-preserving techniques for encrypted traffic inspection over network middleboxes. *arXiv* **2021**, arXiv:2101.04338.
21. Oh, C.; Ha, J.; Roh, H. A survey on TLS-encrypted malware network traffic analysis applicable to security operations centers. *Appl. Sci.* **2021**, *12*, 155. [CrossRef]

22. de Carné de Carnavalet, X.; van Oorschot, P.C. A Survey and Analysis of TLS Interception Mechanisms and Motivations: Exploring how end-to-end TLS is made "end-to-me" for web traffic. *ACM Comput. Surv.* **2023**, *55*, 1–40. [CrossRef]
23. Anderson, B.; McGrew, D. Identifying encrypted malware traffic with contextual flow data. In Proceedings of the 2016 ACM Workshop on Artificial Intelligence and Security, Vienna, Austria, 28 October 2016; pp. 35–46.
24. Anderson, B.; McGrew, D. Machine learning for encrypted malware traffic classification: Accounting for noisy labels and non-stationarity. In Proceedings of the 23rd ACM SIGKDD International Conference on Knowledge Discovery and Data Mining, Halifax, NS, Canada, 13–17 August 2017; pp. 1723–1732.
25. Wang, S.; Chen, Z.; Zhang, L.; Yan, Q.; Yang, B.; Peng, L.; Jia, Z. Trafficav: An effective and explainable detection of mobile malware behavior using network traffic. In Proceedings of the 2016 IEEE/ACM 24th International Symposium on Quality of Service (IWQoS), Beijing, China, 20–21 June 2016; pp. 1–6.
26. Liu, C.; Cao, Z.; Xiong, G.; Gou, G.; Yiu, S.M.; He, L. Mampf: Encrypted traffic classification based on multi-attribute markov probability fingerprints. In Proceedings of the 2018 IEEE/ACM 26th International Symposium on Quality of Service (IWQoS), Banff, AB, Canada, 4–6 June 2018; pp. 1–10.
27. Liu, C.; He, L.; Xiong, G.; Cao, Z.; Li, Z. Fs-net: A flow sequence network for encrypted traffic classification. In Proceedings of the IEEE INFOCOM 2019—IEEE Conference on Computer Communications, Paris, France, 29 April–2 May 2019; pp. 1171–1179.
28. Zhang, W.; Meng, Y.; Liu, Y.; Zhang, X.; Zhang, Y.; Zhu, H. Homonit: Monitoring smart home apps from encrypted traffic. In Proceedings of the 2018 ACM SIGSAC Conference on Computer and Communications Security, Toronto, ON, Canada, 15–19 October 2018; pp. 1074–1088.
29. Cisco. Cisco Encrypted Traffic Analytics White Paper. Available online: https://www.cisco.com/c/en/us/solutions/collateral/enterprise-networks/enterprise-network-security/nb-09-encrytd-traf-anlytcs-wp-cte-en.html (accessed on 18 April 2024).
30. Zheng, W.; Gou, C.; Yan, L.; Mo, S. Learning to classify: A flow-based relation network for encrypted traffic classification. In Proceedings of the Web Conference 2020, Taipei, Taiwan, 20–24 April 2020; pp. 13–22.
31. Fu, Z.; Liu, M.; Qin, Y.; Zhang, J.; Zou, Y.; Yin, Q.; Li, Q.; Duan, H. Encrypted malware traffic detection via graph-based network analysis. In Proceedings of the 25th International Symposium on Research in Attacks, Intrusions and Defenses, Limassol, Cyprus, 26–28 October 2022; pp. 495–509.
32. Qing, Y.; Yin, Q.; Deng, X.; Chen, Y.; Liu, Z.; Sun, K.; Xu, K.; Zhang, J.; Li, Q. Low-Quality Training Data Only? A Robust Framework for Detecting Encrypted Malicious Network Traffic. *arXiv* **2023**, arXiv:2309.04798.
33. Fu, C.; Li, Q.; Xu, K. Detecting unknown encrypted malicious traffic in real time via flow interaction graph analysis. *arXiv* **2023**, arXiv:2301.13686.
34. Anderson, B.; McGrew, D. Tls beyond the browser: Combining end host and network data to understand application behavior. In Proceedings of the Internet Measurement Conference, Amsterdam, The Netherlands, 21–23 October 2019; pp. 379–392.
35. Dimopoulos, G.; Leontiadis, I.; Barlet-Ros, P.; Papagiannaki, K. Measuring video QoE from encrypted traffic. In Proceedings of the 2016 Internet Measurement Conference, Santa Monica, CA, USA, 14–16 November 2016; pp. 513–526.
36. Pan, W.; Cheng, G.; Wu, H.; Tang, Y. Towards QoE assessment of encrypted YouTube adaptive video streaming in mobile networks. In Proceedings of the 2016 IEEE/ACM 24th International Symposium on Quality of Service (IWQoS), Beijing, China, 20–21 June 2016; pp. 1–6.
37. Oche, M.; Noor, R.M.; Chembe, C. Multivariate statistical approach for estimating QoE of real-time multimedia applications in vehicular ITS network. *Comput. Commun.* **2017**, *104*, 88–107. [CrossRef]
38. Shen, M.; Zhang, J.; Xu, K.; Zhu, L.; Liu, J.; Du, X. Deepqoe: Real-time measurement of video qoe from encrypted traffic with deep learning. In Proceedings of the 2020 IEEE/ACM 28th International Symposium on Quality of Service (IWQoS), Hangzhou, China, 15–17 June 2020; pp. 1–10.
39. Wu, H.; Li, X.; Cheng, G.; Hu, X. Monitoring video resolution of adaptive encrypted video traffic based on HTTP/2 features. In Proceedings of the IEEE INFOCOM 2021—IEEE Conference on Computer Communications Workshops (INFOCOM WKSHPS), Vancouver, BC, Canada, 10–13 May 2021; pp. 1–6.
40. Shbair, W.M.; Cholez, T.; Francois, J.; Chrisment, I. A multi-level framework to identify HTTPS services. In Proceedings of the NOMS 2016—2016 IEEE/IFIP Network Operations and Management Symposium, Istanbul, Turkey, 25–29 April 2016; pp. 240–248.
41. Yamauchi, H.; Nakao, A.; Oguchi, M.; Yamamoto, S.; Yamaguchi, S. A study on service identification based on server name indication analysis. In Proceedings of the 2019 Seventh International Symposium on Computing and Networking Workshops (CANDARW), Nagasaki, Japan, 26–29 November 2019; pp. 470–474.
42. Liu, X.; You, J.; Wu, Y.; Li, T.; Li, L.; Zhang, Z.; Ge, J. Attention-based bidirectional GRU networks for efficient HTTPS traffic classification. *Inf. Sci.* **2020**, *541*, 297–315. [CrossRef]
43. Cheng, J.; Wu, Y.; Yuepeng, E.; You, J.; Li, T.; Li, H.; Ge, J. MATEC: A lightweight neural network for online encrypted traffic classification. *Comput. Netw.* **2021**, *199*, 108472. [CrossRef]
44. Panchenko, A.; Lanze, F.; Pennekamp, J.; Engel, T.; Zinnen, A.; Henze, M.; Wehrle, K. Website Fingerprinting at Internet Scale. In NDSS. 2016. Available online: https://nymity.ch/tor-dns/pdf/Panchenko2016a.pdf (accessed on 26 April 2024).
45. Li, S.; Guo, H.; Hopper, N. Measuring information leakage in website fingerprinting attacks and defenses. In Proceedings of the 2018 ACM SIGSAC Conference on Computer and Communications Security, Toronto, ON, Canada, 15–19 October 2018; pp. 1977–1992.

46. Rimmer, V.; Preuveneers, D.; Juarez, M.; Goethem, T.V.; Joosen, W. Automated Website Fingerprinting through Deep Learning. In Proceedings of the Proceedings 2018 Network and Distributed System Security Symposium, San Diego, CA, USA, 18–21 February 2018. [CrossRef]
47. Sirinam, P.; Mathews, N.; Rahman, M.S.; Wright, M. Triplet fingerprinting: More practical and portable website fingerprinting with n-shot learning. In Proceedings of the 2019 ACM SIGSAC Conference on Computer and Communications Security, London, UK, 11–15 November 2019; pp. 1131–1148.
48. Mathews, N.; Holland, J.K.; Oh, S.E.; Rahman, M.S.; Hopper, N.; Wright, M. SoK: A critical evaluation of efficient website fingerprinting defenses. In Proceedings of the 2023 IEEE Symposium on Security and Privacy (SP), San Francisco, CA, USA, 21–25 May 2023; pp. 969–986.
49. Rezaei, S.; Kroencke, B.; Liu, X. Large-scale mobile app identification using deep learning. *IEEE Access* **2019**, *8*, 348–362. [CrossRef]
50. Jiang, M.; Li, Z.; Fu, P.; Cai, W.; Cui, M.; Xiong, G.; Gou, G. Accurate mobile-app fingerprinting using flow-level relationship with graph neural networks. *Comput. Netw.* **2022**, *217*, 109309. [CrossRef]
51. Van Ede, T.; Bortolameotti, R.; Continella, A.; Ren, J.; Dubois, D.J.; Lindorfer, M.; Choffnes, D.; Van Steen, M.; Peter, A. Flowprint: Semi-supervised mobile-app fingerprinting on encrypted network traffic. In Proceedings of the Network and Distributed System Security Symposium (NDSS), San Diego, CA, USA, 23–26 February 2020; Volume 27.
52. Xu, G.; Xu, M.; Chen, Y.; Zhao, J. A Mobile Application-Classifying Method Based on a Graph Attention Network from Encrypted Network Traffic. *Electronics* **2023**, *12*, 2313. [CrossRef]
53. Conti, M.; Mancini, L.V.; Spolaor, R.; Verde, N.V. Ca not you hear me knocking: Identification of user actions on android apps via traffic analysis. In Proceedings of the 5th ACM Conference on Data and Application Security and Privacy, San Antonio, TX, USA, 2–4 March 2015; pp. 297–304.
54. Saltaformaggio, B.; Choi, H.; Johnson, K.; Kwon, Y.; Zhang, Q.; Zhang, X.; Xu, D.; Qian, J. Eavesdropping on {Fine-Grained} user activities within smartphone apps over encrypted network traffic. In Proceedings of the 10th USENIX Workshop on Offensive Technologies (WOOT 16), Austin, TX, USA, 8–9 August 2016.
55. Dubin, R.; Dvir, A.; Pele, O.; Hadar, O. I know what you saw last minute—encrypted http adaptive video streaming title classification. *IEEE Trans. Inf. Forensics Secur.* **2017**, *12*, 3039–3049. [CrossRef]
56. Li, Y.; Huang, Y.; Xu, R.; Seneviratne, S.; Thilakarathna, K.; Cheng, A.; Webb, D.; Jourjon, G. Deep content: Unveiling video streaming content from encrypted wifi traffic. In Proceedings of the 2018 IEEE 17th International Symposium on Network Computing and Applications (NCA), Cambridge, MA, USA, 1–3 November 2018; pp. 1–8.
57. Wu, H.; Wu, Q.; Cheng, G.; Guo, S.; Hu, X.; Yan, S. SFIM: Identify user behavior based on stable features. *Peer Netw. Appl.* **2021**, *14*, 3674–3687. [CrossRef]
58. Scheffler, S.; Mayer, J. Sok: Content moderation for end-to-end encryption. *arXiv* **2023**, arXiv:2303.03979. [CrossRef]
59. Hall, J.L.; Aaron, M.D.; Andersdotter, A.; Jones, B.; Feamster, N.; Knodel, M. A Survey of Worldwide Censorship Techniques. RFC 9505. 2023. Available online: https://www.rfc-editor.org/info/rfc9505 (accessed on 26 April 2024).
60. Wu, M.; Sippe, J.; Sivakumar, D.; Burg, J.; Anderson, P.; Wang, X.; Bock, K.; Houmansadr, A.; Levin, D.; Wustrow, E. How the Great Firewall of China detects and blocks fully encrypted traffic. In Proceedings of the 32nd USENIX Security Symposium (USENIX Security 23), Anaheim, CA, USA, 9–11 August 2023; pp. 2653–2670.
61. Frolov, S.; Wustrow, E. The use of TLS in Censorship Circumvention. In NDSS. 2019. Available online: https://www.freehaven.net/anonbib/papers/ndss2019_03B-2-1_Frolov_paper.pdf (accessed on 26 April 2024).
62. Trustwave. Filter : SNI Extension Feature and HTTPS Blocking. 2015. Available online: https://www3.trustwave.com/software/8e6/hlp/r3000/files/1system_filter.html (accessed on 26 April 2024).
63. Sophos. Sophos Firewall: Web Filtering Basics. 2023. Available online: https://support.sophos.com/support/s/article/KB-000036518?language=en_US (accessed on 26 April 2024).
64. Shbair, W.M.; Cholez, T.; Goichot, A.; Chrisment, I. Efficiently bypassing SNI-based HTTPS filtering. In Proceedings of the 2015 IFIP/IEEE International Symposium on Integrated Network Management (IM), Ottawa, ON, Canada, 11–15 May 2015; pp. 990–995.
65. Morgus, R.; Sherman, J.; Nam, S. Analysis: South Korea's New Tool for Filtering Illegal Internet Content. 2019. Available online: https://www.newamerica.org/cybersecurity-initiative/c2b/c2b-log/analysis-south-koreas-sni-monitoring/ (accessed on 27 April 2024).
66. Bock, D.L.K.; Merino, L.; Fifield, D.; Housmansadr, A.; Levin, D. Exposing and Circumventing China's Censorship of ESNI. 2020. Available online: https://geneva.cs.umd.edu/posts/china-censors-esni/esni/ (accessed on 26 April 2024).
67. Satija, S.; Chatterjee, R. BlindTLS: Circumventing TLS-based HTTPS censorship. In Proceedings of the ACM SIGCOMM 2021 Workshop on Free and Open Communications on the Internet, Virtual, 27 August 2021; pp. 43–49.
68. Waked, L. Analyzing TLS Interception in Middleware Network Appliances. Ph.D. Thesis, Concordia University, Montreal, QC, Canada, 2018.
69. Waked, L.; Mannan, M.; Youssef, A. To intercept or not to intercept: Analyzing tls interception in network appliances. In Proceedings of the 2018 on Asia Conference on Computer and Communications Security, Incheon, Republic of Korea, 4 June 2018; pp. 399–412.
70. Afzal, A.; Hussain, M.; Saleem, S.; Shahzad, M.K.; Ho, A.T.; Jung, K.H. Encrypted network traffic analysis of secure instant messaging application: A case study of signal messenger app. *Appl. Sci.* **2021**, *11*, 7789. [CrossRef]

71. Sarhan, S.A.E.; Youness, H.A.; Bahaa-Eldin, A.M. A framework for digital forensics of encrypted real-time network traffic, instant messaging, and VoIP application case study. *Ain Shams Eng. J.* **2023**, *14*, 102069. [CrossRef]
72. Dierks, T.; Rescorla, E. The Transport Layer Security (TLS) Protocol Version 1.1. RFC 4346. 2006. Available online: https://www.rfc-editor.org/info/rfc4346 (accessed on 26 April 2024).
73. Moriarty, K.; Farrell, S. Deprecating TLS 1.0 and TLS 1.1. RFC 8996. 2021. Available online: https://www.rfc-editor.org/info/rfc8996 (accessed on 19 April 2024).
74. Holz, R.; Hiller, J.; Amann, J.; Razaghpanah, A.; Jost, T.; Vallina-Rodriguez, N.; Hohlfeld, O. Tracking the deployment of TLS 1.3 on the Web: A story of experimentation and centralization. *ACM SIGCOMM Comput. Commun. Rev.* **2020**, *50*, 3–15. [CrossRef]
75. Dowling, B.; Fischlin, M.; Günther, F.; Stebila, D. A cryptographic analysis of the TLS 1.3 handshake protocol. *J. Cryptol.* **2021**, *34*, 37. [CrossRef]
76. Rescorla, E.; Oku, K.; Sullivan, N.; Wood, C.A. TLS Encrypted Client Hello. 2024. Available online: https://datatracker.ietf.org/doc/html/draft-ietf-tls-esni-18 (accessed on 18 May 2024).
77. Bhargavan, K.; Cheval, V.; Wood, C. A symbolic analysis of privacy for tls 1.3 with encrypted client hello. In Proceedings of the 2022 ACM SIGSAC Conference on Computer and Communications Security, Los Angeles, CA, USA, 7–11 November 2022; pp. 365–379.
78. Van Bulck, J.; Minkin, M.; Weisse, O.; Genkin, D.; Kasikci, B.; Piessens, F.; Silberstein, M.; Wenisch, T.F.; Yarom, Y.; Strackx, R. Foreshadow: Extracting the keys to the intel {SGX} kingdom with transient {Out-of-Order} execution. In Proceedings of the 27th USENIX Security Symposium (USENIX Security 18), Baltimore, MD, USA, 15–17 August 2018; pp. 991–1008.
79. Housley, R.; Droms, R. TLS 1.3 Option for Negotiation of Visibility in the Datacenter. Internet-Draft draft-rhrd-tls-tls13-visibility-01, Internet Engineering Task Force. 2018. Available online: https://datatracker.ietf.org/doc/draft-rhrd-tls-tls13-visibility/01/ (accessed on 18 May 2024).
80. ETSI. Middlebox Security Protocol—Part 3: Enterprise Transport Security. 2019. Available online: https://www.etsi.org/deliver/etsi_ts/103500_103599/10352303/01.03.01_60/ts_10352303v010301p.pdf (accessed on 18 May 2024).
81. Migault, D. LURK Extension version 1 for (D)TLS 1.3 Authentication. Internet-Draft draft-mglt-lurk-tls13-06, Internet Engineering Task Force. 2022. Available online: https://datatracker.ietf.org/doc/draft-mglt-lurk-tls13/06/ (accessed on 18 May 2024).
82. Barnes, R.; Iyengar, S.; Sullivan, N.; Rescorla, E. Delegated Credentials for TLS and DTLS. RFC 9345. 2023. Available online: https://www.rfc-editor.org/info/rfc9345 (accessed on 18 May 2024).
83. Bhargavan, K.; Boureanu, I.; Delignat-Lavaud, A.; Fouque, P.A.; Onete, C. A formal treatment of accountable proxying over TLS. In Proceedings of the 2018 IEEE Symposium on Security and Privacy (SP), San Francisco, CA, USA, 20–24 May 2018; pp. 799–816.
84. Lee, H.; Smith, Z.; Lim, J.; Choi, G.; Chun, S.; Chung, T.; Kwon, T.T. maTLS: How to Make TLS Middlebox-Aware? In NDSS. 2019. Available online: https://hw5773.github.io/paper/matls.pdf (accessed on 18 May 2024).
85. Li, J.; Chen, R.; Su, J.; Huang, X.; Wang, X. ME-TLS: Middlebox-enhanced TLS for internet-of-things devices. *IEEE Internet Things J.* **2019**, *7*, 1216–1229. [CrossRef]
86. Grubbs, P.; Arun, A.; Zhang, Y.; Bonneau, J.; Walfish, M. {Zero-Knowledge} Middleboxes. In Proceedings of the 31st USENIX Security Symposium (USENIX Security 22), Boston, MA, USA, 10–12 August 2022; pp. 4255–4272.
87. Zhang, C.; DeStefano, Z.; Arun, A.; Bonneau, J.; Grubbs, P.; Walfish, M. Zombie: Middleboxes that {Don't} Snoop. In Proceedings of the 21st USENIX Symposium on Networked Systems Design and Implementation (NSDI 24), Santa Clara, CA, USA, 16–18 April 2024; pp. 1917–1936.
88. Mozilla. NSS Key Log Format. 2019. Available online: https://nss-crypto.org/reference/security/nss/legacy/key_log_format/index.html (accessed on 20 June 2024).
89. Green, M.; Droms, R.; Housley, R.; Turner, P.; Fenter, S. Data Center Use of Static Diffie-Hellman in TLS 1.3. 2017. Available online: https://datatracker.ietf.org/doc/draft-green-tls-static-dh-in-tls13/ (accessed on 18 May 2024).
90. de Carnavalet, X.D.C.; Mannan, M. Killed by proxy: Analyzing client-end TLS interception software. In Proceedings of the Network and Distributed System Security Symposium, San Diego, CA, USA, 21–24 February 2016.
91. Durumeric, Z.; Ma, Z.; Springall, D.; Barnes, R.; Sullivan, N.; Bursztein, E.; Bailey, M.D.; Halderman, J.A.; Paxson, V. The Security Impact of HTTPS Interception. In NDSS. 2017. Available online: https://git.safemobile.org/crimeflare/cloudflare-tor/raw/commit/020252c3748c37c4b0f2da47f46b3505f82435fa/pdf/2017-The_Security_Impact_of_HTTPS_Interception.pdf (accessed on 19 May 2024).
92. Migault, D. LURK Protocol Version 1. Internet-Draft draft-mglt-lurk-lurk-01, Internet Engineering Task Force. 2021. Available online: https://datatracker.ietf.org/doc/draft-mglt-lurk-lurk/01/ (accessed on 18 May 2024).
93. Migault, D.; Boureanu, I. LURK Extension Version 1 for (D)TLS 1.2 Authentication. Internet-Draft draft-mglt-lurk-tls12-05, Internet Engineering Task Force. 2021. Available online: https://datatracker.ietf.org/doc/draft-mglt-lurk-tls12/05/ (accessed on 18 May 2024).
94. Naylor, D.; Schomp, K.; Varvello, M.; Leontiadis, I.; Blackburn, J.; López, D.R.; Papagiannaki, K.; Rodriguez Rodriguez, P.; Steenkiste, P. Multi-context TLS (mcTLS) enabling secure in-network functionality in TLS. *ACM SIGCOMM Comput. Commun. Rev.* **2015**, *45*, 199–212. [CrossRef]
95. Song, D.X.; Wagner, D.; Perrig, A. Practical techniques for searches on encrypted data. In Proceedings of the 2000 IEEE Symposium on Security and Privacy. S&P 2000, Berkeley, CA, USA, 14–17 May 2000; pp. 44–55.

96. Sherry, J.; Lan, C.; Popa, R.A.; Ratnasamy, S. Blindbox: Deep packet inspection over encrypted traffic. *ACM SIGCOMM Comput. Commun. Rev.* **2015**, *45*, 213–226. [CrossRef]
97. Ning, J.; Poh, G.S.; Loh, J.C.; Chia, J.; Chang, E.C. PrivDPI: Privacy-preserving encrypted traffic inspection with reusable obfuscated rules. In Proceedings of the 2019 ACM SIGSAC Conference on Computer and Communications Security, London, UK, 11–15 November 2019; pp. 1657–1670.
98. Ning, J.; Huang, X.; Poh, G.S.; Xu, S.; Loh, J.C.; Weng, J.; Deng, R.H. Pine: Enabling privacy-preserving deep packet inspection on TLS with rule-hiding and fast connection establishment. In Computer Security–ESORICS 2020: 25th European Symposium on Research in Computer Security, ESORICS 2020, Guildford, UK, 14–18 September 2020; Proceedings, Part I 25; Springer: Berlin/Heidelberg, Germany, 2020; pp. 3–22.
99. Ren, H.; Li, H.; Liu, D.; Xu, G.; Cheng, N.; Shen, X. Privacy-preserving efficient verifiable deep packet inspection for cloud-assisted middlebox. *IEEE Trans. Cloud Comput.* **2020**, *10*, 1052–1064. [CrossRef]
100. Fan, Z.; Zeng, Y.; Zhu, X.; Ma, J. A group key agreement based encrypted traffic detection scheme for Internet of Things. In Proceedings of the 1st ACM International Workshop on Security and Safety for Intelligent Cyber-Physical Systems, Virtual, 16–19 November 2020; pp. 19–26.
101. Kim, J.; Camtepe, S.; Baek, J.; Susilo, W.; Pieprzyk, J.; Nepal, S. P2DPI: Practical and privacy-preserving deep packet inspection. In Proceedings of the 2021 ACM Asia Conference on Computer and Communications Security, Virtual, 7–11 June 2021; pp. 135–146.
102. Canard, S.; Li, C. Towards practical intrusion detection system over encrypted traffic. *IET Inf. Secur.* **2021**, *15*, 231–246. [CrossRef]
103. Chen, D.; Wang, H.; Zhang, N.; Nie, X.; Dai, H.N.; Zhang, K.; Choo, K.K.R. Privacy-preserving encrypted traffic inspection with symmetric cryptographic techniques in IoT. *IEEE Internet Things J.* **2022**, *9*, 17265–17279. [CrossRef]
104. Jia, X.; Zhang, M. Encrypted Packet Inspection Based on Oblivious Transfer. *Secur. Commun. Networks* **2022**, *2022*, 4743078. [CrossRef]
105. Deng, M.; Zhang, K.; Wu, P.; Wen, M.; Ning, J. DCDPI: Dynamic and Continuous Deep Packet Inspection in Secure Outsourced Middleboxes. *IEEE Trans. Cloud Comput.* **2023**, *11*, 3510–3524. [CrossRef]
106. Zhang, X.; Geng, W.; Song, Y.; Cheng, H.; Xu, K.; Li, Q. Privacy-Preserving and Lightweight Verification of Deep Packet Inspection in Clouds. *IEEE/ACM Trans. Netw.* **2023**, *32*, 159–174. [CrossRef]
107. Zhang, K.; Deng, M.; Gong, B.; Miao, Y.; Ning, J. Privacy-Preserving Traceable Encrypted Traffic Inspection in Blockchain-based Industrial IoT. *IEEE Internet Things J.* **2023**, *11*, 3484–3496. [CrossRef]
108. Lan, C.; Sherry, J.; Popa, R.A.; Ratnasamy, S.; Liu, Z. Embark: Securely outsourcing middleboxes to the cloud. In Proceedings of the 13th USENIX Symposium on Networked Systems Design and Implementation (NSDI 16), Santa Clara, CA, USA, 16–18 March 2016; pp. 255–273.
109. Canard, S.; Diop, A.; Kheir, N.; Paindavoine, M.; Sabt, M. BlindIDS: Market-compliant and privacy-friendly intrusion detection system over encrypted traffic. In Proceedings of the 2017 ACM on Asia Conference on Computer and Communications Security, Abu Dhabi, United Arab Emirates, 2–6 April 2017; pp. 561–574.
110. Fan, J.; Guan, C.; Ren, K.; Cui, Y.; Qiao, C. Spabox: Safeguarding privacy during deep packet inspection at a middlebox. *IEEE/ACM Trans. Netw.* **2017**, *25*, 3753–3766. [CrossRef]
111. Yuan, X.; Wang, X.; Lin, J.; Wang, C. Privacy-preserving deep packet inspection in outsourced middleboxes. In Proceedings of the IEEE INFOCOM 2016-The 35th Annual IEEE International Conference on Computer Communications, San Francisco, CA, USA, 10–14 April 2016; pp. 1–9.
112. Akbari, I.; Salahuddin, M.A.; Ven, L.; Limam, N.; Boutaba, R.; Mathieu, B.; Moteau, S.; Tuffin, S. A look behind the curtain: Traffic classification in an increasingly encrypted web. *Proc. ACM Meas. Anal. Comput. Syst.* **2021**, *5*, 1–26. [CrossRef]
113. Chen, Z.; Cheng, G.; Xu, Z.; Guo, S.; Zhou, Y.; Zhao, Y. Length matters: Scalable fast encrypted internet traffic service classification based on multiple protocol data unit length sequence with composite deep learning. *Digit. Commun. Netw.* **2022**, *8*, 289–302. [CrossRef]
114. Yun, X.; Wang, Y.; Zhang, Y.; Zhao, C.; Zhao, Z. Encrypted tls traffic classification on cloud platforms. *IEEE/ACM Trans. Netw.* **2022**, *31*, 164–177. [CrossRef]
115. Shamsimukhametov, D.; Kurapov, A.; Liubogoshchev, M.; Khorov, E. Is encrypted clienthello a challenge for traffic classification? *IEEE Access* **2022**, *10*, 77883–77897. [CrossRef]
116. Piet, J.; Nwoji, D.; Paxson, V. Ggfast: Automating generation of flexible network traffic classifiers. In Proceedings of the ACM SIGCOMM 2023 Conference, New York, NY, USA, 10 September 2023; pp. 850–866.
117. Barut, O.; Luo, Y.; Li, P.; Zhang, T. R1DIT: Privacy-Preserving Malware Traffic Classification With Attention-Based Neural Networks. *IEEE Trans. Netw. Serv. Manag.* **2023**, *20*, 2071–2085. [CrossRef]
118. Mavroudis, V.; Hayes, J. Adaptive Webpage Fingerprinting from TLS Traces. In Proceedings of the 2023 53rd Annual IEEE/IFIP International Conference on Dependable Systems and Networks (DSN), Porto, Portugal, 27–30 June 2023; pp. 445–458.
119. Luxemburk, J.; Čejka, T. Fine-grained TLS services classification with reject option. *Comput. Netw.* **2023**, *220*, 109467. [CrossRef]
120. Li, X.; Guo, J.; Song, Q.; Xie, J.; Sang, Y.; Zhao, S.; Zhang, Y. Listen to Minority: Encrypted Traffic Classification for Class Imbalance with Contrastive Pre-Training. In Proceedings of the 2023 20th Annual IEEE International Conference on Sensing, Communication, and Networking (SECON), Madrid, Spain, 11–14 September 2023; pp. 447–455.
121. Kumar, M.; Kondaiah, C.; Pais, A.R.; Rao, R.S. Machine learning models for phishing detection from TLS traffic. *Clust. Comput.* **2023**, *26*, 3263–3277. [CrossRef]

122. Xie, R.; Wang, Y.; Cao, J.; Dong, E.; Xu, M.; Sun, K.; Li, Q.; Shen, L.; Zhang, M. Rosetta: Enabling robust tls encrypted traffic classification in diverse network environments with tcp-aware traffic augmentation. In Proceedings of the ACM Turing Award Celebration Conference-China 2023, Wuhan, China, 28–30 July 2023; pp. 131–132.
123. Chen, Z.; Cheng, G.; Niu, D.; Qiu, X.; Zhao, Y.; Zhou, Y. WFF-EGNN: Encrypted Traffic Classification based on Weaved Flow Fragment via Ensemble Graph Neural Networks. *IEEE Trans. Mach. Learn. Commun. Netw.* **2023**, *1*, 389–411. [CrossRef]
124. Li, X.; Xie, J.; Song, Q.; Sang, Y.; Zhang, Y.; Li, S.; Zang, T. Let model keep evolving: Incremental learning for encrypted traffic classification. *Comput. Secur.* **2024**, *137*, 103624. [CrossRef]
125. Yuan, Q.; Liu, C.; Yu, W.; Zhu, Y.; Xiong, G.; Wang, Y.; Gou, G. BoAu: Malicious traffic detection with noise labels based on boundary augmentation. *Comput. Secur.* **2023**, *131*, 103300. [CrossRef]
126. Khandkar, V.S.; Hanawal, M.K.; Kulkarni, S.G. State of internet privacy and tales of ECH-TLS. In Proceedings of the 2023 15th International Conference on COMmunication Systems & NETworkS (COMSNETS), Bangalore, India, 3–8 January 2023; pp. 165–170.

Disclaimer/Publisher's Note: The statements, opinions and data contained in all publications are solely those of the individual author(s) and contributor(s) and not of MDPI and/or the editor(s). MDPI and/or the editor(s) disclaim responsibility for any injury to people or property resulting from any ideas, methods, instructions or products referred to in the content.

electronics

MDPI

Article

DistOD: A Hybrid Privacy-Preserving and Distributed Framework for Origin–Destination Matrix Computation

Jongwook Kim

Department of Computer Science, Sangmyung University, Seoul 03016, Republic of Korea; jkim@smu.ac.kr

Abstract: The origin–destination (OD) matrix is a critical tool in understanding human mobility, with diverse applications. However, constructing OD matrices can pose significant privacy challenges, as sensitive information about individual mobility patterns may be exposed. In this paper, we propose DistOD, a hybrid privacy-preserving and distributed framework for the aggregation and computation of OD matrices without relying on a trusted central server. The proposed framework makes several key contributions. First, we propose a distributed method that enables multiple participating parties to collaboratively identify hotspot areas, which are regions frequently traveled between by individuals across these parties. To optimize the data utility and minimize the computational overhead, we introduce a hybrid privacy-preserving mechanism. This mechanism applies distributed differential privacy in hotspot areas to ensure high data utility, while using localized differential privacy in non-hotspot regions to reduce the computational costs. By combining these approaches, our method achieves an effective balance between computational efficiency and the accuracy of the OD matrix. Extensive experiments on real-world datasets show that DistOD consistently provides higher data utility than methods based solely on localized differential privacy, as well as greater efficiency than approaches based solely on distributed differential privacy.

Keywords: origin–destination matrix; differential privacy; distributed privacy-preserving framework

1. Introduction

The origin–destination (OD) matrix captures the flow of individuals between any two regions. This matrix has been extensively applied across a wide range of fields due to its ability to provide valuable insights into mobility patterns [1]. In transportation management, OD matrices serve as the basis for traffic simulation models that enable efficient resource allocation, congestion reduction, and the optimization of public transportation systems [2–5]. In urban planning, OD matrices guide the development of sustainable cities by supporting evidence-based decisions about infrastructure investment and land use. They provide urban planners with critical insights into commuting patterns, enabling more effective and efficient urban design strategies [6,7].

Beyond transportation and urban planning, OD matrices play a critical role in public health and epidemiology, where they are used to model the spread of infectious diseases and assess the impact of human mobility on disease transmission [8,9]. In economic development, OD matrices are critical in modeling spatial interactions, providing insights into the flow of economic activity between locations and enabling the more accurate analysis of regional economic patterns and infrastructure impacts [10]. In addition, OD matrices are used in geographic analysis to represent and explore spatial interactions between locations, enabling the identification of complex flow patterns [11]. These diverse applications underscore the importance of OD matrices in comprehensively understanding and managing human mobility, making them indispensable for both theoretical research and practical implementation.

Despite the widespread utility of the OD matrix, its use can pose significant privacy risks to individuals. Because the OD matrix captures information about movement between regions, it has the potential to reveal sensitive personal information, including users' travel routines and behavioral patterns. This risk arises particularly when the data are used without sufficient protective safeguards, making it possible to re-identify individuals based on their movement data. Researchers have demonstrated that combining mobility data with auxiliary information, such as publicly available demographics or social media check-ins, can make it possible to identify individuals with a high degree of accuracy [12–14]. Therefore, similar privacy concerns arise when collecting and sharing OD matrices, as the aggregated movement data can still reveal patterns that are vulnerable to re-identification attacks [15,16]. This is particularly problematic when OD matrices are shared with external organizations or released for public use, as the risk of unauthorized access, data breaches, or misuse increases [17,18]. In such scenarios, malicious attackers could exploit the published OD matrix data to identify individuals or gain insights into sensitive movement patterns.

Therefore, privacy concerns have become a major obstacle in constructing OD matrices, as many individuals are reluctant to share their location data due to potential misuse. This reluctance stems from the sensitive nature of location data, which can reveal work and home locations, travel patterns, and even personal habits [19,20]. Without sufficient trust in how their data are handled, individuals are less likely to participate in data collection efforts, resulting in incomplete or unreliable datasets [21,22]. As a result, the absence of comprehensive and secure privacy measures can significantly limit the collection of essential movement data, undermining the accuracy and utility of the resulting OD matrices. To overcome these challenges, it is critical to develop privacy-preserving techniques that protect individuals' data while still enabling the generation of OD matrices with high utility.

Recently, the distributed approach has become increasingly popular, allowing multiple parties to work together to achieve a common goal without directly sharing their data. This method ensures that each party's data are kept private, not only from other participants but also from the central server managing the process. As a result, it is particularly useful in situations where a trusted server is unavailable or where privacy concerns are paramount. For example, federated learning is widely used in deep learning to train models across distributed data sources [23–25]. Federated clustering allows data from multiple sources to be grouped together without compromising privacy [26,27]. In addition, secure multiparty computation allows multiple distributed parties to jointly compute a function over their inputs while ensuring that each party's input remains private [28,29].

To address privacy concerns when constructing OD matrices, a distributed solution can be utilized to compute the matrix without sharing sensitive movement data with external, untrusted entities. Figure 1 presents a motivating example for this work, where each party, such as a service provider, maintains a trusted relationship with its users. As a result, each party is able to construct a local OD matrix using the trajectory information provided by its users. To compute an aggregated and global OD matrix, these parties collaborate with each other. Since the central server is not trusted in this scenario, each party shares only a privacy-preserved version of its local OD matrix with external entities, thus preserving their privacy while enabling the computation of the global OD matrix. Here, the privacy-preserved local OD matrix is generated using privacy-preserving mechanisms, such as differential privacy (DP) [30]. In this approach, even if the central server is not fully trusted, as is often the case in real-world applications, it can compute the combined OD matrix from the sanitized data provided by all parties, without having access to the raw OD matrices of individual participants.

Therefore, in this paper, we propose a distributed privacy-preserving framework for the computation of OD matrices using DP, which is the de facto standard for privacy-preserving data collection and publication. The contributions of this paper can be summarized as follows.

- We present DistOD, a distributed privacy-preserving framework for the aggregation and computation of OD matrices in the absence of a trusted central server, a common scenario in real-world applications.

- We propose a distributed method that allows participating parties to collaboratively identify hotspot areas, which represent regions frequently traveled between by individuals across multiple parties.
- To enhance the utility of the resulting OD matrix, our approach employs a hybrid privacy-preserving mechanism. Specifically, we apply distributed DP (DDP) to collect OD data for hotspot areas, while using localized DP for non-hotspot regions. This hybrid approach balances between reducing the computational overhead associated with using only DDP and mitigating the reduced data utility often caused by relying solely on localized DP. By balancing the computational overhead with data utility, the proposed method enables more efficient OD matrix generation while maintaining higher accuracy.
- Finally, we validate the effectiveness of our proposed framework through experiments on real-world datasets, demonstrating that it can accurately compute OD matrices without relying on a trusted central server. This highlights the practical applicability of our approach in real-world scenarios.

The remainder of this paper is organized as follows. Section 2 reviews the related work. Section 3 outlines the necessary background and formally defines the problem addressed in this paper. Section 4 presents the proposed framework for the computation of OD matrices. Section 5 evaluates the proposed approach through experiments conducted on real-world datasets, and Section 6 presents the conclusions of the paper.

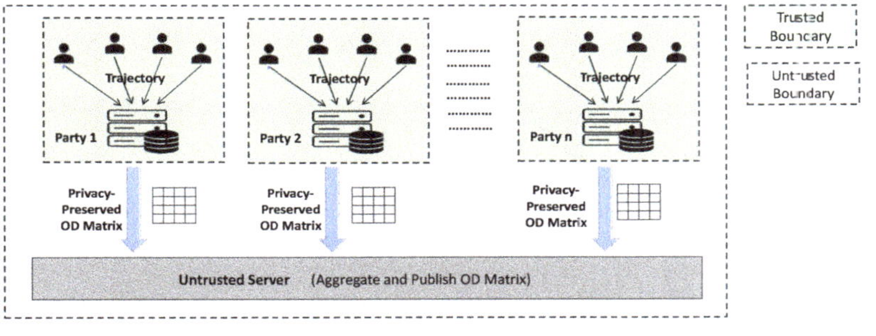

Figure 1. Overview of distributed privacy-preserving OD matrix computation framework.

2. Related Work

2.1. OD Matrix Estimation and Computation

There has been extensive research focused on the estimation and computation of OD matrices. In this section, we briefly summarize some key studies. Mamei et al. [31] explored the estimation of OD matrices using call detail records (CDRs). They introduced two approaches: the time-based approach, which estimates user movements directly from CDRs generated within specific time windows, and the routine-based approach, which uses the routine movements of individuals to compute the OD matrix. Castiglione et al. [32] proposed a method for the estimation of OD matrices by combining principal component analysis (PCA) with a Kalman filter (KF). Their approach uses PCA to capture spatial correlations between variables, while the KF framework effectively handles the nonlinear relationship between traffic data and time-dependent OD flows. To address key challenges in OD matrix estimation, such as underdetermination and lags caused by varying traffic conditions, Xiong et al. [33] proposed an integrated approach that uses deep learning to infer the structures of dynamic OD sequences and applies structural constraints to guide traditional numerical optimization. Sun et al. [34] proposed two bi-level models for the reconstruction of the origin–destination demand in congested networks using both link and route travel times. Tsanakas et al. [35] proposed a data-driven approach to estimating time-dependent OD matrices using floating car data through a data-driven network assignment mechanism, which provides a linear mapping of the OD matrix to link flow observations.

A two-step process for the estimation of bicycle OD matrices was proposed by [36]. The proposed approach first generates a primary OD matrix using a gravity model and then refines it with a path flow estimator to produce the final OD demand. Ros-Roca et al. [37] proposed a new constrained nonlinear optimization model that reduces the number of variables linearly based on the network size, rather than quadratically. By using traffic-related data, the proposed approach avoids the need for traditional traffic assignment and bi-level iterative processes.

With the recent success of deep learning techniques across diverse fields, there has been growing interest in applying these methods to predict OD flow matrices. Li et al. [38] present a generative network-based approach for the accurate prediction of network-wide ride-sourcing passenger demand OD matrices. Their model effectively captures spatiotemporal features and external dependencies, demonstrating superior performance and convergence when evaluated on real-world datasets. OD-GPT [39] is a generative pre-training model inspired by natural language processing that predicts OD flows by framing grid sequence prediction as a next-token prediction task. This approach effectively captures complex spatiotemporal dependencies in urban environments. GODDAG [40] is a framework designed to generate OD flow data in cities lacking historical records, utilizing a graph neural network-based mobility model paired with domain adversarial training. It learns mobility patterns from data-rich source cities and seamlessly transfers this knowledge to estimate OD flows in new urban areas. Chen et al. [41] proposed a framework using an autoencoder network with feature transfer to estimate urban dynamic OD matrices by integrating connected vehicle trajectories and limited automatic vehicle identification data.

2.2. Privacy-Preserving Techniques for OD Matrix Computation

There have been several proposals to address privacy concerns in the publication and estimation of OD matrices. Shaham et al. [18] introduced a technique for the privacy-preserving publication of multi-dimensional OD matrices that capture intermediate points along individual trips. By exploiting DP and taking into account important data properties, such as the density and homogeneity, their method provides robust privacy protection while ensuring high query accuracy. Matet et al. [17] presented an approach for the k-anonymization of OD matrices, addressing privacy concerns in mobility data. By exploiting the low dimensionality of OD data, the proposed method explores a larger solution space than traditional generalization algorithms while maintaining scalability for high-flow matrices. Yin et al. [42] introduced a spatial generalization approach based on k-anonymization to protect the privacy of OD matrices derived from mobile phone location data. Their method addresses the challenge of preserving data utility for mobility analysis while mitigating the risk of re-identification. Kohli et al. [43] developed an algorithm for the construction of differentially private mobility matrices, such as OD matrices, with formal privacy guarantees. They also explored practical strategies to balance privacy and data accuracy, providing valuable guidance for the responsible use of private mobility data.

The method proposed in this paper differs fundamentally from the existing approaches in the way in which it addresses privacy concerns in the handling of OD matrices. Existing methods assume the presence of a trusted central server that manages raw OD matrices and processes them to enhance the privacy. In contrast, the approach proposed in this paper assumes the absence of a trusted central server, necessitating a decentralized solution. As a result, the proposed method provides enhanced privacy protection by ensuring that no party has centralized access to the raw OD data.

2.3. DP in Distributed Systems

DP is widely used in various distributed environments to ensure data privacy, particularly in scenarios where sensitive information is shared across multiple devices, networks, or organizations. Its application spans a variety of areas, including federated learning, federated clustering, and Internet of Things (IoT) networks. In federated learning, DP is commonly used to protect individual user data by adding noise to local model updates before they are aggregated, ensuring that sensitive information remains protected throughout the learning process, without being shared directly with a central server [44–46]. In federated clustering, DP is used to collaboratively perform clustering tasks across distributed data sources, while ensuring that each party's data remain private [47,48]. By adding noise to intermediate results or cluster centers, federated clustering with DP ensures that individual data points are not revealed, even when the collective task is complete. In addition, DP is being used in distributed environments such as cloud and fog layers to securely collect diverse IoT data while maintaining privacy and enabling data analysis and aggregation across multiple sources [49–51]. By integrating DP into these environments, sensitive IoT data, such as health information from wearable devices, smart home data, and location data from mobile sensors, can be collected and processed without compromising individual privacy.

The approach proposed in this paper shares structural similarities with federated learning and federated clustering, as each participating party collaborates to construct a global OD matrix. In addition, it is similar to distributed methods that collect data from diverse sources, as the global OD matrix is built by aggregating the local OD matrices of each participating party. We note that this is the first work to apply DP in the collaborative computation of a global OD matrix in a distributed environment, where the central server is assumed to be untrusted.

2.4. Security Patterns in Distributed Systems

A security pattern is a reusable solution to a common security problem encountered in software design and system architecture [52,53]. These patterns provide a structured framework for the implementation of security practices, enhancing systems' robustness and resilience against potential threats. In this subsection, we provide a brief overview of the existing work on security patterns in distributed systems.

Uzunov et al. [54] presented a pattern-oriented approach to designing authorization infrastructure for distributed systems. They introduced a security solution framework that guides developers in building custom, application-specific authorization models through the incremental application of microprocess and product patterns. Security and Dependability (S&D) Artefacts [55] extended the concept of security patterns by incorporating dependability mechanisms that dynamically adapt to changing contextual conditions. S&D Artefacts are structured to cover the entire system lifecycle, providing a comprehensive library of solutions that enhance both the security and dependability in distributed systems. With the widespread adoption of cloud computing, several studies have focused on developing security patterns for cloud environments [56–59]. Moral-Garcia et al. [57] introduced enterprise security patterns to address recurring security challenges in protecting information systems within cloud-based platforms. Anand et al. [58] proposed a pattern-based cloud security framework that offers practical security solutions, which enable developers to implement them without needing to be security experts. Rath et al. [59] explored security patterns for cloud software as a service (SaaS) that address various security concerns, such as system security, data security, and privacy, and provided guidelines and case studies for the implementation of these patterns on platforms such as AWS and Azure.

3. Preliminaries

In this section, we first present the background information for this paper and then formally define the problem addressed in this paper. In addition, we describe the threat model assumed in this work.

3.1. Differential Privacy

DP is based on a mathematical framework that provides a probabilistic privacy guarantee even in the presence of attackers with arbitrary background knowledge [30]. DP guarantees that an attacker will not be able to determine with certainty whether a particular individual is included in the published dataset. It is defined as follows.

Definition 1 ((ϵ, δ)-DP)**.** *A randomized algorithm $\mathcal{A}$ satisfies (ϵ, δ)-DP if, for (1) any two neighboring datasets, D_1 and D_2, and (2) any possible output O of $\mathcal{A}$, the following condition holds:*

$$Pr[\mathcal{A}(D_1) = O] \leq e^{\epsilon} \times Pr[\mathcal{A}(D_2) = O] + \delta. \quad (1)$$

Two datasets, D_1 and D_2, are defined as neighbors if they differ by only one record. The privacy parameter ϵ, referred to as the privacy budget, controls the strength of the privacy guarantee. This definition ensures that, for any output of the algorithm $\mathcal{A}$, an adversary cannot confidently determine whether the input was D_1 or D_2.

The Gaussian and Laplace mechanisms are two widely used mechanisms in achieving DP. The Gaussian mechanism achieves (ϵ, δ)-DP by adding random noise drawn from the Gaussian distribution.

Definition 2 (Gaussian Mechanism)**.** *Given a function f, the Gaussian mechanism $\mathcal{A}$ releases the following differentially private output:*

$$\mathcal{A}(D) = f(D) + \mathcal{N}(0, \sigma^2) \quad (2)$$

where $\mathcal{N}(0, \sigma^2)$ represents noise drawn from a Gaussian distribution with mean 0 and variance σ^2. The standard deviation σ is defined as

$$\sigma = \frac{\Delta f \cdot \sqrt{2 \ln(1.25/\delta)}}{\epsilon} \quad (3)$$

Here, Δf is the global sensitivity, representing the maximum amount by which the output of f may change when a single record in the dataset is modified. Similarly, the Laplace mechanism achieves (ϵ, 0)-DP by adding noise drawn from a Laplace distribution with mean 0 and scale $\frac{\Delta f}{\epsilon}$.

One of the key characteristics of DP is the composition property, which ensures that the overall privacy guarantee is maintained when multiple differentially private algorithms are applied to the same dataset. However, the total privacy budget accumulates with each application. Specifically, if k mechanisms, each providing (ϵ_i, δ_i)-DP, are applied to the same dataset, the combined privacy guarantee becomes $\left(\sum_{i=1}^{k} \epsilon_i, \sum_{i=1}^{k} \delta_i\right)$-DP. This means that, while the privacy is maintained, the total privacy budget increases with the number of algorithms used.

Variants of Differential Privacy

DP has several variants designed for different privacy needs and scenarios. Two commonly used variants are local differential privacy (LDP) and DDP.

LDP [60,61] provides DP guarantees at the individual data point level. In this approach, noise is added directly to each user's data before they are shared or aggregated. This ensures that privacy protection is applied at the source, without relying on a trusted central server. Because each data point is obfuscated independently, LDP results in a larger loss of data utility due to the significant amount of noise required.

Similar to LDP, DDP [62,63] operates without relying on a trusted central server. However, it differs from LDP in one fundamental way. Noise is added to the combined output, ensuring that the overall result satisfies DP while allowing for more accurate data analysis compared to LDP. Unlike LDP, where each data point is individually protected, DDP guarantees DP only for the aggregated data, making it suitable for scenarios where collaboration among parties is required to compute joint statistics, while protecting the privacy of the entire dataset.

3.2. Problem Definition and Threat Model

Let assume that the entire space is partitioned into non-overlapping regions, denoted as $R = \{r_i \mid i = 1, 2, \ldots, m\}$. The OD matrix contains the directional mobility data, specifying the movement between origins and destinations. Let F be an $m \times m$ matrix, where each element $F[i, j]$ represents the volume of flow from region r_i to region r_j. Typically, an OD matrix captures the mobility patterns between all regions within a given city.

Let us assume that $P = \{p_i \mid i = 1, 2, \ldots, n\}$ represents a set of parties, where each party p_i could be a service provider, such as an application provider, that maintains a trust relationship with its users. Let F_i denote the OD matrix corresponding to each party $p_i \in P$.

The objective of this paper is to compute the combined OD matrix, F, by aggregating the individual OD matrices from each participating party (i.e., $F = \sum_{i=1}^{n} F_i$) under the assumption that the central server is untrusted. In this scenario, the original OD matrices from each party cannot be directly shared with the central server or with other parties due to privacy concerns. Therefore, this paper leverages DP to protect each party's sensitive OD matrix during the aggregation process. By using DP, each party can share a privacy-preserving version of its OD matrix, allowing the central server to compute the combined matrix without accessing the original data.

3.3. Threat Model

Mobility data are highly sensitive and vulnerable to privacy attacks, especially re-identification attacks. Adversaries can leverage auxiliary information to link anonymized mobility patterns to specific individuals [64]. This type of attack poses significant privacy risks and requires the use of privacy mechanisms.

In this paper, we assume two primary adversary models: the honest-but-curious adversary and re-identification attack models. In the honest-but-curious adversary model, the central server and the participating parties are assumed to follow the protocol as specified, but remain curious and may attempt to infer additional information from the data that they receive. In the re-identification attack model, we assume that adversaries may have access to auxiliary data, such as publicly available home and work locations. These adversaries can attempt to re-identify the individuals by correlating the entries in the OD matrix with this external information.

4. Distributed Privacy-Preserving Computation of OD Matrix Without Trusted Central Server

In this section, we introduce a distributed framework for the privacy-preserving computation of OD matrices without the need for a trusted central server. We begin by presenting the baseline approaches and highlighting their limitations. Next, we detail the proposed DistOD framework, which is designed to compute OD matrices efficiently and effectively in distributed environments, balancing the computational overhead with data utility.

4.1. Baseline Approaches

Algorithm 1 presents the pseudocode for the t-th participating party, which is identically applied to all other parties, to distributively compute an OD matrix while ensuring privacy through localized DP. We note that, in our work, localized DP refers to a setting where each party (e.g., a service provider) applies DP to a local dataset collected from its users. This approach differs from LDP [60,61], where noise is added directly to individual data points at the user level before any data aggregation occurs.

The algorithm iterates over each element (i, j) of the OD matrix, adding noise to $F_t[i, j]$ to locally satisfy ϵ-DP (line 5). After perturbing all non-zero entries, the party uploads the perturbed data to the central server for aggregation. Since OD matrices are typically sparse, this approach perturbs and reports only non-zero elements of the OD matrix. We assume that reporting only the non-zero elements poses a minimal privacy risk, as these elements alone are insufficient to reconstruct sensitive individual movement patterns or compromise user privacy in a meaningful way.

Algorithm 1 Aggregation of OD matrix based on localized DP.

```
Each Participating Party Processing:
Initialize O_t as an empty list
for each (i, j) where i, j ∈ {1, 2, ..., m} do
    if F_t[i, j] > 0 then
        Append (i, j, F_t[i, j] + N(0, σ^2)) to O_t
    end if
end for
Report O_t to the central server
```

In Algorithm 1, each party perturbs the elements of its local OD matrix independently to locally satisfy ϵ-DP, which can lead to an excessive amount of noise being added when all perturbed data from multiple parties are aggregated. For example, consider the case where the (i, j) element is non-zero for all parties, such as in the case of popular regions. When the central server aggregates the data from all users, the combined value of the (i, j) element will be $\sum_{t=1}^{n} F_t[i, j] + n \cdot \mathcal{N}(0, \sigma^2)$, which results in an overly noisy aggregated value. Since the goal is to compute the sum of the data across parties, rather than each individual value, it is sufficient to add noise to the final aggregated sum. By satisfying ϵ-DP globally instead of locally, we would only need to add noise $\mathcal{N}(0, \sigma^2)$, which is significantly less than $n \cdot \mathcal{N}(0, \sigma^2)$.

In Algorithm 2, a DDP framework is used with secure multiparty aggregation (SecAgg) to compute the OD matrix in a privacy-preserving manner. Unlike Algorithm 1, where each party independently adds noise to its OD matrix to satisfy ϵ-DP locally, this approach distributes the noise across parties, significantly reducing the total amount of noise introduced during the aggregation process. Each participating party iterates over each element (i, j) of the OD matrix, adding noise drawn from a Gaussian distribution, $\mathcal{N}(0, \frac{\sigma^2}{n})$, where n is the total number of participating parties (line 4). Although the smaller noise added at each party individually does not provide ϵ-DP protection for its data, the aggregated noise across all parties ensures that the final combined result satisfies the ϵ-DP guarantee [62,63]. For example, for the (i, j) element, the combined value across all parties will be $\sum_{t=1}^{n}(F_t[i, j] + \mathcal{N}(0, \frac{\sigma^2}{n})) = \sum_{t=1}^{n} F_t[i, j] + \mathcal{N}(0, \sigma^2)$, which satisfies the ϵ-DP requirement for the aggregated data. Once the noise has been added, each party encrypts its perturbed matrix using the SecAgg protocol (line 6), ensuring that the central server can compute only the aggregated sum of the OD matrices from all participating parties, while preventing access to individual data that may not independently satisfy ϵ-DP.

Algorithm 2 Aggregating OD matrix based on DDP with secure aggregation.

```
1: Each Participating Party Processing:
2: Initialize F'_t as m × m matrix
3: for each (i, j) where i, j ∈ {1, 2, ..., m} do
4:     F'_t[i, j] ← F_t[i, j] + N(0, σ^2/n)
5: end for
6: Encrypt F'_t using SecAgg protocol
7: Report encrypted F'_t to the central server
```

Even though Algorithm 2 reduces the noise added to the data, it incurs a significant computational overhead. First, unlike Algorithm 1, each party cannot simply upload its non-zero elements, since the non-zero entries in each party's OD matrix differ from one another. If parties only reported non-zero elements, when combined by the central server, there would not be enough noise added to satisfy ϵ-DP. Secondly, while there have been significant advances in secure multiparty aggregation techniques, such as those in [65,66], the computational overhead when using these techniques is still considerably high for both the central server and the participating parties. Moreover, the size of the OD matrix can be prohibitively large, making it impractical to report all elements. For instance, if the entire space is divided into a 100-by-100 grid of regions, the corresponding matrix would be 10^4-by-10^4, resulting in a total of 10^8 elements. Reporting such a large number of elements is not feasible due to computational and communication constraints. As a result, while Algorithm 2 effectively reduces the amount of added noise, it remains computationally expensive because of these limitations.

4.2. Proposed DistOD Framework

In this subsection, we introduce the proposed DistOD, a distributed privacy-preserving framework for the computation of OD matrices without relying on a trusted central server. Figure 2 provides an overview of the DistOD process, which consists of two main phases.

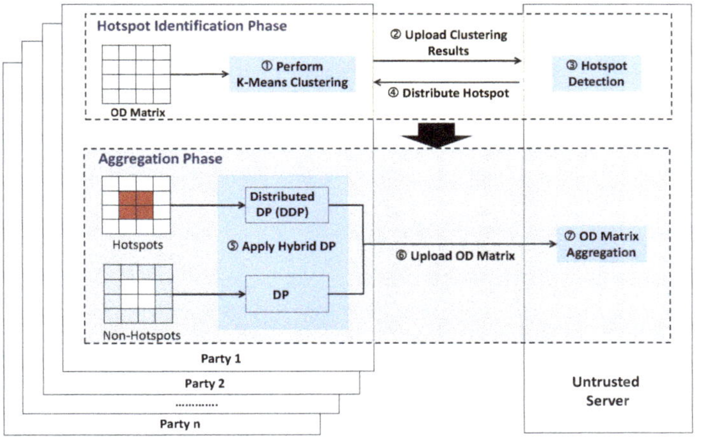

Figure 2. The proposed DistOD framework consists of two main phases. In the hotspot identification phase, hotspot areas are collaboratively identified using location clustering. In the aggregation phase, a hybrid privacy-preserving mechanism is employed by applying DDP to collect OD data for hotspot areas and using localized DP for non-hotspot areas to ensure privacy.

- In the hotspot identification phase, each party performs local clustering and sends the clustering results to the central server. The server then identifies hotspot areas based on the clustering results from all parties and distributes the identified hotspot information back to all parties.
- In the OD matrix aggregation phase, a hybrid privacy-preserving mechanism is employed: DDP is applied to the OD data for hotspot areas, while localized DP is used for non-hotspot areas. After applying the DP mechanisms, each party uploads its OD matrix to the central server, which then aggregates these matrices to compute the global OD matrix.

The rationale behind applying DDP to hotspot areas is as follows. As discussed in the previous subsection, DDP introduces less noise to the raw data compared to localized DP. However, the difference in the amount of noise added by each approach can vary significantly depending on the number of common occurrences shared among parties—for instance, in an extreme case where only one party (e.g., the i-th party) has recorded visits for a particular region pair (r_s, r_e) in the OD matrix, applying localized DP results in noisy data $F_i[s,e] + \mathcal{N}(0, \sigma^2)$. On the other hand, if DDP is applied, the noisy data are expressed as $\sum_{t=1}^{n} F_t[s,e] + n \cdot \mathcal{N}(0, \frac{\sigma^2}{n})$, which is simplified to $F_i[s,e] + \mathcal{N}(0, \sigma^2)$. Thus, in this extreme scenario, there is no advantage of using DDP over localized DP in terms of data utility.

With this in mind, the proposed DistOD approach first identifies hotspot regions that many parties are likely to visit and then applies DDP to these areas to maximize the benefits of using DDP. The detailed steps of each phase are presented below.

4.2.1. Hotspot Identification Phase

In our scenario, the central server is untrusted, and the participating parties do not trust each other. This necessitates a method to identify hotspot areas without directly sharing sensitive raw data. To address this, we employ location clustering techniques. Each party independently clusters its location data and shares only these aggregated results with the untrusted central server, enabling hotspot identification while preserving data privacy. Furthermore, in Section 4.2.3, we extend this clustering-based approach by incorporating DP. This additional layer of protection mitigates the potential for privacy breaches when sharing even the aggregated clustering results with the server. The process of collaboratively identifying hotspot areas consists of local clustering performed by each participating party and hotspot detection performed by the central server.

Local Clustering: Given a region $r_i \in R$, let (x_i, y_i) represent the center coordinates of r_i. Furthermore, let f_i denote the frequency of r_i, which represents the number of times that r_i appears as either an origin or destination in the OD matrix. This frequency can be computed by summing the values in both the row and column corresponding to r_i in the OD matrix as follows:

$$f_i = \sum_{h=1}^{n} F_t[i,h] + \sum_{h=1}^{n} F_t[h,i] \tag{4}$$

Given the dataset $RD = \{(x_i, y_i, f_i) \mid i = 1, 2, \ldots, m\}$, where (x_i, y_i) represents the center coordinates of region r_i and f_i represents the frequency (weight) of visits for region r_i, we apply the k-means algorithm to partition the m regions into k clusters. The k-means algorithm minimizes the following objective function:

$$\text{minimize} \quad \sum_{j=1}^{k} \sum_{r_i \in C_j} f_i \cdot \left\| (x_i, y_i) - (\mu_{j,x}, \mu_{j,y}) \right\|^2 \tag{5}$$

where C_j is the set of points (regions) in cluster j and $(\mu_{j,x}, \mu_{j,y})$ is the centroid of cluster j.

After performing k-means clustering, the clustering result is represented as $CR = \{(\mu_{j,x}, \mu_{j,y}, w_j) \mid j = 1, 2, \ldots, k\}$, where w_j is the weight representing the total visit frequency of all regions assigned to cluster C_j, calculated as $w_j = \sum_{r_i \in C_j} f_i$. This set of cluster centers and weights is then uploaded to the central server for further processing. The clustered regions represent a privacy-preserving version of the users' location data, as only the aggregated cluster centers and their associated weights are shared, rather than the individual raw data.

Hotspot Detection: Upon receiving the k-means clustering results from all participating parties, the central server identifies the hotspots that correspond to the top-l most frequently visited regions. Let $CR = \{CR_1, CR_2, \ldots, CR_n\}$ represent the set of k-means clustering results received from the n participating parties. For each $CR_t \in CR$, the server assigns a weight to each region based on its proximity to the cluster centers. This is performed using a Gaussian kernel, where regions closer to a cluster center are assigned higher weights, effectively prioritizing areas with higher visit densities.

For each clustering result CR_t from the t-th party, the server assigns a weight to each region based on its proximity to all cluster centers. The weight assigned to a region r_i from the clustering result CR_t is calculated as

$$W_t(r_i) = \sum_{(\mu_{j,x}, \mu_{j,y}, w_j) \in CR_t} w_j \times \exp\left(-\frac{(x_i - \mu_{j,x})^2 + (y_i - \mu_{j,y})^2}{2\gamma^2} \right) \tag{6}$$

Here, γ controls the spread of the Gaussian kernel, determining the extent to which each cluster center influences the surrounding regions. As a result, the weight assigned to each region is the cumulative sum of the contributions from all cluster centers in the clustering result CR_t, where each contribution is weighted by the total visit frequency of the regions within its corresponding cluster.

After calculating the weights for each region based on all clustering results in CR, the server aggregates these values to compute the global weight for each region. The global weight for a region r_i is computed by summing the weights assigned to it by all participating parties, as follows:

$$W_{\text{global}}(r_i) = \sum_{t=1}^{n} W_t(r_i). \tag{7}$$

Finally, the server identifies hotspots by selecting the top l regions with the highest global weights. However, selecting regions based on their global weights alone may lead to the inclusion of irrelevant areas, such as regions that are not part of the road network. To prevent this, we first apply a road map filter to exclude any regions that are not on roads, ensuring that only meaningful areas are selected as hotspots. We then sort the remaining regions by their global weights and select the top l regions with the highest weights. This refined set of regions is then returned to each participating party for further analysis.

4.2.2. OD Matrix Aggregation Phase

In the OD matrix aggregation phase, each party first applies a hybrid DP mechanism to its OD matrix. The privacy-preserved OD matrices are then uploaded to the central server, which aggregates them to compute the global OD matrix.

Hybrid DP Mechanism: Algorithm 3 presents the proposed hybrid DP mechanism, which combines DDP for hotspot areas and localized DP for non-hotspot areas, ensuring a balance between computational efficiency and data utility in the aggregation of the OD matrix. Each participating party processes its local OD matrix by iterating over each pair of regions (i, j). For hotspot areas, the party applies DDP by adding Gaussian noise $\mathcal{N}(0, \frac{\sigma^2}{n})$ to the OD matrix entry $F_t[i, j]$ (line 5). For non-hotspot areas, if the value $F_t[i, j]$ is greater than 0, Gaussian noise $\mathcal{N}(0, \sigma^2)$ is added to the OD matrix entry (line 8). After processing, the values in O_t^{DDP} are encrypted using the SecAgg protocol, which ensures the secure aggregation of the DDP results without compromising individual privacy. Finally, both O_t^{DDP} and O_t are reported to the central server for further aggregation.

To improve the utility of the resulting OD matrix, our approach uses a hybrid privacy-preserving mechanism. By applying DDP to high-density regions (hotspots), we ensure that the OD matrix remains highly accurate in these critical areas by reducing the amount of noise introduced. On the other hand, localized DP is applied to non-hotspot areas to protect individual privacy using a simpler and more computationally efficient mechanism, although this comes at the cost of reduced accuracy.

Algorithm 3 Hybrid privacy-preserving mechanism for OD matrix aggregation.

1: **Each Participating Party Processing:**
2: Initialize O_t^{DDP} and O_t as empty lists
3: **for** each (i, j) where $i, j \in \{1, 2, \ldots, m\}$ **do**
4:     **if** r_i and r_j belongs to a hotspot area **then**
5:         Append $(i, j, F_t[i, j] + \mathcal{N}(0, \frac{\sigma^2}{n}))$ to O_t^{DDP}
6:     **else**
7:         **if** $F_t[i, j] > 0$ **then**
8:             Append $(i, j, F_t[i, j] + \mathcal{N}(0, \sigma^2))$ to O_t
9:         **end if**
10:     **end if**
11: **end for**
12: Encrypt O_t^{DDP} using SecAgg protocol
13: Report encrypted O_t^{DDP} and O_t to the central server

Aggregation of the Global OD Matrix: Upon receiving all DP-applied OD matrices from all parties, the central server proceeds to aggregate them to compute the global OD matrix. This process is performed in two distinct steps. First, for the elements of the OD matrix corresponding to hotspot areas, the data received from the parties are encrypted using the SecAgg protocol. Thus, the server collaborates with all participating parties to securely decrypt these data, ensuring that it only accesses the aggregated results, without being able to access the individual data of each party. Secondly, for the elements of the OD matrix corresponding to non-hotspot areas, the server directly aggregates the noisy data provided by each party.

We also note that, in practice, a small number of parties may be adversarial or drop out during the secure aggregation process. In such cases, the server may either receive an inaccurate sum of the noise-added data or be unable to access the aggregated data due to the absence or malfunctioning of certain parties. The issue of dealing with adversarial parties or dropouts has been extensively studied in the literature [62]; therefore, we do not address it in this paper. These techniques can be seamlessly integrated into the proposed method. Instead, this paper focuses on the hybrid approach of using DDP and localized DP in the context of computing the OD matrix, with the goal of balancing the computational overhead and data utility.

4.2.3. Enhancing Privacy in the Hotspot Identification Process

As mentioned earlier, although the proposed DistOD approach shares the cluster results with the untrusted central server rather than the raw data, sharing the cluster centers can still lead to privacy breaches. To enhance the privacy during the hotspot identification process, we can leverage DP to perturb the cluster centers before uploading them to the server. Specifically, after performing k-means clustering, we generate the perturbed clustering result that satisfies (ϵ_1, δ_1)-DP as follows:

$$CR = \left\{ \left(\mu_{j,x} + \mathcal{N}(0, \sigma_1^2), \mu_{j,y} + \mathcal{N}(0, \sigma_1^2), w_j \right) \mid j = 1, 2, \ldots, k \right\} \tag{8}$$

Here, σ_1 is defined as $\frac{\Delta f \cdot \sqrt{2 \ln(1.25/\delta_1)}}{\epsilon_1}$. This ensures that the shared cluster centers are differentially private, minimizing the risk of privacy breaches while still allowing for effective hotspot identification.

Through the composition property of DP, given the total privacy budget ϵ, the remaining privacy budget, $\epsilon_2 (= \epsilon - \epsilon_1)$, is used to perturb the OD matrix, as presented in Algorithm 3. This enhanced privacy inevitably reduces the utility of the aggregated OD matrix, as the accuracy of hotspot identification is affected by the noise added to the true cluster centers, and the reduced privacy budget ϵ_2 is used to perturb the OD matrix during aggregation. In the experimental section, we will evaluate the impact of this enhanced privacy mechanism on the utility of the aggregated OD matrix.

4.2.4. Integration of Security Patterns in DistOD Framework

A security pattern is a reusable solution to a common security problem in software design and system architecture [52,53,56]. These patterns outline recurring security issues and provide best-practice solutions that can be consistently applied in specific contexts to improve the security of system development and operation. In this subsection, we describe how security patterns are integrated into the DistOD framework to provide robust protection against potential security threats. To secure the DistOD framework, we propose to implement security patterns that address the challenges of distributed and privacy-preserving OD matrix computation, ensuring secure interactions, data flow management, and the protection of sensitive information.

Interaction Security Pattern: The decentralized structure of the DistOD framework necessitates that interactions between participating parties and the central server occur in an environment where trust cannot be inherently established. Given this lack of mutual trust, it becomes essential to assume security measures that ensure that only legitimate entities are involved in data exchange and computation. To address this, we propose the use of an authentication and authorization pattern as a fundamental component for secure interactions. In this model, each party undergoes a thorough authentication process, using secure protocols to verify its identity before participating in any data-related activities. Once authenticated, an authorization mechanism must be in place to confirm that the entity has the necessary permissions to access or process specific data. This layered approach to identity verification and access control ensures that only verified and authorized parties are allowed to participate in the distributed computation of OD matrices.

Data Flow Security Pattern: To secure the transmission of data within the DistOD framework, we propose a secure data transmission pattern. This pattern assumes the use of encryption mechanisms to protect the confidentiality of data as they flow between the parties and the untrusted central server. By encrypting all shared data, such as the clustering results and noise-added OD matrices, this pattern prevents eavesdropping and guarantees secure data flows during the computation of OD matrices.

Cryptographic Protection Pattern: In the DistOD framework, while all data transmissions are protected using the data flow security pattern, data associated with hotspot areas require additional protection due to the use of DDP. To address this need, we assume the use of a cryptographic protection pattern that enhances the privacy by ensuring that the central server can only access aggregated results, rather than individual data. This pattern is applied specifically to the OD matrix elements corresponding to hotspot areas, where DDP is used to add noise to each party's data before sharing. By using cryptographic techniques such as the secure aggregation protocol, individual values from the hotspot data remain inaccessible to the central server, which can only access the aggregated sum of these elements.

The security patterns described in this subsection significantly increase the robustness and reliability of the DistOD framework, making it well suited for real-world applications that require strong data security and privacy protections.

5. Experiment

In this section, we present an experimental evaluation of the proposed DistOD method using real-world datasets.

5.1. Experimental Setup

5.1.1. Datasets

We evaluated the effectiveness of the proposed DistOD framework using two different datasets.

- The T-Drive dataset [67] contains one week of trajectory data from 10,357 taxis in Beijing. The T-Drive dataset provides detailed information, including taxi IDs, timestamps, and latitude–longitude coordinates. To generate meaningful origin–destination pairs, we divided the location data into two-hour intervals and used each interval to determine the origin and destination points. This process resulted in 660,000 origin–destination pairs.
- The Porto dataset [68] consists of GPS coordinates collected from 442 taxis operating in Porto, Portugal. For the experiment, we processed these data to extract 1,323,078 origin–destination pairs.

In the experiment, we simulated a scenario with 50 participating parties (i.e., $n = 50$) and distributed the origin–destination pairs evenly among them to create their respective local OD matrices.

For the experiment, we divided the geographic area into four grid sizes, 25×25, 50×50, 75×75, and 100×100, resulting in 625, 2500, 5625, and 10,000 regions, respectively. Each origin or destination location was mapped to the corresponding region to which it belonged. Consequently, the size of the OD matrix used in the experiments was 625×625, 2500×2500, 5625×5625 and $10{,}000 \times 10{,}000$, depending on the grid size.

5.1.2. Baseline and Evaluation Metrics

In the experiments, we evaluated the proposed DistOD against the localized DP-based method (DP_{GM}) in Algorithm 1 and the DDP-based approach (DDP_{ALL}) in Algorithm 2. We note that the DDP_{ALL} used in the experiments is based on methods commonly utilized in federated learning contexts, such as [23]. In addition, we compared DistOD with a localized DP-based method using the Staircase mechanism [69] (DP_{SM}), which is known to introduce less noise into the original data compared to the Gaussian and Laplace mechanisms.

The mean absolute error (MAE), which quantifies the difference between the actual value and the estimated one, was used for evaluation:

$$MAE = \frac{\sum_{g_i \in G} \sum_{g_j \in G} R(g_i) \cdot R(g_j) \cdot |F[i,j] - \hat{F}[i,j]|}{\sum_{g_i \in G} \sum_{g_j \in G} R(g_i) \cdot R(g_j)} \quad (9)$$

Here, F represents the true OD matrix, while $\hat{F}$ denotes the estimated OD matrix generated by the algorithm used in the experiments. In addition, $R(g_i)$ is an indicator function that returns 1 if the region g_i is part of the road network and 0 otherwise. By including the road network in the MAE calculation, we ensured that the MAE was computed meaningfully, considering only valid origin–destination pairs located within the road network.

5.1.3. Experimental Settings

In the experiment, the privacy budget ϵ was varied between 0.25 and 1.0, with δ fixed at 10^{-5}. These values are consistent with standards observed in the DP literature, where ϵ values below 2.0 are typically chosen to balance privacy and utility in practical applications. Lower ϵ values (e.g., 0.25) provide stronger privacy, while higher values allow for moderate privacy, allowing for a range of scenarios to assess the privacy–utility tradeoff. The choice of $\delta = 10^{-5}$ reflects the common practice of setting δ to a small constant, as lower values (e.g., 10^{-5} or less) help to control the probability of significant privacy loss. This ensures that the privacy guarantee is consistently maintained, minimizing the probability of re-identification even under adversarial conditions.

For the identification of hotspot regions in the proposed DistOD method, we set the number of clusters (k) to 50 and the Gaussian kernel parameter (γ) to 10. All algorithms were implemented in Python 3.8, and the experiments were conducted on a system equipped with Intel Xeon 5220R CPUs and 64 GB of RAM.

5.2. Evaluation Results

Figure 3 shows the effect of the varying privacy budget (ϵ) on the MAE. In these experiments, ϵ ranged from 0.25 to 1.0, while the size of the OD matrix was fixed at 10,000 × 10,000. For the proposed DistOD framework, the size of the hotspot areas was varied at between 5% and 20% of the total number of regions (i.e., 10,000). As the value of ϵ decreased (i.e., as the level of privacy increased), the MAE increased for all approaches. This is because stronger privacy guarantees (lower ϵ) introduce more noise into the true data, which reduces the accuracy of the estimated OD matrix. Specifically, as ϵ decreased, the σ of the Gaussian mechanism increased, resulting in more noise being added. On the other hand, as the privacy budget ϵ increased (i.e., as the level of privacy decreased), the σ of the Gaussian mechanism decreased, resulting in less noise being added and thus improving the accuracy.

This tradeoff between data utility and privacy is a well-known characteristic of DP-based methods. Therefore, choosing an appropriate privacy budget requires balancing the desired level of data utility with the required level of privacy, both of which depend on the specific requirements of the application. For example, applications that deal with highly sensitive data may require stronger privacy guarantees, even if this means compromising the accuracy of the results. On the other hand, applications that require accurate data insights for effective decision-making might tolerate a slightly reduced level of privacy in exchange for higher data accuracy.

As expected, among the four different methods, the DDP-based approach (DDP_{ALL}) shows the best performance, while the localized DP-based methods, DP_{GM} and DP_{SM}, show the worst performance. The proposed method, DistOD, performs at an intermediate level within these two categories. However, it is important to note that although the DDP-based approach provides the highest accuracy, this comes at a significant computational cost, making it less practical for large-scale applications. This limitation will be explored in more detail in Section 5.3.

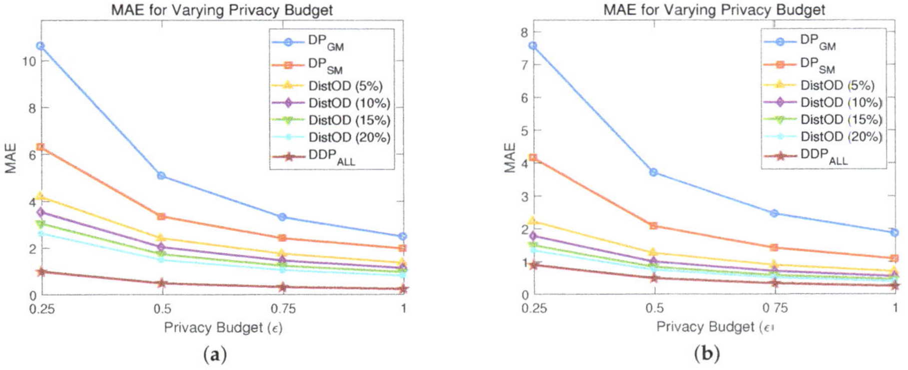

Figure 3. Effect of varying privacy budget (ϵ) on MAE. (**a**) T-Drive dataset. (**b**) Porto dataset.

Furthermore, as the size of the hotspot areas increases, a decrease in the MAE is observed. This is because, in the proposed DistOD, the DDP-based approach is applied to the hotspot areas, which collaboratively adds noise to the true data among the participating parties to satisfy ϵ-DP. As a result, the total error decreases as more regions are covered by the DDP-based approach. However, it is important to note that this improved performance in terms of data utility comes with higher computational costs due to the complexity of the DDP-based approach. As the hotspot size increases, the computational overhead increases because more regions are processed using the DDP mechanism. Therefore, there is a tradeoff between improving the data utility and managing the computational efficiency.

Figure 4 shows the effect of the varying OD matrix sizes on the MAE. In this experiment, the OD matrix size was varied among 625 × 625, 2500 × 2500, 5625 × 5625, and 10,000 × 10,000, while the privacy budget ϵ was fixed at 0.5. As seen in the figure, the DDP-based approach (DDP_{ALL}) consistently achieved the lowest MAE, indicating the best performance, while the localized DP-based methods, DP_{GM} and DP_{SM}, exhibited the highest MAEs, reflecting the worst performance. The proposed method, DistOD, showed intermediate performance between these two categories, following the same trend as observed in Figure 3.

For the Porto dataset, the MAE steadily decreases as the OD matrix size increases. However, for the T-Drive dataset, the relationship between the OD matrix size and MAE does not follow a consistent pattern. Specifically, the MAE decreases as the matrix size increases from 625 × 625 to 5625 × 5625, but then rebounds when the matrix size reaches 10,000 × 10,000. This behavior is explained as follows: when calculating the MAE, only valid origin–destination pairs within the road network are considered, which means that the MAE is influenced more by the number of meaningful origin–destination pairs than by the matrix size itself. In the Porto dataset, the number of valid origin–destination pairs increases proportionally with the matrix size, resulting in a steady decrease in the average MAE. However, in the T-Drive dataset, the number of valid origin–destination pairs reaches a stable point at a matrix size of 5625 × 5625. Beyond this size, the MAE is less dependent on the matrix size and more influenced by the actual data distribution. This observation highlights that the relationship between the matrix size and error is less pronounced when limited to practical, applicable origin–destination pairs within the road network.

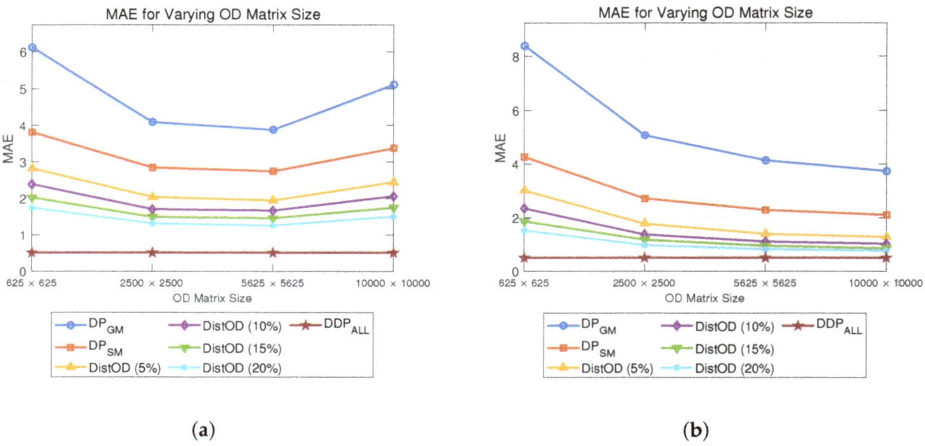

Figure 4. Effect of varying OD matrix size on MAE. (**a**) T-Drive dataset. (**b**) Porto dataset.

Figure 5 shows the experimental results when DP is applied to enhance the privacy during hotspot identification, as discussed in Section 4.2.3. This experiment used the T-Drive dataset with ϵ values ranging from 0.25 to 1.0 and evaluated two OD matrix sizes, 2500×2500 and $10{,}000 \times 10{,}000$. The size of the hotspot areas was fixed at 20% of the total number of regions. In addition, the experiments explored different splits of the total privacy budget between the hotspot identification and OD matrix collection phases, using ratios of 1:9, 2:8, 3:7, 4:6, and 5:5. For example, in Figure 5, DistOD (1:9) indicates that 10% of the privacy budget is allocated to the hotspot identification phase, while the remaining 90% is allocated to the OD matrix collection phase. For comparison, we also plot the results of the DDP-based approach (DDP_{ALL}) and the localized DP-based methods, DP_{GM} and DP_{SM}. Furthermore, the figure also shows the DistOD method, which does not use the DP mechanism during the hotspot identification phase.

As shown in the figure, the MAE increases as a larger portion of the privacy budget is allocated to the hotspot identification phase, leaving less for the OD matrix collection phase. This suggests that, to maintain the data utility in the collected OD matrix, it is more important to minimize the noise during the OD matrix collection phase than to enhance the accuracy of hotspot area identification. This is because the noise introduced during the collection of the OD matrix has a direct impact on the accuracy of the origin–destination estimates. While accurately identifying hotspot areas is valuable, the overall quality of the OD matrix is primarily influenced by how well the collected data capture the actual movement patterns.

Furthermore, as expected, DistOD without the DP mechanism during hotspot identification consistently shows a lower MAE compared to DistOD using the DP mechanism in this phase. More importantly, as shown in the figure, even with a 5:5 privacy budget split between hotspot identification and OD matrix collection, the proposed DistOD still outperforms the localized DP-based approaches. This demonstrates that, despite allocating a significant privacy budget to hotspot identification, DistOD maintains a superior balance between privacy and utility compared to localized methods.

Figure 6 presents the experimental results when applying DP in hotspot identification, where the size of the hotspot regions was varied from 5% to 20% of the total regions. In these experiments, the total privacy budget was divided between the hotspot identification and OD matrix collection phases at a fixed ratio of 1:9. For comparison, the localized DP-based methods, DP_{GM} and DP_{SM}, are also included in the graph.

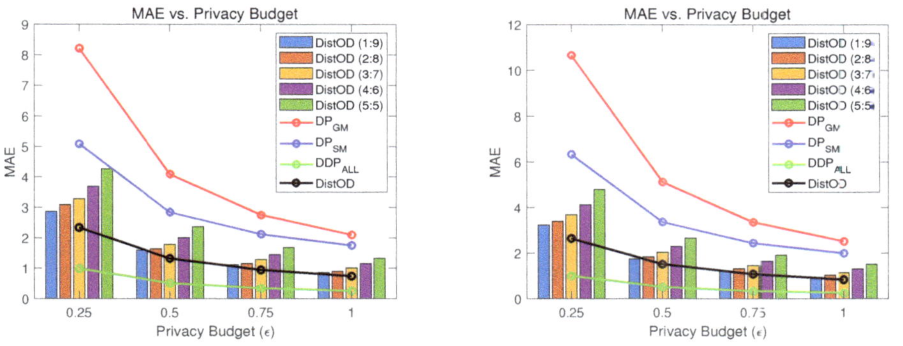

(**a**) (**b**)

Figure 5. Experimental results showing the impact of DP in hotspot identification with the T-Drive dataset: effect of varying the allocation of the total privacy budget between the hotspot identification and OD matrix collection phases. (**a**) OD matrix size = 2500 × 2500. (**b**) OD matrix size = 10,000 × 10,000.

As shown in the figure, there is a slight but consistent increase in the MAE when DP is applied during hotspot identification, compared to when it is not. This increase in error can be attributed to two main factors. First, the introduction of the DP mechanism during hotspot identification adds noise, resulting in the less accurate identification of hotspot areas. Second, a smaller portion of the privacy budget is left for the OD matrix collection phase, further reducing the utility of the collected data. However, despite this slight reduction in utility, the use of DP during hotspot identification can add an important layer of privacy protection, as the true clustering results are not directly shared with the untrusted central server.

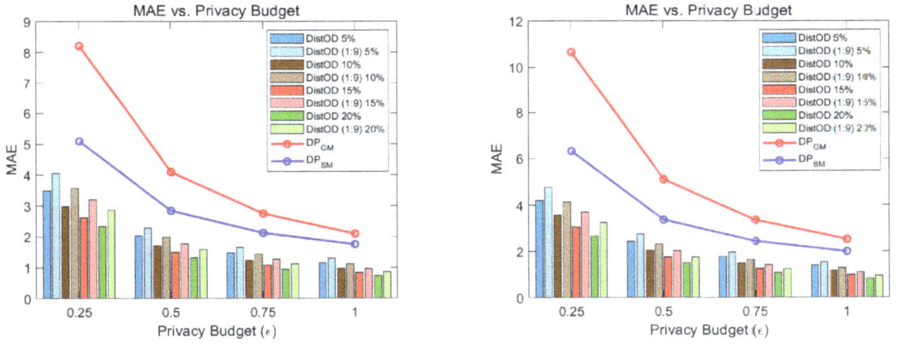

(**a**) (**b**)

Figure 6. Experimental results showing the impact of DP in hotspot identification with the T-Drive dataset: effects of varying hotspot size on MAE. (**a**) OD matrix size = 2500 × 2500. (**b**) OD matrix size = 10,000 × 10,000.

5.3. Performance Analysis Regarding the Communication and Computational Costs

This subsection provides a performance analysis of the communication and computation overheads incurred when using secure aggregation in DDP. Secure aggregation has been extensively studied, and the recent work in [66] introduces a scalable protocol where the communication and computational costs of each participating party depend logarithmically on the number of parties. Specifically, for n parties, the communication and computational costs per party are $O(\log^2 n + L)$ and $O(\log^2 n + L \log n)$, respectively, where L represents the length of the input vectors. Furthermore, the server's communication and computational costs are $O(n(\log^2 n + L))$ and $O(n(\log^2 n + L \log n))$, respectively. Therefore, when the number of participating parties is fixed, the dominant factor affecting the communication and computational overhead of DDP is L, which corresponds to the number of elements in the OD matrix collected using DDP in this work.

Table 1 presents the relative ratio of the number of OD matrix elements where the DDP mechanism is applied under the proposed DistOD method compared to the number of OD matrix elements where the DDP mechanism is applied under the pure DDP-based method (DDP_{ALL}), as described in Algorithm 2. The relative ratio is defined as

$$\text{Relative Ratio} = \frac{\text{Number of elements using DDP with DistOD}}{\text{Number of elements using DDP in with } DDP_{ALL}} \quad (10)$$

This relative ratio quantifies the reduction in the number of elements requiring expensive secure aggregation when using the proposed DistOD method compared to the pure DDP-based approach, DDP_{ALL}.

In Table 1, the size of the hotspot areas for the proposed DistOD method is varied between 5% and 20% of the total number of regions. As expected, as the size of the hotspot areas increases, the relative ratio also increases, indicating a corresponding increase in the communication and computational overhead caused by the use of secure aggregation. More importantly, the relative ratio remains significantly less than 1, demonstrating that the proposed DistOD method significantly reduces the communication and computational overhead associated with secure aggregation compared to the pure DDP-based approach (DDP_{ALL}).

Table 1. The relative ratio of the number of OD matrix elements where the DDP mechanism is applied using the proposed DistOD method compared to the pure DDP-based method (DDP_{ALL}).

	OD Matrix Size			
	625 × 625	**2500 × 2500**	**5625 × 5625**	**10,000 × 10,000**
DistOD (5%)	0.0059	0.0159	0.0189	0.0203
DistOD (10%)	0.0229	0.0520	0.0570	0.0593
DistOD (15%)	0.0503	0.0944	0.1011	0.1089
DistOD (20%)	0.0857	0.1402	0.1546	0.1647

6. Conclusions

In this paper, we have introduced DistOD, a distributed privacy-preserving framework for the computation OD matrices, which addresses the challenge of constructing these matrices without relying on a trusted central server. The proposed DistOD framework employs a hybrid privacy-preserving approach that combines DDP for hotspot regions with localized DP for non-hotspot regions. This method optimizes both the computational efficiency and data utility, achieving a tradeoff between accuracy and privacy. Extensive experiments on real-world datasets demonstrate that DistOD consistently outperforms localized DP-based methods in terms of data utility and surpasses the pure DDP-based approach in terms of efficiency. As a result, DistOD achieves a better balance between utility and efficiency in collecting and computing OD matrices compared to these approaches. The results also highlight the effectiveness of our approach in handling scenarios where no trusted server is available, a common requirement in real-world applications.

For future work, we plan to extend this framework to other domains, such as healthcare and IoT, where privacy concerns are equally important. In the healthcare domain, the framework can be adapted to protect sensitive patient mobility data, which is crucial for epidemiological studies and public health research. In the IoT, it can be used to protect the privacy of location data generated by connected devices, ensuring the safe and responsible use of data in smart environments. In addition, we recognize the significant value in developing formalized security patterns for privacy-preserving computation in distributed systems. Future research will focus on these patterns to further enhance the robustness and reliability of the DistOD framework, supporting broader applications in privacy-sensitive domains.

Funding: This research was funded by a 2023 Research Grant from Sangmyung University (2023-A000-0118).

Data Availability Statement: The original data presented in the study are openly available via Kaggle at https://www.microsoft.com/en-us/research/publication/t-drive-trajectory-data-sample/, (accessed on 1 July 2024).

Conflicts of Interest: The author declares no conflicts of interest.

References

1. Rong, C.; Ding, J.; Li, Y. An interdisciplinary survey on origin-destination flows modeling: Theory and techniques. *ACM Comput. Surv.* **2024**, *57*, 1–49. [CrossRef]
2. Behara, K.N.S.; Bhaskar, A.; Chung, E. A DBSCAN-based framework to mine travel patterns from origin-destination matrices: Proof-of-concept on proxy static OD from Brisbane. *Transp. Res. Part C Emerg. Technol.* **2021**, *131*, 103370. [CrossRef]
3. Alshehri, A.; Owais, M.; Gyani, J.; Aljarbou, M.H.; Alsulamy, S. Residual neural networks for origin–destination trip matrix estimation from traffic sensor tnformation. *Sustainability* **2023**, *15*, 9881. [CrossRef]
4. Lattman, K.; Olsson, L.E.; Friman, M. Development and test of the perceived accessibility scale (PAC) in public transport. *J. Transp. Geogr.* **2016**, *54*, 257–263. [CrossRef]
5. Pereira, F.C.; Rodrigues, F.; Ben-Akiva, M. Using data from the web to predict public transport arrivals under special events scenarios. *J. Intell. Transp. Syst.* **2015**, *19*, 273–288. [CrossRef]
6. Credit, K.; Arnao, Z. A method to derive small area estimates of linked commuting trips by mode from open source LODES and ACS data. *Environ. Plan. B Urban Anal. City Sci.* **2022**, *50*, 709–722. [CrossRef]
7. Yang, T. Understanding commuting patterns and changes: Counterfactual analysis in a planning support framework. *Environ. Plan. B Urban Anal. City Sci.* **2020**, *47*, 1440–1455. [CrossRef]
8. Jia, J.S.; Lu, X.; Yuan, Y.; Xu, G.; Jia, J.; Christakis, N.A. Population flow drives spatio-temporal distribution of COVID-19 in China. *Nature* **2020**, *582*, 389–394. [CrossRef]
9. Li, Z.; Huang, X.; Hu, T.; Ning, H.; Ye, X.; Huang, B.; Li, X. ODT FLOW: Extracting, analyzing, and sharing multi-source multi-scale human mobility. *PLoS ONE* **2021**, *16*, e0255259. [CrossRef]
10. LeSage, J.P.; Fischer, M.M. Spatial econometric methods for modeling origin-destination flows. In *Handbook of Applied Spatial Analysis: Software Tools, Methods and Application*; Springer: Berlin/Heidelberg, Germany, 2009.
11. Vrotsou, K.; Fuchs, G.; Andrienko, N.; Andrienko, G. An interactive approach for exploration of flows through direction-based filtering. *J. Geovisualization Spat. Anal.* **2017**, *1*, 1. [CrossRef]
12. Sapiezynski, P.; Stopczynski, A.; Gatej, R.; Lehmann, S. Tracking human mobility using WiFi signals. *PLoS ONE* **2015**, *10*, e0130824. [CrossRef] [PubMed]
13. Khazbak, Y.; Cao, G. Deanonymizing mobility traces with co-location information. In Proceedings of the IEEE Conference on Communications and Network Security, Las Vegas, NV, USA, 9–11 October 2017.
14. Mattos, E.P.; Domingues, A.C.S.A.; Loureiro, A.A.F. Give me two points and I'll tell you who you are. In Proceedings of the IEEE Intelligent Vehicles Symposium, Paris, France, 9–12 June 2019.
15. Liu, Q.; Yu, J.; Han, J.; Yao, X. Differentially private and utility-aware publication of trajectory data. *Expert Syst. Appl.* **2021**, *180*, 115120. [CrossRef]
16. Qiu, S.; Pi, D.; Wang, Y.; Xu, T. SGTP: A spatiotemporal generalized trajectory publishing method with differential privacy. *J. Ambient Intell. Humaniz. Comput.* **2023**, *14*, 2233–2247. [CrossRef]
17. Matet, B.; Furno, A.; Fiore, M.; Come, E.; Oukhellou, L. Adaptative generalisation over a value hierarchy for the *k*-anonymisation of origin–destination matrices. *Transp. Res. Part C Emerg. Technol.* **2023**, *154*, 104236. [CrossRef]
18. Shaham, S.; Ghinita, G.; Shahabi, C. Differentially-private publication of origin-destination matrices with intermediate stops. In Proceedings of the International Conference on Extending Database Technology, Virtual Event, 29 March–1 April; pp. 131–142.
19. Primault, V.; Boutet, A.; Mokhtar, S.B.; Brunie, L. The long road to computational location privacy: A survey. *IEEE Commun. Surv. Tutor.* **2018**, *21*, 2772–2793. [CrossRef]
20. Kim, J.W.; Edemacu, K.; Jang, B. Privacy-preserving mechanisms for location privacy in mobile crowdsensing: A survey. *J. Netw. Comput. Appl.* **2022**, *200*, 103315. [CrossRef]
21. Kim, J.; Jang, B. Workload-aware indoor positioning data collection via local differential privacy. *IEEE Commun. Lett.* **2019**, *23*, 1352–1356. [CrossRef]
22. Jin, W.; Xiao, M.; Guo, L.; Yang, L.; Li, M. ULPT: A user-centric location privacy trading framework for mobile crowd sensing. *IEEE Trans. Mob. Comput.* **2022**, *21*, 3789–3806. [CrossRef]

23. Truex, S.; Baracaldo, N.; Anwar, A.; Steinke, T.; Ludwig, H.; Zhang, R.; Zhou, Y. A hybrid approach to privacy-preserving federated learning. In Proceedings of the the ACM Workshop on Artificial Intelligence and Security, London, UK, 15 November 2019; pp. 1–11.
24. Banabilah, S.; Aloqaily, M.; Alsayed, E.; Malik, N.; Jararweh, Y. Federated learning review: Fundamentals, enabling technologies, and future applications. *Inf. Process. Manag.* **2022**, *59*, 103061. [CrossRef]
25. Antunes, R.S.; Costa, C.A.; Kuderle, A.; Yari, I.A.; Eskofier, B. Federated learning for healthcare: Systematic review and architecture proposal. *ACM Trans. Intell. Syst. Technol.* **2022**, *13*, 1–23. [CrossRef]
26. Dennis, D.K.; Li, T.; Smith, V. Heterogeneity for the win: One-shot federated clustering. In Proceedings of the International Conference on Machine Learning, Virtual, 18–24 July 2021; pp. 2611–2620.
27. Qiao, D.; Ding, C.; Fan, J. Federated spectral clustering via secure similarity reconstruction. *Adv. Neural Inf. Process. Syst.* **2023**, *36*, 58520–58555.
28. Gao, C.; Yu, J. SecureRC: A system for privacy-preserving relation classification using secure multi-party computation. *Comput. Secur.* **2023**, *128*, 103142. [CrossRef]
29. Sucasas, V.; Aly, A.; Mantas, G.; Rodriguez, J.; Aaraj, N. Secure multi-party computation-based privacy-preserving authentication for smart cities. *IEEE Trans. Cloud Comput.* **2023**, *11*, 3555–3572. [CrossRef]
30. Dwork, C. Differential privacy. In Proceedings of the International Colloquium on Automata, Languages, and Programming, Venice, Italy, 10–14 July 2006; pp. 1–12.
31. Mamei, M.; Bicocchi, N.; Lippi, M.; Mariani, S.; Zambonelli, F. Evaluating origin–destination matrices obtained from CDR data. *Sensors* **2019**, *19*, 4470. [CrossRef] [PubMed]
32. Castiglione, M.; Cantelmo, G.; Qurashi, M.; Nigro, M.; Antoniou, C. Assignment matrix free algorithms for on-line estimation of dynamic origin-destination matrices. *Front. Future Transp.* **2021**, *2*, 640570. [CrossRef]
33. Xiong, Z.; Lian, D.; Chen, E.; Chen, G.; Cheng, X. A DeepLearning framework for dynamic estimation of origin-destination sequence. *arXiv* **2023**, arXiv:2307.05623.
34. Sun, C.; Chang, Y.; Luan, X.; Tu, Q.; Tang, W. Origin-destination demand reconstruction using observed travel time under congested network. *Netw. Spat. Econ.* **2020**, *20*, 733–755. [CrossRef]
35. Tsanakas, N.; Gundlegard, D.; Rydergren, C. O–D matrix estimation based on data-driven network assignment. *Transp. B Transp. Dyn.* **2023**, *11*, 376–407. [CrossRef]
36. Ryu, S. A bicycle origin–destination matrix estimation based on a two-stage procedure. *Sustainability* **2020**, *12*, 2951. [CrossRef]
37. Ros-Roca, X.; Montero, L.; Barcelo, J.; Nokel, K.; Gentile, G. A practical approach to assignment-free dynamic origin–destination matrix estimation problem. *Transp. Res. Part C Emerg. Technol.* **2022**, *134*, 103477. [CrossRef]
38. Li, C.; Zheng, L.; Jia, N. Network-wide ride-sourcing passenger demand origin-destination matrix prediction with a generative adversarial network. *Transp. A Transp. Sci.* **2024**, *20*. [CrossRef]
39. Zhang, M.; Gao, L.; Wang, Q.; Gao, W. Predicting city origin-destination flow with generative pre-training. In Proceedings of the International Conference on Artificial Neural Networks, Lugano, Switzerland, 17–20 September 2024.
40. Rong, C.; Feng, J.; Ding, J. GODDAG: Generating origin-destination flow for new cities via domain adversarial training. *IEEE Trans. Knowl. Data Eng.* **2023**, *35*, 10048–10057. [CrossRef]
41. Chen, P.; Wang, Z.; Zhou, B.; Yu, G. Dynamic origin-destination flow imputation using feature-based transfer learning. *IEEE Trans. Intell. Transp. Syst.* **2024**, *25*, 17147–17159. [CrossRef]
42. Yin, L.; Wang, Q.; Shaw, S.-L.; Fang, Z.; Hu, J.; Tao, Y.; Wang, W. Re-identification risk versus data utility for aggregated mobility research using mobile phone location data. *PLoS ONE* **2015**, *10*, e0140589. [CrossRef] [PubMed]
43. Kohli, N.; Aiken, E.; Blumenstock, J. Privacy guarantees for personal mobility data in humanitarian response. *arXiv* **2023**, arXiv:2306.09471. [CrossRef] [PubMed]
44. Ouadrhiri, A.E.; Abdelhad, A. Differential privacy for deep and federated learning: A survey. *IEEE Access* **2022**, *10*, 22359–22380. [CrossRef]
45. Wei, K.; Li, J.; Ding, M.; Ma, C.; Yang, H.H.; Farokhi, F. Federated learning with differential privacy: Algorithms and performance analysis. *IEEE Trans. Inf. Forensics Secur.* **2020**, *15*, 3454–3469. [CrossRef]
46. Truex, S.; Liu, L.; Chow, K.-H.; Gursoy, M.E.; Wei, W. LDP-Fed: Federated learning with local differential privacy. In Proceedings of the ACM International Workshop on Edge Systems, Analytics and Networking, Heraklion, Greece, 27 April 2020; pp. 61–66.
47. Li, Y.; Wang, S.; Chi, C.-Y.; Quek, T.Q.S. Differentially private federated clustering over non-IID data. *IEEE Internet Things J.* **2024**, *11*, 6705–6721. [CrossRef]
48. Li, Z.; Wang, T.; Li, N. Differentially private vertical federated clustering. *Proc. VLDB Endow.* **2023**, *16*, 1277–1290. [CrossRef]
49. Lyu, L.; Nandakumar, K.; Rubinstein, B.; Jin, J.; Bedo, J.; Palaniswami, M. PPFA: Privacy preserving fog-enabled aggregation in smart grid. *IEEE Trans. Ind. Inform.* **2018**, *14*, 3733–3744. [CrossRef]
50. Yang, M.; Tjuawinata, I.; Lam, K.Y.; Zhao, J.; Sun, L. Secure hot path crowdsourcing with local differential privacy under fog computing architecture. *IEEE Trans. Serv. Comput.* **2022**, *15*, 2188–2201. [CrossRef]
51. Wang, T.; Mei, Y.; Jia, W.; Zheng, X.; Wang, G.; Xie, M. Edge-based differential privacy computing for sensor–cloud systems. *J. Parallel Distrib. Comput.* **2020**, *136*, 75–85. [CrossRef]
52. Gallego-Nicasio, B.; Munoz, A.; Mana, A.; Serrano, D. Security patterns, towards a further level. In Proceedings of the International Conference on Security and Cryptography, Milan, Italy, 7–10 July 2009; pp. 349–356.

53. Papoutsakis, M.; Fysarakis, K.; Spanoudakis, G.; Ioannidis, S.; Koloutsou, K. Towards a collection of security and privacy patterns. *Appl. Sci.* **2021**, *11*, 1396. [CrossRef]
54. Uzunov, A.V.; Fernandez, E.B.; Falkner, K. Security solution frames and security patterns for authorization in distributed, collaborative systems. *Comput. Secur.* **2015**, *55*, 193–234. [CrossRef]
55. Sanchez-Cid, F.; Mana, A.; Spanoudakis, G.; Kloukinas, C.; Serrano, D.; Munoz, A. Representation of security and dependability solutions. *Secur. Dependability Ambient. Intell.* **2009**, *45*, 69–95.
56. Jafari, A.J.; Rasoolzadegan, A. Security patterns: A systematic mapping study. *J. Comput. Lang.* **2020**, *56*, 100938. [CrossRef]
57. Moral-Garcia, S.; Moral-Rubio, S.; Fernandez, E.B.; Fernandez-Medina, E. Enterprise security pattern: A model-driven architecture instance. *Comput. Stand. Interfaces* **2014**, *36*, 748–758. [CrossRef]
58. Anand, P.; Ryoo, J.; Kim, H. Addressing security challenges in cloud computing–A pattern-based approach. In Proceedings of the International Conference on Software Security and Assurance, Suwon, Republic of Korea, 27 July 2015.
59. Rath, A.; Spasic, B.; Boucart, N.; Thiran, P. Security pattern for cloud SaaS: From system and data security to privacy case study in AWS and Azure. *Computers* **2019**, *8*, 34. [CrossRef]
60. Erlingsson, U.; Pihur, V.; Korolova, A. RAPPOR: Randomized aggregatable privacy-preserving ordinal response. In Proceedings of the ACM SIGSAC Conference on Computer and Communications Security, Scottsdale, AZ, USA, 3–7 November 2014; pp. 1054–1067.
61. Wang, T.; Blocki, J.; Li, N.; Jha, S. Locally differentially private protocols for frequency estimation. In Proceedings of the SENIX Conference on Security Symposium, Berkeley, CA, USA, 16–18 August 2017.
62. Goryczka, S.; Xiong, L. A comprehensive comparison of multiparty secure additions with differential privacy. *IEEE Trans. Dependable Secur. Comput.* **2015**, *14*, 463–477. [CrossRef]
63. Wei, Y.; Jia, J.; Wu, Y.; Hu, C.; Dong, C.; Liu, Z.; Chen, X.; Peng, Y.; Wang, S. Distributed differential privacy via shuffling versus aggregation: A curious study. *IEEE Trans. Inf. Forensics Secur.* **2024**, *19*, 2501–2516. [CrossRef]
64. Kim, J.; Jang, B. Privacy-preserving generation and publication of synthetic trajectory microdata: A comprehensive survey. *J. Netw. Comput. Appl.* **2024**, *230*. [CrossRef]
65. Kadhe, S.; Rajaraman, N.; Koyluoglu, O.O.; Ramchandran, K. FastSecAgg: Scalable secure aggregation for privacy-preserving federated learning. *arXiv* **2020**, arXiv:2009.11248.
66. Bell, J.H.; Bonawitz, K.A.; Gascon, A.; Lepoint, T.; Raykova, M. Secure single-server aggregation with (poly)logarithmic overhead. In Proceedings of the ACM SIGSAC Conference on Computer and Communications Security, Virtual Event USA, 9–13 November 2020; pp. 1253–1269.
67. T-Drive Trajectory Data Sample. 2018. Available online: https://www.microsoft.com/en-us/research/publication/t-drive-trajectory-data-sample (accessed on 1 July 2024).
68. Moreira-Matias, L.; Gama, J.; Ferreira, M.; Mendes-Moreira, J.; Damas, L. Predicting taxi–passenger demand using streaming data. *IEEE Trans. Intell. Transp. Syst.* **2013**, *14*, 1393–1402. [CrossRef]
69. Geng, Q.; Kairouz, P.; Oh, S.; Viswanath, P. The staircase mechanism in differential privacy. *IEEE J. Sel. Top. Signal Process.* **2015**, *9*, 1176–1184. [CrossRef]

Disclaimer/Publisher's Note: The statements, opinions and data contained in all publications are solely those of the individual author(s) and contributor(s) and not of MDPI and/or the editor(s). MDPI and/or the editor(s) disclaim responsibility for any injury to people or property resulting from any ideas, methods, instructions or products referred to in the content.

electronics

MDPI

Article

Deep Reinforcement Learning Recommendation System Algorithm Based on Multi-Level Attention Mechanisms

Gaopeng Wang *, Jingyi Ding and Fanlin Hu

Department of Software Engineering, Chongqing University of Posts and Telecommunications, Chongqing 400065, China; s221231012@stu.cqupt.edu.cn (J.D.); s221231021@stu.cqupt.edu.cn (F.H.)
* Correspondence: wanggp@cqupt.edu.cn

Abstract: Traditional recommendation systems, which rely on static user profiles and historical interaction data, frequently face difficulties in adapting to the rapid changes in user preferences that are typical of dynamic environments. In contrast, recommendation algorithms based on deep reinforcement learning are capable of dynamically adjusting their strategies to accommodate real-time fluctuations in user preferences. However, current deep reinforcement learning recommendation algorithms encounter several challenges, including the oversight of item features associated with high long-term rewards that reflect users' enduring interests, as well as a lack of significant relevance between user attributes and item characteristics. This leads to an inadequate extraction of personalized information. To address these issues, this study presents a novel recommendation system known as the Multi-Level Hierarchical Attention Mechanism Deep Reinforcement Recommendation (MHDRR), which is fundamentally grounded in a multi-layer attention mechanism. This mechanism consists of a local attention layer, a global attention layer, and a Transformer layer, allowing for a detailed analysis of individual attributes and interactions within short-term preferred items, while also exploring users' long-term interests. This methodology promotes a comprehensive understanding of users' immediate and enduring preferences, thereby improving the overall effectiveness of the system over time. Experimental results obtained from three publicly available datasets validate the effectiveness of the proposed model.

Keywords: recommendation systems; multi-level attention mechanisms; high-reward item features; deep reinforcement learning

1. Introduction

In contemporary society, the rapid proliferation of information has resulted in users encountering substantial challenges related to information overload, thereby complicating the process of swiftly identifying relevant content within extensive datasets. As a response to this issue, recommendation systems have been developed as sophisticated information-filtering mechanisms, primarily designed to anticipate products or services that may be of interest to users and to deliver personalized recommendations. Through the analysis of users' historical data and behavioral patterns, these systems are capable of generating customized recommendation lists for individual users, thereby enhancing the efficiency of information retrieval and mitigating the challenges associated with information overload [1]. In practical applications, recommendation systems have become essential in various domains, including e-commerce, social networking, and online video platforms [2].

In recent years, recommendation system algorithms have undergone a significant evolution, transitioning from content-based methods to collaborative filtering, matrix factorization, and, more recently, to deep learning and hybrid recommendation approaches [3]. Initially, these systems primarily generated recommendations by analyzing the attributes of items; however, this content-based filtering method encountered limitations in fulfilling the requirements for diversity and novelty. As collaborative filtering and matrix factorization techniques matured, recommendation systems began to utilize user behavior and rating patterns to generate recommendations based on the similarities among users or items. Nevertheless, as the scale of data increased and user behavior became more intricate, traditional collaborative filtering and matrix factorization methods began to reveal limitations in managing sparse data and extensive datasets. The introduction of deep learning has revitalized recommendation systems [4], as neural network models are capable of capturing complex, nonlinear relationships between users and items, while effectively processing unstructured data such as text, images, and videos. Concurrently, hybrid recommendation methods that integrate attention mechanisms have been widely proposed [5–7], further improving the accuracy and diversity of recommendations. However, conventional deep learning approaches predominantly rely on static models, which struggle to adapt to dynamic changes in user preferences, thereby inadequately promoting long-term user satisfaction and the recommendation of long-tail items.

To mitigate these limitations, reinforcement learning has increasingly been integrated into recommendation systems. By conceptualizing the recommendation process as a Markov Decision Process (MDP), these systems can continuously refine their strategies based on user feedback, leading to enhanced outcomes in terms of long-term cumulative rewards and user satisfaction. Notably, deep reinforcement learning (DRL)-based methods have achieved significant advancements in recommendation systems, as researchers leverage the robust representational capabilities of deep learning to manage large datasets and adaptively modify recommendation strategies [8]. Within the realm of DRL recommendation algorithms, numerous innovative approaches have been explored in state representation, such as the incorporation of both positive and negative user feedback and contextual information, including time, location, and device type, thereby enriching the dimensions and complexity of the state model [9–11]. However, the majority of existing methods continue to concentrate primarily on modeling short-term user behavior data. While some initiatives have aimed to enhance recommendation effectiveness by analyzing interaction features between users and items, these approaches are often limited to basic attribute calculations and fail to conduct a thorough analysis of the interrelations among attributes, resulting in a low attribute relevance between users and items and an incomplete extraction of personalized information. To address these challenges, this paper proposes a novel recommendation system with several key contributions: (1) A sophisticated multi-layer attention mechanism has been developed to accurately capture and analyze user preference data. This mechanism specifically integrates the features of items associated with high long-term rewards into the state representation, which are subsequently examined through the Transformer layer within the multi-layer attention framework. These features not only encapsulate users' enduring intrinsic interests but also contribute to stability by mitigating random fluctuations in short-term behaviors, thereby enhancing the robustness and stability of the recommendation algorithm during the training process. (2) By utilizing both local and global attention layers within the multi-layer attention mechanism, we are able to assess the significance of each individual attribute within the feature vectors of users and items, as well as the interactions among these attributes. This approach facilitates the extraction of additional auxiliary information from user behavior data, enabling the capture of comprehensive attribute associations between users and their recently preferred items, which in turn improves the accuracy and depth of personalized recommendations. (3) We have established a novel reinforcement learning-based Markov Decision Process (MDP) framework, upon which we propose a deep reinforcement learning recommendation model known as MHDRR. This model has been empirically validated in real-world scenarios, demonstrating its efficiency and superiority in practical recommendation contexts.

The structure of this paper is organized as follows: Section 2 reviews the related literature; Section 3 examines the application of reinforcement learning frameworks in recommendation systems; Section 4 elaborates on the architecture and training methodologies of the MHDRR model; Section 5 outlines the experimental settings, analyzes the results, and investigates the influence of various factors on model performance; and Section 6 concludes the study while proposing directions for future research.

2. Related Work

2.1. Traditional and Deep Learning Recommendation Technologies

Recent advancements in the domain of recommendation systems have been substantial. Initially, these systems predominantly utilized content-based filtering techniques, which generated recommendations by examining the attributes of items [12]. However, to overcome the shortcomings of content-based approaches, particularly regarding diversity and novelty, collaborative filtering methods were developed. These methods assess behavioral and rating patterns among users or items to generate recommendations based on similarities. This approach gained prominence in the late 1990s. Nevertheless, the rapid expansion of the internet and the increase in data volume revealed the limitations of traditional collaborative filtering techniques in managing large-scale datasets and addressing data sparsity. Consequently, matrix factorization techniques emerged as a solution, becoming prevalent in recommendation systems during the 2000s. By decomposing the user–item interaction matrix into lower-dimensional latent factors, matrix factorization significantly enhanced the capacity to process large datasets and improved recommendation accuracy [13].

The advent of deep learning in the 2010s further transformed recommendation systems. These technologies utilize neural networks to model complex nonlinear relationships between users and items, effectively handling unstructured data such as text, images, and videos, thereby markedly improving the performance and applicability of recommendation systems [4]. For instance, He et al. [5] substituted traditional inner product operations with a multi-layer perceptron to model user-item interactions, resulting in considerable enhancements in implicit feedback-based recommendation systems. Additionally, some researchers have integrated attention mechanisms to leverage auxiliary information embedded in historical data. For example, Kang et al. [6] combined the advantages of Markov chains (MCs) and recurrent neural networks (RNNs) to capture long-term semantics and critical actions in user behavior through attention mechanisms, thereby enhancing recommendation performance across both sparse and dense datasets. Pang et al. introduced a hierarchical attention mechanism to thoroughly analyze user–point of interest (POI) interaction data at various levels, examining the contributions of individual features, feature combinations, and overall features, which significantly enriched the depth and breadth of data mining in recommendation systems [7]. Huang et al. [14] addressed long-tail POI mining and cold-start challenges by employing attention mechanisms to extract and analyze both explicit and implicit features from user data in a structured, local-to-global manner.

Building on these advancements, hybrid recommendation algorithms have gradually emerged. Liu et al. [15] proposed a novel sequential recommendation system, LinRec, based on the Transformer model, which utilized an L2-Normalized Linear Attention mechanism to significantly decrease the computational complexity associated with traditional dot-product attention mechanisms. Wu et al. [16] implemented multi-layer interactive information propagation and holographic embeddings, integrating knowledge graphs and attention mechanisms to effectively incorporate neighboring information and inferred relationships among entities, thereby substantially enhancing the model's ability to utilize multi-source information.

Since the mid-2010s, hybrid recommendation algorithms have emerged as a prominent trend in the research and application of recommendation systems. These algorithms amalgamate various recommendation techniques, including matrix factorization, collaborative filtering, and deep learning, to mitigate the limitations associated with individual methods regarding accuracy and scalability. For instance, Li et al. [17] introduced a personalized course recommendation approach utilizing the BERT model. This method enhances information extraction from course content by integrating deep learning with big data technologies and implementing a domain-specific feature differentiation strategy, thereby improving the performance of the recommendation system. Similarly, Qiu et al. [18] developed a novel recommendation model, DuoRec, which incorporates regularization through the uniformity property in contrastive learning to address distributional challenges in the item embeddings produced by sequential deep learning models.

Nevertheless, the aforementioned recommendation methods predominantly operate under a static model assumption, which inadequately captures dynamic fluctuations in user preferences and fails to effectively accommodate the evolution of user interests. Furthermore, these methods often prioritize the optimization of short-term metrics, such as click-through rates, while overlooking long-term user satisfaction. As a result, they are susceptible to the influence of historical behaviors, leading to a tendency to recommend popular items and encountering difficulties in identifying high-quality long-tail items, which are niche products with significant demand.

2.2. Recommendation Technology Based on Reinforcement Learning

Reinforcement learning (RL) presents a distinctive approach to recommendation systems, diverging from traditional and deep learning-based methodologies. By conceptualizing the recommendation process as a Markov Decision Process (MDP), RL facilitates the continuous adaptation of recommendation strategies in response to user feedback, thereby progressively improving the quality of recommendations. This approach aims to optimize cumulative long-term rewards, allowing for effective adaptation to the evolving interests of users and enhancing overall satisfaction over time [19]. Nevertheless, RL techniques encounter challenges related to limited feature representation capabilities and face computational constraints when addressing extensive state and action spaces in recommendation tasks. To mitigate these limitations, deep reinforcement learning (DRL) integrates the representational strengths of deep learning, employing deep neural networks to analyze intricate user behavior patterns, manage substantial data volumes, and flexibly adjust strategies to accommodate shifts in user preferences, thus enabling more sophisticated and efficient applications within recommendation systems [8].

For instance, Zhao et al. [20] developed a collaborative filtering algorithm utilizing deep generative adversarial networks, which harnesses reinforcement learning to fully leverage users' immediate feedback on current recommendations, employing GANs to satisfy RL's data requirements and optimizing the negative sampling technique. Zhang et al. [9] improved the recommendation efficacy in Deep Q-Network (DQN) state representations by incorporating both positive and negative user feedback. Khurana et al. [21] utilized a Graph Convolutional Network to generate embeddings for users, items, and sessions, and applied Double Deep Q-Network technology to refine recommendation strategies, effectively addressing overestimation bias while preserving recommendation diversity. Gao et al. [22] introduced uncertainty-based weights to penalize unstable Q-values, significantly enhancing long-term user satisfaction in recommendation systems. However, value-based methods that assess Q-values for all potential actions in each state can become inefficient in contexts with extensive action spaces [23]. To address the challenges posed by large action spaces and facilitate efficient single-step updates, researchers have incorporated the Actor–Critic model into recommendation systems. For example, Liu et al. [10] proposed a deep reinforcement learning framework aimed at optimizing interactive recommendation systems, devising four state representation schemes to enhance the learning of recommendation strategies. Xin et al. [24] tackled the challenges of absent negative reward signals and temporal dependencies in reinforcement learning for recommendation systems by integrating supervised negative Q-learning (SNQN) with a negative sampling strategy and supervised advantage Actor–Critic (SA2C). Jiang et al. [11] introduced a deep reinforcement learning recommendation system (UCSRDRL) featuring user–item state representations, thereby improving recommendation quality through the enhanced modeling of user–system interactions. Padhye et al. [25] combined the Actor–Critic framework with the TD3 method, employing convolutional neural network (CNN) layers to capture sequential patterns among documents and achieving low-variance delayed policy updates, which effectively improved document retrieval performance in large action spaces.

Notwithstanding the progress made in the field, a majority of deep reinforcement learning (DRL)-based recommendation systems utilize a variety of innovative strategies to enhance and optimize state representation. These strategies often include the integration of both positive and negative feedback, as well as the incorporation of contextual information such as temporal factors, geographical location, and device type, all aimed at improving the comprehensiveness of state modeling. However, numerous methodologies continue to prioritize short-term user behavior data, frequently neglecting the extraction of features associated with items that yield high long-term rewards, which are essential for accurately capturing users' enduring preferences. Furthermore, although certain studies have attempted to enhance the performance of recommendation systems by examining user–item interaction features, there remains a notable deficiency in the thorough analysis of individual feature attributes and their intricate interactions with other attributes. This shortcoming limits the model's capacity to effectively address more complex and dynamic patterns of user behavior.

3. Reinforcement Learning Recommendation System Modeling

The fundamental component of a reinforcement learning (RL) strategy is the MDP, which is characterized by the tuple (S, A, P, R, γ). In the context of recommendation system, the state space (S) encompasses all potential user preferences and behavioral patterns; the action space (A) consists of all feasible recommendation actions that the system may undertake; the state transition function (P) delineates how states evolve in response to specific actions; the reward function (R) assesses the immediate effectiveness of each recommendation based on user feedback; and the discount factor (γ) evaluates the trade-off between short-term and long-term rewards [8]. In general, it is assumed in the literature that the MDP is fully observable; that is, at any point in time t, the observed value θ_t equals the state S_t, as illustrated in Equation (1); the recommendation system identifies the optimal action at each decision point based on the current state, with the objective of maximizing the long-term cumulative reward.

$$V_\pi(s) = \max_\pi \mathbb{E}_\pi \left[\sum_{k=0}^{\infty} \gamma^k R_{t+k} \mid S_t = s\right], \tag{1}$$

where $\mathbb{E}_\pi$ represents the expected cumulative reward under policy π, R_{t+k} denotes the immediate reward at future time step $t + k$, and $S_t = s$ is the initial state. The MDP for the model described in this paper is defined as follows:

State Space S: $s_t = (I_s, I_l, \text{u})$, where $I_s = \{i_1, i_2, \ldots, i_m\}$ represents the user's history of positive interactions (interests). $I_l = \{i_1, i_2, \ldots, i_n\}$ represents items with special behaviors (high-reward) prior to time step t, and u represents user information.

Action Space A: The action $a_t \in \mathbb{R}^{1\times k}$ is a continuous parameter vector, where k is the dimensionality of the item embeddings. The action a_t is used to compute scores via the dot product with each candidate item $i_t \in \mathbb{R}^{1\times k}$, recommending the item with the highest score to the user.

Transition Probability P: When the recommendation system recommends a product to the user, if the user shows no interest, the state remains unchanged. If the user is interested, I_s is updated to $\{i_2, i_3, \ldots, i_{m+1}\}$. If the user displays a liking (high-reward behavior) for the product, then I_s is updated to $\{i_2, i_3, \ldots, i_{m+1}\}$ and I_l is updated to $\{i_2, i_3, \ldots, i_{n+1}\}$.

Reward R: When the recommendation system executes action a_t and recommends an item to the user, the user's feedback influences the distribution of rewards. Specifically, the reward function $r(s_t, a_t)$ adjusts based on the user's response to the recommendation action, thereby measuring the immediate effectiveness of each recommended action.

Discount Factor γ: $\gamma \in [0, 1]$ is defined as a factor used to balance the importance of immediate and long-term rewards in decision-making. When $\gamma = 0$, the system prioritizes immediate rewards and disregards long-term effects; conversely, when $\gamma = 1$, it considers immediate and long-term rewards as equally important.

4. Model Framework and Training

This section offers a comprehensive examination of the deep reinforcement learning architecture and training methodology employed by the MHDRR model, structured into three principal components. Initially, Section 4.1 provides an in-depth analysis of the state generation module, wherein a multi-layer attention mechanism is utilized to extract state information from user behavior data, thereby furnishing critical input for the decision-making process of the reinforcement learning algorithm. Subsequently, Section 4.2 delineates the architecture of the MHDRR model, elucidating the manner in which these state inputs facilitate the dynamic adjustment of recommendation strategies via the Actor–Critic approach. Lastly, Section 4.3 addresses the training module, elaborating on the model's continuous learning and optimization processes through interaction data, aimed at enhancing the efficacy of the recommendation system.

4.1. Status Module

The architecture of the user state generation module is illustrated in Figure 1. This module comprises an input layer, an embedding layer, and a multi-layer attention mechanism. The input layer incorporates fundamental user information alongside data regarding positively interacted items, which are subsequently encoded into dense vectors via the embedding layer for advanced processing. Central to the state module is the multi-layer attention mechanism, which encompasses a local attention layer, a global attention layer, and a Transformer layer [26]. These components work in concert to facilitate a thorough analysis of user interaction data. The local and global attention layers employ convolutional neural networks (CNNs) and linear transformations for feature extraction: the local attention layer is dedicated to examining users' immediate preferences concerning specific attributes, while the global attention layer addresses interactions among attributes from a more expansive viewpoint, thereby elucidating overarching trends in users' recent preferences. Furthermore, the Transformer layer evaluates features associated with high long-term rewards, thereby capturing users' enduring interests. Ultimately, the features derived from both short-term and long-term analyses are synthesized within the composite attention layer to formulate a comprehensive and nuanced representation of the user state. Subsequent sections will elaborate on each component in detail.

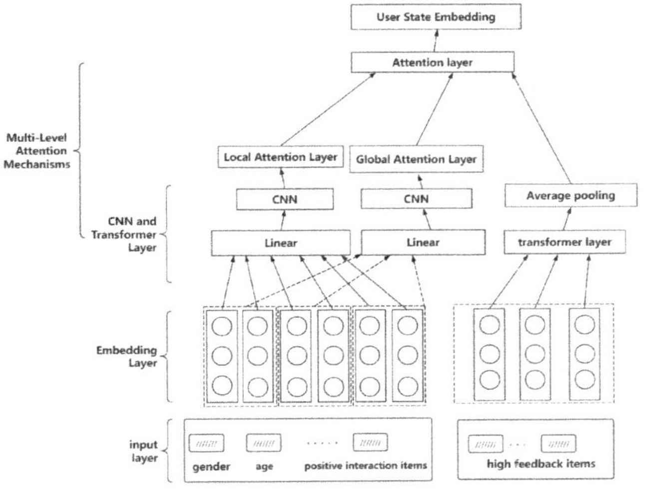

Figure 1. User status generation module.

4.1.1. User and Item Feature Embedding Module

In this model, users and items are encoded as low-dimensional vectors through an embedding layer. Specifically, each item is associated with a low-dimensional vector, termed item embedding $i \in \mathbb{R}^p$, achieved through a learnable embedding matrix $I = \theta^I \in \mathbb{R}^{p \times N}$, where the dimension of I is $p \times N$, p represents the dimensionality of the vector, and N is the number of items. Similarly, the user's embedding vector $u \in \mathbb{R}^q$ is generated through a learnable embedding matrix $U = \theta^U \in \mathbb{R}^{q \times M}$, where q is the vector dimension and M is the total number of users.

4.1.2. Multi-Layer Attention Mechanism for Extracting User's Recent Preference Features Module

The varying significance of different attributes in relation to users and items is noteworthy; for example, the genre of a movie is generally considered more critical than its duration in the context of movie recommendations. Furthermore, the interactions among a movie's attributes are complex, as the overall interpretation of these attributes is often conveyed through their combinations. For instance, a film that incorporates both crime and adventure elements may be particularly appealing to male audiences, whereas the inclusion of romantic or comedic elements could equally attract female viewers. Consequently, this paper proposes a multi-layer attention mechanism to address the challenges associated with individual attributes and their interactions. By analyzing both the local and global features of items that users have recently engaged with positively, this mechanism extracts valuable auxiliary information from the intricate dynamics of attributes. This approach aims to optimize the generation of state representations within the decision-making process, ultimately leading to more accurate recommendation outcomes.

Extraction of Local Features L: In this study, we employ a CNN [27] to extract local features, denoted as L. The feature vector X is constructed by concatenating the user's embedding vector, denoted as u, with the embeddings of m items with which the user has most recently engaged positively. Convolution operations are applied to the input feature vector X_i to extract local features using convolutional kernels $k = (n, 1), n \in z^+$, ensuring that local features are meticulously extracted from each individual feature (i.e., each column), as illustrated in Equation (2).

$$f_{\text{out}}(X_i, C_{\text{out}}) = f_b(C_{\text{out}}) + \sum_{n=1}^{C_{\text{in}}-1} f_w(C_{\text{out}}, (n, 1)) * f_{\text{in}}(X_i, (n, 1)) \tag{2}$$

In this context, C_{in}, C_{out}, $f_b()$, $f_w()$, and $f_{\text{in}}()$ represent the number of input channels, the number of output channels, the bias function, the weight function, and the input preprocessing, respectively. The symbol $*$ denotes cross-correlation, and $X_i \in X$. Subsequently, a ReLU activation function is utilized, resulting in the extraction of the local features as follows:

$$L_i = \text{ReLU}(f_{\text{out}}(X_i, C_{\text{out}}) \cdot W_0 + b_0), \tag{3}$$

where W_0 and b_0 are defined as learnable parameters, while $L_i \in L$ denotes the extracted local features. Ultimately, the contribution of each feature is computed using Equations (4) and (5) to facilitate the adjustment of its weight. Subsequently, all features are aggregated through a weighted summation, as articulated in Equation (6), based on their respective contributions. This process culminates in the formation of the final local feature vector L, which incorporates attention weights.

$$d_i^l = V_l^T \tanh(U_l L_i + b_l), \tag{4}$$

$$a_i^l = \frac{\exp\left(d_i^l\right)}{\sum_{i=0}^{k} \exp\left(d_i^l\right)}, \ 1 \le i \le k, \tag{5}$$

$$L = \sum_{i=0}^{k} a_i \cdot L_i \tag{6}$$

where $\tanh()$ is a nonlinear activation function, V_l, U_l, b_l represent trainable parameters, and k denotes the dimension of L, $\cdot$ representing vector multiplication.

Extraction of Global Features G: To extract the latent information from the overall features, including the combined features, this study establishes the convolutional kernel size as $k = (n, m)$, where $n \in z^+, m \geq 2$. This configuration allows for the scanning of multiple attributes in each iteration, as illustrated in Equation (7).

$$f_{\text{out}}(X_j, C_{\text{out}}) = f_b(C_{\text{out}}) + \sum_{n=1}^{C_{\text{in}}-1} \sum_{m=2}^{c_{\text{in}}-1} f_w(C_{\text{out}}, (n, m)) \cdot f_{\text{in}}(X_j, (n, m)), \tag{7}$$

In this context, let X_j represent the vector constructed from the combination of j features, where $X_i \in X$. Subsequently, as indicated in Equation (8), the Rectified Linear Unit (ReLU) function is employed to derive global features. Analogous to the process of extracting local features, Equations (9)–(11) are utilized to calculate the global feature vector G along with the corresponding attention weights.

$$G_j = \text{ReLU}(f_{\text{out}}(X_j, C_{\text{out}}) W_1 + b_1), \tag{8}$$

$$d_j^g = V_g^T \tanh(U_g G_j + b_g), \tag{9}$$

$$a_j = \frac{\exp\left(d_j^g\right)}{\sum_{j=0}^{k} \exp\left(d_j^g\right)}, \quad 1 \leq j \leq q, \tag{10}$$

$$\text{G} = \sum_{j=0}^{q} a_j \cdot G_j, \tag{11}$$

where W_1, b_1, V_g, U_g, b_g are trainable network parameters and q represents the dimension of the combined features.

4.1.3. The Multi-Layer Attention Mechanism Extracts the User's Long-Term Preference Module for High-Reward Items

Incorporating all high-reward item features prior to time step t as the user's long-term preference state I, each item's feature vector is represented as $\text{Z}_1, \text{Z}_2, \cdots, \text{Z}_\text{N}$. These vectors are subsequently input into a Transformer layer for feature transformation. As illustrated in Figure 2, the position encoding of each item is initially defined through an integer sequence and is then mapped to position embedding vectors $p \in \mathbb{R}^k$ using a learnable embedding matrix, where k denotes the dimension of the item embeddings. These position embedding vectors are combined with the original feature vectors z_i of the items to produce enhanced input feature vectors $y_i = z_i + p_i$. The self-attention layer processes the enhanced feature vectors y_i through three distinct linear transformations to generate the query matrix Q, key matrix K, and value matrix V. The output of the self-attention mechanism is computed as specified in Equation (12).

$$\text{Attention}(Q, K, V) = \text{softmax}\left(\frac{QK^T}{\sqrt{d_k}}\right) V, \tag{12}$$

where d_k represents the dimension of the key vectors and the softmax function is utilized as a nonlinear activation function. Following this, a multi-head attention mechanism is implemented to process the queries, keys, and values. The self-attention output from each attention head is computed as illustrated in Equations (13) and (14) by employing the corresponding weight matrices. These outputs are subsequently aggregated through an output weight matrix.

$$\text{MultiHead}(Q, K, V) = \text{Concat}(head_1, head_2, \ldots, head_h) W^O, \tag{13}$$

$$head_j = \text{Attention}\left(QW_j^Q, KW_j^K, VW_j^V\right), \tag{14}$$

where $head_j$ represents the output from the j-th attention head, while W_j^Q, W_j^K, and W_j^V denote the specific weight matrices associated with that attention head. Additionally, W^O refers to the weight matrix utilized for the output linear transformation. Subsequent to the self-attention module, a feed-forward network is employed, as illustrated in Equation (15), which serves to augment the model's capacity for nonlinear processing.

$$FFN(x) = max(0, xW_1 + b_1)W_2 + b_2, \tag{15}$$

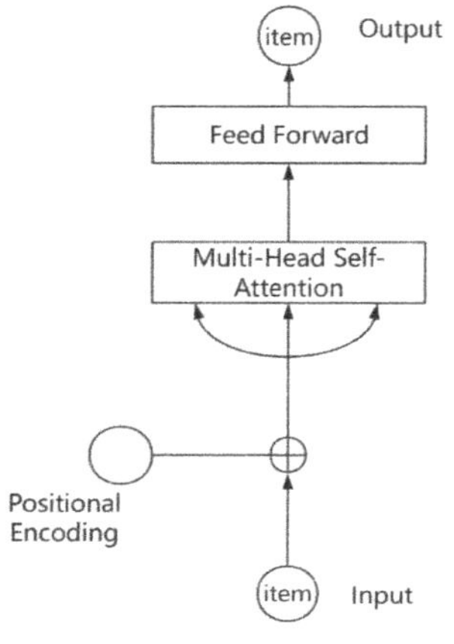

Figure 2. Structure diagram of Transformer layer.

In the context of the feed-forward network, W_1 and W_2 represent the weight matrices, while b_1 and b_2 denote the bias vectors. The function $\max(0, x)$ corresponds to the ReLU activation function. Furthermore, in accordance with Equation (16), average pooling is performed across all item feature vectors.

$$h_{pool} = \frac{1}{N}\sum_{i=1}^{N} h_i'', \tag{16}$$

where h_i'' denotes the output item feature vectors derived from the Transformer layer, while h_{pool} represents the average of all item feature vectors. It is posited that h_{pool} encapsulates the user's long-term preferences for high-reward item features; therefore, we define $I = h_{pool}$.

4.1.4. Feature Fusion Module of Multi-Layer Attention Mechanism

To effectively integrate the user's recent local features L, global features G, and long-term high-reward features I, we utilize an attention layer to weight and combine these features. Specifically, we define the following fusion formula Equation (17):

$$A = \alpha \cdot L + \beta \cdot G + \gamma \cdot I, \tag{17}$$

where α, β, and γ are the weight coefficients learned through the attention mechanism, calculated as per Equations (18)–(20):

$$\alpha = \text{softmax}(e_L, e_G, e_I), \tag{18}$$

$$\beta = \text{softmax}(e_L, e_G, e_I), \tag{19}$$

$$\gamma = \text{softmax}(e_L, e_G, e_I), \tag{20}$$

where e_L, e_G, e_I are the unnormalized weight values computed by a feed-forward neural network.

4.2. MHDRR Recommendation Process

The architecture of the recommendation model presented in this paper is illustrated in Figure 3. The Actor network generates actions based on the current state, which is produced by the state module. The state s_t is processed through two ReLU layers to enhance its nonlinear processing capabilities, followed by a Tanh layer to adjust the output range, thereby ensuring that the action values remain within an appropriate interval. Ultimately, the action a_t is determined by the equation $a_t = \pi_\theta(s_t)$, where π_θ represents the policy network and θ denotes the parameters of the policy network. To enhance exploration efficiency and mitigate the risk of converging to local optima during training, an ε-greedy strategy [28] is employed, which introduces a degree of randomness in the action selection process. The action $a_t \in \mathbb{R}^{1*k}$ is represented as a continuous parameter vector, where k denotes the dimension of item embeddings. Furthermore, a_t is utilized to compute scores through the dot product with each item $i_t \in \mathbb{R}^{1*k}$ in the candidate set, as specified in Equation (21), for the purpose of selecting recommended items.

$$score_t = i_t a_t^T, \tag{21}$$

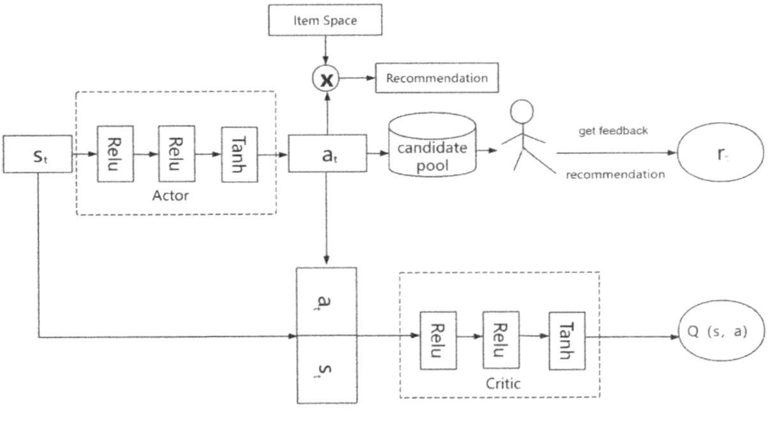

Figure 3. Working principle diagram of MHDRR model.

The item exhibiting the highest dot product score will be recommended to the user. Upon acceptance of a recommended item by the user, the system acquires the user's immediate feedback, denoted as r_t, which functions as a reward signal to assess the immediate impact of the recommendation. To enhance the training and optimization of the recommendation algorithm, the triplet (s_t, a_t, r_t) is documented and stored in an experience pool. The parameters θ of the Actor network are updated via policy gradient, in accordance with Equation (22).

$$\nabla_\theta J(\pi_\theta) \approx \frac{1}{N}\sum_t \nabla_a Q_\omega(s,a)|_{s=s_t,a=\pi_\theta(s_t)} \nabla_\theta \pi_\theta(s_t), \tag{22}$$

In this context, let N represent the batch size and $Q_\omega(s_t, a_t)$ denote the Q-value derived from the Critic network. The Critic network, which is a deep Q network, plays a crucial role in evaluating the efficacy of the action policies generated by the Actor network. It approximates the true state–action value function $Q_\omega(s_t, a_t)$, commonly referred to as the Q-function, utilizing a deep neural network parameterized as $Q_\pi(s_t, a_t)$. The Critic network computes the Q-value based on the current state s_t and the action taken a_t, in conjunction with the immediate reward r_t and the expected reward for the subsequent state s_{t+1}. The Q-value is then updated in accordance with Equation (23).

$$Q_\omega(s_t, a_t) = r_t + \gamma \mathbb{E}_{s_{t+1}\sim\mathcal{E}}[Q_{\omega'}(s_{t+1}, \pi_\theta(s_{t+1}))], \tag{23}$$

where γ denotes the discount factor, while $\mathbb{E}_{s_{t+1}\sim\mathcal{E}}$ signifies the expected value of achieving the subsequent state s_{t+1} following a transition from the current state s_t and action a_t. To facilitate the training of the Critic network, this study employs the Temporal Difference (TD) learning algorithm, which utilizes a loss function L grounded in the mean squared error between the target Q-value y_i and the Q-value estimated by the Critic network, denoted as $Q_\omega(s_i, a_i)$. The target Q-value, y_i, is computed according to Equation (24).

$$y_i = r_i \gamma Q_{\omega'}(s_{i+1}, \pi_\theta(s_{i+1})), \tag{24}$$

where $Q_{\omega'}$ is the target Critic network and ω' represents the parameters of the target Critic network. The loss function L for the Critic network is shown in Equation (25):

$$L = \frac{1}{N}\sum\nolimits_i (y_i - Q_\omega(s_i, a_i))^2, \tag{25}$$

where y_i represents the target Q-value, N denotes the batch size, and Q_ω signifies the Q-value as determined by the current Critic network. The parameters ω of the Critic network are adjusted through the minimization of this loss function, thereby enhancing the accuracy of the predictions regarding the expected return for various state–action pairs.

4.3. Training Module

The algorithm is trained utilizing the Deep Deterministic Policy Gradient (DDPG) method [29]. Algorithm 1 delineates the training technique employed by the proposed model. The process commences with the initialization of the networks, wherein the Actor network, denoted as π_θ, and the Critic network, represented as Q_ω, are assigned random initial weights. Concurrently, the target networks, $\pi_{\theta'}$ and $Q_{\omega'}$, are initialized based on the weights of the original networks to ensure the synchronization of their parameters (lines 1–2). Furthermore, the replay buffer, denoted as D, is initialized to store state transitions, thereby facilitating the experience replay mechanism (line 3).

In each session, the initial state is established based on the user interaction history or predetermined environmental settings (line 5). The Actor network utilizes the policy $\pi_\theta(s_t)$ in conjunction with the current state s_t to ascertain the action a_t at each time step (line 7). The action a_t is employed to recommend products, prompting the environment to yield a new state s_{t+1} and the associated reward r_t (lines 8–9). The newly generated state and reward information are subsequently recorded and stored in the replay buffer D for future training iterations (line 10).

During the training process, the replay buffer is periodically sampled in batches to facilitate the training of the Actor and Critic networks. The update of the parameters of the Critic network entails the computation of the target Q-value y_i and the minimization of the mean squared error between the predicted Q-values and the target Q-values (lines 11–13). In the case of the Actor network, the policy gradient method modifies the action policy based on the gradient information supplied by the Critic network, thereby improving decision-making performance (line 14).

Furthermore, a weighted average with a parameter τ is employed to gradually update the parameters of the target networks. This approach alleviates fluctuations in the learning process by partially integrating weights, thereby enhancing the stability of the learning process (lines 16–17). The entire procedure concludes upon the completion of all scheduled sessions, resulting in the return of the trained network parameters θ and ω (line 20). These returned network parameters are subsequently utilized in a practical recommendation system to facilitate decision support.

Algorithm 1. Training Process of the MHDRR

Set random weights for the actor network π_θ and the critic network Q_ω;
Set up the target networks $\pi_{\theta'}$ and $Q_{\omega'}$ with weights $\theta' \leftarrow \theta$ and $\omega' \leftarrow \omega$;
Set up the replay buffer D;
for session $= 1, \mathrm{M}$ **do**
Based on the history of user interactions, set the initial state s_0;
for t $= 1, \mathrm{T}$ **do**
The actor selects an action a_t according to the current policy $\pi_\theta(s_t)$;
Execute action a_t, recommend items, and observe the reward $\mathrm{r_t} = \mathrm{R(s_t, a_t)}$;
Set s_{t+1} according to the defined state transition function;
Store the state transition (s_t, a_t, r_t, s_{t+1}) in D;
Take a sample from D of a mini-batch of N transitions (s_t, a_t, r_t, s_{t+1});
Set $y_i = r_i + \gamma Q_{\omega'}(s_{i+1}, \pi_{\theta'}(s_{i+1}))$;
Utilizing Equation (25), update the critic network;
Utilizing Equation (22), update the critic network;
Modify the target networks' parameters:
$\theta' \leftarrow \tau\theta + (1-\tau)\theta'$;
$\omega' \leftarrow \tau\omega + (1-\tau)\omega'$;
end for
end for
return θ and ω;

5. Experiments and Analysis

5.1. Experimental Setup

The MHDRR algorithm was implemented utilizing Python 3.6 and TensorFlow 2.5.0. All experimental procedures were conducted on a personal computer featuring an Intel i7-10875H CPU and an NVIDIA RTX 3060 GPU. During the training of the model, the average utilization rates for the CPU and GPU were recorded at 70% and 80%, respectively. Each iteration involved the processing of a mini-batch consisting of 32 samples, with an average processing duration of approximately 3 s per batch.

For the experimental analysis, three distinct versions of the Movielens dataset were employed: ML_100k, ML_1M, and ML_10M. Detailed information regarding these datasets is presented in Table 1. In the data preparation phase, users who had provided fewer than 10 total ratings were excluded from the dataset. The datasets were subsequently divided into training and testing subsets, with 80% of the data randomly allocated for model training and the remaining 20% designated for testing purposes. It is important to note that users were not represented in both the training and testing sets concurrently.

$$r_t = r(s_t, a_t) = \frac{1}{2}(rating - 3), \tag{26}$$

where rating is the score a user gives to an item. Prior to time step t, the ten most recent items that received ratings above 3 are utilized to represent the state of recent interest. Additionally, all items rated as 5 before time step t are regarded as indicative of the state of long-term high-reward preferences. Two independent Adam optimizers are employed to update the parameters of the Actor and Critic networks, respectively. To mitigate the risk of overfitting, L2 regularization is incorporated during the optimization process. The learning rate for the Actor network is established at 1×10^{-4}, whereas the learning rate for the Critic network is set at 1×10^{-3}. The discount factor γ is assigned a value of 0.9 to modulate the contribution of future rewards. In the multi-head attention layer of the Transformer architecture, n = 4 heads are utilized. During the recommendation process, the system considers all movies within the candidate set, with the exception of those that have been previously recommended.

Table 1. Introduction to the dataset.

Dataset	Users	Items	Ratings	Scale
ML_100K	943	1682	100,000	[1–5]
ML_1M	6040	3952	1,000,209	[1–5]
ML_10M	69,878	10,677	10,000,054	[1–5]

5.2. Evaluation Metrics

This paper utilizes HR@K and NDCG@K as evaluation metrics. HR@K denotes the ratio of positive ratings provided by users among the top K items recommended by the recommendation system, whereas NDCG@K signifies the normalized discounted cumulative gain, which evaluates the quality of the ranking within the recommendation list. The calculations for these metrics are presented in Equations (27)–(29).

$$HR@K = \frac{NumberOfHits@K}{GT}, \tag{27}$$

$$DCG@K = \frac{1}{N}\sum_{u=1}^{N}\sum_{i=1}^{K}\frac{2^{rel_i}-1}{\log_2(i+1)}, \tag{28}$$

$$NDCG@K = \frac{DCG@K}{IDCG}, \tag{29}$$

The variable NumberOfHits@k denotes the quantity of items within the top K recommendations that align with the user's actual interests, while GT represents the total number of items in the test set that the user finds appealing, with reli $\in [0,1]$. Additionally, the term represents the reward value for the i-th movie, and IDCG refers to the ideal discounted cumulative gain (DCG) for the optimal arrangement of recommendations.

5.3. Comparative Models

This study utilizes several baseline models for comparative analysis, categorized into three distinct groups: traditional collaborative filtering-based recommendation models, deep learning-based recommendation models, and deep reinforcement learning-based recommendation models. The specific models employed include PMF [30], SVD++ [5], NCF [31], GRU4Rec [32], SASRec [6], DQN [33], DEERS [9], and DRR [10].

PMF: Probabilistic Matrix Factorization (PMF) interprets the process of matrix decomposition by breaking down the user interaction matrix into a product of low-rank latent factor matrices corresponding to users and items. This methodology, when integrated with a restricted Boltzmann machine model, markedly enhances the accuracy of recommendations for users who exhibit sparse rating patterns.

SVD++: SVD++ is an enhancement of the latent factor model that incorporates neighborhood models and extends its functionality to leverage both explicit and implicit user feedback. This integration significantly improves the accuracy of recommendations.

NCF: Neural Collaborative Filtering (NCF) utilizes a multi-layer perceptron to learn the interaction function between users and items, thereby introducing nonlinearity to augment the model's expressive capacity.

GRU4Rec: The first model to apply recurrent neural networks within a recommendation system, specifically designed for contexts that rely on short-term session data as opposed to extensive long-term user histories.

SASRec: A sequence model that employs self-attention mechanisms to identify pertinent items from relatively brief user action histories, utilizing this information to forecast the subsequent item.

DQN: A deep reinforcement learning algorithm that combines deep learning techniques with Q-learning. It processes environmental states using a neural network model, generates Q-values for each potential action, and selects actions based on these Q-values.

DEERS: The first model designed to dynamically acquire optimization strategies through user feedback, employing reinforcement learning techniques. This model places a specific emphasis on the effective integration of both positive and negative feedback to enhance the quality of recommendations.

DRR: A model grounded in the Actor–Critic framework; however, it fails to account for long-term features and the interactions between user and item attributes within its state modeling.

5.4. Experimental Results and Analysis

The comparative experimental results are shown in Tables 2–4. Across the different sizes of the MovieLens datasets (100 k, 1 M, and 10 M), the MHDRR model consistently demonstrated superior performance, particularly on the larger 1 M and 10 M datasets, where it outperformed all other models in both HR@10 and NDCG@10 metrics. Even on the smaller 100 k dataset, where user–item interactions are relatively limited, the MHDRR model was still able to provide highly accurate recommendations. When applied to the larger 1 M and 10 M datasets, this model significantly improved the generalization capability and accuracy of the recommendation system by effectively utilizing the extensive user interaction data. This highlights the clear advantage of the MHDRR model in handling large-scale datasets and demonstrates its ability not only to predict user interest points more accurately but also to prioritize items in the recommendation list that users are likely to find more appealing, thereby delivering more personalized recommendation results.

Table 2. MovieLens_100k experiment results.

Models	K = 5		K = 10	
	HR	**NDCG**	**HR**	**NDCG**
PMF	0.3182	0.2157	0.4691	0.2641
SVD++	0.2721	0.1828	0.4253	0.2310
NCF	0.4891	0.3467	0.6601	0.4024
GRU4Rec	0.5185	0.3611	0.6807	0.4236
SASRec	0.5269	0.3706	0.6910	0.4243
DQN	0.2813	0.1802	0.4324	0.2290
DEERS	0.5060	0.3585	0.6595	0.4084
DRR	0.7198	0.4963	0.7853	0.5457
MHDRR	0.7102	0.4988	0.8012	0.5749

Among the various models based on collaborative filtering, Probabilistic Matrix Factorization (PMF) and SVD++ predominantly utilize historical interaction data for linear predictions, which constrains their ability to effectively address nonlinear and complex relationships. In contrast, Neural Collaborative Filtering (NCF) leverages deep learning techniques to introduce nonlinearity, demonstrating superior performance compared to PMF and SVD++ across two datasets of varying sizes. Furthermore, the MHDRR model integrates both deep learning and reinforcement learning methodologies. This integration not only enables the capture of nonlinear and complex relationships between users and items but also facilitates the dynamic adjustment of recommendation strategies in response to changes in user behavior. Consequently, MHDRR exhibits an enhanced adaptability and efficiency in managing large datasets compared to PMF, SVD++, and NCF.

Table 3. MovieLens_1M experiment results.

Models	K = 5		K = 10	
	HR	NDCG	HR	NDCG
PMF	0.3019	0.1995	0.4521	0.2479
SVD++	0.2434	0.1635	0.3709	0.2044
NCF	0.5030	0.3512	0.6682	0.4050
GRU4Rec	0.6602	0.4857	0.8057	0.5329
SASRec	0.6676	0.4936	0.8063	0.5389
DQN	0.2969	0.1942	0.4513	0.2421
DEERS	0.4918	0.3497	0.6543	0.4023
DRR	0.6936	0.4468	0.8116	0.4045
MHDRR	0.7259	0.5121	0.8397	0.5511

Table 4. MovieLens_10M experiment results.

Models	K = 5		K = 10	
	HR	NDCG	HR	NDCG
PMF	0.4775	0.3318	0.6434	0.3854
SVD++	0.3836	0.2828	0.5072	0.3330
NCF	0.7635	0.5809	0.8816	0.6194
GRU4Rec	0.7937	0.6212	0.8989	0.6566
SASRec	0.8240	0.6567	0.9143	0.6862
DQN	0.4909	0.3407	0.6573	0.3947
DEERS	0.7224	0.5708	0.8389	0.6085
DRR	0.8697	0.7182	0.9387	0.7543
MHDRR	0.8854	0.7551	0.9428	0.7792

Among the various deep learning-based recommendation models, the SASRec model demonstrates superior performance across both datasets. The SASRec model utilizes a self-attention mechanism that effectively identifies significant items from brief sequences of user behavior, suggesting that the modeling of short-term interests can improve recommendation accuracy. However, traditional deep learning algorithms typically update their recommendation strategies solely during the training phase, which restricts their adaptability to shifts in user preferences. In contrast, the strength of the MHDRR model resides in its capacity to integrate both short-term behavioral sequences and long-term high-reward feedback. Through its dynamic adjustment capabilities derived from reinforcement learning, the MHDRR model significantly enhances the understanding of and responsiveness to users' long-term preferences, thereby achieving substantial improvements in sequence prediction accuracy and long-term user satisfaction.

Among the three models based on deep reinforcement learning, the MHDRR model is distinguished from both DQN and DEERS by its integration of value-based and policy-based reinforcement learning algorithms. This model incorporates evaluation mechanisms specifically designed to address the potential challenges associated with high variance and local optima that may arise during policy evaluation. In contrast, although the DRR model also utilizes the Actor–Critic framework, it inadequately accounts for the long-term high-reward characteristics of users and fails to effectively represent comprehensive state information. The MHDRR model, through its multi-level attention mechanism and the integration of long-term high-reward item features, offers a more nuanced analysis of user behavior patterns. This capability enables the recommendation system to more accurately predict and adapt to fluctuations in user preferences.

5.5. Ablation Experiment and Analysis

In order to assess the efficacy of the multi-layer attention mechanism in identifying short-term preference characteristics and long-term high-reward feedback attributes within the MHDRR framework, a series of experiments were performed utilizing the MovieLens-1M dataset. These experiments involved the selective retention of one or more components of the multi-layer attention mechanism, specifically the local feature module, the global feature module, and the long-term high-reward feedback feature module. A comprehensive summary of the configurations employed in each model is presented in Table 5.

Table 5. Models used in the ablation experiment.

Model	Local Features of Multiple Layers of Attention	Multi-Layer Global Features of Attention	Long-Term High-Reward Feedback Characteristics
HDRR			√
MDRR	√	√	
MHDRR-L	√		√
MHDRR-G		√	√
MHDRR	√	√	√

The results of the ablation experiments, as illustrated in Figures 4 and 5, indicate that the HDRR model exhibits the lowest performance. This finding suggests that relying exclusively on the capture of long-term preferences, without considering short-term user behavior, fails to adequately address the requirements of recommendation systems. In contrast, while the MDRR model incorporates a multi-level attention mechanism to capture short-term preference features, its performance diminishes relative to the comprehensive MHDRR model when long-term high-reward feedback features are excluded. This observation underscores the critical importance of these features in enhancing the quality of recommendations. Furthermore, the comparison between MHDRR-L and MHDRR-G, both of which retain long-term high-reward feedback features, reveals that MHDRR-G outperforms MHDRR-L. This finding affirms the significant role of the global features of short-term preferences, as captured by the multi-level attention mechanism, in comprehending broader user preferences. Notably, MHDRR demonstrates superior performance across all evaluated metrics, thereby validating that the integration of short-term local and global features with long-term high-reward feedback features is essential for an effective recommendation system. This evidence illustrates the synergistic effect of these features in improving recommendation accuracy and user satisfaction, thereby confirming the efficacy of the multi-level attention mechanism and long-term high-reward feedback.

5.6. Hyperparameter Experiment and Analysis

In this study, we explored the impact of embedding dimensions on the performance of the MHDRR framework by conducting experiments on three movie-rating datasets of varying sizes (Movies-100k, Movies-1M, and Movies-10M), with embedding dimensions set at 16, 32, 64, 100, 150, and 200. The experimental results are shown in Figures 6–8. The results indicate that as the embedding dimensions increased from 16 to 100, both the hit rate (HR@10) and normalized discounted cumulative gain (NDCG@10) improved significantly across all three datasets, suggesting that higher embedding dimensions effectively capture complex user–item interaction relationships. However, when the embedding dimensions reached 150 and 200, the improvement in recommendation performance began to plateau, likely indicating that the model had reached its learning capacity given the current data, and further increases in embedding dimensions might lead to overfitting and wasted resources. Therefore, based on a balance of performance and efficiency, an embedding dimension of 100 was determined to be optimal, ensuring the best trade-off between recommendation accuracy and computational resource utilization.

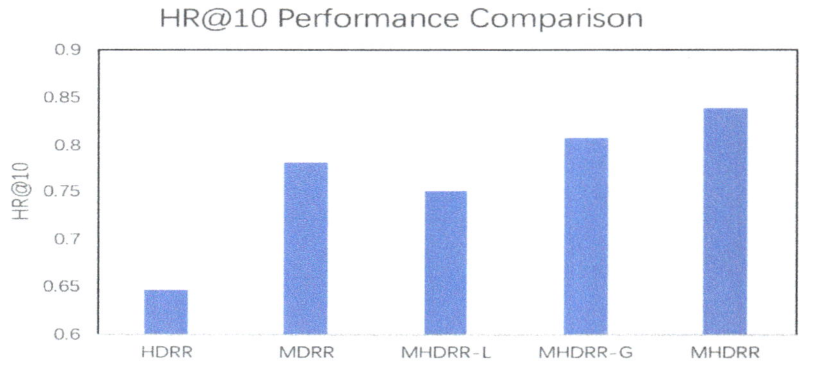

Figure 4. HR performance of different models.

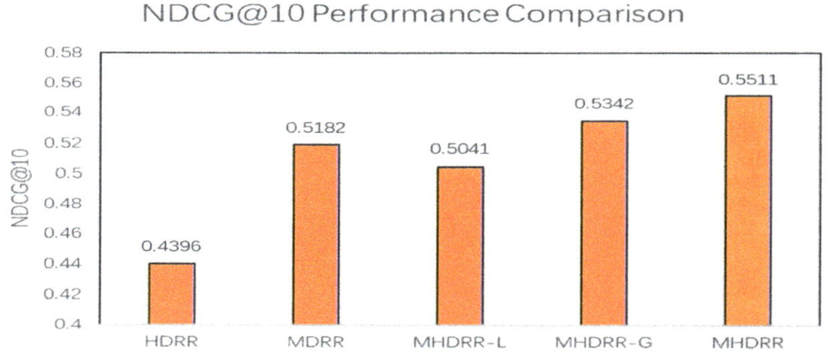

Figure 5. NDCG performance of different models.

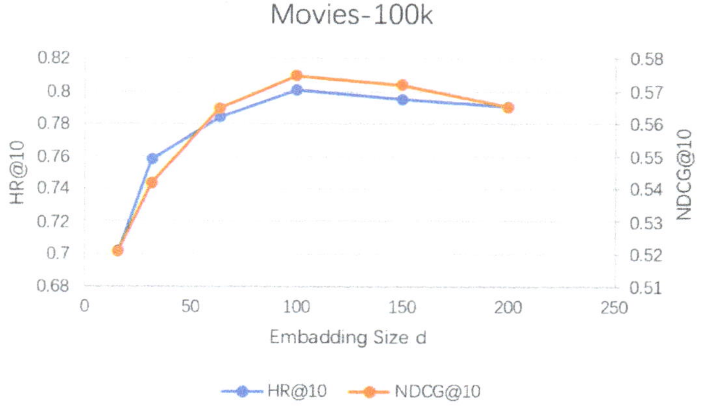

Figure 6. Parameter study on embedding size d on the MovieLens-100k datasets.

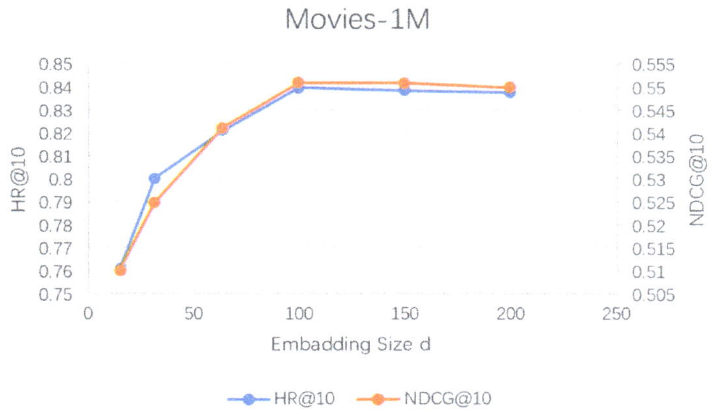

Figure 7. Parameter study on embedding size d on the MovieLens-1M datasets.

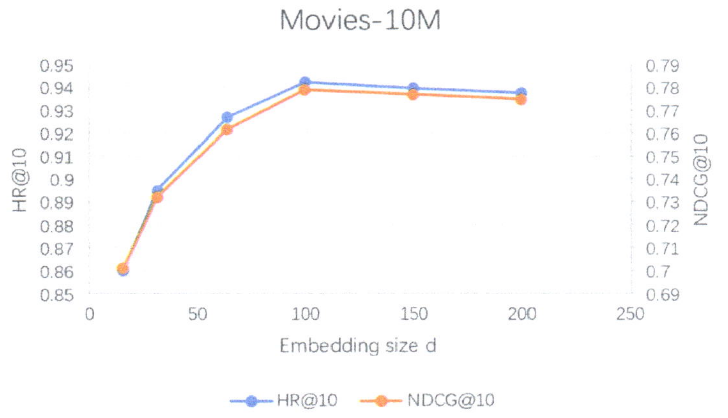

Figure 8. Parameter study on embedding size d on the MovieLens-10M datasets.

6. Conclusions

This paper presents a novel recommendation system, referred to as MHDRR, which integrates a multi-level attention mechanism with deep reinforcement learning algorithms. This integration significantly enhances the system's ability to extract key information from user feedback data and effectively captures the intricate relationships between users and items. Additionally, the system incorporates features related to long-term high-reward items, enabling it to accurately identify and respond to users' inherent interests, thereby optimizing the long-term benefits of the recommendation system. The model was evaluated using the publicly available MovieLens-100K, MovieLens-1M, and MovieLens-10M datasets, and comparative analyses with other models indicate that MHDRR substantially improves both the accuracy of recommendations and the normalized discounted cumulative gain metrics.

In recommendation systems, diversity serves as a critical metric for evaluating the quality of a recommendation list. A recommendation list characterized by high diversity encompasses a wide and varied array of items, thereby providing users with diverse options that enrich their exploration experience and overall satisfaction [34]. Future research will concentrate on improving the diversity of recommendation systems to more effectively address the extensive needs of users.

Author Contributions: Conceptualization, J.D.; Methodology, G.W.; Software, J.D.; Validation, F.H.; Data curation, F.H.; Writing—original draft, J.D.; Writing—review & editing, F.H.; Project administration, G.W.; Funding acquisition, G.W. All authors have read and agreed to the published version of the manuscript.

Funding: This research was funded by the Chongqing Science and Technology Bureau 2020 Science and Technology Enterprise Technological Innovation and Application Development Special Project. The funding number: cstc2020kqiscx-phxmX0142.

Data Availability Statement: The data that support the findings of this study are openly available at https://grouplens.org/datasets/movielens/ (accessed on 20 November 2024).

Conflicts of Interest: The authors declare no conflicts of interest.

References

1. Ko, H.; Lee, S.; Park, Y.; Choi, A. A survey of recommendation systems: Recommendation models, techniques, and application fields. *Electronics* **2022**, *11*, 141. [CrossRef]
2. Ricci, F.; Rokach, L.; Shapira, B. Introduction to recommender systems handbook. In *Recommender Systems Handbook*; Springer: Boston, MA, USA, 2010; pp. 1–35.
3. Roy, D.; Dutta, M. A systematic review and research perspective on recommender systems. *J. Big Data* **2022**, *9*, 59 [CrossRef]
4. Martins, G.B.; Papa, J.P.; Adeli, H. Deep learning techniques for recommender systems based on collaborative filtering. *Expert Syst.* **2020**, *37*, e12647. [CrossRef]
5. Koren, Y. Factorization meets the neighborhood: A multifaceted collaborative filtering model. In Proceedings of the 14th ACM SIGKDD International Conference on Knowledge Discovery and Data Mining, Las Vegas, NV, USA, 24–27 August 2008; pp. 426–434.
6. Kang, W.C.; McAuley, J. Self-attentive sequential recommendation. In Proceedings of the 2018 IEEE International Conference on Data Mining (ICDM), Singapore, 17–20 November 2018; IEEE: Piscataway, NJ, USA, 2018; pp. 197–206.
7. Pang, G.; Wang, X.; Hao, F.; Wang, L.; Wang, X. Efficient point-of-interest recommendation with hierarchical attention mechanism. *Appl. Soft Comput.* **2020**, *96*, 106536. [CrossRef]
8. Afsar, M.M.; Crump, T.; Far, B. Reinforcement learning based recommender systems: A survey. *ACM Comput. Surv.* **2022**, *55*, 1–38. [CrossRef]
9. Zhao, X.; Zhang, L.; Ding, Z.; Xia, L.; Tang, J.; Yin, D. Recommendations with negative feedback via pairwise deep reinforcement learning. In Proceedings of the 24th ACM SIGKDD International Conference on Knowledge Discovery & Data Mining, London, UK, 19–23 August 2018; pp. 1040–1048.
10. Liu, F.; Tang, R.; Li, X.; Zhang, W.; Ye, Y.; Chen, H.; Guo, H.; Zhang, Y.; He, X. State Representation Modeling for Deep Reinforcement Learning Based Recommendation. *Knowl. Based Syst.* **2020**, *205*, 106170. [CrossRef]
11. Jiang, P.; Ma, J.; Zhang, J. Deep Reinforcement Learning based Recommender System with State Representation. In Proceedings of the 2021 IEEE International Conference on Big Data (Big Data), Orlando, FL, USA, 15–18 December 2021; IEEE: Piscataway, NJ, USA, 2021; pp. 5703–5707.
12. Javed, U.; Shaukat, K.; Hameed, I.A.; Iqbal, F.; Alam, T.M.; Luo, S. A review of content-based and context-based recommendation systems. *Int. J. Emerg. Technol. Learn. (IJET)* **2021**, *16*, 274–306. [CrossRef]
13. Koren, Y.; Rendle, S.; Bell, R. Advances in collaborative filtering. In *Recommender Systems Handbook*; Springer: Berlin/Heidelberg, Germany, 2021; pp. 91–142.
14. Huang, Z.; Xu, X.; Zhu, H.; Zhou, M. An efficient group recommendation model with multiattention-based neural networks. *IEEE Trans. Neural Netw. Learn. Syst.* **2020**, *31*, 4461–4474. [CrossRef] [PubMed]
15. Liu, L.; Cai, L.; Zhang, C.; Zhao, X.; Gao, J.; Wang, W.; Lv, Y.; Fan, W.; Wang, Y.; He, M.; et al. Linrec: Linear attention mechanism for long-term sequential recommender systems. In Proceedings of the 46th International ACM SIGIR Conference on Research and Development in Information Retrieval, Taipei, Taiwan, 23–27 July 2023; pp. 289–299.
16. Wu, Z. An efficient recommendation model based on knowledge graph attention-assisted network (kgatax). *arXiv* **2024**, arXiv:2409.15315.
17. Li, B.; Li, G.; Xu, J.; Li, X.; Liu, X.; Wang, M.; Lv, J. A personalized recommendation framework based on MOOC system integrating deep learning and big data. *Comput. Electr. Eng.* **2023**, *106*, 108571. [CrossRef]
18. Qiu, R.; Huang, Z.; Yin, H.; Wang, Z. Contrastive learning for representation degeneration problem in sequential recommendation. In Proceedings of the Fifteenth ACM International Conference on Web Search and Data Mining, Tempe, AZ, USA, 21–25 February 2022; pp. 813–823.
19. Sutton, R.S.; Barto, A.G. *Reinforcement Learning: An Introduction*, 2nd ed.; MIT Press: Cambridge, MA, USA, 2018.
20. Zhao, J.; Li, H.; Qu, L.; Zhang, Q.; Sun, Q.; Huo, H.; Gong, M. DCFGAN: An adversarial deep reinforcement learning framework with improved negative sampling for session-based recommender systems. *Inf. Sci.* **2022**, *596*, 222–235. [CrossRef]
21. Khurana, P.; Gupta, B.; Sharma, R.; Bedi, P. Session-aware recommender system using double deep reinforcement learning. *J. Intell. Inf. Syst.* **2024**, *62*, 403–429. [CrossRef]

22. Gao, C.; Xu, K.; Zhou, K.; Li, L.; Wang, X.; Yuan, B.; Zhao, P. Value penalized q-learning for recommender systems. In Proceedings of the 45th International ACM SIGIR Conference on Research and Development in Information Retrieval, Madrid, Spain, 11–15 July 2022; pp. 2008–2012.
23. Dulac-Arnold, G.; Evans, R.; van Hasselt, H.; Sunehag, P.; Lillicrap, T.; Hunt, J.; Mann, T.; Weber, T.; Degris, T.; Coppin, B. Deep reinforcement learning in large discrete action spaces. *arXiv* **2015**, arXiv:1512.07679.
24. Xin, X.; Karatzoglou, A.; Arapakis, I.; Jose, J.M. Supervised advantage actor-critic for recommender systems. In Proceedings of the Fifteenth ACM International Conference on Web Search and Data Mining, Tempe, AZ, USA, 21–25 February 2022; pp. 1186–1196.
25. Padhye, V.; Lakshmanan, K. A deep actor critic reinforcement learning framework for learning to rank. *Neurocomputing* **2023**, *547*, 126314. [CrossRef]
26. Wu, L.; Li, S.; Hsieh, C.J.; Sharpnack, J. SSE-PT: Sequential recommendation via personalized transformer. In Proceedings of the 14th ACM Conference on Recommender Systems, Virtual Event, Brazil, 22–26 September 2020.
27. Alzubaidi, L.; Zhang, J.; Humaidi, A.J.; Al-Dujaili, A.; Duan, Y.; Al-Shamma, O.; Santamaría, J.; Fadhel, M.A.; Al-Amidie, M.; Farhan, L. Review of deep learning: Concepts, CNN architectures, challenges, applications, future directions. *J. Big Data* **2021**, *8*, 1–74. [CrossRef] [PubMed]
28. Tokic, M. Adaptive ε-greedy exploration in reinforcement learning based on value differences. In *KI 2010: Advances in Artificial Intelligence, Proceedings of the Annual Conference on Artificial Intelligence, Atlanta, GA, USA, 11–15 July 2010*; Springer: Berlin/Heidelberg, Germany, 2010; pp. 203–210.
29. Hou, Y.; Liu, L.; Wei, Q.; Xu, X.; Chen, C. A novel DDPG method with prioritized experience replay. In Proceedings of the 2017 IEEE International Conference on Systems, Man, and Cybernetics (SMC), Banff, AB, Canada, 5–8 October 2017; IEEE: Piscataway, NJ, USA, 2017; pp. 316–321.
30. Mnih, A.; Salakhutdinov, R.R. Probabilistic matrix factorization. *Adv. Neural Inf. Process. Syst.* **2007**, *20*, 1257–1264.
31. He, X.; Liao, L.; Zhang, H.; Nie, L.; Hu, X.; Chua, T.S. Neural collaborative filtering. In Proceedings of the 26th International Conference on World Wide Web, Perth, Australia, 3–7 April 2017; pp. 173–182.
32. Hidasi, B. Session-based Recommendations with Recurrent Neural Networks. *arXiv* **2015**, arXiv:1511.06939.
33. Mnih, V.; Kavukcuoglu, K.; Silver, D.; Rusu, A.A.; Veness, J.; Bellemare, M.G.; Graves, A.; Riedmiller, M.; Fidjeland, A.K.; Ostrovski, G.; et al. Human-level control through deep reinforcement learning. *Nature* **2015**, *518*, 529–533. [CrossRef] [PubMed]
34. Zheng, Y.; Wang, D.X. A survey of recommender systems with multi-objective optimization. *Neurocomputing* **2022**, *474*, 141–153. [CrossRef]

Disclaimer/Publisher's Note: The statements, opinions and data contained in all publications are solely those of the individual author(s) and contributor(s) and not of MDPI and/or the editor(s). MDPI and/or the editor(s) disclaim responsibility for any injury to people or property resulting from any ideas, methods, instructions or products referred to in the content.

electronics

MDPI

Article

A Practically Secure Two-Factor and Mutual Authentication Protocol for Distributed Wireless Sensor Networks Using PUF

Jiaqing Mo [1,*], Zhihua Zhang [2] and Yuhua Lin [2]

[1] School of Computer Science and Software, Zhaoqing University, Zhaoqing 526061, China
[2] Center of Modern Educational Technology, Zhaoqing University, Zhaoqing 526061, China; zzh@zqu.edu.cn (Z.Z.); lyh@zqu.edu.cn (Y.L.)
* Correspondence: mojiaqing@126.com

Abstract: In a distributed wireless sensor network (DWSN), sensors continuously perceive the environment, collect data, and transmit it to remote users through the network so as to realize real-time monitoring of the environment or specific targets. However, given the openness of wireless channels and the sensitivity of collecting data, designing a robust user authentication protocol to ensure the legitimacy of user and sensors in such DWSN environments faces serious challenges. Most of the current authentication schemes fail to meet some important and often overlooked security features, such as resisting physical impersonation attack, resisting smartcard loss attack, and providing forward secrecy. In this work, we put forward a practically secure two-factor authentication scheme using a physically unclonable function to prevent a physical impersonation attack and sensor node capture attack, utilize Chebyshev chaotic mapping to provide forward secrecy, and improve the efficiency and security of session key negotiation. Furthermore, we use the fuzzy verifier technique to prevent attackers from offline guessing attacks to resist smartcard loss attacks. In addition, a BAN logic proof and heuristic security analysis show that the scheme achieves mutual authentication and key agreement as well as prevents known attacks. A comparative analysis with state-of-the-art schemes shows that the proposal not only achieves desired security features but also maintains better efficiency.

Keywords: authentication protocol; physical impersonation attack; physically unclonable function; Chebyshev chaotic mapping; distributed wireless sensor networks

1. Introduction

The development of microelectronics technology, computing technology, and wireless transmission technologies has promoted the rapid development of low-power multifunctional sensors for integrating various functions such as information collection, environmental sensing, and wireless communication in miniaturized volumes [1]. A distributed wireless sensor network consists of users, gateways, and many static or mobile microsensors that form a multihop self-organizing network through wireless communication, realize data collection and data aggregation, and transmit the data through a wireless channel by a gateway to a remote user for further analysis and processing [2]; its architecture is shown in Figure 1. A DWSN has a wide range of application scenarios, such as industrial Internet of Things [3], wireless medical sensor networks [4], smart homes [5], mine monitoring [6], etc. Note that since a WSN is the foundation of a DWSN, this paper also discusses the security of a WSN in the related works section. In a DSWN, wireless sensors are characterized by limited energy, computing power, and transmission bandwidth, and they are typically deployed in unmanned or harsh environments. Because the data gathered by wireless sensors are often important and sensitive and are transmitted wirelessly, it is easy for attackers to launch malicious attacks, such as eavesdropping, blocking, tampering, and replaying, during the communication process [7,8]. In a DWSN, the most serious case is that the node is subjected to a physical impersonation attack. By capturing the wireless sensor node in the network, the attacker obtains all the information (including the key) in the node, clones it, disguises it as a legitimate node, and participates in various network activities. Due to its legitimate information, the cloned node cannot be identified by ordinary security authentication methods. Although IEEE 802.15.4 provides some security services for the lower layers of the WSN stack, it also has some security defects [9]. Moreover, the openness of wireless networks and the scanty resources of wireless sensors make it necessary to establish appropriate authentication and key agreement mechanisms at the application layer to ensure secure communication between legitimate users and the sensors.

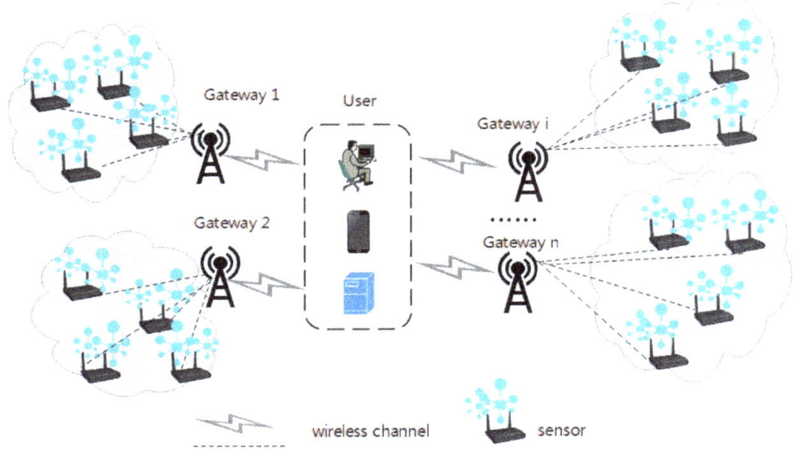

Figure 1. The typical architecture of a DWSN.

1.1. Related Works

As the key technology of network security, the user authentication protocol verifies the user's legality and encrypts the transmission data between communication parties. It is crucial to ensure network security, and this is a prerequisite for ensuring the secure transmission of data and access by authorized users. In recent years, as sensor-based IoT technologies have been increasingly widely used in industrial and other scenarios, designing user authentication protocols for DWSNs has attracted the attention of the research community. In general, for DWSN user authentication protocols, in addition to being suitable for the actual needs and capable of user anonymity, mutual authentication, and high efficiency, they should also be able to defend against malicious attacks, like insider attacks, replay attacks, and physical impersonation attacks [10]. It is worth noting that the sensor node physical impersonation attack is easily overlooked.

Researchers have proposed various user authentication protocol schemes based on the hash function to address the challenges posed by the high-security requirements and resource constraints imposed by wireless sensors due to data sensitivity in the WSN environment [11–21]. Although these schemes are efficient in computation cost, they are still subject to some attacks, resulting in session key leakage or failure to meet the relevant security properties of the session key, which cannot guarantee the session key's security negotiated by the two parties. For example, Das [22] proposed a three-factor (password, smartcard, biometrics) authentication protocol for a large-scale DWSN, but we found that Das's scheme suffered from smartcard loss attack, failed to provide sensor node anonymity, and could not thwart a physical impersonation attack. Md. et al. [23] also found that Das's scheme failed to resist a known session-specific temporary information attack and replay attack; the scheme [13] lacks forward secrecy; that is, if the system key is obtained by an attacker, the attacker can calculate the session key shared by the user and the sensor; protocols [12,14,15,19,20] are vulnerable to a temporary information leakage attack; protocols [11,16–18] cannot withstand a session key leakage attack; and protocols [15,19–21] could not thwart a physical impersonation attack. To address the security flaws of these authentication schemes by using the hash function, Wang et al. emphasized that public key operations should be employed to construct an authentication protocol in universal circumstances [24]. Compared with RSA and other public key cryptosystems, elliptic curve cryptography (ECC) has the merits of a shorter key length and faster computing speed, and it has been widely employed in various authentication protocols [25–33]. However, this kind of user authentication, using an ECC protocol for the WSN environment, still has the problem of high computation cost. Moreover, related research has shown that these authentication schemes based on ECC still lack anonymity and cannot resist security risks like a user impersonation attack and insider attack. Thus, designing a DWSN authentication protocol that not only can resist various known attacks and satisfy favorable security properties but also achieve a good trade-off between security and efficiency is a very challenging task.

Because public key cryptography with Chebyshev chaotic mapping has the merits of not relying on large prime numbers, faster computation, and shorter encryption length under the same security strength compared with modular exponential and ECC in public key cryptosystems, some researchers have proposed user authentication schemes using chaotic mapping [34,35]. Wang et al. [34] reported that a previous scheme lacked forward secrecy and was insecure to resist a session key leakage attack, impersonation attack, sensor node impersonation attack, desynchronization attack, and temporary information leakage attack; additionally, they suggested an improved anonymous authentication protocol to surmount these defects. However, our examination revealed that Wang et al.'s scheme fails to resist a gateway impersonation attack and temporary information leakage attack. To overcome the lack of forward secrecy, lack of three-factor (password, smartcard, biometric) security, and other defects in the previous scheme, Xu et al. [35] suggested a three-factor authentication protocol with chaotic mapping; however, the attacker can launch a replay attack because their scheme lacks a timestamp mechanism, and when insiders obtain registration information and the smartcard, they can recover some secret information and launch a user impersonation attack correspondingly. Li et al. [36] suggested an enhanced scheme with chaotic mapping to overcome the shortcomings in the previous scheme. Unfortunately, we point out that Li et al.'s solution is not appropriate in practice because, in their architecture, the user is capable of communicating directly with the sensor without having to go through a gateway, which shows that the communication distance is too far and that the signal transmission needs to consume more energy, resulting in the rapid depletion of the scanty energy of the sensor. Over the past few years, several enhanced authentication schemes [37–39] have been devised to eliminate the security weaknesses of previous protocols and to improve their efficiency using chaotic mapping in recent years. These schemes provide better security features compared to [10,27–30], but we note that none of them can defend against a sensor node physical impersonation attack.

Because sensors in the current DWSN are still at risk of being captured and physically impersonated by attackers, a new technique called PUF is being used in sensor nodes to improve the security of WSN authentication protocols. Recently, Shao et al. [40] put forward a mutual anonymous authentication protocol using PUF and a fuzzy extractor to thwart a desynchronization attack and privileged-insider attack for a wireless medical sensor network environment. In their scheme, both the user and the sensor use PUF to negotiate a session key to secure real-time data transmission between them. However, their scheme is not resistant to a desynchronization attack, and it is expensive to deploy because PUF is used on both the user and sensor sides. To resolve the faultiness of physical-layer security and over-centralized problem of the wireless medical sensor network, Wang et al. [41] devised a lightweight authentication protocol using PUF and blockchain technology with dynamic identity updates. Although this solution successfully addressed the physical-layer security of the sensor, all three participants in the authentication process needed to save many challenge response pairs in advance, which undoubtedly took up plenty of storage space for each of them. Lee et al. [42] presented a three-factor anonymous authentication scheme with PUF to ensure the secure communication of a wireless medical sensor network. It is possible for Lee et al.'s protocol to eliminate a sensor node capture attack within their protocol; however, the challenge response pairs saved in the gateway note are not updated during the authentication process, which exposes their scheme to potential risks such as an insider attack. In [43], a multifactor authentication scheme utilized PUF for an IoT-enabled WSN to provide a solution for accessing remote sensors through a base station. Recently, to address security shortcomings in three different schemes, Tyagi et al. [44] suggested an authentication scheme using PUF and ECC. However, we discovered that Tyagi et al.'s solution did not renew the challenge response pair as Lee et al.'s scheme [42], and the sensors directly communicate with the user as the scheme [36]. Although their scheme may protect against a sensor node physical impersonation attack, the high computation cost and communication cost or inner design flaws make them impractical in deployment.

1.2. Research Motivation and Contribution

Due to the huge application potential of a DWSN in many scenarios, some authentication protocols applied to the DWSN environment still have security defects, so it is extremely necessary to design authentication protocols with high security that are suitable for the DWSN environment. On the one hand, due to the scant energy and computation capability of wireless sensors, traditional network security technologies cannot be directly employed in a DWSN; thus, an authentication protocol for a DWSN should be designed to be efficient and lightweight. On the other hand, the data collected and transmitted by wireless sensors are frequently sensitive and can even lead to serious problems such as privacy disclosure and personal security, so there is a higher demand for security. In addition, compared to other public key cryptography systems such as ECC, Chebyshev chaotic mapping not only reduces computation cost on a wireless sensor with limited resources but also improves computation efficiency of the authentication scheme while maintaining higher security. In particular, sensor nodes are easily captured by attackers to launch a physical impersonation attack, so an authentication protocol must be able to defend against a physical impersonation attack. To solve these problems, we propose a DWSN anonymous authentication scheme using PUF and Chebyshev chaotic mapping.

The following are the contributions of this paper:

1. We put forward an anonymous user authentication scheme for a DWSN utilizing PUF, Chebyshev chaotic mapping, and two factors, i.e., password and smartcard. Our scheme uses PUF only on sensor nodes to thwart a physical impersonation attack, and there is no need to prepare many challenge response pairs in advance. The challenge-response information of the sensor node is also not fixed but varies during each authentication process to guarantee the sensor node's physical security, and this does not require a special additional phase. In addition, we use the public key cryptography system Chebyshev chaotic mapping, which can not only prevent the

guessing attacks caused by the simple use of the hash function to generate the shared session key but can also ensure the same security with only one-third of the operation cost compared with an ECC.
2. We demonstrate the security of our scheme by using the BAN logic and heuristic analysis to demonstrate that it not only achieves secure session key negotiation and mutual authentication but also has the ability of preventing various known attacks while possessing the desired security features.
3. We analyze the performance by comparing our protocol with that of state-of-the-art relevant protocols to indicate that our protocol produces a better trade-off between efficiency and security.

2. Preliminaries

2.1. Chebyshev Chaotic Mapping

Let p and t be variables, and $p \in Z^+$, $t \in [-1, 1]$. The definition of p degree Chebyshev polynomial is as follows: $T_p(t)$: $[-1,1] \to [-1, 1]$, $T_p(t) = cos(parccos(t))$ [45]. When $p \geq 2$, the equivalent iterative relation is $T_p\ (t) = 2\ t\ T_{p-1}(t) - T_{p-2}(t)$, where $T_1(t) = t$ and $T_0(t) = 1$. Chebyshev polynomial satisfies the following semigroup property: $T_q(T_p(t)) = T_{qp}(t) = T_{pq}(t) = T_p(T_q(t))$, where q and $p \in Z^+$. When $p > 1$, the Chebyshev polynomial is also called the Chebyshev chaotic mapping.

For example, we set $p = 0, 1, 2, \ldots$, and $t = 0.3$; thus, $T_0(t) = 1$, $T_1(t) = 0.3$, $T_2(t) = 2tT_1(t) - T_0(t) = -0.82$, $T_3(t) = -0.792$, $T_4(t) = 0.3448$, $T_5(t) = 0.99888$, $T_6(t) = 0.2545$, and $T_6(t) = T_3(T_2(t)) = T_2(T_3(t)) = 0.2545$. By repeating this process, a series of values can be obtained that satisfy the semigroup property, and as the number of iterations increases, the output will exhibit complex and unpredictable characteristics.

In 2008, Zhang [46] proved that the Chebyshev polynomial still satisfies the semigroup property if the variable t is extended to the interval $(-\infty, +\infty)$. The extended Chebyshev polynomial is described as $T_p\ (t) = 2tT_{p-1}(t) - T_{p-2}(t)$ mod P, where P is a large prime and $t \in (-\infty, +\infty)$. For convenience, mod P is left out in the subsequent subsections. The security of the extended Chebyshev polynomial is mainly based on the following two mathematical problems as follows:

Discrete Logarithm Problem (DLP): Given a, $b = T_r(a)$, P, and $a \in (-\infty,+\infty)$, find r in polynomial time such that $b \equiv T_r(a)$ is infeasible.

Diffie–Hellman Problem (DHP): Given a, $T_r(a)$, $T_s(a)$, P, and $a \in (-\infty,+\infty)$, find b in polynomial time such that $b \equiv T_{rs}(a)$ is infeasible.

2.2. Physically Unclonable Function

A physically unclonable function (PUF) is a function that uses structured differences within a physical circuit so that any input challenge outputs a unique and unpredictable response [47]. A PUF's output response is based on the intrinsic properties of the physical system, so each PUF is unique, unpredictable, and difficult to replicate or simulate. The PUF can also realize several traditional public key encryption functions while reducing the computation and communication overhead. The PUF is embedded as the basic unit in the computing device, which enhances the security of the protocol, and the computing time can be negligible. The PUF can be expressed as a functional relationship between the input challenge C and the output response R, i.e., $R = PUF(C)$.

2.3. Adversary Model

To facilitate the reader's comprehension of the cryptanalysis of our proposal in Section 4, an adversary model depicting the attacker's capabilities is presented here according to the relevant literature.

1. The attacker can completely manipulate the public channel; that is, the attacker can intercept, block, tamper, and retransmit the message on the public channel [48,49].
2. The attacker can draw out the secret parameters on the smartcard [50].
3. To facilitate memory, the identity and password set by the user often have low entropy, so the attacker can conduct an offline guessing attack on the user's identity and password simultaneously by enumeration [24,51,52].
4. The lengths of the random numbers and keys chosen by each communicating entity are large enough that an attacker cannot successfully guess them in polynomial time [53].
5. When considering an insider attack, insiders can derive the registration message sent by the user during the registration phase [54,55].

2.4. Security Requirements

In light of the literature [48,53], an efficient and robust DWSN user authentication protocol should meet the security requirements as follows.

1. Provide N-factor security: For an N-factor (password, smartcard, biometric information, etc.) authentication protocol for the DWSN, even if an attacker obtains $N - 1$ factors, the attack cannot log into the system.
2. Defense against known attacks: The DWSN authentication protocol should be robust enough to defend against known attacks like an impersonation attack, an insider attack, a temporary information leakage attack, and a replay attack.
3. Provide forward secrecy: If the master key of the system is leaked, an attacker should either be unable to recover the previous session keys or be unable to calculate future session keys.
4. Prevent a sensor node capture attack: If an attacker captures a sensor node, other sensor nodes are not affected.
5. User anonymity: The attacker cannot disclose the real identities of users.
6. Mutual authentication and key agreement: Mutual authentication between the sensor and the user is achieved, and a shared session key is negotiated.

3. Our Proposed Scheme

In this section, we suggest a two-factor (password, smartcard) authentication protocol for the DWSN. Our scheme improves security and efficiency mainly in three aspects:

1. We use PUF to thwart a physical impersonation attack and sensor node capture attack.
2. Because it is imperative that the public key algorithm is used to improve the security of the protocol [24], we adopt the Chebyshev chaotic mapping algorithm, which is superior to other public key algorithms in terms of efficiency, to improve efficiency and provide forward secrecy.
3. We utilize a fuzzy verifier mechanism to eliminate an offline guessing attack caused by the loss/stolen smartcard being acquired by attackers.

Our solution consists of five phases: system setup, user registration, sensor node registration, login and authentication, and password update.

The meanings of the symbols used in this article are listed in Table 1.

Table 1. The meaning of notations.

Notation	Meaning
GW_i	The ith gateway node
U_i	ith user
S_j	jth sensor node
ID_i	U_i's identity
PW_i	U_i's password
SID_j	S_j's identity
K_{Gi}	GW_i's master key
K_j	S_j's secret password key
$h()$	A secure one-way hash function
T_i	Timestamp, $i = 1, 2, \ldots$.
$\|\|$	Concatenation
$\oplus$	Bitwise XOR operation
$\rightarrow$	The public channel

3.1. System Setup

The ith gateway node GW_i selects the master key K_{Gi}, a large prime number α_i, a Chebyshev polynomial parameter $\beta_i \in (-\infty,+\infty)$, calculates $G_P = T_{KGi}(\beta_i)$, and stores $\{K_{Gi}, \alpha_i\}$ secretly and publishes $\{G_P, \beta_i\}$.

3.2. User Registration

1. U_i sets the identity ID_i and password PW_i and then delivers a registration request message $\{ID_i\}$ to the GW_i via a secure channel.
2. On receiving the message, GW_i checks whether ID_i is in the database. If ID_i already exists, GW_i aborts the registration. Otherwise, it stores ID_i in the database and selects random numbers x and R_g, calculates $DID_i = h(ID_i \| R_g)$, $UID_i = DID_i \oplus h(x \| K_{Gi})$, $P_i = h(UID_i \| K_{Gi})$, stores $\{P_i, x\}$ into the database, and stores $\{UID_i, DID_i, h(), \beta_i\}$ into the smartcard. Finally, GW_i delivers the card to U_i through a secure channel.
3. After receiving the smartcard, the user chooses a random number r and calculates $A_i = h(PW_i \| r)$, selects $\delta \in [2^8, 2^{10}]$, calculates $R_i = r \oplus h(ID_i \| PW_i) \bmod \delta$, $H_i = DID_i \oplus h(PW_i \| ID_i \| r)$, $L_i = UID_i \oplus h(ID_i \| A_i)$, $V_i = h(A_i \| ID_i)$, replaces $\{UID_i, DID_i\}$ with $\{H_i, L_i\}$ in the smartcard, and keeps (R_i, V_i, δ) in the smartcard.

3.3. Sensor Node Registration

1. S_j chooses the identity SID_j and a random number R_j, calculates $PR_j = h(SID_j \| R_j)$, and sends the registration request information $\{SID_j, PR_j\}$ to the GW_i.
2. After receiving $\{SID_j, PR_j\}$, GW_i calculates $KS_j = h(PR_j \| K_{Gi})$, $P_j = h(SID_j \| K_{Gi})$, stores $\{P_j, PR_j\}$ in the database, and then transmits $\{KS_j, C_s\}$ to S_j via a secure channel, where C_s is a challenge.
3. On receiving $\{KS_j, C_s\}$, S_j computes $R_s = PUF(C_s)$, sends to GW_i, and stores $\{PR_j, KS_j\}$ in memory.
4. GW_i stores $\{C_s, R_s\}$ in the database.

3.4. Login and Authentication

1. U_i inserts the smartcard, inputs ID_i and PW_i, calculates $r^* = R_i \oplus h(ID_i \| PW_i) \bmod \delta$, $A_i^* = h(PW_i \| r^*)$, $V_i^* = h(A_i^* \| ID_i)$, and verifies that $V_i^* == V_i$ holds. If not, U_i terminates this session. Otherwise, U_i selects random number a and timestamp T_1, computes $A_1 = T_a(\beta_i)$, $DID_i = H_i \oplus h(PW_i \| ID_i \| r^*)$, $UID_i = L_i \oplus h(ID_i \| A_i^*)$, $V_1 = h(DID_i \| UID_i \| A_1 \| T_1)$, $M_1 = (UID_i \| SID_j \| V_1) \oplus T_a(G_P)$, and transmits a login request $\{A_1, M_1, T_1\}$ to GW_i.

2. On receiving the user's login request, GW_i uses the current timestamp T_1' to verify $|T_1' - T_1| \leq \Delta T$, decrypts M_1 by computing $M_1 \oplus T_{KGi}(A_1)$ to obtain UID_i, SID_j, V_1, calculates $P_i = h(UID_i || K_{Gi})$, $P_j = h(SID_j || K_{Gi})$, retrieves the secret value x according to P_i, retrieves $\{C_s, R_s, PR_j\}$ according to P_j, calculates $KS_j = h(PR_j || K_{Gi})$, $DID_i = UID_i \oplus h(x || K_{Gi})$, $V_1' = h(DID_i || UID_i || A_1 || T_1)$, and verifies whether $V_1' == V_1$ holds. If the stipulation is false, GW_i aborts the session; otherwise, GW_i chooses random number b and timestamp T_2, $M_2 = (h(b || DID_i) || C_s) \oplus h(KS_j || SID_j)$, $V_2 = h(SID_j || h(b || DID_i) || A_1 || R_s || T_2)$, and finally delivers $\{M_2, A_1, V_2, T_2\}$ to S_j.
3. On receiving the incoming message, S_j verifies $|T_2' - T_2| \leq \Delta T$ with the current timestamp T_2' and calculates $(h(b || DID_i)' || C_s') = M_2 \oplus h(KS_j || SID_j)$, $R_s' = PUF(C_s')$, $V_2' = h(SID_j || h(b || DID_i)' || A_1 || R_s || T_2)$, and verifies whether $V_2' == V_2$ holds. If not, S_j ends the session; otherwise, S_j selects random number c and timestamp T_3, computes $C_s^{new} = h(C_s || h(b || DID_i)')$, $R_s^{new} = PUF(C_s^{new})$, $A_2 = T_c(y)$, session key $SK_{su} = h(h(b || DID_i)' || A_1 || A_2 || T_c(A_1))$, $V_3 = h(R_s^{new} || KS_j || h(b || DID_i)' || A_2 || T_3)$, $L_j = R_s^{new} \oplus KS_j$, $M_3 = h(A_1 || A_2 || SK_{su})$, and finally sends the message $\{A_2, L_j, V_3, M_3, T_3\}$ to GW_i.
4. On receiving the message, GW_i verifies that $|T_3' - T_3| \leq \Delta T$, where T_3' is the current timestamp, calculates $R_s^{new} = L_j \oplus KS_j$, $V_3' = h(R_s^{new} || KS_j || h(b || DID_i)' || A_2 || T_3)$, and determines whether V_3' and V_3 are equal. If not, GW_i ends the session. Otherwise, GW_i obtains the current timestamp T_4, and calculates $C_s^{new} = h(C_s || h(b || DID_i)')$, $M_4 = h(b || DID_i) \oplus h(DID_i || UID_i || T_4)$, $V_4 = h(M_3 || DID_i || T_4)$, replaces $\{P_j, C_s, R_s, PR_j\}$ with $\{P_j, C_s^{new}, R_s^{new}, PR_j\}$, and finally sends $\{A_2, M_4, V_4, T_4\}$ to U_i.
5. Upon receiving the message from GW_i, U_i uses the current timestamp T_4' to verify $|T_4' - T_4| \leq \Delta T$, calculates $h(b || DID_i)'' = M_4 \oplus h(DID_i || UID_i || T_4)$, $SK_{us} = h(h(b || DID_i)'' || A_1 || A_2 || T_a(A_2))$, $V_4' = h(h(A_1 || A_2 || SK_{us}) || DID_i || T_4)$, and compares $V_{4'}$ and V_4 for equality. If V_4' and V_4 are equal, U_i accepts SK_{us} as the session key with S_j; otherwise, U_i terminates the session.

This phase is illustrated in Figure 2.

3.5. Password Update

If the user intends to renew the password, the subsequent steps are necessary.

1. U_i inserts the smartcard into the card reader and types his ID_i and password PW_i. The smartcard calculates $r = R_i \oplus h(ID_i || PW_i) \bmod \delta$, $A_i = h(PW_i || r)$, $DID_i = H_i \oplus h(PW_i || ID_i || r)$, $UID_i = L_i \oplus h(ID_i || A^*)$, $V_i' = h(A_i || ID_i)$, and compares V_i' and V_i for equality. If the two are equal, the smartcard executes the next step; otherwise, the card ends this session.
2. U_i inputs his ID_i and new password PW_i^{new}, calculates $A_i^{new} = h(PW_i^{new} || r)$, $R_i^{new} = r \oplus h(ID_i || PW_i^{new}) \bmod \delta$, $H_i^{new} = DID_i \oplus h(PW_i^{new} || ID_i || r)$, $L_i^{new} = UID_i \oplus h(ID_i || A_i^{new})$, and $V_i^{new} = h(A_i^{new} || ID_i)$.
3. U_i replaces $\{H_i, L_i, R_i, V_i\}$ with $\{H_i^{new}, L_i^{new}, R_i^{new}, V_i^{new}\}$ on the card.

U_i	GW_i	S_j
Inserts the smartcard Inputs ID_i, PW_i $r^* = R_i \oplus h(ID_i \| PW_i) \bmod \delta$ $A_i^* = h(PW_i \| r^*)$ $V_i^* = h(A_i^* \| ID_i)$ Checks $V_i^* ? = V_i$ Selects a and T_1 $A_1 = T_a(\beta_i)$ $DID_i = H_i \oplus h(PW_i \| ID_i \| r^*)$ $UID_i = L_i \oplus h(ID_i \| A_i^*)$ $V_1 = h(DID_i \| UID_i \| A_1 \| T_1)$ $M_1 = (UID_i \| SID_j \| V_1) \oplus T_a(G_P)$ $\{A_1, M_1, T_1\} \longrightarrow$		
	Checks $\mid T_1' - T_1 \mid \leq \Delta T$ $UID_i \| SID_j \| V_1 = M_1 \oplus T_{KGi}(A_1)$ $P_i = h(UID_i \| K_{Gi})$ $P_j = h(SID_j \| K_{Gi})$ Retrieves x Retrieves $\{C_s, R_s, PR_j\}$ $KS_j = h(PR_j \| K_{Gi})$ $DID_i = UID_i \oplus h(x \| K_{Gi})$ $V_1' = h(DID_i \| UID_i \| A_1 \| T_1)$ Checks $V_1' ? = V_1$ Selects b and T_2 $M_2 = (h(b \| DID_i) \| C_s) \oplus h(KS_j \| SID_j)$ $V_2 = h(SID_j \| h(b \| DID_i) \| A_1 \| R_s \| T_2)$ $\{M_2, A_1, V_2, T_2\} \longrightarrow$	
		Checks $\mid T_2' - T_2 \mid \leq \Delta T$ $(h(b \| DID_i)' \| C_s') = M_2 \oplus h(KS_j \| SID_j)$ $R_s' = PUF(C_s')$ $V_2' = h(SID_j \| h(b \| DID_i)' \| A_1 \| R_s \| T_2)$ Checks $V_2' ? = V_2$ Selects c and T_3 $C_s^{new} = h(C_s \| h(b \| DID_i)')$ $R_s^{new} = PUF(C_s^{new})$ $A_2 = T_c(\beta_i)$ $SK_{su} = h(h(b \| DID_i)' \| A_1 \| A_2 \| T_c(A_1))$ $V_3 = h(R_s^{new} \| KS_j \| h(b \| DID_i)' \| A_2 \| T_3)$ $L_j = R_s^{new} \oplus R_s'$ $M_3 = h(A_1 \| A_2 \| SK_{su})$ $\longleftarrow \{A_2, L_j, V_3, M_3, T_3\}$
	Checks $\mid T_3' - T_3 \mid \leq \Delta T$ $R_s^{new} = L_j \oplus R_s$ $V_3' = h(KS_j \| h(b \| DID_i) \| A_2 \| T_3)$ Checks $V_3' ? = V_3$ Selects T_4 $C_s^{new} = h(C_s \| h(b \| DID_i)')$ $M_4 = h(b \| DID_i) \oplus h(DID_i \| UID_i \| T_4)$ $V_4 = h(M_3 \| DID_i \| T_4)$ replaces $\{P_j, C_s, R_s, PR_j\}$ with $\{P_j, C_s^{new}, R_s^{new}, PR_j\}$ $\longleftarrow \{A_2, M_4, V_4, T_4\}$	
Checks $\mid T_4' - T_4 \mid \leq \Delta T$ $h(b \| DID_i)'' = M_4 \oplus h(DID_i \| UID_i \| T_4)$ $SK_{us} = h(h(b \| DID_i)'' \| A_1 \| A_2 \| T_a(A_2))$ $V_4 = h(h(A_1 \| A_2 \| SK_{us}) \| DID_i \| T_4)$ Checks $V_4' ? = V_4$ Accepts SK_{us}		

Figure 2. The login and authentication phase.

4. Security Analysis

In this section, we first employ BAN (Burrows_Abadi_Needham) logic [48] to demonstrate the security of the proposal, and then, we perform a heuristic analysis to show that the proposal can thwart known attacks and satisfies the security requirements of DWSNs.

4.1. Security Proof

BAN logic is a belief-based modal logic that has been widely used in the formal analysis of key agreement security of cryptographic authentication protocols. We employ the BAN logic to prove the security property of mutual authentication and key agreement in the proposal. To save space, we use the BAN symbols and rules in [48] to perform the security proof of the proposal.

We define the following goals of our protocol:

Goal 1: $U_i \mid\equiv S_j \mid\equiv (U_i \overset{SK}{\leftrightarrow} S_j)$

Goal 2: $U_i \mid\equiv (U_i \overset{SK}{\leftrightarrow} S_j)$

Goal 3: $S_j \mid\equiv U_i \mid\equiv (U_i \overset{SK}{\leftrightarrow} S_j)$

Goal 4: $S_j \mid\equiv (U_i \overset{SK}{\leftrightarrow} S_j)$

The idealized form of the messages transmitted by each communication participant during the authentication process is described as below:

Msg1: $U_i \rightarrow GW_i$: $<A_1, M_1, T_1>_{DIDi}$

Msg2: $GW_i \rightarrow S_j$: $<h(b \mid\mid DID_i), A_1, V_2, T_2>_{KSj}$

Msg3: $S_j \rightarrow GW_i$: $<A_2, L_j, V_3, M_3, T_3>_{KSj}$

Msg4: $GW_i \rightarrow U_i$: $<A_2, h(b \mid\mid DID_i), V_5, T_4>_{UIDi}$

According to the initial state of the proposal, we make the following assumptions:

1. H_1: $U_i \mid\equiv \#(T_4)$
2. H_2: $GW_i \mid\equiv \#(T_1)$
3. H_3: $S_j \mid\equiv \#(T_2)$
4. H_4: $GW_i \mid\equiv \#(T_3)$
5. H_5: $GW_i \mid\equiv GW_i \overset{DID_i}{\leftrightarrow} U_i$
6. H_6: $S_j \mid\equiv GW_i \overset{KS_j}{\leftrightarrow} S_j$
7. H_7: $GW \mid\equiv GW_i \overset{KS_j}{\leftrightarrow} S_j$
8. H_8: $U_i \mid\equiv S_j \mid\equiv U_i \overset{SK}{\leftrightarrow} S_j$
9. H_9: $U_i \mid\equiv U_i \overset{UID_i}{\leftrightarrow} GW_i$
10. H_{10}: $S_j \mid\equiv U_i \mid\equiv U_i \overset{SK}{\leftrightarrow} S_j$

The validity of the proposal on the basis of the above definition and the BAN logic rules is carried out as follows.

From *Msg1*, we obtain S_1:

$$GW_i \triangleleft <A_1, M_1, T_1>_{DIDi}$$

Thus, according to S_1, H_5, and the message meaning rule, we obtain S_2:

$$GW_i \mid\equiv U_i \mid\sim <UID_i, DID_i, A_1, T_1>$$

According to S_2, H_2, and the freshness-conjuncatenation rule, we obtain S_3:

$$GW_i \mid\equiv \# <UID_i, DID_i, A_1, T_1>$$

According to S_2, S_3, and the brief rule, we obtain S_4:

$$GW_i \mid \equiv U_i \mid \equiv <UID_i, DID_i, A_1, T_1>$$

From *Msg2*, we obtain S_5:

$$S_j \triangleleft <h(b \mid\mid DID_i), A_1, V_2, T_2>_{KSj}$$

According to S_5, H_6, and the message meaning rule, we obtain S_6:

$$S_j \mid \equiv GW_i \mid \sim <h(b \mid\mid DID_i), A_1, V_2, T_2>$$

According to S_6, H_3, and the freshness-conjuncatenation rule, we obtain S_7:

$$S_j \mid \equiv \# <h(b \mid\mid DID_i), A_1, V_2, T_2>$$

According to S_6, S_7, and the brief rule, we obtain S_8:

$$S_j \mid \equiv GW_i \mid \equiv <h(b \mid\mid DID_i), A_1, V_2, T_2>$$

From *Msg3*, we obtain S_9:

$$GW_i \triangleleft <A_2, L_j, V_3, M_3, T_3>_{KSj}$$

According to S_9, H_7, and the message meaning rule, we obtain S_{10}:

$$GW_i \mid \equiv S_j \mid \sim <A_2, L_j, V_3, M_3, T_3>$$

According to S_{10}, H_4, and the freshness-conjuncatenation rule, we obtain S_{11}:

$$GW_i \mid \equiv \# <A_2, L_j, V_3, M_3, T_3>$$

According to S_{10}, S_{11}, and the brief rule, we obtain S_{12}:

$$GW_i \mid \equiv S_j \mid \equiv <A_2, L_j, V_3, M_3, T_3>$$

From *Msg4*, we obtain S_{13}:

$$U_i \triangleleft <A_2, h(b \mid\mid DID_i), V_5, T_4>_{UIDi}$$

According to S_{13}, H_9, and the message meaning rule, we obtain S_{14}:

$$U_i \mid \equiv GW_i \mid \sim <A_2, h(b \mid\mid DID_i), V_5, T_4>$$

According to S_{14}, H_1, and the freshness-conjuncatenation rule, we obtain S_{15}:

$$U_i \mid \equiv \# <A_2, h(b \mid\mid DID_i), V_5, T_4>$$

According to S_{14}, S_{15}, and the brief rule, we obtain S_{16}:

$$U_i \mid \equiv GW_i \mid \equiv <h(b \mid\mid DID_i), A_1, V_2, T_2>$$

Because $SK = h(h(b \mid\mid DID_i) \mid\mid A_1 \mid\mid A_2 \mid\mid T_{a1}(A_2))$, and according to S_{12} and S_{16}, we obtain S_{17}:

$$U_i| \equiv S_j| \equiv (U_i \overset{SK}{\leftrightarrow} S_j)\ (Goal\ 1)$$

According to S_{17}, H_8, and the Jurisdiction rule, we obtain S_{18}:

$$U_i| \equiv (U_i \overset{SK}{\leftrightarrow} S_j)\ (Goal\ 2)$$

According to S_4 and S_8 and because $SK = h(h(b||DID_i)||A_1||A_2||T_{a1}(A_2))$, we obtain S_{19}:

$$S_j| \equiv U_i| \equiv (U_i \overset{SK}{\leftrightarrow} S_j)\ (Goal\ 3)$$

Finally, according to S_{19}, H_{10}, and the Jurisdiction rule, we obtain S_{20}:

$$S_j| \equiv (U_i \overset{SK}{\leftrightarrow} S_j)\ (Goal\ 4)$$

Therefore, Goals 1–4 have been proven successfully, and it means that, in the proposal, U_i and S_j not only authenticate mutually but also generate a session key between them.

4.2. Security Analysis

We analyze the security of our scheme and finally compare it with related protocols with regard to security properties.

1. *Smartcard loss attack*: Assume that the attacker derives the smartcard of the legitimate user and retrieves the secret data $\{H_i, L_i, R_i, V_i, h(), \delta, \beta_i\}$ on the card through the side channel analysis technique [50], where $H_i = DID_i \oplus h(PW_i||ID_i||r)$, $L_i = UID_i \oplus h(ID_i||A_i)$, $V_i = h(A_i||ID_i)$, and $A_i = h(PW_i||r)$, $R_i = r \oplus h(ID_i||PW_i)$ mod δ. If the attacker intends to guess ID_i and PW_i through H_i and L_i because the attacker knows nothing about the secret parameter r of the user U_i and the secret parameters (x, R_g) and the master key K_{Gi} of the GW_i, the attack will not succeed. In addition, if the attacker intends to guess ID_i and PW_i through V_i, first, r must be found by calc unnecessary ulating $r = R_i \oplus h(ID_i||PW_i)$ mod δ. However, due to the protection of the fuzzy verifier technique, the probability of the attacker's guessing success is very trivial and can be ignored [24]. Therefore, our scheme can defend against a smartcard loss attack.
2. *N-factor security*: Our protocol is a two-factor (password, smartcard) scheme; thus, $N = 2$. On the one hand, if the attacker only acquires the password, clearly, the attacker cannot log in to the system. On the other hand, if the attacker only obtains the smartcard, although the attacker can extract the secret parameters on the smartcard, as analyzed in item 1 of Section 4.2, the attacker still cannot guess the user's password and cannot log into the system. Thus, our scheme can provide N-factor security.
3. *Insider attack*: Suppose the insider obtains the user's registration request $\{ID_i\}$, temporarily derives the user's smartcard, retrieves the secret parameters $\{H_i, L_i, R_i, V_i, h(), \delta, \beta_i\}$ on the card through a side channel analysis attack, and then prepares to guess the user's password PW_i through the parameters (H_i, L_i, R_i, V_i), as analyzed in item 1 of Section 4.2, due to the protection of the fuzzy verifier mechanism, the attacker will fail to acquire r so that the correct PW_i cannot be guessed, and finally, the two important parameters (DID_i, UID_i) of the user cannot be disclosed. In addition, we suppose an insider has obtained the sensor information $\{P_j, C_s, R_s, PR_j\}$ stored in GW_i and eavesdrops on the interaction messages $\{M_2, A_1, V_2, T_2\}$ and $\{A_2, L_j, V_3, M_3, T_3\}$ between GW_i and the sensor. Although the attacker can obtain the updated PUF response by computing $R_s^{new} = L_j \oplus R_s$, because the calculation of the session key involves parameters A_1 and A_2 and the attacker cannot break the DLP and DHP problems, the attacker cannot calculate the session key based on $h(h(b||DID_i)'||A_1||A_2||T_c(A_1))$.

   Therefore, our protocol can protect against an insider attack.

4. *Forward secrecy and backward secrecy*: In our protocol, if an attacker acquires U_i's smartcard, the attacker cannot launch a successful guessing attack on ID_i and PW_i, so our protocol does not suffer from the forward secrecy issue as in Kwon et al.'s scheme. On the other hand, even if the master key K_{Gi} of the GW_i is disclosed to the attacker, because the session key $SK = h(h(b \| DID_i)' \| A_1 \| A_2 \| T_c(A_1))$ and the attacker cannot obtain PR_j, the attacker is incapable of calculating KS_j; as a result, $h(b \| DID_i)$ cannot be obtained by calculating $M_2 \oplus h(KS_j \| SID_j)$. More importantly, although the attacker can eavesdrop on the messages containing A_1 and A_2 in the public channel, the attacker still cannot calculate SK because calculating $T_c(A_1)$ is equivalent to solving the DLP problem and the DHP problem. In summary, our scheme can provide forward and backward secrecy for session keys.
5. *Mutual authentication*: In some schemes, like Kwon et al.'s protocol [15], the mutual authentication among U_i, GW_i, and S_j relies on the single secret parameter HID_i. Once the attacker acquires the parameter HID_i, the attacker can impersonate a legal user to deliver a valid login request to GW_i and pass the authentication of GW_i and S_j and, finally, generate a shared session key with S_j. In our scheme, the authentication of GW_i to U_i depends on these secret parameters (α_i, P_i, x, K_{Gi}); the mutual authentication of GW_i and S_j depends on the two parameters of KS_j and SID_j, and SID_j transmitted on the open channel is not in clear text; the authentication of U_i to GW_i relies on two secret parameters of UID_i and DID_i. It can be observed that the mutual authentication among communication entities in our scheme does not depend on a single parameter but on multiple sets of mutually independent secret parameters. This makes it extremely difficult for attackers to spoof messages to deceive communication entities and pass their verification. Thus, our scheme achieves mutual authentication among the three communication participants U_i, GW_i, and S_j.
6. *Desynchronization attack*: Since our scheme does not need to synchronously update the related information between GW_i and the user's smartcard in each authentication process to keep user anonymity and to prevent the attacker from tracing, our scheme can defend against a desynchronization attack.
7. *Replay attack*: In our scheme, the messages sent by U_i, GW_i, and S_j all contain timestamps, and the timestamps are protected using a hash function in V_i ($i = 1, 2, 3, 4$). Upon receiving the message, the receiver must not only check the freshness of the timestamps but must also check the corresponding hash value V_i. If the attacker intends to conduct a replay attack by intercepting the message and changing the timestamp and retransmitting the message to the receiver, it will cause the V_i calculated by the hash function at the receiver's side using the timestamp as a parameter to be inconsistent with the received V_i, and the session will be ended. Thus, our scheme can prevent a replay attack.
8. *Sensor node capture Attack*: If the attacker captures the sensor node S_j, the attacker can read the key KS_j from the sensor's memory and restore $h(b \| DID_i)$ of the three parameters needed to reveal the session key based on the eavesdropped messages $\{M_2, A_1, V_2, T_2\}$ and $\{A_2, L_j, V_3, M_3, T_3\}$. Because the session key $SK = h(h(b \| DID_i)'' \| A_1 \| A_2 \| T_a(A_2))$, the attacker is still unable to reveal the session key as the attacker also faces both the DLP problem and the DHP problem. In addition, due to the features of PUF, the attacker cannot produce R_s or R_s^{new} from C_s or C_s^{new}, which is necessary to generate the valid authenticators V_2 and V_3, respectively. In this way, even if the sensor S_j is captured by an attacker, it will not affect the secure communication between other sensor nodes and U_i. Thus, our protocol can defend against a sensor node capture attack.

9. *Man-in-the-middle attack*: Assuming the attacker blocks the user's login request message $\{A_1, M_1, T_1\}$, because he does not obtain $\{K_{Gi}, \alpha_i\}$, he or she cannot decrypt M_1 to obtain relevant information (UID_i, SID_j, V_1). In addition, if the attacker obtains $\{K_{Gi}, \alpha_i\}$ by some means, but because $V_1 = h(DID_i || UID_i || A_1 || T_1)$ and the attacker cannot obtain x, it is not feasible to fake V_1. Hence, our proposal can thwart a man-in-the-middle attack.
10. *User anonymity*: Suppose the attacker eavesdrops on four messages, $\{A_1, M_1, T_1\}$, $\{M_2, A_1, V_2, T_2\}$, $\{A_2, L_j, V_3, M_3, T_3\}$, and $\{A_2, M_4, V_4, T_4\}$, in the login and authentication phase, since M_1 is ciphertext, other parameters are generated using random numbers (a, b, c), timestamps, and hash functions, and the message in each user login process is different. In addition, there is no user identity information that allows for the attacker to track the user according to these messages, and the attacker also cannot determine whether different login request messages are delivered by the same user. Thus, the proposal achieves user anonymity.
11. *User Impersonation Attack*: In the proposal, if the attacker is going to conduct a user impersonation attack to deceive GW_i, the attacker must first produce a valid login request message $\{A_1, M_1, T_1\}$. However, without knowledge of the user's ID_i, PW_i, and parameters (DID_i, UID_i), the attacker cannot produce a valid login request message. In addition, it has been pointed out in item 1 of Section 4.2 that, even if the user's smartcard is stolen by the attacker, the guessing attack on ID_i and PW_i will not be successful. It is also pointed out in item 2 of Section 4.2 that, even if the user's ID_i and smartcard are obtained by the attacker and the attacker starts guessing the password, he or she will fail due to the protection of the fuzzy verifier technique. Hence, the proposal can thwart a user impersonation attack.
12. *Physical impersonation attack*: This attack indicates that an attacker can imitate the sensor to send a fake message $\{A_2, L_j, V_3, M_3, T_3\}$ to GW_i and pass the validation of GW_i. However, if the attacker intends to recreate the same wireless sensor as the original wireless sensor with the PUF, the fake message $\{A_2, L_j, V_3, M_3, T_3\}$ generated by the attacker through the invalid PUF will be discriminated and rejected by the GW_i Hence, the proposed scheme can defend against a physical impersonation attack.
13. *DoS attack*: In our scheme, an attacker might send a previously valid message $\{A_1, M_1, T_1\}$ to GW_i repeatedly to consume the target's resources. If the attacker alters T_1 to T_1' so that $T_{ct} - T_1' \leq \Delta t$ is valid, where T_{ct} is the current time and Δt represents a very small time interval, although GW_i passes the verification of timestamp T_1', GW_i also calculates $V_1' = h(DID_i || UID_i || A_1 || T_1')$ according to T_1' and then determines whether $V_1' = V_1$ is valid. Obviously, since $V_1 = h(DID_i || UID_i || A_1 || T_1)$, $V_1' = h(DID_i || UID_i || A_1 || T_1')$, and $T_1' \neq T_1$ and the attacker does not know DID_i and UID_i, the attacker cannot forge V_1 to pass authentication. So $V_1' = V_1$ does not hold, and GW_i terminates the session. Similarly, if an attacker repeatedly sends messages $\{M_2, A_1, V_2, T_2\}$, $\{A_2, L_j, V_3, M_3, T_3\}$, and $\{A_2, M_4, V_4, T_4\}$ to the sensor, gateway, and user to launch a DoS (Denial of Service) attack, it will also be unsuccessful. The analysis process is similar to the above. Therefore, our scheme can prevent a DoS attack.
14. *Comparison of security features*: According to the above security analysis, we compare the proposal with state-of-the-art schemes [28,29,33,40,42–44] with respect to security features, and the result is as exhibited in Table 2, where "$\surd$" means that the attack can be thwarted or the security property can be satisfied, while "x" means that the attack cannot be resisted or the security property cannot be satisfied. It can be observed from Table 2 that the scheme [44] cannot prevent a physical impersonation attack, though it uses the PUF function on the user side. Although the scheme [40] uses the PUF

function on both the user side and sensor side, it is not resistant to a desynchronization attack. Furthermore, compared with other related schemes, our scheme can defend against more attacks and satisfy more security properties, while other schemes are subject to some security flaws, more or less.

Table 2. Comparison of security features.

Security Features	[28]	[29]	[33]	[40]	[42]	[43]	[44]	Ours
S1	√	√	√	×	×	√	√	√
S2	√	√	√	×	×	√	√	√
S3	√	√	√	√	√	√	√	√
S4	×	×	×	√	√	√	×	√
S5	√	√	√	×	×	√	×	√
S6	√	√	√	√	√	√	√	√
S7	×	√	√	√	√	√	√	√
S8	√	√	√	√	√	×	√	√
S9	√	×	√	√	√	√	√	√
S10	√	√	√	√	×	×	√	√
S11	√	√	√	√	×	×	√	√
S12	×	×	×	√	√	√	×	√
S13	√	√	√	√	√	√	√	√
S14	×	√	√	√	×	√	√	√

S1: Resist smartcard loss attack; S2: Resist user impersonation attack; S3: Resist *GW* impersonation attack; S4: Resist sensor node capture attack; S5: Resist desynchronization attack; S6: Provide forward secrecy; S7: Resist replay attack; S8: Resist insider attack; S9: Resist man-in-the-middle attack; S10: User anonymity; S11: Sensor node anonymity; S12: Resist physical impersonation attack; S13: Mutual authentication and key agreement; S14: Resist DoS attack.

When considering the influence of the external environment on the proposal, various states can be constructed, such as the user sends an authentication request, the gateway verifies the authenticity of the user's identity, the sensor verifies the authenticity of the gateway and the user, the gateway verifies the authenticity of the sensor's identity, the user verifies the authenticity of the gateway's identity, and then the Markov chain is established. If the external environment changes, such as an increase in network latency or an attacker attempts brute-force intercepted messages, the timestamp mechanism resolves these issues. Although this may affect the probability of transition, the future state depends only on the current state, not on past states and historical information, so the execution process of the proposal conforms to the Markovian effect and does not conform to the non-Markovian effect [56]. These are left for a future in-depth analysis.

5. Performance Analysis

In this section, we compare the performance of the proposal with state-of-the-art schemes [28,29,33,40,42–44] with respect to the login and authentication phase in four aspects: computation overhead, communication overhead, sensor throughput, and storage overhead.

5.1. Computation Overhead

For convenience, we use the running time of various cryptographic operations in the literature [34,35] as the benchmark to calculate the computation overhead of each scheme. Suppose that T_H, T_P, T_C, T_F, and T_S denote the execution times of a hash function, an elliptic curve point multiplication, a Chebyshev polynomial calculation, a Rep function of the fuzzy extractor, and the symmetric encryption/decryption, respectively, and their values are 0.5 ms, 63.08 ms, 21.02 ms, 63.08 ms, and8.7 ms, respectively. Since the XOR operation takes very little time, we ignore its time overhead. Table 2 shows the comparison results between the proposal and relevant protocols in terms of computation overhead. For ease of understanding, we show Table 3 as a graph in Figure 3.

Table 3. Comparison of computation overhead.

	[28]	[29]	[33]	[40]	[42]	[43]	[44]	Ours
U_i	$7T_H + 3T_P$	$6T_H + T_F + 2T_P + 2T_S$	$13T_H + T_F + 2T_P$	$13T_H + T_F$	$18T_H + T_F$	$9T_H$	$12T_H + T_F + 2T_P$	$9T_H + 3T_C$
GW_i	$9T_H + T_P$	$3T_H + 6T_S$	$10T_H + 2T_P$	$17T_H + T_F$	$22T_H$	$15T_H + 2T_S + 3T_F$	$8T_H$	$12T_H + T_C$
S_j	$8T_H + 2T_P$	$2T_H + 2T_P + 2T_S$	$6T_H$	$8T_H + T_F$	$12T_H + T_F$	$9T_H + T_F + T_S$	$6T_H + 2T_P$	$6T_H + 2T_C$
Total cost	$24T_H + 6T_P$	$11T_H + T_F + 4T_P + 10T_S$	$29T_H + T_F + 4T_P$	$38T_H + 3T_F$	$52T_H + 2T_F$	$33T_H + 4T_F + 3T_S$	$26T_H + T_F + 4T_P$	$27T_H + 6T_C$
Computation overhead (ms)	390.48	407.9	329.9	208.24	467.56	286.22	328.4	139.62

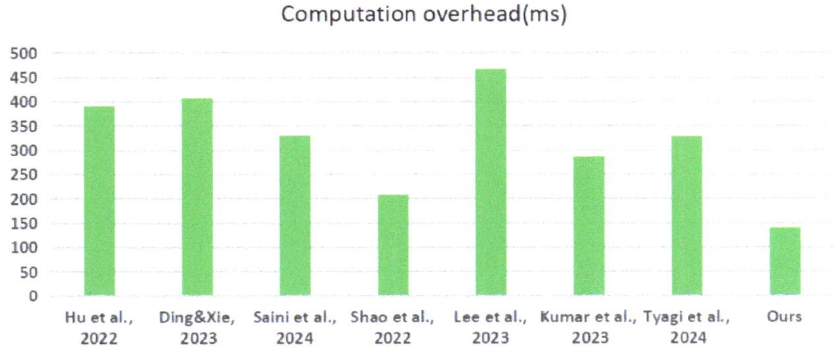

Figure 3. Comparison of computation overhead [28,29,33,40,42–44].

5.2. Communication Overhead

According to [34], we set the length of the random number, elliptic curve, hash value, Chebyshev polynomial, identity, timestamp, and encrypted block lengths to 128 bits, 320 bits, 160 bits, 128 bits, 32 bits, 32 bits, and 128 bits, respectively. Table 3 shows the comparison results of communication overhead between the proposal and relevant schemes [28,29,33,40,42–44]. Moreover, for the sake of understanding, we present Table 4 as a graph, as shown in Figure 4.

Table 4. Comparison of communication overhead.

	[28]	[29]	[33]	[40]	[42]	[43]	[44]	Ours
Communication overhead (bits)	3252	3456	1952	2752	2016	5120	2656	1952

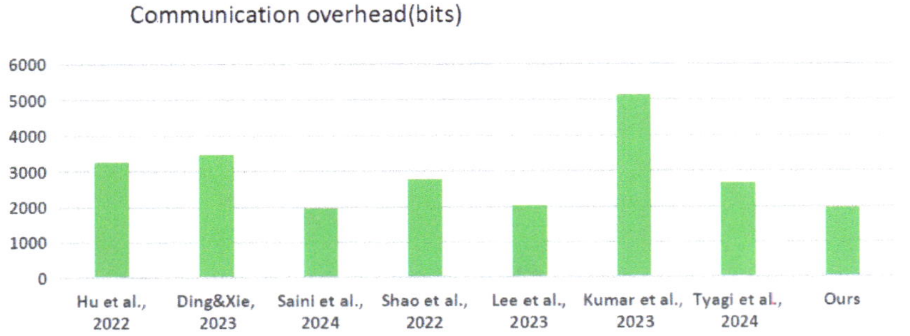

Figure 4. Comparison of communication overhead [28,29,33,40,42–44].

5.3. Sensor Throughput

Because wireless sensors are often deployed in unattended environments, it is difficult for users to replenish their energy in real time. A wireless sensor consumes a certain amount of energy to receive and send data, so its network throughput is closely related to its life cycle. Therefore, we analyze the network throughput to examine its impact on the life cycle of the sensor node. The comparison results of the sensor node throughput between the proposed scheme and the other schemes [28,29,33,40,42–44] are shown in Table 5 and Figure 5.

Table 5. Comparison of sensor node throughput.

	[28]	[29]	[33]	[40]	[42]	[43]	[44]	Ours
Receive	928	640	384	896	512	1024	1152	480
Send	852	896	352	512	192	864	960	480
Total (bits)	1780	1536	736	1408	704	1888	2112	960

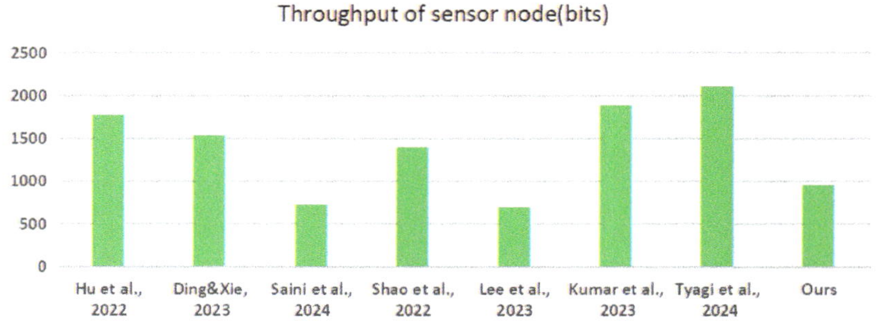

Figure 5. Comparison of sensor node throughput [28,29,33,40,42–44].

5.4. Storage Overhead

By comparing the proposal with state-of-the-art protocols [28,29,33,40,42–44] in terms of their own storage overhead for the three communication participants U_i, GW_i, and S_j, the results are illustrated in Table 6 and Figure 6.

Table 6. Comparison of storage overhead.

	[28]	[29]	[33]	[40]	[42]	[43]	[44]	Ours
Smartcard	544	736	960	832	640	2464	1728	746
Gateway	640	608	832	1312	896	2016	448	1204
Sensor	192	192	352	320	512	192	480	320
Total	1376	1536	2144	2464	2048	4672	2656	2270

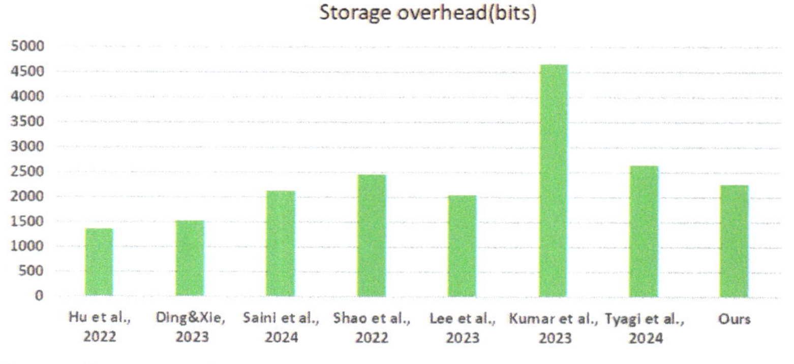

Figure 6. Comparison of storage overhead [28,29,33,40,42–44].

5.5. Comprehensive Analysis

From the performance comparison of the four aspects mentioned above, we can see that our scheme has favorable performance. From Table 3 and Figure 3, we can see that the proposal requires the least computation time of 139.62 ms. Compared with that of the other schemes, the computation overhead of our protocol has a significant advantage over that of the other schemes [28,29,33,40,42–44]. Furthermore, from Figures 4 and 5, we can see that our protocol and Saini et al.'s scheme [33] have the lowest communication overhead among all the protocols, our protocol is slightly higher than protocols [33,42] in terms of sensor throughput, and Figure 6 also shows that our protocol is slightly higher than protocols [28,29,33,42] but better than protocols [40,43,44] in terms of storage overhead. Although schemes [40,44] use PUF to ensure the security of authentication, it can be seen from Figure 3 to Figure 6 that they have no advantage in terms of computation overhead, communication overhead, sensor node throughput, and storage overhead compared with our scheme, and the computation cost of [42] is three times that of our scheme. Moreover, the computation overhead and communication overhead of [43] are almost 2.5 times greater than those of our scheme, and their storage overhead is 2 times greater than that of our scheme. In addition, as can be seen from Table 2, scheme [40] fails to avoid a smartcard loss attack and user impersonation attack. Both scheme [42] and scheme [43] cannot provide user anonymity and sensor node anonymity, which makes it difficult for them to protect user privacy and the sensor does face some potential attacks; thus, these schemes cannot fully meet the security requirements of a DWSN. In summary, our scheme is more efficient than most of the related schemes while satisfying comprehensive security requirements. Compared with other related protocols, our protocol can achieve a better trade-off between performance and security, so it is more suitable for deployment in the WSN application environment.

6. Conclusions

In this study, we suggest an anonymous authentication scheme with PUF and Chebyshev chaotic mapping for a DWSN to resist some security defects, especially the easily overlooked physical impersonation attack, and we use BAN logic to prove the security of the protocol. In addition, our protocol is compared with related protocols in five aspects, security features, computation overhead, communication overhead, sensor throughput, and storage overhead. The results show that, although our protocol is not the most efficient compared with the competitive schemes, it can fulfill the security requirements that are needed for DWSN circumstances. Consequently, our protocol is more suitable for actual deployment than the related schemes. The countermeasure we took to eliminate the security defects is suitable for addressing the security weaknesses in similar authentication protocols, and this countermeasure can also be used as a reference for designing new protocols in the future.

In future work, we plan to use a more advanced public key algorithm to reduce the runtime of the public key operation and to improve the performance of this protocol. In addition, we will build an environment suitable for conducting DWSN experiments, such as connecting dedicated wireless sensors to actual hardware, such as Arduino or Raspberry Pi, for testing or using simulation software NS-3 3.40 to simulate network behavior, simulate various attack scenarios (such as node capture attack, replay attacks, etc.), verify the security of the protocol, and measure indicators such as computation overhead, communication overhead, and energy consumption for performance evaluation.

Author Contributions: Conceptualization, J.M.; methodology, J.M. and Z.Z.; software, Z.Z.; validation, Z.Z. and Y.L.; formal analysis, J.M. and Y.L.; writing—original draft preparation, J.M.; writing—review and editing, Z.Z.; supervision, Y.L. and J.M. All authors have read and agreed to the published version of the manuscript.

Funding: This research received no external funding.

Data Availability Statement: The data presented in this study are available in this article.

Acknowledgments: The authors would like to thank the anonymous reviewers for their constructive comments and recommendations.

Conflicts of Interest: The authors declare no conflicts of interest.

References

1. Sadeghi Ghahroudi, M.; Shahrabi, A.; Ghoreyshi, S.M.; Alfouzan, F.A. Distributed node deployment algorithms in mobile wireless sensor networks: Survey and challenges. *ACM Trans. Sens. Netw.* **2023**, *19*, 1–26. [CrossRef]
2. Talmale, R.; Bhat, M.N. Energy attentive and pre-fault recognize mechanism for distributed wireless sensor network using fuzzy logic approach. *Wirel. Pers. Commun.* **2022**, *124*, 1263–1280. [CrossRef]
3. Peter, O.; Pradhan, A.; Mbohwa, C. Industrial internet of things (IIoT): Opportunities, challenges, and requirements in manufacturing businesses in emerging economies. *Procedia Comput. Sci.* **2023**, *217*, 856–865. [CrossRef]
4. Anitha, R.; Tapas Bapu, B. Blockchain-based light-weight authentication approach for a multiple wireless sensor network. *IETE J. Res.* **2024**, *70*, 1480–1494. [CrossRef]
5. Magara, T.; Zhou, Y. Internet of Things (IoT) of Smart Homes: Privacy and Security. *J. Electr. Comput. Eng.* **2024**, *2024*, 7716956. [CrossRef]
6. Huo, Y.; Xu, Y.; Zhao, X.; Sun, Y.; Li, S. Path Loss Estimation of Wireless Sensor Networks in Coal Mine Collapsed Zone. *IEEE Sens. J.* **2024**, *24*, 9002–9015. [CrossRef]
7. Alimoradi, P.; Barati, A.; Barati, H. A hierarchical key management and authentication method for wireless sensor networks. *Int. J. Commun. Syst.* **2022**, *35*, e5076. [CrossRef]
8. Wang, C.; Wang, D.; Duan, Y.; Tao, X. Secure and Lightweight User Authentication Scheme for Cloud-Assisted Internet of Things. *IEEE Trans. Inf. Foren. Sec.* **2023**, *18*, 2961–2976. [CrossRef]
9. Reziouk, A.; Laurent, E.; Demay, J.-C. Practical security overview of IEEE 802.15. 4. In Proceedings of the 2016 International Conference on Engineering & MIS (ICEMIS), Agadir, Morocco, 22–24 September 2016; IEEE: Piscataway, NJ, USA, 2016; pp. 1–9.
10. Li, X.; Liu, S.; Kumari, S.; Chen, C.-M. PSAP-WSN: A provably secure authentication protocol for 5g-based wireless sensor networks. *CMES-Comput. Model. Eng. Sci.* **2023**, *135*, 711. [CrossRef]
11. Huang, W. ECC-based three-factor authentication and key agreement scheme for wireless sensor networks. *Sci. Rep.* **2024**, *14*, 1787. [CrossRef]
12. Yu, S.J.; Park, Y.H. SLUA-WSN: Secure and Lightweight Three-Factor-Based User Authentication Protocol for Wireless Sensor Networks. *Sensors* **2020**, *20*, 4143. [CrossRef]
13. Wu, F.; Li, X.; Xu, L.; Vijayakumar, P.; Kumar, N. A Novel Three-Factor Authentication Protocol for Wireless Sensor Networks With IoT Notion. *IEEE Syst. J.* **2020**, *15*, 1120–1129. [CrossRef]
14. Darbandeh, F.G.; Safkhani, M. SAPWSN: A secure authentication protocol for wireless sensor networks. *Comput. Netw.* **2023**, *220*, 109469. [CrossRef]
15. Kwon, D.K.; Yu, S.J.; Lee, J.Y.; Son, S.H.; Park, Y.H. WSN-SLAP: Secure and Lightweight Mutual Authentication Protocol for Wireless Sensor Networks. *Sensors* **2021**, *21*, 936. [CrossRef]
16. Wu, T.-Y.; Yang, L.; Lee, Z.; Chu, S.-C.; Kumari, S.; Kumar, S. A provably secure three-factor Authentication protocol for wireless sensor networks. *Wirel. Commun. Mob. Com.* **2021**, *2021*, 5537018. [CrossRef]
17. Kumar, D. A secure and efficient user authentication protocol for wireless sensor network. *Multimed. Tools Appl.* **2021**, *80*, 27131–27154. [CrossRef]
18. Goyat, R.; Kumar, G.; Saha, R.; Conti, M. Pribadi: A decentralized privacy-preserving authentication in wireless multimedia sensor networks for smart cities. *Clust. Comput.* **2024**, *27*, 4823–4839. [CrossRef]
19. Nyangaresi, V.O.; Yenurkar, G.K. Anonymity preserving lightweight authentication protocol for resource-limited wireless sensor networks. *High-Confid. Comput.* **2024**, *4*, 100178. [CrossRef]
20. Thakur, G.; Prajapat, S.; Kumar, P.; Chen, C.-M. A Privacy-Preserving Three-Factor Authentication System for IoT-Enabled Wireless Sensor Networks. *J. Syst. Archit.* **2024**, *154*, 103245. [CrossRef]
21. Mostefa, B.; Abdelkader, G.; Mohamed, B. User-Authentication Protocol to Secure Wireless Sensor Network Access in the Internet of Things Context. *J. Commun. Softw. Syst.* **2024**, *20*, 186–197. [CrossRef]

22. Das, A.K. A secure and efficient user anonymity-preserving three-factor authentication protocol for large-scale distributed wireless sensor networks. *Wirel. Pers. Commun.* **2015**, *82*, 1377–1404. [CrossRef]
23. Shafiullah, S.M.; Reddy, M.C.M.; Gorripati, R.; Bapana, S.; Naresh, M.; Vorugunti, C.S. A secure and light weight three factor authentication protocol for Large Scale Distributed wireless sensor networks. In Proceedings of the 2016 International Conference on Wireless Communications, Signal Processing and Networking (WiSPNET), Chennai, India, 23–25 March 2016; IEEE: Piscataway, NJ, USA, 2016; pp. 1944–1949.
24. Wang, D.; Wang, P. Two birds with one stone: Two-factor authentication with security beyond conventional bound. *IEEE Trans. Depend. Secure* **2016**, *15*, 708–722. [CrossRef]
25. Abdi Nasib Far, H.; Bayat, M.; Kumar Das, A.; Fotouhi, M.; Pournaghi, S.M.; Doostari, M.-A. LAPTAS: Lightweight anonymous privacy-preserving three-factor authentication scheme for WSN-based IIoT. *Wirel. Netw.* **2021**, *27*, 1389–1412. [CrossRef]
26. Wang, C.; Xu, G.; Li, W. A secure and anonymous two-factor authentication protocol in multiserver environment. *Secur. Commun. Netw.* **2018**, *2018*, 9062675. [CrossRef]
27. Fan, Q.; Chen, J.; Xu, F.; Li, L.; Luo, M. A biometrics-based anonymous authentication and key agreement scheme for wireless sensor networks. *Concurr. Comput. Pract. Exp.* **2022**, *34*, e6178. [CrossRef]
28. Hu, B.; Tang, W.; Xie, Q. A two-factor security authentication scheme for wireless sensor networks in IoT environments. *Neurocomputing* **2022**, *500*, 741–749. [CrossRef]
29. Ding, Z.; Xie, Q. Provably Secure Dynamic Anonymous Authentication Protocol for Wireless Sensor Networks in Internet of Things. *Sustainability* **2023**, *15*, 5734. [CrossRef]
30. Ghahramani, M.; Javidan, R. Time dependency: An efficient biometric-based authentication for secure communication in wireless healthcare sensor networks. *J. Comput. Virol. Hacki.* **2023**, *19*, 303–317. [CrossRef]
31. Thakur, G.; Prajapat, S.; Kumar, P.; Das, A.K.; Shetty, S. An efficient lightweight provably secure authentication protocol for patient monitoring using wireless medical sensor networks. *IEEE Access* **2023**, *11*, 114662–114679. [CrossRef]
32. Xie, Q.; Xie, Q. Security Analysis on a Three-Factor Authentication Scheme of 5G Wireless Sensor Networks for IoT System. *IEEE Internet Things* **2024**, *11*, 15038–15042. [CrossRef]
33. Saini, K.K.; Kaur, D.; Kumar, D.; Kumar, B. An efficient three-factor authentication protocol for wireless healthcare sensor networks. *Multimed. Tools Appl.* **2024**, *83*, 63699–63721. [CrossRef]
34. Wang, F.; Xu, G.; Xu, G. A provably secure anonymous biometrics-based authentication scheme for wireless sensor networks using chaotic map. *IEEE Access* **2019**, *7*, 101596–101608. [CrossRef]
35. Xu, G.; Wang, F.; Zhang, M.; Peng, J. Efficient and provably secure anonymous user authentication scheme for patient monitoring using wireless medical sensor networks. *IEEE Access* **2020**, *8*, 47282–47294. [CrossRef]
36. Li, J.; Zhang, W.; Kumari, S.; Choo, K.K.R.; Hogrefe, D. Security analysis and improvement of a mutual authentication and key agreement solution for wireless sensor networks using chaotic maps. *Trans. Emerg. Telecommun. Technol.* **2018**, *29*, e3295. [CrossRef]
37. Mo, J.; Hu, Z.; Shen, W. A provably secure three-factor authentication protocol based on chebyshev chaotic mapping for wireless sensor network. *IEEE Access* **2022**, *10*, 12137–12152. [CrossRef]
38. Tyagi, G.; Kumar, R. An improved multifactor user authentication scheme for wireless sensor networks. *Wirel. Pers. Commun.* **2022**, *123*, 1311–1343. [CrossRef]
39. Tyagi, G.; Kumar, R. Multi-factor user authentication and key agreement scheme for wireless sensor networks using Chinese remainder theorem. *Peer Peer Netw.* **2023**, *16*, 260–276. [CrossRef]
40. Shao, X.; Guo, Y.; Guo, Y. A PUF-based anonymous authentication protocol for wireless medical sensor networks. *Wirel. Netw.* **2022**, *28*, 3753–3770. [CrossRef]
41. Wang, W.; Chen, Q.; Yin, Z.; Srivastava, G.; Gadekallu, T.R.; Alsolami, F.; Su, C. Blockchain and PUF-based lightweight authentication protocol for wireless medical sensor networks. *IEEE Internet Things* **2021**, *9*, 8883–8891. [CrossRef]
42. Lee, J.; Oh, J.; Park, Y. A secure and anonymous authentication protocol based on three-factor wireless medical sensor networks. *Electronics* **2023**, *12*, 1368. [CrossRef]
43. Kumar, R.; Singh, S.; Singh, P.K. A secure and efficient computation based multifactor authentication scheme for Intelligent IoT-enabled WSNs. *Comput. Electr. Eng.* **2023**, *105*, 108495. [CrossRef]
44. Tyagi, G.; Kumar, R. An efficient user authentication and key agreement scheme for wireless sensor networks using physically unclonable function. *Int. J. Inf. Secur.* **2024**, *23*, 935–962. [CrossRef]
45. Mason, J.C.; Handscomb, D.C. *Chebyshev Polynomials*; CRC Press: Boca Raton, FL, USA, 2002.
46. Zhang, L. Cryptanalysis of the public key encryption based on multiple chaotic systems. *Chaos Soliton Fract.* **2008**, *37*, 669–674. [CrossRef]
47. Herder, C.; Yu, M.-D.; Koushanfar, F.; Devadas, S. Physical unclonable functions and applications: A tutorial. *Proc. IEEE* **2014**, *102*, 1126–1141. [CrossRef]

48. Wang, C.; Xu, G.; Jing, S. An Enhanced Three-Factor User Authentication Scheme Using Elliptic Curve Cryptosystem for Wireless Sensor Networks. *Sensors* **2017**, *17*, 2946. [CrossRef]
49. Amin, R.; Islam, S.H.; Biswas, G.P.; Khan, M.K.; Leng, L.; Kumar, N. Design of an anonymity-preserving three-factor authenticated key exchange protocol for wireless sensor networks. *Comput. Netw.* **2016**, *101*, 42–62. [CrossRef]
50. Kim, T.H.; Kim, C.; Park, I. Side channel analysis attacks using AM demodulation on commercial smart cards with SEED. *J. Syst. Software* **2012**, *85*, 2899–2908. [CrossRef]
51. Mangard, S.; Oswald, E.; Popp, T. *Power Analysis Attacks: Revealing the Secrets of Smart Cards*; Springer Science & Business Media: New York, NY, USA, 2008; Volume 31, Available online: https://link.springer.com/book/10.1007/978-0-387-38162-6 (accessed on 21 September 2024).
52. Li, W.; Shen, Y.; Wang, P. Breaking Three Remote user Authentication Systems for Mobile Devices. *J. Signal Process. Syst.* **2018**, *90*, 1179–1190. [CrossRef]
53. Jiang, Q.; Zeadally, S.; Ma, J.; He, D. Lightweight Three-Factor Authentication and Key Agreement Protocol for Internet-Integrated Wireless Sensor Networks. *IEEE Access* **2017**, *5*, 3376–3392. [CrossRef]
54. Mo, J.; Chen, H. A lightweight secure user authentication and key agreement protocol for wireless sensor networks. *Secur. Commun. Netw.* **2019**, *2019*, 2136506. [CrossRef]
55. Choi, Y.; Lee, Y.; Moon, J.; Won, D. Security enhanced multi-factor biometric authentication scheme using bio-hash function. *PLoS ONE* **2017**, *12*, e0176250. [CrossRef]
56. Gardiner, C.W.; Zoller, P. *Quantum Noise: A Handbook of Markovian and Non-Markovian Quantum Stochastic Methods with Applications to Quantum Optics*; Springer: Berlin/Heidelberg, Germany, 2004.

Disclaimer/Publisher's Note: The statements, opinions and data contained in all publications are solely those of the individual author(s) and contributor(s) and not of MDPI and/or the editor(s). MDPI and/or the editor(s) disclaim responsibility for any injury to people or property resulting from any ideas, methods, instructions or products referred to in the content.

electronics

MDPI

Review

State of the Art in Parallel and Distributed Systems: Emerging Trends and Challenges

Fei Dai [1,*], Md Akbar Hossain [1] and Yi Wang [2]

[1] School of Computing, Eastern Institute of Technology, Napier 4104, New Zealand; ahossain@eit.ac.nz
[2] School of Mathematical and Computational Sciences, Massey University, Palmerston North 4410, New Zealand; y.wang24@massey.ac.nz
* Correspondence: tdai@eit.ac.nz

Abstract

Driven by rapid advancements in interconnection, packaging, integration, and computing technologies, parallel and distributed systems have significantly evolved in recent years. These systems have become essential for addressing modern computational demands, offering enhanced processing power, scalability, and resource efficiency. This paper provides a comprehensive overview of parallel and distributed systems, exploring their interrelationships, their key distinctions, and the emerging trends shaping their evolution. We analyse four parallel computing paradigms—heterogeneous computing, quantum computing, neuromorphic computing, and optical computing—and examine emerging distributed systems such as blockchain, serverless computing, and cloud-native architectures. The associated challenges are highlighted, and potential future directions are outlined. This work serves as a valuable resource for researchers and practitioners aiming to stay informed about trends in parallel and distributed computing while understanding the challenges and future developments in the field.

Keywords: parallel computing; distributed systems; emerging trends; system challenges; future directions

1. Introduction

In the continually advancing field of computing, parallel and distributed systems have emerged as indispensable tools for addressing the escalating demands for computational power, scalability, and efficient resource utilisation. For instance, the rapid growth of artificial intelligence (AI) workloads has driven the need for computing systems capable of processing datasets exceeding petabyte scales, such as those required for training large language models like GPT-4, which involves hundreds of billions of parameters [1]. With advancements in interconnection networks, packaging technologies, system integration, and computational architectures, these systems have demonstrated remarkable improvements in performance, enabling the management of increasingly large-scale and complex workloads [2]. By facilitating the concurrent execution of tasks across multiple processors and nodes, parallel and distributed systems underpin modern solutions to critical computational challenges, including big data analytics, AI, real-time simulations, and cloud-based services.

The significance of parallel and distributed systems extends beyond their computational capabilities, as they play a pivotal role in driving innovation across various industries. For example, in high-performance computing (HPC), these systems enable climate modelling [3] and molecular dynamics simulations [4], while distributed architectures power applications like global-scale content delivery networks [5] and decentralised finance [6]. A recent study indicates that distributed systems in finance have great potential to improve processing speeds for decentralised applications [7]. However, these benefits come with significant challenges, including scalability, security, interoperability, fault tolerance, legal compliance, and the integration of diverse and heterogeneous resources [7]. Addressing these challenges is essential for ensuring the sustained evolution and utility of parallel and distributed systems.

Despite their critical importance, many existing reviews of parallel and distributed systems either focus narrowly on specific aspects or lack comprehensive analyses of their historical development, emerging trends, and future challenges. This paper aims to bridge this gap by providing a holistic overview of these systems and exploring their evolution, interrelationships, and distinctions. Furthermore, it examines key challenges associated with parallel and distributed systems and proposes actionable future research directions to guide the field's continued advancement.

The organisation of this paper is illustrated in Figure 1, which provides a clear roadmap of the topics discussed. Section 2 defines parallel and distributed systems, introduces key categories, and explores their interrelationships and distinctions. Section 3 examines emerging trends in parallel systems, focusing on heterogeneous computing, quantum computing, neuromorphic computing, and optical computing. Section 4 explores emerging trends in distributed systems, highlighting blockchain and distributed ledgers, serverless computing, cloud-native architectures, and distributed AI and machine learning (ML) systems. Section 5 discusses the primary challenges facing these systems, providing specific metrics and real-world examples. Section 6 outlines actionable future research directions to address these challenges. Finally, Section 7 concludes this paper.

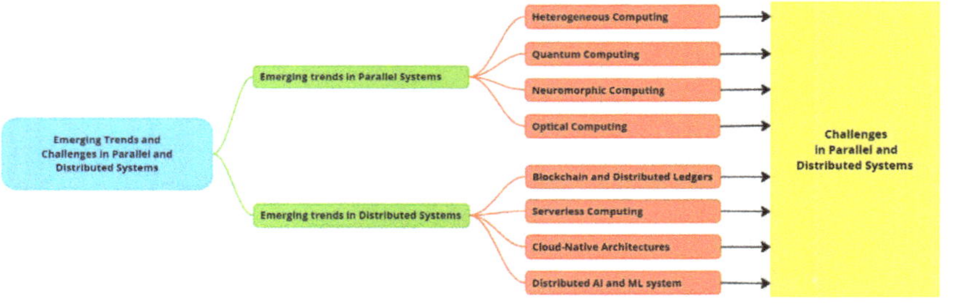

Figure 1. Logical overview of this paper's structure. This figure illustrates the organisation of sections, their interdependencies, and the logical progression of topics in this review.

2. Overview of Parallel and Distributed Systems

This section defines parallel and distributed systems, introduces various categories and common architectures, and explores their relationships and synergies. This foundational understanding sets the stage for a deeper examination of their historical context, key concepts, and terminologies.

2.1. Parallel Systems

Parallel systems are computational architectures designed to execute multiple tasks simultaneously by dividing computations into smaller sub-tasks processed concurrently across multiple processors or cores within a single machine or a closely connected cluster [8]. Their primary objective is to reduce computation time and improve performance efficiency, with applications in scientific simulations, image processing, and large-scale data analysis [9]. Key features of parallel systems include concurrency, coordination among processors, and efficient utilisation of shared resources.

Traditional parallel systems can be categorised into three main types: *Shared Memory Systems*, where multiple processors share a common memory space, allowing for direct communication through shared variables—examples include multi-core processors and symmetric multiprocessors (SMPs); *Distributed Memory Systems*, in which each processor has its own private memory and communicates with others by passing messages—examples include cluster computing and massively parallel processing (MPP) systems; and *Hybrid Systems*, which combine shared and distributed memory approaches, often seen in modern supercomputers and HPC clusters to leverage the advantages of both architectures. Common architectures include *Central Processing Units (CPUs)*, found in everyday devices like laptops and smartphones, enabling parallel task execution to improve performance and efficiency; *General-Purpose Graphics Processing Units (GPGPUs)*, used in gaming, video rendering, and AI applications to perform massive parallel computations; *Application-Specific Integrated Circuits (ASICs)*, custom-designed hardware optimised for specific applications such as cryptocurrency mining and specialised AI algorithms, providing high performance and energy efficiency; and *Field-Programmable Gate Arrays (FPGAs)*, which are reconfigurable silicon devices that can be electrically programmed to implement various digital circuits or systems [10], commonly used in scientific research, aerospace, and defence.

The origins of parallel computing can be traced back to the late 1950s with the advent of vector processors and early supercomputers like the IBM Stretch [11] and the CDC 6600 [12]. Significant advancements occurred in the 1980s with the introduction of MPP systems [13], including the Connection Machine [14] and the Cray series [15]. These systems utilised thousands of processors to perform simultaneous computations, paving the way for modern parallel architectures. In the 1990s and 2000s, the development of multi-core processors [16] and GPGPUs [17] revolutionised parallel computing by making it more accessible and efficient. The rise of ML, big data, and deep learning advancements led to a surge in demand for high-performance parallel processing hardware. However, traditional parallel hardware began to show limitations in providing the necessary processing capacity for AI training. Challenges such as insufficient interconnection bandwidth between cores and processors and the "memory wall" problem—where memory bandwidth cannot keep up with processing speed—became critical bottlenecks. To address these challenges, scientists and engineers have been developing innovative parallel computing systems tailored for AI and other demanding applications. Recent innovations, including heterogeneous computing, quantum computing, neuromorphic systems, and optical computing, aim to address these limitations, as discussed in Section 3.

2.2. Distributed Systems

Distributed systems are computational architectures where multiple autonomous computing nodes, often geographically separated, collaborate to achieve a common objective [18]. These nodes communicate and coordinate their actions by passing messages over a network [19]. Distributed systems emphasise fault tolerance, scalability, and resource sharing, making them essential for various applications, including cloud computing, distributed databases, and blockchain networks. Key features of distributed systems include the ability to handle node failures gracefully, scale out by adding more nodes, and efficiently manage distributed resources.

Distributed systems can be categorised into several types: *Client–Server Systems*, where clients request services and resources from centralised servers—examples include web applications and enterprise software; *Peer-to-Peer (P2P) Systems*, in which nodes act as both clients and servers, sharing resources directly without centralised control—examples include file-sharing networks and blockchain platforms; *Cloud Computing Systems*, which provide scalable and flexible resources over the Internet—examples include Amazon Web Services (AWS) and Google Cloud Platform (GCP); and *Edge Computing Systems*, which process data near the source of generation to reduce latency and bandwidth usage—examples include Internet of Things (IoT) devices and real-time analytics systems. Common architectures in distributed systems include the *Client–Server Model*, used in web services where web browsers (clients) communicate with web servers to fetch and display content; *Cloud Infrastructure*, utilised for on-demand resource provisioning, hosting applications, and data storage, as seen in platforms like AWS and GCP; and *IoT Networks*, which connect various smart devices, enabling them to communicate and perform tasks collaboratively in real-time.

The concept of distributed systems emerged in the 1970s with the development of ARPANET, the precursor to the modern Internet [20]. Early distributed systems focused on resource sharing and remote access to computational power. The 1980s and 1990s witnessed the growth of distributed databases [21] and the Client–Server Model [22], which became fundamental in enterprise computing. The 2000s marked the rise of cloud computing and big data, epitomising the distributed system paradigm by providing scalable, on-demand computing resources over the Internet [23]. Technologies like Hadoop and MapReduce [24] enhanced the capability to process large datasets in a distributed manner. More recently, edge computing [25] and the IoT [26] have extended the reach of distributed systems to the periphery of networks, enabling real-time processing and decision-making at the edge. The development of digital cryptocurrencies and advancements in AI have further propelled the growth of distributed systems. In this paper, we focus on emerging trends such as blockchain and distributed ledgers, serverless computing, cloud-native architectures, and distributed AI and ML systems, which will be explored in Section 4.

2.3. Relationship and Synergy Between Parallel and Distributed Systems

Parallel and distributed systems are integral to modern computing, each contributing to efficiently executing large-scale and complex tasks. While they serve distinct purposes, their relationship is characterised by complementary roles and overlapping functionalities. Parallel systems are designed to maximise computational speed within a single machine or tightly coupled cluster [27]. By dividing a large task into smaller sub-tasks and processing them simultaneously across multiple processors, parallel systems achieve significant reductions in computation time. This makes them ideal for HPC applications like AI training and real-time data processing. Distributed systems, on the other hand, are engineered to leverage multiple autonomous nodes that collaborate over a network to achieve a common goal. This architecture prioritises scalability, fault tolerance, and resource sharing, making distributed systems suitable for applications that require robust, scalable, and reliable infrastructure, such as cloud computing and distributed databases.

In some scenarios, parallel and distributed systems can overlap, creating hybrid systems that combine the strengths of both architectures. For instance, a distributed system might employ parallel processing within individual nodes to further enhance performance. Conversely, a parallel system might distribute tasks across closely connected clusters, incorporating distributed computing elements. Both parallel and distributed systems aim to improve computational efficiency and handle large-scale problems, but they do so with different focuses and methods. The primary distinction between parallel and distributed systems lies in their architecture and operational focus:

- *Architecture*: Parallel systems use multiple processors or cores within a single machine or a closely connected cluster to perform concurrent computations [8]. Distributed systems, on the other hand, involve multiple independent machines that communicate over a network [19].

- *Coordination and communication*: In parallel systems, communication between processors is typically fast and direct due to their close proximity. Distributed systems require communication over potentially large distances, often leading to higher latency and the need for sophisticated communication protocols.
- *Scalability and fault tolerance*: Distributed systems are designed to scale out by adding more nodes and are built with fault tolerance in mind [28], allowing them to continue functioning even if some nodes fail. Parallel systems focus on scaling up by adding more processors to a single machine [29], with fault tolerance often a secondary consideration.
- *Resource sharing*: Distributed systems emphasise resource sharing and collaboration among independent nodes, each potentially equipped with its own local resources, such as distributed memory. Parallel systems concentrate resources within a single system, focusing on components like cache systems to enhance computational power.

Understanding the relationship and differences between parallel and distributed systems is crucial for engineers, researchers, and students as they explore the diverse applications and challenges within these fields. Both systems play vital roles in advancing computational capabilities and addressing the demands of modern technology.

3. Emerging Trends in Parallel Systems

The development of parallel systems has primarily followed two main directions: enhancing existing computing architectures and creating new parallel architectures to adapt to new applications, such as ML. Industry leaders like Intel, AMD, and NVIDIA exemplify this trend by producing new products based on advanced architectures annually, targeting general tasks, servers, AI training, etc. The rapid development of deep learning has spurred the proposal of many innovative architectures, such as near-memory computing architecture, heterogeneous computing architecture, quantum computing architecture, neuromorphic computing architecture, and optical computing architecture, aimed at overcoming the memory wall of traditional Von Neumann architecture [30]. In response to the increasing volumes of processing data and advancements in AI, we explore the emerging trends in parallel systems across four key areas: heterogeneous computing, quantum computing, neuromorphic computing, and optical computing.

3.1. Heterogeneous Computing

Heterogeneous computing integrates different types of processors and specialised computing units to work together, leveraging their unique strengths to enhance overall system performance and efficiency. As new architectures are proposed and technological advancements continue, heterogeneous computing continues to evolve. To explore the emerging trend of heterogeneous computing within parallel systems, we first examine the evolution of computing and then focus on advanced ultra-heterogeneous computing (UHC). Specifically, we discuss the software and hardware architectures that support UHC and provide an outlook on its future developments.

Figure 2 outlines the evolution of computing, beginning with single-engine serial processing followed by homogeneous computing then heterogeneous computing, and culminating in UHC. The evolution of heterogeneous computing can be described in four stages. In the first stage, a single processor handles all computational tasks sequentially, limiting performance to the capabilities of a single processing unit. As the demand for higher performance grew, this led to the second stage, which marked the introduction of homogeneous parallel processing. Here, multiple cores of the same type, such as multicore CPUs or ASICs, work together to perform tasks in parallel. This approach improves performance by distributing workloads across several identical processors. However, the need to optimise diverse tasks pushed the transition to the third stage: heterogeneous computing. In this stage, two types of processors, such as CPUs and GPUs, are combined to handle various computational tasks more effectively, with each processor type optimised for specific operations, thereby enhancing overall efficiency. Finally, as applications became more complex and diverse, the necessity to maximise computational efficiency and performance led to the final stage: UHC. This stage integrates multiple types of processors, such as CPUs, GPUs, neural processing units (NPUs), and data processing units (DPUs), combining their specialised strengths to address complex computational needs.

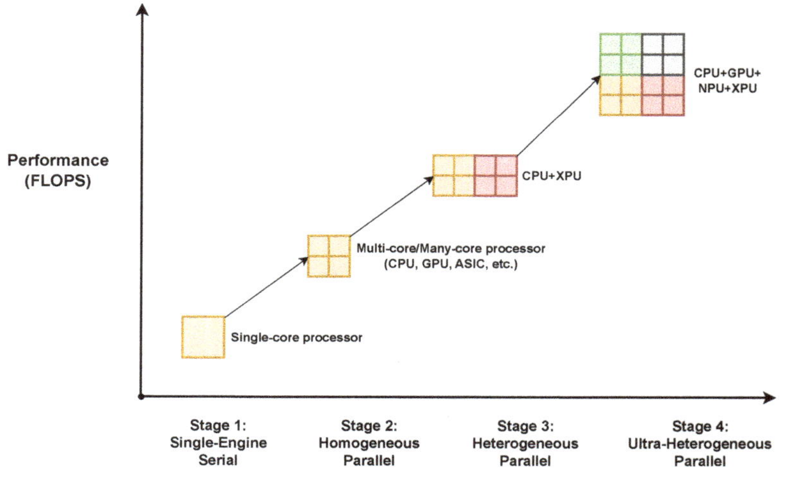

Figure 2. Evolution of various computing eras. This figure outlines the evolution of computing, from single-engine serial processing to ultra-heterogeneous parallel processing, highlighting key stages in this transformation. The different colours in the squares represent various processor types utilized in each stage.

With the development of technology, we are entering the early stages of UHC, which promises higher performance than in previous eras. For instance, systems integrating CPUs, GPUs, and DPUs have already demonstrated significant improvements in handling various AI tasks [31]. However, such systems rely on the support of both software and hardware. Figure 3 illustrates the software and hardware layers required for UHC systems. The software layer is responsible for effectively managing and optimising diverse processing units. Software frameworks support seamless communication and coordination between different types of processors, allowing tasks to be dynamically assigned to the most suitable processing unit. Advancements in frameworks like CUDA and OpenCL have significantly enhanced interoperability and workload allocation across processors, enabling efficient dynamic task management [32]. This involves developing sophisticated schedulers, resource managers, and communication protocols that can handle the complexities of UHC environments. Additionally, programming models and languages (e.g., CUDA, OpenCL, OpenMP, MPI, etc.) must evolve to provide abstractions that simplify the development of applications for UHC systems, enabling developers to leverage the full potential of diverse computing resources without needing to manage low-level hardware details [33].

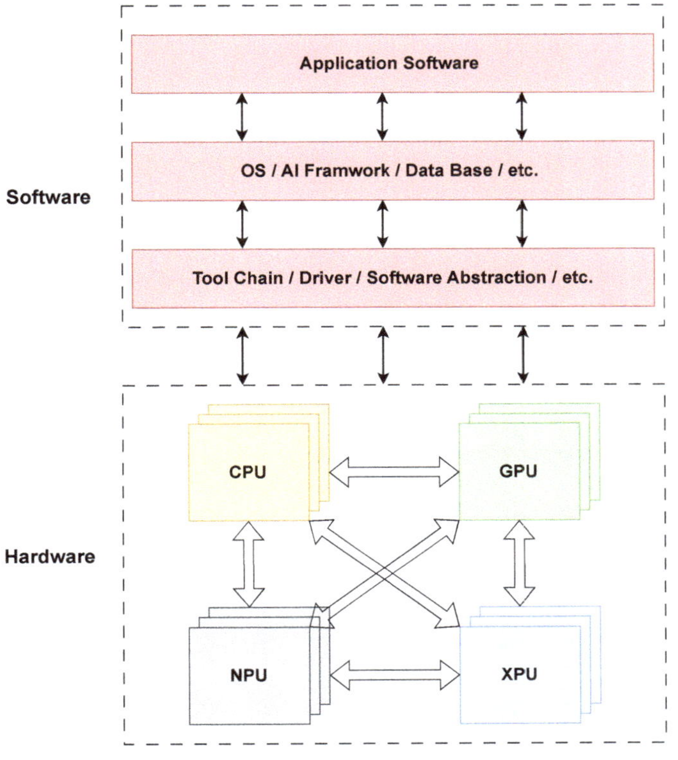

Figure 3. Hardware and software layers of UHC. This figure depicts the essential software and hardware components required for UHC systems, emphasising interoperability and workload distribution.

The hardware architectures for UHC integrate multiple processing units into a cohesive system. This involves designing interconnects that provide high-bandwidth, low-latency communication between CPUs, GPUs, NPUs, DPUs, and other specialised processors. Memory architectures will also evolve to support efficient data sharing and movement between different processing units, minimising bottlenecks and maximising throughput. Innovations like 3D stacking and advanced co-packaging technologies play a pivotal role in enabling UHC systems by reducing communication delays and improving system performance [34].

The future of UHC is promising, with potential applications spanning various fields, including AI, scientific computing, and real-time data processing. As demand grows for more powerful and efficient systems, UHC architectures are poised to become increasingly prevalent. Advances in both technological infrastructure and development frameworks will be instrumental in driving this evolution, facilitating systems that seamlessly integrate diverse processing units to deliver unparalleled performance and efficiency.

3.2. Quantum Computing

Quantum computing represents a significant departure from classical computing paradigms, utilising the principles of quantum mechanics to perform computations. Unlike classical computers that process information as binary bits (0's and 1's), quantum computers leverage quantum bits (qubits), which can exist in multiple states simultaneously due to the phenomenon of superposition. This enables quantum computers to process vast amounts of information in parallel, making them particularly powerful for certain types of computations. Quantum computing research began in the 1980s [35]. Although its initial development was slow due to technological barriers, it has accelerated rapidly in recent decades with the scaling up of qubit numbers in superconducting systems [36]. To explore the emerging trends in quantum computing, we start by discussing quantum computers and their applications, followed by an explanation of the different types of qubits and their development trends. Finally, we conclude with an overview of the current state and future prospects of quantum computing.

Quantum computers leverage qubits, which can exist in multiple states simultaneously (superposition) and be entangled with one another, enabling exponential increases in computational power for certain types of problems [37]. To illustrate superposition, consider a coin spinning in the air: unlike a classical bit that is either heads or tails, a qubit remains in a combination of both states until measured. Similarly, entanglement can be visualised as a pair of dice that always show the same number, regardless of their distance from each other. Despite these advantages, qubits are highly sensitive to environmental noise and interactions, leading to stability issues and significant error rates. These limitations present a major challenge to the development of practical quantum systems, as maintaining coherence and minimising errors often require complex error correction protocols and cryogenic environments.

Quantum gates are designed to manipulate the coefficients of basis states, performing general functions akin to logic gates in traditional computing systems [38]. Another essential concept, quantum interference, allows quantum algorithms to amplify correct solutions while cancelling out incorrect ones, significantly improving computational efficiency. Quantum algorithms specifically exploit the principles of superposition, entanglement, and quantum interference to execute computations more efficiently than classical computers [39]. Building on these unique properties, quantum computing holds promise for solving complex problems currently intractable for classical computers, such as large-scale optimisation, cryptography, and quantum physical system simulation [40]. Major technology companies and research institutions are heavily investing in quantum computing research, driving rapid advancements in practical quantum computers and efficient quantum algorithms.

There are various physical systems to realise qubits, each offering distinct advantages and contributing to the overall progress in quantum computing. Superconducting qubits utilise superconducting circuits and are among the most mature technologies in this domain [36]. However, they require extremely low temperatures, increasing operational complexity and cost. Silicon qubits, based on semiconductor technology similar to classical computer chips [41], offer compatibility with existing fabrication techniques but face scalability challenges, as quantum coherence deteriorates with size. Trapped-ion qubits use ions trapped in electromagnetic fields and manipulated with lasers [42], known for their high fidelity, but their operations are inherently slower, posing limitations for large-scale computations. Neutral atom qubits employ neutral atoms trapped in optical lattices [43], facilitating scalable quantum computing, yet achieving consistent trapping and manipulation across large arrays remains challenging. Diamond-based qubits utilise nitrogen-vacancy centres in diamonds [44], which can be manipulated at room temperature but often suffer from low qubit density and complex fabrication. Photonic qubits use photons to encode quantum information [45], providing advantages in communication due to their speed and low loss, but their integration into computational frameworks and achieving scalable photonic processors remain significant hurdles.

The current state of quantum computing demonstrates a promising trajectory, with continuous advancements in qubit technology and quantum algorithms. Despite earlier bottlenecks in qubit stability, fidelity, and scalability, ongoing research has successfully addressed many of these issues, enabling steady progress in increasing qubit numbers. As depicted in Figure 4, the number of qubits in quantum processors has been steadily increasing across different technologies. IBM's roadmap outlines plans to scale its Flamingo systems to 1000 qubits by 2027 and deliver quantum-centric supercomputers with thousands of logical qubits by 2030 and beyond [46]. This trend highlights quantum computing's potential to revolutionise fields requiring immense computational power, such as materials science, AI, and high-energy physics.

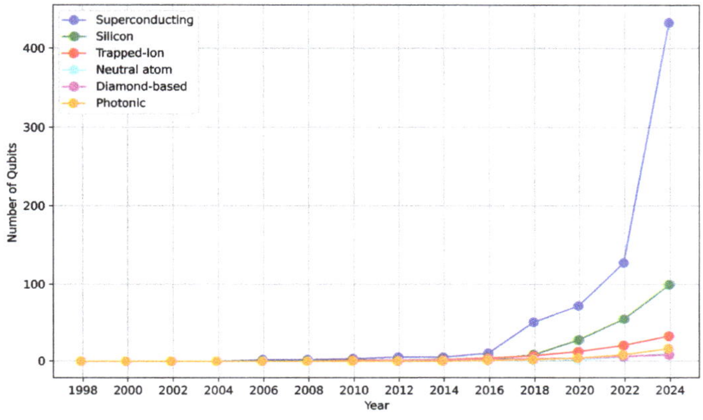

Figure 4. Qubit growth in quantum computers over recent years. This figure presents the increasing number of qubits in quantum processors, reflecting advancements in quantum computing technology.

Current applications of quantum computers span a wide range of domains, demonstrating tangible benefits in solving complex problems that challenge classical systems. In cryptography, quantum computers are revolutionising secure communication by exploiting superposition and entanglement to enhance encryption and decryption processes [47]. Similarly, in molecular simulation, quantum algorithms enable precise modelling of molecular structures and interactions, crucial for drug discovery [48], materials science [49], and other chemistry-related fields [50]. These advancements hold the potential to accelerate breakthroughs in healthcare, energy, and environmental sustainability. Moreover, financial modelling is another promising domain, where quantum computers optimise portfolios, predict market trends, and manage risk with unprecedented speed and accuracy [51].

The rise of quantum machine learning (QML) adds a new dimension to the application of quantum computers. QML leverages quantum algorithms to enhance ML tasks such as classification, pattern recognition, and autonomous decision-making [52]. By leveraging quantum speed-ups, QML can process complex datasets more efficiently than classical methods, offering advantages in fields such as finance, healthcare, and AI. Figure 5 illustrates the workflow of QML, highlighting the interaction between quantum data, quantum gates, and ML models in tasks such as image classification and dynamic decision-making in autonomous systems.

In conclusion, quantum computing represents one of the most transformative trends in the evolving landscape of parallel systems. By harnessing the fundamental principles of quantum mechanics, quantum computing is poised to complement classical HPC, unlocking unprecedented computational power for scientific discovery and industrial applications.

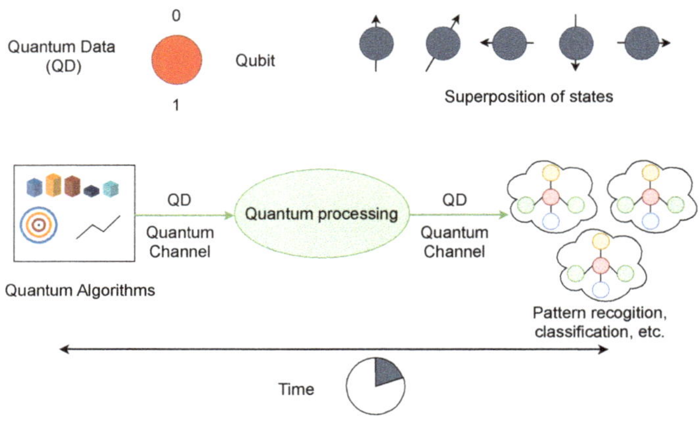

Figure 5. Overview of QML. This figure illustrates the integration of quantum computing principles in ML, showing how quantum algorithms leverage qubit-based computation. The green arrows indicate the data flow of quantum information between processing units.

3.3. Neuromorphic Computing

Neuromorphic computing is a class of brain-inspired computing architectures which, at a certain level of abstraction, simulate the biological computations of the brain. This approach enhances the efficiency of compatible computational tasks and achieves computational delays and energy consumption with biological computation. The term "neuromorphic" was introduced by Carver Mead in the late 1980s [53,54], referring to mixed analogue–digital implementations of brain-inspired computing. Over time, as technology evolved, it came to encompass a wider range of brain-inspired hardware implementations. Specifically, unlike the von Neumann architecture's CPU–memory separation and synchronous clocking, neuromorphic computing utilises neurons and synapses, the fundamental components, to integrate computation and memory. It employs an event-driven approach based on asynchronous event-based spikes, which is more efficient for the brain-like sparse and massively parallel computing, significantly reducing energy consumption. At the algorithmic level, the brain-inspired Spike Neural Network (SNN) serves as an essential algorithm deployed on neuromorphic hardware, efficiently completing ML tasks [55,56] and other operations [57,58]. Recent advancements in VLSI technology and AI have propelled neuromorphic computing towards large-scale development [59]. This introduces developments in neuromorphic computing from both hardware and algorithmic perspectives and discusses future trends.

IBM TrueNorth is based on distributed digital neural models designed to address cognitive tasks in real time [60]. Its chip contains 4096 neurosynaptic cores, each core featuring 256 neurons, with each neuron having 256 synaptic connections. On the one hand, the intra-chip network integrates 1 million programmable neurons and 256 million trainable synapses; on the other hand, the inter-chip interface supports seamless multi-chip communication of arbitrary size, facilitating parallel computation. By using offline learning, various common algorithms such as convolutional networks, restricted Boltzmann machines, hidden Markov models, and multi-modal classification have been mapped to TrueNorth, achieving good results in real-time multi-object detection and classification tasks with milliwatt-level energy consumption.

Neurogrid, a tree-structured neuromorphic computing architecture, fully considers neural features such as the axonal arbor, synapse, dendritic tree, and ion channels to maximise synaptic connections [61]. Neurogrid uses analogue signals to save energy and a tree structure to maximise throughput, allowing it to simulate 1 million neurons and billions of synaptic connections with only 16 neurocores and a power consumption of only 3 watts. Neurogrid's hardware is suitable for real-time simulation, while its software can be used for interactive visualisation.

As one of the neuromorphic computing platforms contributing to the European Union Flagship Human Brain Project (HBP), SpiNNaker is a parallel computation architecture with a million cores [62]. Each SpiNNaker node has 18 cores, connected by a system network-on-chip. Nodes select 1 neural core to act as the monitor processor, assigned an operating system support role, while the other 16 cores support application roles, with the 18th core reserved as a fault-tolerance spare. Nodes communicate through a router to complete parallel data exchange. SpiNNaker can be used as an interface with AER sensors and for integration with robotic platforms.

Intel's Loihi is a neuromorphic research processor supporting multi-scale SNNs, achieving performance comparable to mainstream computing architectures [63,64]. Loihi features a maximum of 128,000 neurons per chip with 128 million synapses. Its unique capabilities include a highly configurable synaptic memory with variable weight precision, support for a wide range of plasticity rules, and graded reward spikes that facilitate learning. Loihi has been evaluated in various applications, such as adaptive robot arm control, visual–tactile sensory perception, modelling diffusion processes for scientific computing applications, and solving hard optimisation problems like railway scheduling. Loihi2 [65], as a new generation of neuromorphic computing and an upgrade of Loihi, is equipped with generalised event-based messaging, greater neuron model programmability, enhanced learning capabilities, numerous capacity optimisations to improve resource density, and faster circuit speeds. Importantly, besides the features from Loihi1, Loihi2 has shared synapses for convolution, which is ideal for deep convolutional neural networks.

SNNs are an essential algorithmic component of neuromorphic computing. To accomplish a task, we should consider how to define a tailored SNN and deploy it on hardware [54]. From a training perspective, algorithms can be categorised into online learning and offline learning. The offline-learning approach first deploys the SNN on neuromorphic hardware and then uses the plasticity features to approximate backpropagation. This is a real-time method for optimising hardware simulation of plasticity. Offline learning involves training an Artificial Neural Network (ANN) on a CPU or GPU based on specific tasks and data, then converting the ANN to an equivalent SNN and deploying it on neuromorphic hardware. As a key to training algorithms, various studies have analysed backpropagation.

An Energy-Efficient Backpropagation approach successfully implemented backpropagation on TrueNorth hardware [56]. Importantly, this method treats spikes and discrete synapses as continuous probabilities, allowing the trained network to map to neuromorphic hardware through probability sampling. This training method achieved 99.42% accuracy on the MNIST dataset with only 0.268 mJ per image. Furthermore, backpropagation through time (BPTT) has been implemented on neuromorphic datasets, providing a training method for recurrent structures on neuromorphic platforms [66]. Benefiting from these training optimisations, SNNs in neuromorphic computing have been applied in various ML tasks such as Simultaneous Velocity and Texture Classification [67], Real-time Facial Expression Recognition [68], and EMG Gesture Classification [69]. Similarly, they have been used in neuroscience research [70,71]. SNN-based neuromorphic computing is also utilised in non-ML tasks. Benefiting from the neuromorphic vertex–edge structure, graph theory problems can be mapped onto the hardware [58,72,73]. Additionally, it has been applied to solving NP-complete problems [74].

Neuromorphic computing often aims to replicate aspects of biological neural processing in hardware, but there is an ongoing debate over how strictly such systems must adhere to biophysical plausibility versus employing more abstract ML methods. On the one hand, SNN models, such as the Izhikevich formulation [75], focus on capturing the temporal dynamics of real neurons, which can yield insights into how biological brains encode and process information. Research has shown that such models can replicate a variety of neuronal firing patterns with computational efficiency, providing a bridge between computational neuroscience and neuromorphic engineering [76]. On the other hand, more traditional ML algorithms, such as Bayesian inference [77], support vector machines [78], or the large language models [79] dominating modern AI, tend to trade some fidelity to biological detail for mathematical tractability, scalability, and often better empirical performance on a range of industrial tasks.

Despite the proven feasibility of neuromorphic computing in many tasks, it remains largely experimental. In today's landscape of energy-consuming AI driven by GPU clusters, bringing neuromorphic computing out of the lab and achieving performance equal to or better than GPU-based AI with low energy consumption is a significant trend [80–82]. Standardised hardware protocols and community-maintained software will be crucial. From a neuroscience research perspective, neuromorphic computing simulates brain structures to varying degrees. Leveraging these simulations could provide new insights into neural mechanisms and brain function. Neuromorphic computing has a close-loop relationship with both AI and neuroscience, drawing inspiration from and serving both fields, tightly linking their development and advancing our understanding of intelligence.

3.4. Optical Computing

Optical computing utilises the properties of light to perform parallel computations, providing the potential to significantly exceed the speed and efficiency of electronic computing [83]. Unlike electronic computing, which relies on the movement of electrical charges, optical computing uses photons to carry and process information. Because light travels faster and experiences minimal resistance, optical computing has the potential to significantly improve processing speeds and energy efficiency. Research in optical computing can be traced back to the early 1960s [84]. Over the years, the primary focus of optical computing has been on integrating optical components for communication within computer systems or incorporating optical functions due to advances in electronic technology [84]. Although these elements remain under development and have yet to mature, the adaptation and exploration of optical computing, especially in AI, have grown rapidly in recent years due to the boom in AI and the limitations of traditional electrical architectures. To explore the emerging trends in optical computing, we first examine the different categories of optical computing systems and then discuss the potential and outlook of optical computing in AI.

Optical computing systems can be categorised into analogue, digital, and hybrid optical computing systems (OCS). Each category differs in how it processes information, balancing speed, precision, and scalability. Analogue optical computing systems (AOCS) utilise the continuous nature of light to perform computations, leveraging properties such as intensity, phase, and wavelength to represent and process data. This enables high precision and real-time processing capabilities, making AOCS suitable for signal processing and image recognition applications. On the other hand, digital optical computing systems (DOCS) operate on binary principles similar to traditional electronic computers, where light is used to represent binary data (0's and 1's) and perform logical operations through optical gates. DOCS can achieve exceptionally high-speed processing and parallelism, ideal for tasks requiring rapid data computation. However, scalability and integration difficulties pose significant challenges for DOCS, particularly in large-scale systems. Hybrid optical computing systems (HOCS) combine the strengths of both analogue and digital approaches, integrating continuous and discrete data representations to optimise performance across a broader range of applications. By leveraging the unique advantages of light, such as its speed and bandwidth, these hybrid systems can enhance computational efficiency and open new frontiers in fields such as telecommunications, AI, and scientific simulations. Table 1 summarises the features of these three systems.

Table 1. Comparison of optical computing systems. This table compares analogue optical computing systems (AOCS), digital optical computing systems (DOCS), and hybrid optical computing systems (HOCS) based on key characteristics such as data type, speed, error susceptibility, complexity, integration challenges, and applications.

Feature	AOCS	DOCS	HOCS
Data type	Continuous	Discrete (binary)	Both continuous and discrete
Speed	Very high	High	High
Error susceptibility	Higher	Lower	Balanced
Complexity	Lower	Higher	Medium
Integration	Challenging	Easier	Moderate
Applications	Real-time processing, imaging	Logic operations, data storage	Neural networks, adaptive optics

Optical computing also leverages optical components such as microring resonators (MRRs) and Mach–Zehnder interferometers (MZIs) to design essential elements such as logic gates, switches, storage devices, routers, and photonic integrated circuits. Microring resonators act as miniature loops that guide and filter light, while Mach–Zehnder interferometers function as optical switches, enabling precise control over light-based computations. The development of these components has been pivotal in advancing the field, leading to the creation of more compact and powerful photonic circuits. Initially, research focused on the fundamental properties of light and how it could be manipulated for computation. Over time, advancements in materials science and nanofabrication have enabled greater miniaturisation and improved integration of optical components.

Optical computing is making significant strides across multiple domains, particularly in telecommunications, AI, and HPC. Key areas of impact include the following: *1. Telecommunications:* Optical components enhance data transmission speeds and network capacity. Photonic technologies in fibre-optic networks reduce latency and increase bandwidth, making them integral to modern communication infrastructures [85]. *2. AI:* Optical neural networks, particularly those utilising MZIs, enable AI computations at speeds beyond conventional electronic processors. One notable example is the use of optical matrix multiplication for accelerating deep learning models, significantly reducing energy consumption in AI training [86]. *3. HPC:* The integration of photonic integrated circuits (PICs) and photonic–electronic co-design is advancing HPC infrastructures [87]. The adoption of optical interconnects in HPC provides high bandwidth and lower energy consumption, significantly improving data transfer efficiency for large-scale simulations and AI training [88]. Despite these advancements, optical computing still faces challenges, including manufacturing complexities, optical loss, and crosstalk, which hinder large-scale adoption [89]. However, ongoing research in photonic materials and integrated circuit design continues to address these limitations, paving the way for more scalable optical computing solutions.

Optical computing has evolved significantly with advances in component technology, growing applications, and increasing research interest. While it is not yet poised to replace electronic computing entirely, it is expected to play a complementary role, particularly in areas demanding ultra-fast, energy-efficient computations. As research progresses, breakthroughs in nanophotonics, integrated optical chips, and AI-driven photonic computing will likely drive optical computing toward mainstream adoption. With further improvements in scalability and integration, optical computing may soon redefine HPC, revolutionising fields such as AI, communications, and beyond. For readers interested in a more in-depth exploration of optical computing, the review papers [84,86,90], as well as the book [91], provide comprehensive insights into its fundamentals and applications.

4. Emerging Trends in Distributed Systems

In the rapidly evolving landscape of computing, distributed systems have become integral to handling the scale, complexity, and diversity of modern applications. By leveraging multiple interconnected computing resources, distributed systems provide scalable, resilient, and efficient solutions that traditional centralised systems cannot offer. As data volumes grow exponentially and applications demand real-time processing and decision-making, innovative approaches in distributed computing are essential. This section explores the emerging trends in distributed systems, focusing on four key areas: blockchain and distributed ledgers, serverless computing, cloud-native architectures, and distributed AI and ML systems. These advancements are redefining how data are managed, processed, and secured across various industries, enabling new possibilities while addressing critical scalability, efficiency, security, and privacy challenges.

4.1. Blockchain and Distributed Ledgers

The concept of the blockchain was first coined by Satoshi Nakamoto in 2008 after the failure of the global financial system in 2007 [92]. Though he did not formally define the blockchain, he demonstrated the blockchain concept for electronic cash (called Bitcoin) transfers where no central authority is needed to prevent double-spending. The first successful Bitcoin transaction took place in 2009 when Satoshi Nakamoto transferred 10 BTC (Bitcoin) to Hal Finney. Satoshi uses a peer-to-peer network to timestamp transactions through a hash-based Proof-of-Work chain, which acts as an unchangeable record unless the Proof of Work is redone. However, the concept of blockchain is fundamentally based on three elements: (i) blind signature, a cryptographic concept proposed by David Chaum in 1989 for automation of payment [93]; (ii) timestamped documents which secure digital documents by stamping the documents with the date [94]; and (iii) Reusable Proof of Work (RPoW), a mechanism for preventing double-spending and securing decentralized networks, later extended into a reusable format by Hal Finney in 2004 [95]. Therefore, researchers formally defined the blockchain as a meta-technology which combines several computing techniques [96]. However, the most widely adopted definition of blockchain is a distributed digital ledger technology with a ledger of transactions, or blocks, that form a systematic, linear chain of all transactions ever made. Blockchain presents timestamped and immutable blocks of highly encrypted and anonymised data not owned or mediated by any specific person or groups [97,98]. A block in a blockchain is primarily identified by its block header hash or block hash, a cryptographic hash made by hashing the block header twice through the SHA256 algorithm. In addition, a block can also be identified by the block height, which is its position in the blockchain or the number of blocks preceding it in the blockchain. The Merkle tree offers a secure and efficient way to create a digital fingerprint for the complete set of transactions. A blockchain structure is shown in Figure 6, where blocks are connected through their respective hash code.

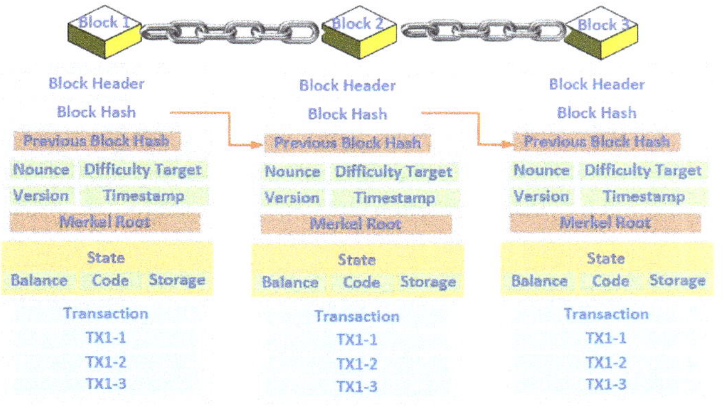

Figure 6. Basic structure of a blockchain block. This figure presents the fundamental components of a blockchain block, explaining how distributed ledger technology ensures security and integrity in decentralised networks.

Distributed ledger technology (DLT) is the underlying generalised concept that makes the blockchain work in a distributed platform. The concept of DLT incorporates principles from "The Byzantine General Problem", described by Lamport et al. [99], which evaluates the strategies for achieving consensus in distributed systems despite conflicting information in an adversarial environment. Consensus protocols, like Proof of Stake, allow participants to achieve a shared view of the ledger without intermediaries. Emerging mechanisms, such as Proof of Space and Proof of Authority [100], have gained attention for their lower energy consumption and faster transaction verification times compared to Proof of Work. These mechanisms aim to address the inefficiencies and environmental impacts associated with traditional methods, offering tailored solutions for specific use cases. Additionally, cryptographic techniques, such as the Schnorr Signature Scheme and Merkle Tree, enhance data integrity and trust within blockchain frameworks, reinforcing secure data verification processes [101]. A distributed ledger is a digital record maintained across a network of machines, known as nodes, with any updates being reflected simultaneously for all participants and authenticated through cryptographic signatures [102].

Beyond cryptocurrencies, blockchain's applications span a wide range of industries, including eHealth [103,104], intellectual property [105,106], education, digital identity, finance [107–109], supply chain [110–112], IoT [113–115], etc. In supply chain management, blockchain frameworks such as IBM Food Trust provide end-to-end traceability, ensuring transparency and accountability. Case studies, such as Walmart's use of blockchain to track food provenance, have quantified significant reductions in tracing times, from days to seconds, illustrating blockchain's potential to streamline operations and mitigate fraud. In healthcare, blockchain's anonymity and immutability features make it unparalleled for secure information sharing among different providers, forming the foundation of modern healthcare, alternatively termed Healthcare 5.0. Numerous frameworks such as MeDShare [116], Medblock [117], HealthBlock [118], and BLOSOM [119] have been developed to secure patient records. BCIF-EHR, an interoperable blockchain-based framework proposed in [103], facilitates seamless sharing and integration of electronic health records (EHRs) while preserving privacy and security. However, the framework requires a decentralised authentication and access control mechanism to restrict access to authorised entities only. Addressing this limitation, TrustHealth [104] integrates blockchain with a trusted execution environment, designing a secure database that ensures the confidentiality and integrity of EHRs. TrustHealth also incorporates a secure session key generation protocol, enabling secure communication channels between healthcare providers and the trusted execution environment. Such advancements exemplify blockchain's ability to transform healthcare by improving interoperability, security, and trust.

Despite its broad applicability, blockchain faces challenges such as latency and high energy consumption, particularly in Proof-of-Work-based systems. These issues can hinder real-time applications and raise concerns about environmental sustainability. Additionally, blockchain's reliance on distributed consensus mechanisms can lead to cold-start issues in networks with low node participation, delaying transaction validation. Overall, blockchain's transformative potential lies in its ability to provide secure, transparent, and decentralised solutions across diverse sectors, fundamentally changing how data integrity and trust are managed.

4.2. Serverless Computing

The concept of serverless computing emerged in the mid-2000s with cloud services like Amazon S3 and EC2, which simplified infrastructure management for developers [120]. However, a major breakthrough came in 2014 with the introduction of AWS Lambda [121], which established the Function-as-a-Service (FaaS) model. This allowed developers to execute code in response to events without managing servers, providing automatic scaling and reducing operational overhead [122]. IBM OpenWhisk (2016) later expanded on this concept by offering an open-source alternative that prioritised flexibility [123]. Further advancements included Microsoft Azure Functions [124] and Google Cloud Run [125], which integrated containerised workloads to extend serverless capabilities.

Serverless computing provides automatic scalability, eliminating the need for manual resource management. A key advantage of this model is its "pay-as-you-go" pricing structure, where users pay only for the compute time they consume rather than pre-allocated resources, significantly reducing costs for variable workloads [126]. These benefits make serverless computing ideal for applications such as web services [127], IoT [128], and large-scale data processing [129]. Industries including finance, healthcare, and e-commerce utilise serverless computing to enable rapid scaling and resource efficiency. Major companies like Netflix and Airbnb rely on serverless architectures to handle fluctuating traffic loads, ensuring a smooth user experience during peak demand [130]. Studies indicate that serverless platforms can handle up to 10,000 concurrent function executions while maintaining response times below 500 ms, making them suitable for real-time applications [131].

Despite its advantages, serverless computing presents several challenges. One major concern is cold-start latency, which occurs when an idle function is invoked and requires initialisation. To mitigate this, techniques such as function pre-warming, optimising container configurations, and adjusting function granularity have been developed, reducing cold-start delays by up to 50% in production environments [132,133]. Another issue is vendor lock-in, where applications become dependent on proprietary cloud provider implementations. To overcome this, multi-cloud serverless frameworks like Knative and OpenFaaS have emerged, allowing developers to deploy serverless workloads across multiple providers, increasing flexibility and reducing dependency risks [134]. Furthermore, serverless architectures are not well suited for long-running processes, as they impose execution time limits. Hybrid serverless–edge computing models are increasingly being explored to process latency-sensitive workloads closer to the data source, particularly for IoT applications [135].

Ongoing advancements aim to enhance serverless computing's flexibility and performance. AI-based function pre-warming, such as Alibaba Cloud's Function Compute prediction models, proactively warms up instances to reduce startup delays [136]. Federated serverless architectures provide cost-effectiveness and resource efficiency [137].

Additionally, confidential computing techniques like secure enclaves are being integrated to enhance function-level security, mitigating multi-tenant isolation concerns [138]. For high-frequency workloads, the unpredictable costs of serverless computing can sometimes make traditional cloud computing a more economical option. Research into more transparent and cost-efficient serverless pricing structures is ongoing [139].

Overall, while serverless computing offers scalability, cost efficiency, and operational flexibility, its adoption requires addressing challenges related to latency, vendor dependence, and security. Continued advancements in optimisation techniques, multi-cloud interoperability, and pricing models will further enhance its impact on the future of cloud computing.

4.3. Cloud-Native Architectures

Cloud-native architectures began with distributed systems research in the 1990s [140] and the introduction of virtualisation by VMware in 1998 [141]. In 2006, AWS launched EC2 and S3, making on-demand cloud services widely available [120]. DevOps ideas took off around 2009 [142], combining development and operations to speed up software delivery. Docker emerged in 2013 as a platform for packaging applications into lightweight containers [143], followed by Google's open-source release of Kubernetes in 2014 to orchestrate and manage containerized workloads [144].

Docker emerged in 2013 for packaging applications into lightweight containers [143], followed by Google's open-source release of Kubernetes in 2014 to orchestrate and manage containerised workloads [144]. The Cloud Native Computing Foundation (CNCF) formed in 2015 and made Kubernetes its first project [144], while AWS Lambda (launched in 2014) introduced serverless computing [121], and service meshes emerged to handle microservice communication [128].

Today, cloud-native architecture optimises cloud application performance by integrating microservices, containerisation, and continuous integration/continuous delivery (as shown in Figure 7) [145,146]. These techniques enable modularity, scalability, and reliability. Microservices divide applications into independent, manageable services, containerisation ensures consistent deployment, and CI/CD accelerates the development life cycle, creating a robust framework for efficiently handling dynamic workloads. Tools like Docker and Kubernetes simplify container orchestration, streamline scaling, and accelerate deployment pipelines [147]. Unlike traditional monolithic structures, cloud-native applications are modular, allowing components to be managed, scaled, and updated independently. This makes cloud-native architectures highly effective in dynamic environments demanding rapid iteration and resilient deployment [148–150].

Alongside these core components, advanced communication paradigms such as Partitioned Global Address Space (PGAS) models and Remote Direct Memory Access (RDMA) further enhance cloud-native platforms [151]. PGAS models provide a shared memory abstraction across distributed systems, emphasising data locality and reducing communication overhead, making them particularly suitable for high-performance applications in cloud environments. RDMA further enhances infrastructure efficiency by enabling direct memory-to-memory transfers between nodes, bypassing CPU involvement to minimise latency and maximise throughput. These technologies are critical for optimising the performance of modern distributed systems and are increasingly adopted in cloud-native platforms.

Cloud-native architectures also play a pivotal role in Industry 4.0, where real-time data processing across IoT and edge devices matters most. These architectures realise smooth integration in distributed systems, hence managing large-scale, latency-sensitive data efficiently [152]. By incorporating PGAS and RDMA, these architectures can handle complex data flows and resource-intensive tasks with greater efficiency, supporting the scalability demands of Industry 4.0. One of the prominent design elements of cloud-native designs is the multi-cloud and distributed cloud models that, for instance, enable the deployment of applications across multiple cloud providers [153]. This increases availability and avoids vendor lock-in, giving flexibility and resilience to enterprises by utilising unique services across cloud platforms [154].

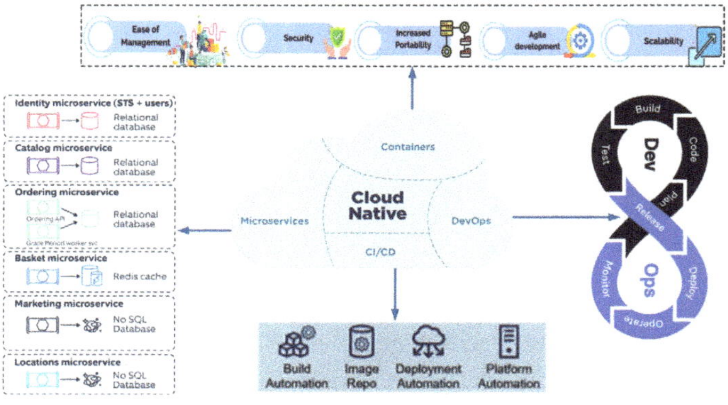

Figure 7. Key building blocks of a cloud-native architecture. This figure illustrates the four fundamental components of cloud-native systems: containers, microservices, DevOps, and CI/CD. These elements enable scalability, automation, and continuous deployment in modern cloud computing environments.

On top of this, cloud-native architectures leverage Platform-as-a-Service (PaaS) environments to simplify infrastructure management and scaling [155]. Cloud federation strategies improve interoperability across providers, enabling seamless service migration and management in heterogeneous systems [156]. Infrastructure as Code (IaC) automates resource provisioning, ensuring efficient and secure application deployment [157]. By combining these methods with advanced communication paradigms, cloud-native architectures offer robust fault tolerance and high resource utilisation, supporting a range of workloads from e-commerce to scientific computing.

Despite these benefits, cloud-native approaches come with their own set of challenges. Integrating PGAS and RDMA can be complex, requiring specialised hardware and in-depth expertise, which may raise costs and limit portability across diverse platforms. Deploying microservices at scale also necessitates comprehensive observability solutions to handle complex debugging and performance monitoring tasks. In multi-cloud scenarios, while the flexibility is appealing, organisations may still encounter partial vendor lock-in due to unique service integrations. Security remains a prominent concern, as misconfigurations in container orchestration or vulnerabilities within microservices can open pathways for data breaches. Additionally, the rapid pace of innovation in the cloud-native ecosystem demands continual learning and adaptation, placing pressure on both developers and operators to stay abreast of emerging tools and best practices [144]. Balancing these challenges with the clear advantages of agility, scalability, and resilience is essential for successful adoption across various industries.

4.4. Distributed AI and ML Systems

Distributed AI and ML systems are the backbone for scalable training and deployment of complex models across decentralised networks [158]. Unlike the centralised approach, this architecture allows the computation to be distributed among different nodes, reducing the latency in training and efficiently processing large datasets [159]. This ML approach can optimise learning and AI inference, particularly for resource-constrained devices such as IoT or edge computing devices used in real-time applications [160]. It aligns with the principles of federated learning, which allow for collaborative model training without the need to share raw data, thus preserving data privacy and reducing bandwidth demands [161]. By leveraging intelligent agents in a distributed environment, these systems can significantly reduce model training time while maintaining robust fault tolerance [162]. Moreover, distributed learning algorithms applied in different application areas, such as 6G [163] and smart grid systems [164], illustrate how these methods can optimise resource usage and enable real-time decision-making with minimal latency. Advanced variants, such as AutoDAL, enable automatic hyperparameter tuning within distributed learning frameworks, addressing scalability and efficiency challenges in large-scale data analysis [165].

Federated learning is an emerging area in distributed AI, allowing model training across decentralised devices or servers without centralising raw data. This approach improves privacy and reduces data transfer costs, with models trained locally on edge devices and only shared parameters sent back to central servers, as shown in Figure 8 [166]. Federated learning is especially valuable in applications with strict privacy requirements, such as healthcare and finance, where regulatory constraints limit centralised data storage [167]. However, federated systems face significant challenges in balancing privacy preservation and model accuracy. Privacy-preserving techniques, such as differential privacy and secure multi-party computation, introduce noise or encryption that can reduce model performance [168]. To address this, privacy-aware optimisation algorithms, such as those incorporating adaptive noise levels or secure aggregation protocols, have been proposed to maintain accuracy while ensuring data security [169,170]. Another critical challenge in federated systems is communication overhead, especially in scenarios involving frequent synchronisation of model updates across devices. This overhead can significantly increase latency and reduce efficiency in large-scale systems. Potential solutions include strategies like periodic aggregation, where updates are transmitted at predefined intervals rather than continuously [171], and selective model updates, which prioritise transmitting critical updates based on gradient sparsity or importance [172]. Additionally, techniques such as gradient compression and quantised updates can minimise communication costs without sacrificing accuracy, making federated learning more scalable and efficient in distributed environments [173,174]. These advancements demonstrate that federated learning can address privacy and efficiency challenges effectively, paving the way for its widespread adoption in privacy-sensitive domains.

Distributed training systems enable simultaneous model training across multiple nodes, significantly accelerating the development of complex AI models. Techniques like data parallelism, model parallelism, and pipeline parallelism optimise resource usage, making them essential for large-scale training tasks in fields like natural language processing and computer vision, where computational demands are exceptionally high [175]. By distributing workloads across multiple nodes, these systems reduce the dependence on centralised infrastructures, promoting scalable, efficient, and resource-adaptive ML [176]. Despite these advantages, distributed training systems face several challenges that limit their efficiency and effectiveness. Communication overhead, caused by frequent synchronisation of parameters across nodes, can result in increased latency and inefficient bandwidth utilisation, particularly in large-scale systems [177]. Techniques like gradient sparsification [178], optimised collective communication protocols [31], and Asynchronous Stochastic Gradient Descent (ASGD) [179,180] aim to mitigate these issues by reducing the volume of data transmitted during updates and allowing nodes to operate more independently.

However, these methods often struggle to maintain model accuracy due to inconsistent parameter updates [181], requiring advanced consistency management algorithms, such as dynamic weighting of updates, to address this trade-off. Another significant challenge is managing data heterogeneity, as data distributed across nodes are often non-IID (non-independent and identically distributed), leading to skewed model updates that hinder training effectiveness [182]. Solutions like adaptive loss functions, dynamic weighting of local models, and frameworks such as AdaFed [183] dynamically adjust the contributions of local models based on data quality, improving convergence. Privacy-preserving methods, such as differential privacy and secure multi-party computation, add further complexity by introducing noise or encryption to protect sensitive data, which can degrade model accuracy [184]. Privacy-aware optimisation strategies such as PSDF [185] are being developed to balance security with performance. Resource optimisation is another critical issue [186], particularly in decentralised environments with heterogeneous hardware capabilities and network reliability. Adaptive resource allocation frameworks that dynamically adjust computation and communication parameters based on workload demands and node capacities [187] are essential for efficient resource utilisation, but implementing these frameworks requires robust scheduling algorithms and real-time monitoring. Addressing these challenges through innovative algorithms, resource management strategies, and privacy-aware techniques is essential for unlocking the full potential of distributed training systems.

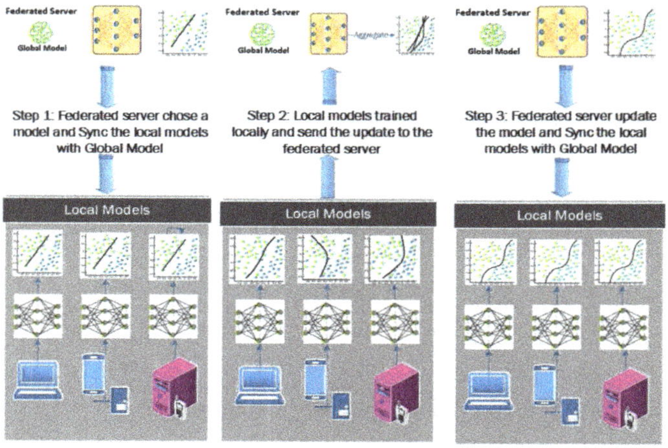

Figure 8. Step-by-step illustration of federated ML. This figure explains the federated learning process, highlighting key stages such as local model training, aggregation, and privacy-preserving updates.

In summary, distributed AI and ML systems offer transformative potential by enabling scalable, efficient, and secure training across decentralised networks, while challenges such as communication overhead, data heterogeneity, and synchronisation remain, ongoing advancements in adaptive algorithms and privacy-preserving methods continue to address these issues, paving the way for widespread adoption in sectors like healthcare, finance, and IoT.

5. Challenges in Parallel and Distributed Systems

Parallel and distributed systems have revolutionised the way computational tasks are performed, enabling the handling of complex and large-scale applications. However, these systems face several challenges that can hinder their efficiency and effectiveness. This section delves into the key challenges in parallel and distributed systems, including scalability and performance, security and privacy, fault tolerance and reliability, interoperability and standardisation, energy efficiency, and ethical concerns.

5.1. Scalability and Performance

Achieving scalability while maintaining high performance is one of the foremost challenges in parallel and distributed systems. As the number of processors or nodes increases, bottlenecks can arise due to limitations in network bandwidth, synchronisation overhead, and resource contention [188]. These issues can significantly degrade system performance, negating the benefits of adding more computational resources. A notable example of scalability challenges is in distributed AI systems, where training large-scale models like GPT3 involves 175 billion parameters spread across thousands of GPUs [189,190]. Synchronisation overhead during gradient updates can significantly impact training efficiency, especially as the number of GPUs increases [191]. Studies have shown that communication overhead during parameter updates and gradient synchronisation can dominate the training time in large-scale distributed systems, reducing the benefits of scaling out [192]. Additionally, memory bandwidth and latency constraints exacerbate the problem, reducing the overall efficiency of these systems [175].

Addressing these challenges requires integrated solutions that consider the distinct demands of heterogeneous, quantum, neuromorphic, and optical computing paradigms. In heterogeneous computing, task scheduling algorithms ensure efficient workload distribution among diverse processing units (e.g., CPUs, GPUs, DPUs) to prevent resource underutilisation [193]. Advanced scheduling algorithms dynamically assign tasks to appropriate processors, optimising execution and guaranteeing energy consumption [194]. For quantum computing, modular quantum architectures and hybrid quantum–classical systems help manage the scalability of qubit systems while reducing error propagation [195]. In neuromorphic computing, innovations such as photonics integration, online learning, and 3D stacking enhance the scalability of ANNs by increasing density and reducing power consumption [196]. For optical computing, material advancements such as silicon photonics and integrated photonic circuits enable the scaling of optical interconnects while minimising crosstalk and optical loss. Hardware/software co-design innovations further enhance the performance of optical computing systems [87]. Optimising communication protocols [197], dynamic resource allocation [198], and adaptive scheduling algorithms [199] improve data transfer and task management. Gradient compression techniques in distributed AI systems reduce communication delays, while optical interconnects [85] and optical wireless communication [200] provide high-bandwidth, low-latency data transfer, enhancing overall system efficiency. Together, these advancements improve workload distribution, enabling parallel and distributed systems to scale efficiently and meet the demands of complex modern applications.

5.2. Security and Privacy

Security and privacy are paramount concerns in distributed environments where data and resources are shared across multiple nodes [201]. Threats such as unauthorised access, data breaches, and malicious attacks can compromise the integrity and confidentiality of the system. Distributed systems are particularly vulnerable due to their open and interconnected nature, which can be exploited by attackers. A notable case involved a major cloud service provider experiencing downtime across its network due to a coordinated ransomware attack, resulting in financial losses exceeding USD 1.85 million and extensive recovery efforts [202]. Similarly, in parallel systems used for HPC, side-channel attacks that exploit shared memory vulnerabilities have exposed sensitive data, highlighting the need for enhanced security measures [203].

To address these challenges, robust security solutions should span hardware, software, and cryptographic advancements [204]. Encryption methods such as AES-256 and secure communication protocols like TLS ensure data protection during storage and transmission, while authentication mechanisms, including multi-factor authentication, enhance access control [205]. Zero-trust architectures and Trusted Execution Environments limit attack surfaces by isolating sensitive computations and continuously validating user and device credentials [206]. In distributed systems like blockchain, mechanisms such as Merkle trees and Proof-of-Stake consensus algorithms maintain data integrity and ensure secure transaction validation [207]. With the advent of quantum computing, post-quantum cryptography, including lattice-based cryptography, and quantum key distribution are critical for securing communications and future-proofing systems against quantum-enabled threats [208]. These solutions, when integrated into parallel and distributed systems, provide resilience against evolving cyber threats, safeguarding user privacy and ensuring system reliability.

5.3. Fault Tolerance and Reliability

Fault tolerance and reliability are critical in ensuring that parallel and distributed systems continue to operate correctly even in the presence of component failures [209]. Hardware malfunctions, network issues, or software errors can lead to system downtime or data loss, which is unacceptable in mission-critical applications. For instance, distributed systems supporting global financial transactions need to maintain uninterrupted operation despite hardware failures or network disruptions, as downtime can result in significant financial and reputational losses [210].

Many methods have been proposed to address these challenges in various distributed computing scenarios. Redundancy and replication ensure high availability and data integrity by maintaining multiple copies of critical data across nodes [206], while checkpointing periodically saves system states, enabling recovery without restarting entire processes [211]. Self-healing algorithms and dynamic task migration mitigate the impact of hardware and software failures by redistributing workloads to healthy nodes or components [212]. Similarly, modular architectures and error-correcting codes enhance the reliability of quantum systems by addressing decoherence and qubit failures [209]. Neuromorphic systems benefit from fault-tolerant designs and techniques that accommodate various types of resistive random-access memory faults [213]. Optical interconnect systems rely on the ONOS SDN controller for dynamic provisioning of data connectivity services and advanced automatic failure recovery [214]. Middleware solutions, such as those supporting distributed frameworks (e.g., Apache Spark) or blockchain consensus algorithms (e.g., Proof of Stake), enhance robustness against node failures and maintain consistency across distributed systems [210]. By integrating these strategies, parallel and distributed systems can enhance reliability, minimise disruptions, and meet the demands of modern mission-critical applications.

5.4. Interoperability and Standardisation

In heterogeneous environments where diverse systems and technologies coexist, interoperability becomes a significant challenge [215]. Orchestrating operations across different platforms, protocols, and interfaces requires careful coordination. Without standardisation, integrating new components or scaling the system can lead to incompatibilities and increased complexity. Managing heterogeneity in UHC systems, where CPUs, GPUs, NPUs, and DPUs have to collaborate seamlessly, exacerbates these challenges.

To address these challenges, adopting standardised communication protocols and resource allocation frameworks is essential [216]. Protocols like MPI and NCCL enable efficient data exchange in parallel systems [197], while resource allocation frameworks such as Kubernetes facilitate task distribution in distributed systems [144]. Middleware solutions abstract hardware and platform differences, simplifying the integration of components in heterogeneous and distributed environments [206]. For quantum systems, modular architectures and standardised quantum gates ensure compatibility between quantum and classical components, enabling hybrid quantum–classical workflows [217]. Neuromorphic systems require different neural coding schemes for achieving the best performance of neuromorphic systems under different design constraints [218]. In optical systems, the optical gates, photonic integrated circuits, and optical architectures are still evolving, and the development of standards and related protocols is ongoing [89]. Industry standards and open architectures promote interoperability, allowing diverse systems to work together while fostering collaborative innovation. For example, distributed frameworks like Apache Hadoop and TensorFlow support heterogeneous hardware, ensuring compatibility across CPUs, GPUs, and accelerators [219]. Such standardisation efforts reduce development costs, streamline integration, and enable parallel and distributed systems to scale efficiently, incorporating emerging technologies with minimal complexity.

5.5. Energy Efficiency

As parallel and distributed systems scale up, power consumption becomes a growing concern [220]. High energy usage not only increases operational costs but also has environmental implications due to the carbon footprint associated with large data centres and computing clusters. A notable example is the training of large-scale AI models like GPT-3, which reportedly consumed approximately 1287 megawatt-hours (MWh) of electricity during its training phase, emitting over 550 metric tons of carbon dioxide if powered by non-renewable sources [221]. This substantial energy use underscores the importance of implementing energy-efficient solutions across all parallel and distributed systems.

Addressing energy-efficiency challenges in parallel and distributed systems requires a holistic approach that integrates energy-efficient hardware, intelligent algorithms, dynamic power management, and sustainable infrastructure. Hardware innovations, such as neuromorphic chips like Intel's Loihi [63] and optical network processors [222,223], significantly reduce energy consumption through specialised designs and advanced technologies. Energy-aware algorithms, such as SkipTrain in decentralised learning [224], enhance efficiency by strategically skipping certain training rounds and replacing them with synchronisation rounds. Quantum algorithms like QAOA further minimise computational overhead, improving overall energy efficiency [216]. At the infrastructure level, renewable-powered data centres [220] and dynamic workload migration support sustainable operations. Additionally, techniques such as dynamic voltage and frequency scaling (DVFS) and adaptive power gating optimise energy usage by adjusting power levels based on workload demands [225]. For blockchain systems, energy-efficient consensus protocols such as Proof of Authority reduce power consumption while maintaining security and operational viability [100], helping to mitigate their environmental impact.

5.6. Emerging Ethical Concerns

As AI becomes increasingly integrated into parallel and distributed systems, ethical concerns have emerged as a critical challenge [226]. Issues such as algorithmic bias, misuse of sensitive user data, and lack of transparency in decision-making processes can undermine trust, fairness, and accountability in AI-driven systems [227]. For example, biased AI models deployed in distributed healthcare platforms can lead to unequal treatment outcomes, disproportionately disadvantaging marginalised groups [228]. Similarly, inadequate data governance in cloud-based AI systems can result in privacy violations, exposing sensitive user information to misuse or unauthorised access [229].

Addressing these challenges requires a multi-faceted approach across governance, technology, and collaboration. Robust governance frameworks and adherence to ethical guidelines throughout the AI life cycle are essential for ensuring accountability. Explainable AI (XAI) techniques can improve transparency by providing interpretable insights into decision-making processes, reducing the risk of biased or opaque outcomes [230]. Privacy-preserving technologies, such as federated learning, allow data to remain decentralised, mitigating risks associated with data misuse or breaches [167]. Federated learning has shown promise in fields like healthcare, enabling collaborative model training without compromising data privacy [231]. Additionally, interdisciplinary collaborations among technologists, ethicists, and policymakers are vital for establishing standards and policies that promote equitable and responsible AI deployment. Standards such as fairness metrics, model validation protocols, and data auditing mechanisms ensure AI systems align with ethical principles. For instance, blockchain-based audit trails can improve accountability in distributed systems by recording data usage and decision-making processes securely and transparently [232]. By integrating these strategies, parallel and distributed systems can address emerging ethical concerns, fostering trust and ensuring sustainable, equitable development.

6. Future Directions

Building on the challenges outlined in this paper, it is evident that significant advancements are still needed to overcome scalability, energy efficiency, and security limitations in parallel and distributed systems. As these systems evolve, several emerging technologies and research areas show promise for addressing current obstacles and driving innovation. This section discusses the future directions of each class of parallel and distributed systems.

- *Heterogeneous computing:* As computing moves towards UHC architectures integrating diverse processors such as CPUs, GPUs, TPUs, FPGAs, and specialised accelerators, significant advancements are required to address challenges in scalability, energy efficiency, and complexity [233]. These architectures have the potential to revolutionise computing by leveraging the unique strengths of each processor type; however, their successful implementation depends on overcoming several critical obstacles. One key research direction is the development of hybrid scheduling algorithms [234]. These algorithms should dynamically adapt to varying computational demands, both online and offline, while optimising energy efficiency and performance [235]. Additionally, designing energy-aware resource management frameworks that minimise power consumption without compromising computational throughput is crucial for meeting sustainability goals [236]. Another vital area of focus is high-bandwidth, low-latency interconnect technologies, which are essential for seamless data exchange among heterogeneous components [237]. Innovations such as photonic interconnects and 3D packaging can alleviate bandwidth bottlenecks and reduce latency, enabling efficient communication between processors [238]. To enhance developer adoption and simplify programming for heterogeneous systems, further refinement of frameworks such as CUDA, OpenCL, SYCL, and oneAPI, as well as emerging unified programming models like CodeFlow [239], is essential. These frameworks should provide robust abstractions, allowing developers to harness the full potential of diverse architectures without dealing with low-level hardware complexities. Finally, synergies among quantum computing, neuromorphic systems, optical computing, and optical interconnects present exciting opportunities for future exploration. Advancing these interdisciplinary technologies will be critical in shaping the next generation of high-performance, energy-efficient computing architectures.

- *Quantum computing:* The future trajectory of quantum computing is shaped by several critical technological and practical imperatives. At the hardware level, the ongoing development of diverse qubit technologies—including superconducting, silicon-based, trapped-ion, and photonic implementations—remains essential for advancing quantum computing capabilities [36,42,43]. While these platforms have demonstrated significant progress, challenges such as noise reduction, high error rates, and decoherence should be effectively addressed to realise practical quantum advantage [37] Current quantum error correction protocols require substantial qubit overhead, necessitating innovative approaches that can scale efficiently with system size [240] Industry roadmaps, such as IBM's plan to develop processors with thousands of qubits [46], highlight the importance of achieving fault tolerance while maintaining quantum coherence across larger qubit arrays. The integration of quantum computing with classical computing represents a promising direction for near-term applications. Hybrid quantum–classical systems, particularly in ML and optimisation tasks, can leverage the complementary strengths of both paradigms [217]. To facilitate broader adoption, the field will address interconnected challenges, including quantum infrastructure development. Establishing robust quantum networking protocols and leveraging optical interconnects will be crucial for scaling quantum systems beyond single-processor implementations [195]. Additionally, the development of standardised quantum software frameworks and advanced error mitigation techniques will be instrumental in enhancing accessibility and usability [240]. Beyond technical advancements, the socioeconomic implications of quantum computing warrant careful consideration. The transformative potential of quantum technologies spans multiple industries, with significant applications in cryptography [47] and molecular simulation [48]. Ensuring equitable access to quantum resources and fostering a skilled quantum workforce will be critical in maximising the societal benefits of quantum computing across diverse sectors and regions.
- *Neuromorphic computing:* Inspired by the brain's architecture, neuromorphic computing is rapidly emerging as a promising solution for achieving energy-efficient, event-driven processing, particularly in AI and ML tasks [53]. Despite its potential, scalability remains a significant hurdle, as building larger neuromorphic systems demands advancements in technological infrastructure, development tools, and integration strategies [59]. Future progress should focus on enhancing the programmability of neuromorphic hardware to enable larger, more complex systems capable of addressing diverse AI and ML workloads [241]. This includes improving the flexibility and accessibility of programming environments to facilitate adoption by a broader range of developers and researchers. In parallel, the development of SNNs as foundational algorithms requires further exploration, particularly in areas such as backpropagation [56] and online learning [242], to enhance their adaptability, scalability, and real-time performance. The practical adoption of neuromorphic hardware faces challenges such as the lack of standardised protocols and the high costs of chip fabrication. Initiatives like Intel's Loihi 2 platform have demonstrated progress in commercialising neuromorphic computing [65], but broader collaboration among academia, industry, and policymakers will be necessary to standardise frameworks, reduce costs, and accelerate adoption. Integrating neuromorphic computing with photonics presents a promising avenue for addressing key challenges, including scalability, energy efficiency, precision, and standardised performance benchmarks [196]. As the technology evolves, addressing ethical concerns and promoting the responsible

use of brain-inspired systems will be critical [243]. Ensuring equitable access, avoiding misuse, and fostering transparency in neuromorphic applications will help ensure that the technology benefits society responsibly.

- *Optical computing:* The future of optical computing holds transformative potential for meeting the escalating demands of modern computing systems, particularly in AI, telecommunications, and HPC [84]. Advancing this technology requires addressing several critical research challenges through innovative solutions and interdisciplinary collaboration. A key research direction is the development of next-generation photonic integrated circuits, with a particular focus on advancing core components such as MRRs and MZIs [238]. These components will evolve to meet stringent requirements for scalability, efficiency, and reliability. The advancement of all-optical processing presents promising opportunities, including the development of optical gates and logical units, high bit-rate signal processing, and optical quantum computing [89]. High-performance optical interconnects offer significant advantages over traditional electrical interconnects, enabling efficient data transmission in large-scale systems such as data centres, supercomputers, and quantum networks [85]. Industry adoption is already underway, as demonstrated by Google's integration of photonic components in data centres and the emergence of optical neural network research prototypes [88]. In the quantum computing domain, optical components play a crucial role in facilitating high-bandwidth communication between quantum processors, addressing key challenges related to quantum network scalability and efficiency [195]. To accelerate the practical deployment of optical computing systems, research efforts should focus on three key areas: miniaturisation techniques, advanced materials development, and scalable manufacturing processes. These technological advancements are essential for achieving cost-effective, energy-efficient solutions that can expand access to HPC capabilities. This expansion is particularly crucial for small and medium-sized enterprises and academic institutions, which stand to benefit significantly from more accessible advanced computing resources. As optical computing technologies mature, they are poised to revolutionise industries by delivering unprecedented computational power, sustainability, and accessibility. This evolution represents a major step toward meeting the growing computational demands of modern society while aligning with global sustainability goals.
- *Blockchain and distributed ledgers:* Blockchain and DLTs present a decentralised, tamper-resistant way to ensure security and transparency in distributed systems [102]. These technologies eliminate intermediaries and offer immutable transaction records, enabling trustless environments in applications like cloud computing, IoT, and supply chain management. However, challenges such as latency, high energy consumption in Proof-of-Work-based systems, and cold-start delays hinder their scalability and responsiveness. Future research should prioritise the development of scalable blockchain architectures with energy-efficient consensus mechanisms [244]. Innovations such as Proof of Stake and sharding can significantly reduce energy consumption while maintaining robust security and enabling high transaction throughput [245]. These advancements are essential to ensuring blockchain's feasibility in real-time applications and resource-constrained environments. Another promising direction is the creation of tailored blockchain frameworks for specific distributed computing applications. Decentralised file systems, for example, can leverage blockchain to ensure data availability, integrity, and secure sharing [246], while decentralised cloud services can benefit from blockchain's capabilities in managing resource allocation and security [113]. Interoperability among blockchain networks is another key area, requiring standardised protocols and cross-chain communication to enable multi-

platform applications. Practical use cases, such as supply chain management and IoT, already demonstrate blockchain's potential to enhance traceability, secure resource sharing, and improve trust [110]. Efforts to minimise blockchain's environmental impact through energy-efficient mechanisms and green blockchain initiatives further align with global sustainability goals. By addressing these challenges, blockchain and DLTs can revolutionise distributed systems, transforming how data integrity, transparency, and trust are managed across industries.

- *Serverless computing:* Serverless computing, which abstracts infrastructure management and allows developers to focus solely on code execution, is emerging as a transformative paradigm in parallel and distributed systems. By automatically scaling based on demand, serverless architectures are particularly well suited for distributed applications with highly variable workloads, providing cost efficiency, flexibility, and ease of deployment [134]. However, serverless computing faces challenges such as cold-start latency, latency associated with initialising functions, and difficulties in managing stateful, resource-intensive applications [132,135]. Future advancements should address these limitations. Improving the latency and scalability of serverless frameworks is essential, particularly for HPC and real-time distributed systems [132]. Fine-grained resource management techniques and enhanced serverless orchestration mechanisms are needed to efficiently handle parallel tasks across distributed nodes, ensuring optimised workload distribution and responsiveness [236]. Serverless systems show significant potential in AI/ML workflows, enabling seamless deployment of ML models and distributed training pipelines [247]. Their adoption in multi-cloud environments can ensure interoperability across cloud platforms, reducing vendor lock-in and improving resource utilisation [248]. Additionally, techniques like container pre-warming, lightweight virtualisation, and predictive scaling can mitigate cold-start issues, making serverless computing viable for latency-sensitive and resource-constrained environments [132]. By overcoming these challenges, serverless computing can significantly contribute to the evolution of parallel and distributed systems, enabling more scalable, efficient, and adaptable architectures across a wide range of industries.
- *Cloud-native architectures:* Cloud-native architectures are transforming distributed computing by leveraging microservices, containerisation, and orchestration tools like Kubernetes to enable auto-scaling, fault tolerance, and resilience. By decomposing applications into smaller, independent components, these architectures provide flexibility and adaptability, ensuring consistent performance even under varying workload demands [146]. Future advancements should enhance the coordination and orchestration of microservices to ensure data consistency across geographically dispersed cloud resources. For instance, an optimised communication solution has been proposed to enhance inter-service communication in microservices [249]. Synergies with large generative AI models are essential to enable dynamic load balancing between cloud and edge nodes, optimising costs of goods sold and improving resource accessibility [250]. Multi-cloud orchestration initiatives, such as the expansion of the Kubernetes ecosystem [144] and platforms like Google's Anthos [251], demonstrate the feasibility of cross-cloud collaboration for managing complex workloads. Energy efficiency is a critical challenge as cloud-native systems scale. Green computing strategies, such as intelligent container scheduling and life-cycle management, can reduce energy consumption and environmental impact [225]. Additionally, improved container orchestration algorithms that dynamically allocate resources are vital for aligning these architectures with sustainability goals [252]. Security and privacy are paramount due to the decentralised nature of microservices [253], which increases vulnerabilities in

inter-service communication. Robust encryption, authentication, and real-time monitoring are needed to mitigate risks, particularly in sensitive domains like healthcare and finance. By addressing these challenges and fostering synergies with emerging technologies, cloud-native architectures can drive innovation and sustainability across industries such as smart cities, real-time analytics, and scientific research. These systems will remain a cornerstone of distributed computing, delivering efficiency, resilience, and adaptability.

- *Distributed AI and ML:* The future of distributed AI and ML presents transformative opportunities alongside significant technical challenges that require innovative solutions. As distributed workloads grow in scale and complexity, addressing fundamental issues in model synchronisation, communication efficiency, and computational overhead becomes increasingly critical [158,177]. A key research direction is the development of advanced distributed learning frameworks, with a particular emphasis on federated learning architectures, which enable privacy-preserving training across decentralised nodes [171]. These frameworks will evolve to handle heterogeneous data distributions and varying computational capabilities across nodes while maintaining model consistency and performance. Establishing standardised benchmarks for federated learning, particularly in sensitive domains such as healthcare and financial services, will be crucial for validating system robustness and reliability [167]. Such benchmarks should assess not only model accuracy but also critical metrics such as communication efficiency, privacy preservation, and resource utilisation. Another crucial research direction is the advancement of edge AI technologies, which enable sophisticated AI processing at the network edge [160]. This paradigm shift toward edge-centric AI architectures promises significant improvements in latency reduction and bandwidth optimisation, particularly for real-time applications in autonomous systems and IoT networks. Future research should focus on developing lightweight, efficient models capable of operating within the resource constraints of edge devices while maintaining high-performance standards [160]. The integration of distributed AI with emerging computing paradigms opens new avenues for innovation. Hybrid architectures combining classical systems with quantum processors hold promise for solving complex optimisation problems [217], while neuromorphic computing offers potential for energy-efficient, event-driven processing [56]. These integrations require interdisciplinary research efforts to address challenges in cross-platform optimisation, data flow management, and system interoperability. Additionally, the development of standardised interfaces and programming abstractions will be essential to enabling seamless integration across these diverse computing platforms. To fully realise the potential of these advancements, the field should also address broader socio-technical challenges. This includes developing robust frameworks for ethical AI deployment [254], ensuring equitable access to distributed AI resources, and establishing clear guidelines for responsible innovation. The long-term success of distributed AI systems will ultimately depend on balancing technical advancements with practical considerations of cost, scalability, and societal impact.

7. Conclusions

This paper has provided a comprehensive overview of parallel and distributed systems, emphasising their pivotal role in meeting the escalating computational demands of modern applications. By exploring their interrelationships and key distinctions, we established a foundation for understanding the emerging trends shaping their evolution. In the domain of parallel systems, we analysed four emerging paradigms: heterogeneous computing, quantum computing, neuromorphic computing, and optical computing. In the sphere of distributed systems, we examined several emerging trends: blockchain and distributed ledgers, serverless computing, cloud-native architectures, and distributed AI and ML systems. Additionally, we discussed the challenges that persist in these systems, including scalability limitations, security and privacy concerns, fault tolerance, interoperability issues, and energy efficiency demands. Addressing these challenges is crucial for the continued evolution and broader adoption of parallel and distributed systems.

Future research should focus on advancing software frameworks, developing innovative hardware architectures, optimising communication protocols, and designing efficient algorithms. By embracing these emerging trends and proactively tackling associated challenges, we can develop more powerful, efficient, and adaptable computing systems. Such advancements will drive innovation across various sectors, contribute to scientific and technological progress, and meet the complex demands of the future computational landscape.

Author Contributions: Conceptualisation, F.D.; methodology, F.D.; validation, F.D., M.A.H., and Y.W.; investigation, F.D., M.A.H., and Y.W.; resources, F.D.; data curation, F.D.; writing—original draft preparation, F.D.; writing—review and editing, F.D., M.A.H., and Y.W.; visualisation, F.D. and M.A.H.; funding acquisition, F.D. All authors have read and agreed to the published version of the manuscript.

Funding: This research received no external funding.

Data Availability Statement: Data sharing is not applicable to this article as no new data were created or analysed in this study.

Acknowledgments: The authors sincerely thank the editors of *Electronics* Journal for their valuable support. We are also deeply grateful to the reviewers for their insightful comments and constructive feedback, which have greatly enhanced the quality of this work.

Conflicts of Interest: The authors declare no conflicts of interest.

References

1. Achiam, J.; Adler, S.; Agarwal, S.; Ahmad, L.; Akkaya, I.; Aleman, F.L.; Almeida, D.; Altenschmidt, J.; Altman, S.; Anadkat, S.; et al. Gpt-4 technical report. *arXiv* **2023**, arXiv:2303.08774.
2. Das, A.; Palesi, M.; Kim, J.; Pande, P.P. Chip and Package-Scale Interconnects for General-Purpose, Domain-Specific and Quantum Computing Systems-Overview, Challenges and Opportunities. *IEEE J. Emerg. Sel. Top. Circuits Syst.* **2024**, *14*, 354–370. [CrossRef]
3. Michalakes, J. Hpc for weather forecasting. *Parallel Algorithms Comput. Sci. Eng.* **2020**, *2*, 297–323. [CrossRef]
4. Pronk, S.; Pouya, I.; Lundborg, M.; Rotskoff, G.; Wesen, B.; Kasson, P.M.; Lindahl, E. Molecular simulation workflows as parallel algorithms: The execution engine of Copernicus, a distributed high-performance computing platform. *J. Chem. Theory Comput.* **2015**, *11*, 2600–2608. [CrossRef] [PubMed]
5. Scellato, S.; Mascolo, C.; Musolesi, M.; Crowcroft, J. Track globally, deliver locally: Improving content delivery networks by tracking geographic social cascades. In Proceedings of the 20th International Conference on World Wide Web, Hyderabad, India, 28 March–1 April 2011; pp. 457–466.
6. Sharma, R.; Singh, A. Blockchain Technologies and Call for an Open Financial System: Decentralised Finance. In *Decentralized Finance and Tokenization in FinTech*; IGI Global: Hershey, PA, USA, 2024; pp. 21–32.
7. Raj, K.B.; Mehta, K.; Siddi, S.; Sharma, M.; Sharma, D.K.; Adhav, S.; Gonzáles, J.L. Optimizing Financial Transactions and Processes Through the Power of Distributed Systems. In *Meta Heuristic Algorithms for Advanced Distributed Systems*; Wiley Online Library: Hoboken, NJ, USA, 2024; pp. 289–303.
8. Hockney, R.W.; Jesshope, C.R. *Parallel Computers 2: Architecture, Programming and Algorithms*; CRC Press: Boca Raton, FL, USA, 2019.
9. Navarro, C.A.; Hitschfeld-Kahler, N.; Mateu, L. A survey on parallel computing and its applications in data-parallel problems using GPU architectures. *Commun. Comput. Phys.* **2014**, *15*, 285–329. [CrossRef]
10. Farooq, U.; Marrakchi, Z.; Mehrez, H.; Farooq, U.; Marrakchi, Z.; Mehrez, H. FPGA architectures: An overview. In *Tree-Based Heterogeneous FPGA Architectures: Application Specific Exploration and Optimization*; Springer: Midtown Manhattan, NY, USA, 2012; pp. 7–48.

11. Halsted, D. The origins of the architectural metaphor in computing: Design and technology at IBM, 1957–1964. *IEEE Ann. Hist. Comput.* **2018**, *40*, 61–70. [CrossRef]
12. Chawan, M.P.; Patle, B.; Cholake, V.; Pardeshi, S. Parallel Computer Architectural Schemes. *Int. J. Eng. Res. Technol.* **2012**, *1*, 9.
13. Batcher. Design of a massively parallel processor. *IEEE Trans. Comput.* **1980**, *100*, 836–840.
14. Leiserson, C.E.; Abuhamdeh, Z.S.; Douglas, D.C.; Feynman, C.R.; Ganmukhi, M.N.; Hill, J.V.; Hillis, D.; Kuszmaul, B.C.; St. Pierre, M.A.; Wells, D.S.; et al. The network architecture of the Connection Machine CM-5. In Proceedings of the Fourth Annual ACM Symposium on Parallel Algorithms and Architectures, San Diego, CA, USA, 29 June–1 July 1992; pp. 272–285.
15. Alverson, B.; Froese, E.; Kaplan, L.; Roweth, D. *Cray XC Series Network*; White Paper WP-Aries01-1112; Cray Inc.: Seattle, WA, USA, 2012.
16. Keckler, S.W.; Hofstee, H.P.; Olukotun, K. *Multicore Processors and Systems*; Springer: Berlin/Heidelberg, Germany, 2009.
17. McClanahan, C. History and evolution of gpu architecture. *Surv. Pap.* **2010**, *9*, 1–7.
18. Kshemkalyani, A.D.; Singhal, M. *Distributed Computing: Principles, Algorithms, and Systems*; Cambridge University Press: Cambridge, UK, 2011.
19. Ali, M.F.; Khan, R.Z. Distributed computing: An overview. *Int. J. Adv. Netw. Appl.* **2015**, *7*, 2630.
20. Paloque-Bergès, C.; Schafer, V. Arpanet (1969–2019). *Internet Hist.* **2019**, *3*, 1–14. [CrossRef]
21. Bonifati, A.; Chrysanthis, P.K.; Ouksel, A.M.; Sattler, K.U. Distributed databases and peer-to-peer databases: Past and present. *Acm Sigmod Rec.* **2008**, *37*, 5–11. [CrossRef]
22. Oluwatosin, H.S. Client-server model. *Iosr J. Comput. Eng.* **2014**, *16*, 67–71. [CrossRef]
23. Qian, L.; Luo, Z.; Du, Y.; Guo, L. Cloud computing: An overview. In Proceedings of the Cloud Computing: First International Conference, CloudCom 2009, Beijing, China, 1–4 December 2009; Proceedings 1; Springer: Berlin/Heidelberg, Germany, 2009; pp. 626–631.
24. Dittrich, J.; Quiané-Ruiz, J.A. Efficient big data processing in Hadoop MapReduce. *Proc. Vldb Endow.* **2012**, *5*, 2014–2015. [CrossRef]
25. Cao, K.; Liu, Y.; Meng, G.; Sun, Q. An overview on edge computing research. *IEEE Access* **2020**, *8*, 85714–85728. [CrossRef]
26. Madakam, S.; Ramaswamy, R.; Tripathi, S. Internet of Things (IoT): A literature review. *J. Comput. Commun.* **2015**, *3*, 164–173. [CrossRef]
27. Roosta, S.H. *Parallel Processing and Parallel Algorithms: Theory and Computation*; Springer Science & Business Media: Berlin/Heidelberg, Germany, 2012.
28. Burns, B. *Designing Distributed Systems: Patterns and Paradigms for Scalable, Reliable Services*; O'Reilly Media, Inc.: Sebastopol, CA, USA, 2018.
29. Parhami, B. *Introduction to Parallel Processing: Algorithms and Architectures*; Springer Science & Business Media: Berlin/Heidelberg, Germany, 1999; Volume 1.
30. Santoro, G.; Turvani, G.; Graziano, M. New logic-in-memory paradigms: An architectural and technological perspective. *Micromachines* **2019**, *10*, 368. [CrossRef]
31. Ben-Nun, T.; Hoefler, T. Demystifying parallel and distributed deep learning: An in-depth concurrency analysis. *Acm Comput. Surv. Csur* **2019**, *52*, 1–43. [CrossRef]
32. Asaduzzaman, A.; Trent, A.; Osborne, S.; Aldershof, C.; Sibai, F.N. Impact of CUDA and OpenCL on parallel and distributed computing. In Proceedings of the 2021 8th International Conference on Electrical and Electronics Engineering (ICEEE), Antalya, Turkey, 9–11 April 2021; IEEE: Piscataway, NJ, USA, 2021; pp. 238–242.
33. Fang, J.; Huang, C.; Tang, T.; Wang, Z. Parallel programming models for heterogeneous many-cores: A comprehensive survey. *CCF Trans. High Perform. Comput.* **2020**, *2*, 382–400. [CrossRef]
34. Prasad, A.; Muzio, C.; Ton, P.; Razdaan, S. Advanced 3D Packaging of 3.2 Tbs Optical Engine for Co-packaged Optics (CPO) in Hyperscale Data Center Networks. In Proceedings of the 2024 IEEE 74th Electronic Components and Technology Conference (ECTC), Denver, CO, USA, 28–31 May 2024; IEEE: Piscataway, NJ, USA, 2024; pp. 101–106.
35. Horowitz, M.; Grumbling, E. *Quantum Computing: Progress and Prospects*; The National Academies Press: Washington, DC, USA, 2019.
36. Huang, H.L.; Wu, D.; Fan, D.; Zhu, X. Superconducting quantum computing: A review. *Sci. China Inf. Sci.* **2020**, *63*, 180501. [CrossRef]
37. Yang, Z.; Zolanvari, M.; Jain, R. A survey of important issues in quantum computing and communications. *IEEE Commun. Surv. Tutor.* **2023**, *25*, 1059–1094. [CrossRef]
38. Radtke, T.; Fritzsche, S. Simulation of n-qubit quantum systems. I. Quantum registers and quantum gates. *Comput. Phys. Commun.* **2005**, *173*, 91–113. [CrossRef]
39. Mosca, M. Quantum Computer Algorithms. Ph.D. Thesis, University of Oxford, Oxford, UK, 1999.
40. Nofer, M.; Bauer, K.; Hinz, O.; van der Aalst, W.; Weinhardt, C. Quantum Computing. *Bus. Inf. Syst. Eng.* **2023**, *65*, 361–367. [CrossRef]

41. Gonzalez-Zalba, M.; De Franceschi, S.; Charbon, E.; Meunier, T.; Vinet, M.; Dzurak, A. Scaling silicon-based quantum computing using CMOS technology. *Nat. Electron.* **2021**, *4*, 872–884. [CrossRef]
42. Schäfer, V.; Ballance, C.; Thirumalai, K.; Stephenson, L.; Ballance, T.; Steane, A.; Lucas, D. Fast quantum logic gates with trapped-ion qubits. *Nature* **2018**, *555*, 75–78. [CrossRef] [PubMed]
43. Graham, T.; Song, Y.; Scott, J.; Poole, C.; Phuttitarn, L.; Jooya, K.; Eichler, P.; Jiang, X.; Marra, A.; Grinkemeyer, B.; et al. Multi-qubit entanglement and algorithms on a neutral-atom quantum computer. *Nature* **2022**, *604*, 457–462. [CrossRef] [PubMed]
44. Chu, Y.; Lukin, M.D. Quantum optics with nitrogen-vacancy centers in diamond. In *Quantum Optics and Nanophotonics*; Harvard of University: Cambridge, MA, USA, 2015; pp. 229–270.
45. Lukens, J.M.; Lougovski, P. Frequency-encoded photonic qubits for scalable quantum information processing. *Optica* **2017**, *4*, 8–16. [CrossRef]
46. AbuGhanem, M. IBM quantum computers: Evolution, performance, and future directions. *arXiv* **2024**, arXiv:2410.00916.
47. Easttom, C. Quantum computing and cryptography. In *Modern Cryptography: Applied Mathematics for Encryption and Information Security*; Springer: Berlin/Heidelberg, Germany, 2022; pp. 397–407.
48. Blunt, N.S.; Camps, J.; Crawford, O.; Izsák, R.; Leontica, S.; Mirani, A.; Moylett, A.E.; Scivier, S.A.; Sunderhauf, C.; Schopf, P.; et al. Perspective on the current state-of-the-art of quantum computing for drug discovery applications. *J. Chem. Theory Comput.* **2022**, *18*, 7001–7023. [CrossRef]
49. Bauer, B.; Bravyi, S.; Motta, M.; Chan, G.K.L. Quantum algorithms for quantum chemistry and quantum materials science. *Chem. Rev.* **2020**, *120*, 12685–12717. [CrossRef] [PubMed]
50. Ollitrault, P.J.; Miessen, A.; Tavernelli, I. Molecular quantum dynamics: A quantum computing perspective. *Accounts Chem. Res.* **2021**, *54*, 4229–4238. [CrossRef]
51. Orús, R.; Mugel, S.; Lizaso, E. Quantum computing for finance: Overview and prospects. *Rev. Phys.* **2019**, *4*, 100028. [CrossRef]
52. Cerezo, M.; Verdon, G.; Huang, H.Y.; Cincio, L.; Coles, P.J. Challenges and opportunities in quantum machine learning. *Nat. Comput. Sci.* **2022**, *2*, 567–576. [CrossRef]
53. Mead, C. Neuromorphic electronic systems. *Proc. IEEE* **1990**, *78*, 1629–1636. [CrossRef]
54. Schuman, C.D.; Kulkarni, S.R.; Parsa, M.; Mitchell, J.P.; Kay, B. Opportunities for neuromorphic computing algorithms and applications. *Nat. Comput. Sci.* **2022**, *2*, 10–19. [CrossRef]
55. Shrestha, A.; Ahmed, K.; Wang, Y.; Qiu, Q. Stable spike-timing dependent plasticity rule for multilayer unsupervised and supervised learning. In Proceedings of the 2017 International Joint Conference on Neural Networks (IJCNN), Anchorage, AK, USA, 14–19 May 2017; IEEE: Piscataway, NJ, USA, 2017; pp. 1999–2006.
56. Esser, S.K.; Appuswamy, R.; Merolla, P.; Arthur, J.V.; Modha, D.S. Backpropagation for energy-efficient neuromorphic computing. *Adv. Neural Inf. Process. Syst.* **2015**, *28*. Available online: https://proceedings.neurips.cc/paper_files/paper/2015/hash/10a5ab2db37feedfdeaab192ead4ac0e-Abstract.html (accessed on 7 January 2025).
57. Alom, M.Z.; Van Essen, B.; Moody, A.T.; Widemann, D.P.; Taha, T.M. Quadratic unconstrained binary optimization (QUBO) on neuromorphic computing system. In Proceedings of the 2017 International Joint Conference on Neural Networks (IJCNN), Anchorage, AK, USA, 14–19 May 2017; IEEE: Piscataway, NJ, USA, 2017; pp. 3922–3929.
58. Corder, K.; Monaco, J.V.; Vindiola, M.M. Solving vertex cover via ising model on a neuromorphic processor. In Proceedings of the 2018 IEEE International Symposium on Circuits and Systems (ISCAS), Florence, Italy, 27–30 May 2018; IEEE: Piscataway, NJ, USA, 2018; pp. 1–5.
59. Furber, S. Large-scale neuromorphic computing systems. *J. Neural Eng.* **2016**, *13*, 051001. [CrossRef] [PubMed]
60. Merolla, P.A.; Arthur, J.V.; Alvarez-Icaza, R.; Cassidy, A.S.; Sawada, J.; Akopyan, F.; Jackson, B.L.; Imam, N.; Guo, C.; Nakamura, Y.; et al. A million spiking-neuron integrated circuit with a scalable communication network and interface. *Science* **2014**, *345*, 668–673. [CrossRef]
61. Benjamin, B.V.; Gao, P.; McQuinn, E.; Choudhary, S.; Chandrasekaran, A.R.; Bussat, J.M.; Alvarez-Icaza, R.; Arthur, J.V.; Merolla, P.A.; Boahen, K. Neurogrid: A mixed-analog-digital multichip system for large-scale neural simulations. *Proc. IEEE* **2014**, *102*, 699–716. [CrossRef]
62. Furber, S.B.; Galluppi, F.; Temple, S.; Plana, L.A. The spinnaker project. *Proc. IEEE* **2014**, *102*, 652–665. [CrossRef]
63. Davies, M.; Wild, A.; Orchard, G.; Sandamirskaya, Y.; Guerra, G.A.F.; Joshi, P.; Plank, P.; Risbud, S.R. Advancing neuromorphic computing with loihi: A survey of results and outlook. *Proc. IEEE* **2021**, *109*, 911–934. [CrossRef]
64. Davies, M.; Srinivasa, N.; Lin, T.H.; Chinya, G.; Cao, Y.; Choday, S.H.; Dimou, G.; Joshi, P.; Imam, N.; Jain, S.; et al. Loihi: A neuromorphic manycore processor with on-chip learning. *IEEE Micro* **2018**, *38*, 82–99. [CrossRef]
65. Davies, M. Taking neuromorphic computing to the next level with Loihi2. *Intel Labs' Loihi* **2021**, *2*. 1–7.
66. Zenke, F.; Neftci, E.O. Brain-inspired learning on neuromorphic substrates. *Proc. IEEE* **2021**, *109*, 935–950. [CrossRef]
67. Brayshaw, G.; Ward-Cherrier, B.; Pearson, M.J. Simultaneous Velocity and Texture Classification from a Neuromorphic Tactile Sensor Using Spiking Neural Networks. *Electronics* **2024**, *13*, 2159. [CrossRef]

68. Smith, H.; Seekings, J.; Mohammadi, M.; Zand, R. Realtime Facial Expression Recognition: Neuromorphic Hardware vs. Edge AI Accelerators. In Proceedings of the 2023 International Conference on Machine Learning and Applications (ICMLA), Jacksonville, FL, USA, 15–17 December 2023; IEEE: Piscataway, NJ, USA, 2023; pp. 1547–1552.
69. Bezugam, S.S.; Shaban, A.; Suri, M. Neuromorphic recurrent spiking neural networks for emg gesture classification and low power implementation on loihi. In Proceedings of the 2023 IEEE International Symposium on Circuits and Systems (ISCAS), Monterey, CA, USA, 21–25 May 2023; IEEE: Piscataway, NJ, USA, 2023; pp. 1–5.
70. Frady, E.P.; Sommer, F.T. Robust computation with rhythmic spike patterns. *Proc. Natl. Acad. Sci. USA* **2019**, *116*, 18050–18059. [CrossRef]
71. Yakopcic, C.; Rahman, N.; Atahary, T.; Taha, T.M.; Beigh, A.; Douglass, S. High speed cognitive domain ontologies for asset allocation using loihi spiking neurons. In Proceedings of the 2019 International Joint Conference on Neural Networks (IJCNN), Budapest, Hungary, 14–19 July 2019; IEEE: Piscataway, NJ, USA, 2019; pp. 1–8.
72. Kay, B.; Date, P.; Schuman, C. Neuromorphic graph algorithms: Extracting longest shortest paths and minimum spanning trees. In *Proceedings of the 2020 Annual Neuro-Inspired Computational Elements Workshop*; Association for Computing Machinery: New York, NY, USA, 2020; pp. 1–6.
73. Cong, G.; Lim, S.H.; Kulkarni, S.; Date, P.; Potok, T.; Snyder, S.; Parsa, M.; Schuman, C. Semi-supervised graph structure learning on neuromorphic computers. In Proceedings of the International Conference on Neuromorphic Systems, Knoxville, TN, USA, 27–29 July 2022; pp. 1–4.
74. Aimone, J.B.; Date, P.; Fonseca-Guerra, G.A.; Hamilton, K.E.; Henke, K.; Kay, B.; Kenyon, G.T.; Kulkarni, S.R.; Mniszewski, S.M.; Parsa, M.; et al. A review of non-cognitive applications for neuromorphic computing. *Neuromorphic Comput. Eng.* **2022**, *2*, 032003. [CrossRef]
75. Izhikevich, E.M. Simple model of spiking neurons. *IEEE Trans. Neural Netw.* **2003**, *14*, 1569–1572. [CrossRef] [PubMed]
76. Gerstner, W.; Kistler, W.M. *Spiking Neuron Models: Single Neurons, Populations, Plasticity*; Cambridge University Press: Cambridge, UK, 2002.
77. Box, G.E.; Tiao, G.C. *Bayesian Inference in Statistical Analysis*; John Wiley & Sons: Hoboken, NJ, USA, 2011.
78. Cortes, C. Support-Vector Networks. *Mach. Learn.* **1995**, *20*, 273–297. [CrossRef]
79. Zhao, W.X.; Zhou, K.; Li, J.; Tang, T.; Wang, X.; Hou, Y.; Min, Y.; Zhang, B.; Zhang, J.; Dong, Z.; et al. A survey of large language models. *arXiv* **2023**, arXiv:2303.18223.
80. Destrycker, N.; Benoot, W.; Mattias, J.; Rodriguez, I.; Steenari, D. EDGX-1: A New Frontier in Onboard AI Computing with a Heterogeneous and Neuromorphic Design. In Proceedings of the 2023 European Data Handling & Data Processing Conference (EDHPC), Juan-Les-Pins, France, 2–6 October 2023; IEEE: Piscataway, NJ, USA, 2023; pp. 1–6.
81. Ng, L.K.; Chow, S.S. {GForce}:{GPU-Friendly} oblivious and rapid neural network inference. In Proceedings of the 30th USENIX Security Symposium (USENIX Security 21), Online, 11–13 August 2021; pp. 2147–2164.
82. Luo, T.; Wong, W.F.; Goh, R.S.M.; Do, A.T.; Chen, Z.; Li, H.; Jiang, W.; Yau, W. Achieving green ai with energy-efficient deep learning using neuromorphic computing. *Commun. Acm* **2023**, *66*, 52–57. [CrossRef]
83. Guenther, B.D.; Steel, D. *Encyclopedia of Modern Optics*; Academic Press: Cambridge, MA, USA, 2018.
84. Kazanskiy, N.L.; Butt, M.A.; Khonina, S.N. Optical computing: Status and perspectives. *Nanomaterials* **2022**, *12*, 2171. [CrossRef]
85. Mekawey, H.; Elsayed, M.; Ismail, Y.; Swillam, M.A. Optical interconnects finally seeing the light in silicon photonics: Past the hype. *Nanomaterials* **2022**, *12*, 485. [CrossRef] [PubMed]
86. Xia, C.; Chen, Y.; Zhang, H.; Zhang, H.; Dai, F.; Wu, J. Efficient neural network accelerators with optical computing and communication. *Comput. Sci. Inf. Syst.* **2023**, *20*, 513–535. [CrossRef]
87. Ning, S.; Zhu, H.; Feng, C.; Gu, J.; Jiang, Z.; Ying, Z.; Midkiff, J.; Jain, S.; Hlaing, M.H.; Pan, D.Z.; et al. Photonic-electronic integrated circuits for high-performance computing and ai accelerators. *J. Light. Technol.* **2024**, *42*, 7834–7859. [CrossRef]
88. Cheng, Q.; Bahadori, M.; Glick, M.; Rumley, S.; Bergman, K. Recent advances in optical technologies for data centers: A review. *Optica* **2018**, *5*, 1354–1370. [CrossRef]
89. Minzioni, P.; Lacava, C.; Tanabe, T.; Dong, J.; Hu, X.; Csaba, G.; Porod, W.; Singh, G.; Willner, A.E.; Almaiman, A.; et al. Roadmap on all-optical processing. *J. Opt.* **2019**, *21*, 063001. [CrossRef]
90. Wu, J.; Lin, X.; Guo, Y.; Liu, J.; Fang, L.; Jiao, S.; Dai, Q. Analog optical computing for artificial intelligence. *Engineering* **2022**, *10*, 133–145. [CrossRef]
91. Li, X.; Shao, Z.; Zhu, M.; Yang, J. *Fundamentals of Optical Computing Technology*; Springer: Singapore 2018.
92. Nakamoto, S. *Bitcoin: A Peer-to-Peer Electronic Cash System*; Satoshi Nakamoto: Online, 2008. Available online: https://www.bitcoin.org (accessed on 7 December 2024).
93. Chaum, D. Blind signatures for untraceable payments. In *Advances in Cryptology: Proceedings of Crypto 82*; Springer: Boston, MA, USA, 1983.
94. Haber, S.; Stornetta, W.S. *How to Time-Stamp a Digital Document*; Springer: Berlin/Heidelberg, Germany, 1991.

95. Finney, H. *RPOW—Reusable Proofs of Work*; Nakamoto Institute: Online, 2004. Available online: https://nakamotoinstitute.org/finney/rpow/index.html (accessed on 7 December 2024).
96. Mougayar, W. *The Business Blockchain: Promise, Practice, and Application of the next INTERNET Technology*; John Wiley & Sons: Hoboken, NJ, USA, 2016.
97. Zhao, J.L.; Fan, S.; Yan, J. Overview of business innovations and research opportunities in blockchain and introduction to the special issue. *Financ. Innov.* **2016**, *2*, 28. [CrossRef]
98. Tripathi, G.; Ahad, M.A.; Casalino, G. A comprehensive review of blockchain technology: Underlying principles and historical background with future challenges. *Decis. Anal. J.* **2023**, *9*, 100344. [CrossRef]
99. Lamport, L.; Shostak, R.; Pease, M. The Byzantine generals problem. In *Concurrency: The Works of Leslie Lamport*; Association for Computing Machinery: New York, NY, USA, 2019 ; pp. 203–226.
100. Alrubei, S.; Ball, E.; Rigelsford, J. Securing IoT-blockchain applications through honesty-based distributed proof of authority consensus algorithm. In Proceedings of the 2021 International Conference on Cyber Situational Awareness, Data Analytics and Assessment (CyberSA), Virtual, 14–18 June 2021; IEEE: Piscataway, NJ, USA, 2021; pp. 1–7.
101. Garg, N.; Nehra, A.; Baza, M.; Kumar, N. Secure and efficient data integrity verification scheme for cloud data storage. In Proceedings of the 2023 IEEE 20th Consumer Communications & Networking Conference (CCNC), Las Vegas, NV, USA, 8–11 January 2023; IEEE: Piscataway, NJ, USA, 2023; pp. 1–6.
102. Benčić, F.M.; Žarko, I.P. Distributed ledger technology: Blockchain compared to directed acyclic graph. In Proceedings of the 2018 IEEE 38th International Conference on Distributed Computing Systems (ICDCS), Vienna, Austria, 2–5 July 2018; IEEE: Piscataway, NJ, USA, 2018; pp. 1569–1570.
103. Reegu, F.A.; Abas, H.; Gulzar, Y.; Xin, Q.; Alwan, A.A.; Jabbari, A.; Sonkamble, R.G.; Dziyauddin, R.A. Blockchain-based framework for interoperable electronic health records for an improved healthcare system. *Sustainability* **2023**, *15*, 6337. [CrossRef]
104. Li, J.; Luo, X.; Lei, H. TrustHealth: Enhancing eHealth Security with Blockchain and Trusted Execution Environments. *Electronics* **2024**, *13*, 2425. [CrossRef]
105. Maesa, D.D.F.; Tietze, F. Automating Intellectual Property License Agreements with DLT. In Proceedings of the 2023 IEEE International Conference on Decentralized Applications and Infrastructures (DAPPS), Athens, Greece, 17–20 July 2023; IEEE: Piscataway, NJ, USA, 2023; pp. 48–56.
106. Ito, K.; O'Dair, M. A critical examination of the application of blockchain technology to intellectual property management. In *Business Transformation Through Blockchain: Volume II*; Palgrave Macmillan: Cham, Switzerland, 2019; pp. 317–335.
107. Xu, R.; Zhu, J.; Yang, L.; Lu, Y.; Xu, L.D. Decentralized finance (DeFi): A paradigm shift in the Fintech. *Enterp. Inf. Syst.* **2024**, *18*, 2397630. [CrossRef]
108. Daugaard, T.V.; Jensen, J.B.; Kauffman, R.J.; Kim, K. Blockchain solutions with consensus algorithms and immediate finality: Toward Panopticon-style monitoring to enhance anti-money laundering. *Electron. Commer. Res. Appl.* **2024**, *65*, 101386. [CrossRef]
109. Rijanto, A. *Blockchain Technology Roles to Overcome Accounting, Accountability and Assurance Barriers in Supply Chain Finance*; Asian Review of Accounting; Emerald Group Publishing Ltd.: Bingley, UK, 2024.
110. Trollman, H.; Garcia-Garcia, G.; Jagtap, S.; Trollman, F. Blockchain for ecologically embedded coffee supply chains. *Logistics* **2022**, *6*, 43. [CrossRef]
111. Herbe, A.; Estermann, Z.; Holzwarth, V.; vom Brocke, J. How to effectively use distributed ledger technology in supply chain management? *Int. J. Prod. Res.* **2024**, *62*, 2522–2547. [CrossRef]
112. Odimarha, A.C.; Ayodeji, S.A.; Abaku, E.A. The role of technology in supply chain risk management: Innovations and challenges in logistics. *Magna Sci. Adv. Res. Rev.* **2024**, *10*, 138–145. [CrossRef]
113. Selvarajan, S.; Shankar, A.; Uddin, M.; Alqahtani, A.S.; Al-Shehari, T.; Viriyasitavat, W. A smart decentralized identifiable distributed ledger technology-based blockchain (DIDLT-BC) model for cloud-IoT security. *Expert Syst.* **2024**, *42*, e13544. [CrossRef]
114. Fitzpatrick, P.; Thorpe, C. An Investigation into the Feasibility of using Distributed Digital Ledger technology for Digital Forensics for Industrial IoT. In Proceedings of the European Conference on Cyber Warfare and Security, Jyvaskyla, Finland, 27–28 June 2024; Volume 23, pp. 827–835.
115. Ling, X.; Le, Y.; Zhang, B.; Wang, J.; Gao, X. Blockchain-Enhanced Open Internet of Things Access Architecture. U.S. Patent 11,954,681, 9 April 2024.
116. Xia, Q.; Sifah, E.B.; Asamoah, K.O.; Gao, J.; Du, X.; Guizani, M. MeDShare: Trust-less medical data sharing among cloud service providers via blockchain. *IEEE Access* **2017**, *5*, 14757–14767. [CrossRef]
117. Fan, K.; Wang, S.; Ren, Y.; Li, H.; Yang, Y. Medblock: Efficient and secure medical data sharing via blockchain. *J. Med. Syst.* **2018**, *42*, 136. [CrossRef]
118. Abdelgalil, L.; Mejri, M. HealthBlock: A framework for a collaborative sharing of electronic health records based on blockchain. *Future Internet* **2023**, *15*, 87. [CrossRef]
119. Johari, R.; Kumar, V.; Gupta, K.; Vidyarthi, D.P. BLOSOM: BLOckchain technology for Security of Medical records. *Ict Express* **2022**, *8*, 56–60. [CrossRef]

120. Li, Y.; Lin, Y.; Wang, Y.; Ye, K.; Xu, C. Serverless computing: State-of-the-art, challenges and opportunities. *IEEE Trans. Serv. Comput.* **2022**, *16*, 1522–1539. [CrossRef]
121. Serverless Function, FaaS Serverless—AWS Lambda. Available online: https://aws.amazon.com/lambda/ (accessed on 31 October 2024).
122. Patil, R.; Chaudhery, T.S.; Qureshi, M.A.; Sawant, V.; Dalvi, H. Serverless computing and the emergence of function-as-a-service. In Proceedings of the 2021 International Conference on Recent Trends on Electronics, Information, Communication & Technology (RTEICT), Bangalore, India, 27–28 August 2021; IEEE: Piscataway, NJ, USA, 2021; pp. 764–769.
123. Sadowski, M.; Frantzell, L.; Sadowski, M.; Frantzell, L. Apache OpenWhisk–Open Source Project. In *Serverless Swift: Apache OpenWhisk for iOS Developers*; Apress: Berkeley, CA, USA, 2020; pp. 37–57.
124. Kumar, V.; Agnihotri, K. *Serverless Computing Using Azure Functions: Build, Deploy, Automate, and Secure Serverless Application Development with Azure Functions (English Edition)*; BPB Publications: Noida, India, 2021.
125. Bisong, E.; Bisong, E. An overview of google cloud platform services. In *Building Machine Learning and Deep Learning Models on Google Cloud Platform: A Comprehensive Guide for Beginners*; Apress: Berkeley, CA, USA, 2019; pp. 7–10.
126. Rajan, R.A.P. Serverless architecture-a revolution in cloud computing. In Proceedings of the 2018 Tenth International Conference on Advanced Computing (ICoAC), Chennai, India, 13–15 December 2018; IEEE: Piscataway, NJ, USA, 2018; pp. 88–93.
127. Sok, C.; d'Orazio, L.; Tekin, R.; Tombroff, D. WebAssembly serverless join: A Study of its Application. In Proceedings of the 36th International Conference on Scientific and Statistical Database Management, Rennes France, 10–12 July 2024; pp. 1–4.
128. Ouyang, R.; Wang, J.; Xu, H.; Chen, S.; Xiong, X.; Tolba, A.; Zhang, X. A Microservice and Serverless Architecture for Secure IoT System. *Sensors* **2023**, *23*, 4868. [CrossRef]
129. Werner, S.; Tai, S. A reference architecture for serverless big data processing. *Future Gener. Comput. Syst.* **2024**, *155*, 179–192. [CrossRef]
130. Guhan, T.; Sekhar, G.C.; Revathy, N.; Baranidharan, K.; Aancy, H.M. Financial and Economic Analysis on Serverless Computing System Services. In *Essential Information Systems Service Management*; IGI Global: Hershey, PA, USA, 2025; pp. 83–112.
131. Lee, C.; Zhu, Z.; Yang, T.; Huo, Y.; Su, Y.; He, P.; Lyu, M.R. SPES: Towards Optimizing Performance-Resource Trade-Off for Serverless Functions. *arXiv* **2024**, arXiv:2403.17574.
132. Golec, M.; Walia, G.K.; Kumar, M.; Cuadrado, F.; Gill, S.S.; Uhlig, S. Cold start latency in serverless computing: A systematic review, taxonomy, and future directions. *Acm Comput. Surv.* **2024**, *57*, 1–36. [CrossRef]
133. Karamzadeh, A.; Shameli-Sendi, A. Reducing cold start delay in serverless computing using lightweight virtual machines. *J. Netw. Comput. Appl.* **2024**, *232*, 104030. [CrossRef]
134. Lyu, S.; Rzeznik, A. Going Serverless with the Amazon AWS Rust SDK. In *Practical Rust Projects: Build Serverless, AI, Machine Learning, Embedded, Game, and Web Applications*; Springer: Berlin/Heidelberg, Germany, 2023; pp. 201–246.
135. Aslanpour, M.S.; Toosi, A.N.; Cicconetti, C.; Javadi, B.; Sbarski, P.; Taibi, D.; Assuncao, M.; Gill, S.S.; Gaire, R.; Dustdar, S. Serverless edge computing: Vision and challenges. In Proceedings of the 2021 Australasian Computer Science Week Multiconference, Dunedin, New Zealand, 1–5 February 2021; pp. 1–10.
136. Lekkala, C. AI-Driven Dynamic Resource Allocation in Cloud Computing: Predictive Models and Real-Time Optimization. *J. Artif. Intell. Mach. Learn. Data Sci.* **2024**, *2*, 450–456. [CrossRef]
137. Grafberger, A.; Chadha, M.; Jindal, A.; Gu, J.; Gerndt, M. Fedless: Secure and scalable federated learning using serverless computing. In Proceedings of the 2021 IEEE International Conference on Big Data (Big Data), Orlando, FL, USA, 15–18 December 2021; IEEE: Piscataway, NJ, USA, 2021; pp. 164–173.
138. Li, X.; Leng, X.; Chen, Y. Securing serverless computing: Challenges, solutions, and opportunities. *IEEE Netw.* **2022**, *37*, 166–173. [CrossRef]
139. Liu, F.; Niu, Y. Demystifying the cost of serverless computing: Towards a win-win deal. *IEEE Trans. Parallel Distrib. Syst.* **2023**, *35*, 59–72. [CrossRef]
140. Kosińska, J.; Baliś, B.; Konieczny, M.; Malawski, M.; Zieliński, S. Toward the observability of cloud-native applications: The overview of the state-of-the-art. *IEEE Access* **2023**, *11*, 73036–73052. [CrossRef]
141. Fazuludeen, N.; Banu, S.S.; Gupta, A.; Swathi, V. Challenges And Issues of Managing the Virtualization Environment Through Vmware Vsphere. *Nanotechnol. Perceptions* **2024**, *20*, 281–292.
142. Krishna Kaiser, A. Introduction to devops. In *Reinventing ITIL® and DevOps with Digital Transformation: Essential Guidance to Accelerate the Process*; Springer: Berlin/Heidelberg, Germany, 2023; pp. 3–38.
143. Pandey, B.; Mishra, A.K.; Yadav, A.; Tiwari, D.; Pandey, M.S. Virtualization using Docker container. In *Emerging Real-World Applications of Internet of Things*; CRC Press: Boca Raton, FL, USA, 2022; pp. 157–181.
144. Hightower, K.; Burns, B.; Beda, J. *Kubernetes: Up and Running Dive into the Future of Infrastructure*; Oreilly Media Inc.: Sebastopol, CA, USA, 2017.
145. Balalaie, A.; Heydarnoori, A.; Jamshidi, P. Microservices architecture enables devops: Migration to a cloud-native architecture. *IEEE Softw.* **2016**, *33*, 42–52. [CrossRef]

146. Pahl, C.; Brogi, A.; Soldani, J.; Jamshidi, P. Cloud container technologies: A state-of-the-art review. *IEEE Trans. Cloud Comput.* **2017**, *7*, 677–692. [CrossRef]
147. Bernstein, D. Containers and cloud: From lxc to docker to kubernetes. *IEEE Cloud Comput.* **2014**, *1*, 81–84. [CrossRef]
148. Oyeniran, C.; Adewusi, A.O.; Adeleke, A.G.; Akwawa, L.A.; Azubuko, C.F. Microservices architecture in cloud-native applications: Design patterns and scalability. *Comput. Sci. IT Res. J.* **2024**, *5*, 2107–2124. [CrossRef]
149. Bharadwaj, D.; Premananda, B. Transition of cloud computing from traditional applications to the cloud native approach. In Proceedings of the 2022 IEEE North Karnataka Subsection Flagship International Conference (NKCon), Vijayapura, India, 20–21 November 2022; IEEE: Piscataway, NJ, USA, 2022; pp. 1–8.
150. Goniwada, S.R.; Goniwada, S.R. Enterprise Cloud Native Software Engineering. In *Cloud Native Architecture and Design: A Handbook for Modern Day Architecture and Design with Enterprise-Grade Examples*; Apress: Berkeley, CA, USA, 2022; pp. 495–522.
151. Farreras, M.; Almási, G.; Cascaval, C.; Cortes, T. Scalable RDMA performance in PGAS languages. In Proceedings of the 2009 IEEE International Symposium on Parallel & Distributed Processing, Rome, Italy, 23–29 May 2009; IEEE: Piscataway, NJ, USA, 2009; pp. 1–12.
152. Gil, G.; Corujo, D.; Pedreiras, P. Cloud native computing for industry 4.0: Challenges and opportunities. In Proceedings of the 2021 26th IEEE International Conference on Emerging Technologies and Factory Automation (ETFA), Vasteras, Sweden, 7–10 September 2021; IEEE: Piscataway, NJ, USA, 2021; pp. 01–04.
153. Alonso, J.; Orue-Echevarria, L.; Casola, V.; Torre, A.I.; Huarte, M.; Osaba, E.; Lobo, J.L. Understanding the challenges and novel architectural models of multi-cloud native applications–A systematic literature review. *J. Cloud Comput.* **2023**, *12*, 6. [CrossRef]
154. Pham, X.Q.; Nguyen, T.D.; Huynh-The, T.; Huh, E.N.; Kim, D.S. Distributed cloud computing: Architecture, enabling technologies, and open challenges. *IEEE Consum. Electron. Mag.* **2022**, *12*, 98–106. [CrossRef]
155. Deng, S.; Zhao, H.; Huang, B.; Zhang, C.; Chen, F.; Deng, Y.; Yin, J.; Dustdar, S.; Zomaya, A.Y. Cloud-native computing: A survey from the perspective of services. *Proc. IEEE* **2024**, *112*, 12–46. [CrossRef]
156. Sana, K.; Hassina, N.; Kadda, B.B. Towards a reference architecture for interoperable clouds. In Proceedings of the 2021 8th International Conference on Electrical and Electronics Engineering (ICEEE), Antalya, Turkey, 9–11 April 2021; IEEE: Piscataway, NJ, USA, 2021; pp. 229–233.
157. Tankov, V.; Valchuk, D.; Golubev, Y.; Bryksin, T. Infrastructure in code: Towards developer-friendly cloud applications. In Proceedings of the 2021 36th IEEE/ACM International Conference on Automated Software Engineering (ASE), Melbourne, Australia, 15–19 November 2021; IEEE: Piscataway, NJ, USA, 2021; pp. 1166–1170.
158. Verbraeken, J.; Wolting, M.; Katzy, J.; Kloppenburg, J.; Verbelen, T.; Rellermeyer, J.S. A survey on distributed machine learning. *Acm Comput. Surv. Csur* **2020**, *53*, 1–33. [CrossRef]
159. Dai, F.; Chen, Y.; Huang, Z.; Zhang, H. Wrht: Efficient all-reduce for distributed DNN training in optical interconnect systems. In Proceedings of the 52nd International Conference on Parallel Processing, Salt Lake City, UT, USA, 7–10 August 2023; pp. 556–565.
160. Filho, C.P.; Marques, E., Jr.; Chang, V.; Dos Santos, L.; Bernardini, F.; Pires, P.F.; Ochi, L.; Delicato, F.C. A systematic literature review on distributed machine learning in edge computing. *Sensors* **2022**, *22*, 2665. [CrossRef] [PubMed]
161. Hudson, N.; Hossain, M.J.; Hosseinzadeh, M.; Khamfroush, H.; Rahnamay-Naeini, M.; Ghani, N. A framework for edge intelligent smart distribution grids via federated learning. In Proceedings of the 2021 International Conference on Computer Communications and Networks (ICCCN), Athens, Greece, 19–22 July 2021; IEEE: Piscataway, NJ, USA, 2021; pp. 1–9.
162. Reijonen, J.; Opsenica, M.; Morabito, R.; Komu, M.; Elmusrati, M. Regression training using model parallelism in a distributed cloud. In Proceedings of the 2019 IEEE Intl Conf on Dependable, Autonomic and Secure Computing, Intl Conf on Pervasive Intelligence and Computing, Intl Conf on Cloud and Big Data Computing, Intl Conf on Cyber Science and Technology Congress (DASC/PiCom/CBDCom/CyberSciTech), Fukuoka, Japan, 5–8 August 2019; IEEE: Piscataway, NJ, USA, 2019. pp. 741–747.
163. Majumdar, S.; Trivisonno, R.; Poe, W.Y.; Carle, G. Distributing intelligence for 6G network automation: Performance and architectural impact. In Proceedings of the ICC 2023-IEEE International Conference on Communications, Rome, Italy, 28 May–1 June 2023; IEEE: Piscataway, NJ, USA, 2023; pp. 6224–6229.
164. Gholizadeh, N.; Musilek, P. Distributed learning applications in power systems: A review of methods, gaps, and challenges. *Energies* **2021**, *14*, 3654. [CrossRef]
165. Chen, X.; Wujek, B. Autodal: Distributed active learning with automatic hyperparameter selection. In Proceedings of the AAAI Conference on Artificial Intelligence, New York, NY, USA, 7–12 February 2020; Volume 34, pp. 3537–3544.
166. McMahan, H.B.; Moore, E.; Ramage, D.; Hampson, S.; y Arcas, B.A. Communication-efficient learning of deep networks from decentralized data. In Proceedings of the Artificial Intelligence and Statistics, Fort Lauderdale, FL, USA, 20–22 April 2017; PMLR:W&CP; pp. 1273–1282.
167. Li, T.; Sahu, A.K.; Talwalkar, A.; Smith, V. Federated learning: Challenges, methods, and future directions. *IEEE Signal Process. Mag.* **2020**, *37*, 50–60. [CrossRef]

168. Bonawitz, K.; Ivanov, V.; Kreuter, B.; Marcedone, A.; McMahan, H.B.; Patel, S.; Seth, K. Practical secure aggregation for privacy-preserving machine learning. In Proceedings of the 2017 ACM SIGSAC Conference on Computer and Communications Security, Dallas, TX, USA, 30 October–3 November 2017; ACM: New York, NY, USA, 2017; pp. 1175–1191.
169. Geyer, R.C.; Klein, T.; Nabi, M. Differentially private federated learning: A client level perspective. *arXiv* **2017**, arXiv:1712.07557.
170. Truex, S.; Baracaldo, N.; Anwar, A.; Steinke, T.; Ludwig, H.; Zhang, R.; Zhou, Y. A hybrid approach to privacy-preserving federated learning. In Proceedings of the 12th ACM Workshop on Artificial Intelligence and Security, London, UK, 15 November 2019; pp. 1–11.
171. Konečný, J.; McMahan, H.B.; Yu, F.X.; Richtárik, P.; Suresh, A.T.; Bacon, D. Federated learning: Strategies for improving communication efficiency. *arXiv* **2016**, arXiv:1610.05492.
172. Shokri, R.; Shmatikov, V. Privacy-preserving deep learning. In Proceedings of the 22nd ACM SIGSAC Conference on Computer and Communications Security, Denver, CO, USA, 12–16 October 2015; ACM: New York, NY, USA, 2015; pp. 1310–1321.
173. Lin, Y.; Han, S.; Mao, H.; Wang, Y.; Dally, W.J. Deep gradient compression: Reducing the communication bandwidth for distributed training. *arXiv* **2017**, arXiv:1712.01887.
174. Alistarh, D.; Grubic, D.; Li, J.; Tomioka, R.; Vojnovic, M. QSGD: Communication-efficient SGD via gradient quantization and encoding. In Proceedings of the Advances in Neural Information Processing Systems, Long Beach, CA, USA, 4–9 December 2017; pp. 1709–1720.
175. Dean, J.; Corrado, G.; Monga, R.; Chen, K.; Devin, M.; Mao, M.; Ranzato, M.; Senior, A.; Tucker, P.; Yang, K.; et al. Large scale distributed deep networks. In *Advances in Neural Information Processing Systems*; 2012 ; Volume 25. Available online: https://proceedings.neurips.cc/paper_files/paper/2012/hash/6aca97005c68f1206823815f66102863-Abstract.html (accessed on 7 November 2024).
176. Zhang, C.; Patras, P.; Haddadi, H. Deep learning in mobile and wireless networking: A survey. *IEEE Commun. Surv. Tutorials* **2019**, *21*, 2224–2287. [CrossRef]
177. Cao, X.; Başar, T.; Diggavi, S.; Eldar, Y.C.; Letaief, K.B.; Poor, H.V.; Zhang, J. Communication-efficient distributed learning: An overview. *IEEE J. Sel. Areas Commun.* **2023**, *41*, 851–873. [CrossRef]
178. Chouvardas, S.; Slavakis, K.; Kopsinis, Y.; Theodoridis, S. A sparsity promoting adaptive algorithm for distributed learning. *IEEE Trans. Signal Process.* **2012**, *60*, 5412–5425. [CrossRef]
179. Zhang, S.; Zhang, C.; You, Z.; Zheng, R.; Xu, B. Asynchronous stochastic gradient descent for DNN training. In Proceedings of the 2013 IEEE International Conference on Acoustics, Speech and Signal Processing, Vancouver, BC, Canada, 26–31 May 2013; IEEE: Piscataway, NJ, USA, 2013; pp. 6660–6663.
180. Du, Y.; You, K. Asynchronous stochastic gradient descent over decentralized datasets. *IEEE Trans. Control. Netw. Syst.* **2021**, *8*, 1212–1224. [CrossRef]
181. Ko, Y.; Choi, K.; Seo, J.; Kim, S.W. An in-depth analysis of distributed training of deep neural networks. In Proceedings of the 2021 IEEE International Parallel and Distributed Processing Symposium (IPDPS), Portland, OR, USA, 17–21 May 2021; IEEE: Piscataway, NJ, USA, 2021; pp. 994–1003.
182. Mahmoudi, A.; Ghadikolaei, H.S.; Fischione, C. Cost-efficient distributed optimization in machine learning over wireless networks. In Proceedings of the ICC 2020–2020 IEEE International Conference on Communications (ICC), Dublin, Ireland, 7–11 June 2020; IEEE: Piscataway, NJ, USA, 2020; pp. 1–7.
183. Giuseppi, A.; Della Torre, L.; Menegatti, D.; Pietrabissa, A. AdaFed: Performance-based adaptive federated learning. In Proceedings of the the 5th International Conference on Advances in Artificial Intelligence, Virtual, 20–22 November 2021; pp. 38–43.
184. Byrd, D.; Polychroniadou, A. Differentially private secure multi-party computation for federated learning in financial applications. In Proceedings of the First ACM International Conference on AI in Finance, New York, NY, USA, 15–16 October 2020; pp. 1–9.
185. Xu, X.; Liu, W.; Zhang, Y.; Zhang, X.; Dou, W.; Qi, L.; Bhuiyan, M.Z.A. Psdf: Privacy-aware iov service deployment with federated learning in cloud-edge computing. *Acm Trans. Intell. Syst. Technol. Tist* **2022**, *13*, 1–22. [CrossRef]
186. Qiao, D.; Li, M.; Guo, S.; Zhao, J.; Xiao, B. Resources-efficient Adaptive Federated Learning for Digital Twin-Enabled IIoT. *IEEE Trans. Netw. Sci. Eng.* **2024**, *11*, 3639–3652. [CrossRef]
187. Ao, Y.; Wu, Z.; Yu, D.; Gong, W.; Kui, Z.; Zhang, M.; Ye, Z.; Shen, L.; Ma, Y.; Wu, T.; et al. End-to-end adaptive distributed training on paddlepaddle. *arXiv* **2021**, arXiv:2112.02752.
188. Jin, Y.; Wang, H.; Tang, X.; Hoefler, T.; Liu, X.; Zhai, J. Identifying scalability bottlenecks for large-scale parallel programs with graph analysis. In Proceedings of the 25th ACM SIGPLAN Symposium on Principles and Practice of Parallel Programming, San Diego, CA, USA, 22–26 February 2020; pp. 409–410.
189. Jiang, Z.; Lin, H.; Zhong, Y.; Huang, Q.; Chen, Y.; Zhang, Z.; Peng, Y.; Li, X.; Xie, C.; Nong, S.; et al. {MegaScale}: Scaling large language model training to more than 10,000 {GPUs}. In Proceedings of the 21st USENIX Symposium on Networked Systems Design and Implementation (NSDI 24), Santa Clara, CA, USA, 16–18 April 2024; pp. 745–760.

190. Narayanan, D.; Shoeybi, M.; Casper, J.; LeGresley, P.; Patwary, M.; Korthikanti, V.; Vainbrand, D.; Kashinkunti, P.; Bernauer, J.; Catanzaro, B.; et al. Efficient large-scale language model training on gpu clusters using megatron-lm. In Proceedings of the International Conference for High Performance Computing, Networking, Storage and Analysis, St. Louis, MO, USA, 14–21 November 2021; pp. 1–15.
191. Dai, F.; Chen, Y.; Huang, Z.; Zhang, H.; Zhang, F. Efficient all-reduce for distributed DNN training in optical interconnect systems. In Proceedings of the 28th ACM SIGPLAN Annual Symposium on Principles and Practice of Parallel Programming, Montreal, QC, Canada, 25 February 2023–1 March 2023; pp. 422–424.
192. Hoefler, T.; Belli, R. Scientific benchmarking of parallel computing systems: Twelve ways to tell the masses when reporting performance results. In Proceedings of the International Conference for High Performance Computing, networking, Storage and Analysis, Austin, TX, USA, 15–20 November 2015; pp. 1–12.
193. Xie, G.; Xiao, X.; Peng, H.; Li, R.; Li, K. A survey of low-energy parallel scheduling algorithms. *IEEE Trans. Sustain. Comput.* **2021**, *7*, 27–46. [CrossRef]
194. Li, C.; Chen, L. Optimization for energy-aware design of task scheduling in heterogeneous distributed systems: A meta-heuristic based approach. *Computing* **2024**, *106*, 2007–2031. [CrossRef]
195. Sakuma, D.; Taherkhani, A.; Tsuno, T.; Sasaki, T.; Shimizu, H.; Teramoto, K.; Todd, A.; Ueno, Y.; Hajdušek, M.; Ikuta, R.; et al. An Optical Interconnect for Modular Quantum Computers. *arXiv* **2024**, arXiv:2412.09299.
196. Brunner, D.; Shastri, B.J.; Qadasi, M.A.A.; Ballani, H.; Barbay, S.; Biasi, S.; Bienstman, P.; Bilodeau, S.; Bogaerts, W.; Böhm, F.; et al. Roadmap on Neuromorphic Photonics. *arXiv* **2025**, arXiv:2501.07917.
197. Thakur, R.; Rabenseifner, R.; Gropp, W. Optimization of collective communication operations in MPICH. *Int. J. High Perform. Comput. Appl.* **2005**, *19*, 49–66. [CrossRef]
198. Wang, X.; Martínez, J.F. XChange: A market-based approach to scalable dynamic multi-resource allocation in multicore architectures. In Proceedings of the 2015 IEEE 21st International Symposium on High Performance Computer Architecture (HPCA), Burlingame, CA, USA, 7–11 February 2015; IEEE: Piscataway, NJ, USA, 2015; pp. 113–125.
199. Reuther, A.; Byun, C.; Arcand, W.; Bestor, D.; Bergeron, B.; Hubbell, M.; Jones, M.; Michaleas, P.; Prout, A.; Rosa, A.; et al. Scalable system scheduling for HPC and big data. *J. Parallel Distrib. Comput.* **2018**, *111*, 76–92. [CrossRef]
200. Shamim, M.S.; Muralidharan, J.; Ganguly, A. An interconnection architecture for seamless inter and intra-chip communication using wireless links. In Proceedings of the 9th International Symposium on Networks-on-Chip, Vancouver, BC, Canada, 28–30 September 2015; pp. 1–8.
201. Belapurkar, A.; Chakrabarti, A.; Ponnapalli, H.; Varadarajan, N.; Padmanabhuni, S.; Sundarrajan, S. *Distributed Systems Security: Issues, Processes and Solutions*; John Wiley & Sons: Hoboken, NJ, USA, 2009.
202. Sophos. The State of Ransomware 2021. In *Technical Report*; Sophos Group: Abingdon, UK, 2021. Available online: https://news.sophos.com/en-us/2021/04/27/the-state-of-ransomware-2021/ (accessed on 7 January 2025).
203. Baviskar, S.; Sanoj, R.; Nath, H.V. A Survey on Harnessing High-Performance Computing and Machine Learning for Detecting Stealthy Cache-Based Side-Channel Attacks. In Proceedings of the 2024 IEEE International Conference on Blockchain and Distributed Systems Security (ICBDS), Pune, India, 17–19 October 2024; IEEE: Piscataway, NJ, USA, 2024; pp. 1–6.
204. Kakoulli, E.; Zacharioudakis, E. Survey on Cryptoprocessors Advances and Technological Trends. In Proceedings of the The International Conference on Innovations in Computing Research, Madrid, Spain, 4–6 September 2024; Springer: Berlin/Heidelberg, Germany, 2024; pp. 411–430.
205. Swanzy, P.N.; Abukari, A.M.; Ansong, E.D. Data Security Framework for Protecting Data in Transit and Data at Rest in the Cloud. *Curr. J. Appl. Sci. Technol.* **2024**, *43*, 61–77. [CrossRef]
206. Egwutuoha, I.P.; Levy, D.; Selic, B.; Chen, S. A survey of fault tolerance mechanisms and checkpoint/restart implementations for high performance computing systems. *J. Supercomput.* **2013**, *65*, 1302–1326. [CrossRef]
207. Lashkari, B.; Musilek, P. A comprehensive review of blockchain consensus mechanisms. *IEEE Access* **2021**, *9*, 43620–43652. [CrossRef]
208. Chahar, S. Exploring the future trends of cryptography. In *Next Generation Mechanisms for Data Encryption*; CRC Press: Boca Raton, FL, USA, 2025; pp. 234–257.
209. Gärtner, F.C. Fundamentals of fault-tolerant distributed computing in asynchronous environments. *Acm Comput. Surv. CSUR* **1999**, *31*, 1–26. [CrossRef]
210. Bazgir, E.; Haque, E.; Uddin, M.S. Analysis of Distributed Systems. *Int. J. Comput. Appl.* **2024**, *975*, 8887. [CrossRef]
211. Jayasekara, S.; Karunasekera, S.; Harwood, A. Optimizing checkpoint-based fault-tolerance in distributed stream processing systems: Theory to practice. *Softw. Pract. Exp.* **2022**, *52*, 296–315. [CrossRef]
212. Kirti, M.; Maurya, A.K.; Yadav, R.S. Fault-tolerance approaches for distributed and cloud computing environments: A systematic review, taxonomy and future directions. *Concurr. Comput. Pract. Exp.* **2024**, *36*, e8081. [CrossRef]
213. Liu, M.; Xia, L.; Wang, Y.; Chakrabarty, K. Fault tolerance in neuromorphic computing systems. In Proceedings of the 24th Asia and South Pacific Design Automation Conference, Tokyo, Japan, 21–24 January 2019; pp. 216–223.

214. Campanella, A.; Yan, B.; Casellas, R.; Giorgetti, A.; Lopez, V.; Zhao, Y.; Mayoral, A. Reliable optical networks with ODTN: Resiliency and fail-over in data and control planes. *J. Light. Technol.* **2020**, *38*, 2755–2764. [CrossRef]
215. March, S.; Hevner, A.; Ram, S. Research commentary: An agenda for information technology research in heterogeneous and distributed environments. *Inf. Syst. Res.* **2000**, *11*, 327–341. [CrossRef]
216. Razon, A.; Thomas, T.; Banunarayanan, V. Advanced distribution management systems: Connectivity through standardized interoperability protocols. *IEEE Power Energy Mag.* **2019**, *18*, 26–33. [CrossRef]
217. Pulicharla, M.R. Hybrid Quantum-Classical Machine Learning Models: Powering the Future of AI. *J. Ournal Sci. Technol.* **2023**, *4*, 40–65. [CrossRef]
218. Guo, W.; Fouda, M.E.; Eltawil, A.M.; Salama, K.N. Neural coding in spiking neural networks: A comparative study for robust neuromorphic systems. *Front. Neurosci.* **2021**, *15*, 638474. [CrossRef] [PubMed]
219. Wang, Z.; Liu, K.; Li, J.; Zhu, Y.; Zhang, Y. Various frameworks and libraries of machine learning and deep learning: A survey. *Arch. Comput. Methods Eng.* **2019**, *31*, 1–24. [CrossRef]
220. Sheikh, H.F.; Tan, H.; Ahmad, I.; Ranka, S.; Bv, P. Energy-and performance-aware scheduling of tasks on parallel and distributed systems. *Acm J. Emerg. Technol. Comput. Syst. JETC* **2012**, *8*, 1–37. [CrossRef]
221. Alzoubi, Y.I.; Mishra, A. Green artificial intelligence initiatives: Potentials and challenges. *J. Clean. Prod.* **2024**, *468*, 143090. [CrossRef]
222. Krishnamoorthy, A.; Schwetman, H.; Zheng, X.; Ho, R. Energy-efficient photonics in future high-connectivity computing systems. *J. Light. Technol.* **2015**, *33*, 889–900. [CrossRef]
223. Gu, H.; Chen, K.; Yang, Y.; Chen, Z.; Zhang, B. MRONoC: A low latency and energy efficient on chip optical interconnect architecture. *IEEE Photonics J.* **2017**, *9*, 1–12. [CrossRef]
224. Dhasade, A.; Dini, P.; Guerra, E.; Kermarrec, A.M.; Miozzo, M.; Pires, R.; Sharma, R.; de Vos, M. Energy-Aware Decentralized Learning with Intermittent Model Training. *arXiv* **2024**, arXiv:2407.01283.
225. Bambagini, M.; Marinoni, M.; Aydin, H.; Buttazzo, G. Energy-aware scheduling for real-time systems: A survey. *Acm Trans. Embed. Comput. Syst. TECS* **2016**, *15*, 1–34. [CrossRef]
226. Yellu, R.R.; Maruthi, S.; Dodda, S.B.; Thuniki, P.; Reddy, S.R.B. AI Ethics-Challenges and Considerations: Examining ethical challenges and considerations in the development and deployment of artificial intelligence systems. *Afr. J. Artif. Intell. Sustain. Dev.* **2021**, *1*, 9–16.
227. Mensah, G.B. Artificial intelligence and ethics: A comprehensive review of bias mitigation, transparency, and accountability in AI Systems. *Africa Journal For Regulatory Affairs (AJFRA)* **2024**, *1*, 32–45.
228. Celi, L.A.; Cellini, J.; Charpignon, M.L.; Dee, E.C.; Dernoncourt, F.; Eber, R.; Mitchell, W.G.; Moukheiber, L.; Schirmer, J.; Situ, J.; et al. Sources of bias in artificial intelligence that perpetuate healthcare disparities—A global review. *PloS Digit. Health* **2022**, *1*, e0000022. [CrossRef]
229. Salako, A.O.; Fabuyi, J.A.; Aideyan, N.T.; Selesi-Aina, O.; Dapo-Oyewole, D.L.; Olaniyi, O. Advancing Information Governance in AI-Driven Cloud Ecosystem: Strategies for Enhancing Data Security and Meeting Regulatory Compliance. *Asian J. Res. Comput. Sci.* **2024**, *17*, 66–88. [CrossRef]
230. Patidar, N.; Mishra, S.; Jain, R.; Prajapati, D.; Solanki, A.; Suthar, R.; Patel, K.; Patel, H. Transparency in AI Decision Making: A Survey of Explainable AI Methods and Applications. *Adv. Robot. Technol.* **2024**, *2*, 1 .
231. Xu, J.; Glicksberg, B.S.; Su, C.; Walker, P.; Bian, J.; Wang, F. Federated learning for healthcare informatics. *J. Healthc. Inform. Res.* **2021**, *5*, 1–19. [CrossRef] [PubMed]
232. Turker, I.; Bicer, A.A. How to use blockchain effectively in auditing and assurance services. In *Digital Business Strategies in Blockchain Ecosystems: Transformational Design and Future of Global Business*; Springer International Publishing: Cham, Switzerland, 2020; pp. 457–471.
233. Mzukwa, A. Exploring Next-Generation Architectures for Advanced Computing Systems: Challenges and Opportunities. *J. Adv. Comput. Syst.* **2024**, *4*, 9–18.
234. Singh, H.; Tyagi, S.; Kumar, P.; Gill, S.S.; Buyya, R. Metaheuristics for scheduling of heterogeneous tasks in cloud computing environments: Analysis, performance evaluation, and future directions. *Simul. Model. Pract. Theory* **2021**, *111*, 102353. [CrossRef]
235. Kocot, B.; Czarnul, P.; Proficz, J. Energy-aware scheduling for high-performance computing systems: A survey. *Energies* **2023**, *16*, 890. [CrossRef]
236. Shabestari, F.; Navimipour, N.J. An Energy-Aware Resource Management Strategy Based On Spark and YARN in Heterogeneous Environments. *IEEE Trans. Green Commun. Netw.* **2023**, *8*, 635–644. [CrossRef]
237. Lu, P.J.; Lai, M.C.; Chang, J.S. A survey of high-performance interconnection networks in high-performance computer systems. *Electronics* **2022**, *11*, 1369. [CrossRef]
238. Mahajan, R.; Li, X.; Fryman, J.; Zhang, Z.; Nekkanty, S.; Tadayon, P.; Jaussi, J.; Shumarayev, S.; Agrawal, A.; Jadhav, S.; et al. Co-packaged photonics for high performance computing: Status, challenges and opportunities. *J. Light. Technol.* **2021**, *40*, 379–392. [CrossRef]

239. Wang, Z.; Zhao, J. Fork is All You Needed in Heterogeneous Systems. *arXiv* **2024**, arXiv:2404.05085.
240. Cai, Z.; Babbush, R.; Benjamin, S.C.; Endo, S.; Huggins, W.J.; Li, Y.; McClean, J.R.; O'Brien, T.E. Quantum error mitigation. *Rev. Mod. Phys.* **2023**, *95*, 045005. [CrossRef]
241. Abreu, S.; Pedersen, J.E. Neuromorphic Programming: Emerging Directions for Brain-Inspired Hardware. In Proceedings of the 2024 International Conference on Neuromorphic Systems (ICONS), Arlington, VA, USA, 30 July–2 August 2024; IEEE: Piscataway, NJ, USA, 2024; pp. 358–365.
242. Imam, N.; Cleland, T.A. Rapid online learning and robust recall in a neuromorphic olfactory circuit. *Nat. Mach. Intell.* **2020**, *2*, 181–191. [CrossRef] [PubMed]
243. Rabadán, A.T.; Ammar, A. Neurochips: An Ethical Consideration. In *Learning and Career Development in Neurosurgery: Values-Based Medical Education*; Springer: Cham, Switzerland, 2022; pp. 101–109.
244. Fernández-Caramés, T.M.; Fraga-Lamas, P. A Comprehensive Survey on Green Blockchain: Developing the Next Generation of Energy Efficient and Sustainable Blockchain Systems. *arXiv* **2024**, arXiv:2410.20581.
245. Asif, R.; Hassan, S.R. Shaping the future of Ethereum: Exploring energy consumption in Proof-of-Work and Proof-of-Stake consensus. *Front. Blockchain* **2023**, *6*, 1151724. [CrossRef]
246. Ismail, A.; Toohey, M.; Lee, Y.C.; Dong, Z.; Zomaya, A.Y. Cost and performance analysis on decentralized file systems for blockchain-based applications: State-of-the-art report. In Proceedings of the 2022 IEEE International Conference on Blockchain (Blockchain), Espoo, Finland, 22–25 August 2022; IEEE: Piscataway, NJ, USA, 2022; pp. 230–237.
247. Dulam, N.; Shaik, B.; Allam, K. Serverless AI: Building Scalable AI Applications Without Infrastructure Overhead. *J.-Assist. Sci. Discov.* **2022**, *2*, 519–542.
248. Soltani, B.; Ghenai, A.; Zeghib, N. Towards distributed containerized serverless architecture in multi cloud environment. *Procedia Comput. Sci.* **2018**, *134*, 121–128. [CrossRef]
249. Weerasinghe, S.; Perera, I. Optimized Strategy in Cloud-Native Environment for Inter-Service Communication in Microservices. *Int. J. Online Biomed. Eng.* **2024**, *20*, *1*. [CrossRef]
250. Lu, Y.; Bian, S.; Chen, L.; He, Y.; Hui, Y.; Lentz, M.; Li, B.; Liu, F.; Li, J.; Liu, Q.; et al. Computing in the Era of Large Generative Models: From Cloud-Native to AI-Native. *arXiv* **2024**, arXiv:2401.12230.
251. Gulli, A. *Google Anthos in Action: Manage Hybrid and Multi-Cloud Kubernetes Clusters*; Simon and Schuster: New York, NY, USA, 2023.
252. Kaul, D. AI-Driven Self-Healing Container Orchestration Framework for Energy-Efficient Kubernetes Clusters. *Emerg. Sci. Res.* **2024**, *2024*, 1–13.
253. Theodoropoulos, T.; Rosa, L.; Benzaid, C.; Gray, P.; Marin, E.; Makris, A.; Cordeiro, L.; Diego, F.; Sorokin, P.; Girolamo, M.D.; et al. Security in Cloud-Native Services: A Survey. *J. Cybersecur. Priv.* **2023**, *3*, 758–793. [CrossRef]
254. Peters, D.; Vold, K.; Robinson, D.; Calvo, R.A. Responsible AI—Two frameworks for ethical design practice. *IEEE Trans. Technol. Soc.* **2020**, *1*, 34–47. [CrossRef]

Disclaimer/Publisher's Note: The statements, opinions and data contained in all publications are solely those of the individual author(s) and contributor(s) and not of MDPI and/or the editor(s). MDPI and/or the editor(s) disclaim responsibility for any injury to people or property resulting from any ideas, methods, instructions or products referred to in the content.

electronics

MDPI

Article

Tensor-Based Uniform and Discrete Multi-View Projection Clustering

Linlin Ma [1,†], Haomin Li [2,†], Wenke Zang [1,*], Xincheng Liu [1] and Minghe Sun [3]

1 School of Business, Shandong Normal University, Jinan 250014, China; linlinsummer0520@163.com (L.M.); xincheng0524@163.com (X.L.)
2 Haide College, Ocean University of China, Qingdao 266100, China; 19854205837@163.com
3 Carlos Alvarez College of Business, The University of Texas at San Antonio, San Antonio, TX 78249, USA; minghe.sun@utsa.edu
* Correspondence: wink@sdnu.edu.cn
† These authors contributed equally to this work.

Abstract

Multi-view graph clustering (MVGC) utilizes affinity graphs to efficiently obtain information between views. Although various excellent MVGC methods have been proposed, they still have many limitations. To surmount these limitations, this work develops a novel tensor-based unified and discrete multi-view projection clustering (TUDMPC) approach. Specifically, TUDMPC uses projection and the $L_{2,1}$-norm for feature selection to reduce the effects of redundancy and noise. Meanwhile, the differences among similar graphs are minimized through the tensor kernel norm to better leverage information across views and capture high-order correlations. In addition, the rank constraint is applied to keep the affinity graphs with a discrete cluster structure, and the clustering results are obtained directly in a unified joint framework. Finally, an efficient optimization algorithm is proposed to obtain the clustering results. Experiments are conducted to compare the clustering results of TUDMPC with seven baseline methods. The results show that TUDMPC outperforms the existing methods.

Keywords: multi-view clustering; tensor kernel norm; projection learning; graph learning

1. Introduction

For the majority of applications, the collected data are from various sources with different formats. For example, a website can include images, audio, and other types of data in various ways, and may be considered multi-view data. Consensus cluster structures among different view data can be found by multi-view clustering (MVC) methods. Different views of data may have consistent information in a specific underlying data structure. Capturing information on inter-view consistency and complementarity is one of the hotspots in multi-view clustering studies.

Graphs are a crucial data structure for visually displaying the connections of data. Multi-view graph clustering (MVGC), with outstanding performance and widespread applications in numerous industries [1], can use affinity graphs to efficiently obtain consistent and complementary information [2].

Numerous MVGC approaches have demonstrated promising performance. Kumar et al. [3], by developing Co-regMSC, used feature factorization to obtain latent embedding, learn affinity graphs by reducing the differences in low-dimensional latent embedding of various views, and achieve decent performance. However, Co-regMSC does not distinguish the weights of various views. Nie et al. [4] proposed to distribute weights to various views in an adaptable manner. However, this approach uses preset similarity graphs, and, hence, its clustering performance is heavily influenced by the initial graphs. Jing et al. [5] used hypergraph embedding to select important features while fusing all views in the Grassmann space. However, these approaches still have the following two limitations. (1) Learning affinity graphs in high-dimensional spaces with redundant and high-dimensional features can lead to the curse of dimensionality and feature spoofing problems. (2) Most affinity graphs can only consider the shared information but cannot capture the higher-order correlations, making the generated affinity matrix poor-quality.

To address the high dimensionality issue, a large number of dimensionality reduction techniques [6–8] have been applied to MVC. Yuan et al. [9] presented an unsupervised feature selection method that simultaneously removes irrelevant features. Gao et al. [8] transformed high-dimensional data into a subspace using a projection matrix but did not care about the local structure and complementarity. To use higher-order and complementary information, researchers presented the tensor kernel norm methods [10–14]. Wu et al. [15] learned uniform graph and low-rank tensor, which reduces the dimensionality of data and retains higher-order information, but does not perform feature selection for dimensionality reduction, with performance susceptible to noise. Liu et al. [14] used tensor constraints to capture the global structure of views under deep learning.

High-order information among different views can be captured by tensors. The existing tensor-based methods do not consider redundant information, and most of them do not directly obtain clustering results during optimization but use other clustering algorithms subsequently, such as K-means or spectral clustering, to obtain the results. In order to perform feature selection and structure preservation in a unified framework and capture both complementary and higher-order information without subsequent steps to obtain clustering results, this study proposes a brand-new MVC approach called tensor-based unified and discrete multi-view projection clustering (TUDMPC). As depicted in Figure 1, the approach uses projection to learn low-dimensional spatial features and uses the $L_{2,1}$-norm for feature selection to eliminate the effects of redundancy and noise. Meanwhile, the divergence between similar graphs is minimized by a tensor kernel norm to better utilize the high-order correlations and complementary information of related graphs with different views. In addition, the Laplace rank constraints are imposed to ensure that the affinity graphs have discrete cluster structures and that the clustering results are obtained directly in a unified framework. This work makes the following major contributions:

- The high-dimensional data in the view are mapped to a low-dimensional potential space by projection learning to reduce the complexity of the method and to avoid dimensional catastrophes. Meanwhile, the $L_{2,1}$-norm is utilized for feature selection to remove the problem of outliers and redundant data on the clustering. The use of post-fusion in the low-dimensional space can adaptively and more accurately learn affinity graphs while maintaining the popular structure.
- The proposed TUDMPC minimizes the differences between views by using the tensor kernel norm, which makes excellent use of complementarity and captures the high-order correlations.
- The affinity graph generated from TUDMPC representing the clustering structure and the clustering results can be obtained in a unified framework without subsequent processing.
- An efficient iterative algorithm is developed to implement TUDMPC. The experimental results show that TUDMPC outperforms some of the baseline methods using datasets from the literature and from online websites.

The rest of this paper is structured as follows. In Section 2, related work is briefly reviewed. The details of TUDMPC, along with its background knowledge, are described in Section 3. The optimized iterative algorithm is described in Section 4. Experimental experiments are reported in Section 5. Conclusions are provided in Section 6.

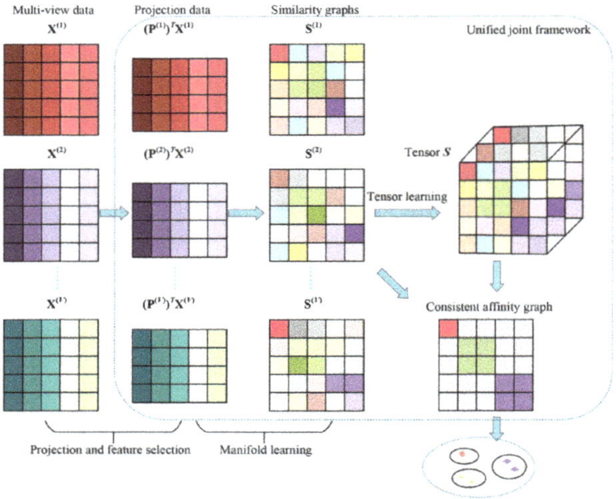

Figure 1. Flowchart of the TUDMPC algorithm.

2. Related Works

Numerous MVC methods have been developed, which can be generally classified into graph-based [1,3,16–24], subspace-based [4,25–30], and matrix decomposition-based [6,14,31–33].

The graph-based methods use graph topology to construct consistent similarity matrices. Wang et al. [20] advocated the learning of each view-specific and consistent affinity matrices in a mutually reinforcing approach. Xia et al. [21] exploited an MVC network that facilitates joint self-supervised learning and blocks the diagonal representation of data. Ren et al. [18] introduced the low-dimensional space with energy-conserving properties into clustering, using energy-preserving feature projection-based techniques to solve high-dimensional and corrupted data problems. Sang et al. [22] suggested an automatic weighted multi-view projection clustering approach that allows simultaneous manifold learning, dimensionality reduction, and consistent graph learning. Zhao et al. [23] extracted local information of binary codes to obtain the best clustering results by orthogonalizing the mapping matrix to remove redundant data and embedding bipartite graphs into a unified clustering framework.

Multi-view clustering based on matrix factorization tries to find the subspace where most of the data points are located by factorizing the original data as a product of two non-negative, including the base and the coefficient, matrices and utilizing the coefficient matrix to acquire the clustering results. Deng et al. [31] presented unconstrained non-negative matrix factorization guided multi-view clustering without non-negative restrictions by employing mapping functions that meet the non-negativity requirement, which allows extending the optimization method and employing learning rates to guide the optimization. Liu et al. [32] linked matrix factorization with probabilistic latent semantic analysis to improve clustering performance. Shi et al. [33] reconstructed non-negative and orthogonal graphs and updated the soft label matrix to create a superior similarity matrix.

Multi-view subspace clustering approaches consider that the data are not distributed uniformly but are distributed in the underlying subspace, and thus the clustering structure can be found in the potential low-dimensional subspace. Lv et al. [28] proposed partition fusion, where multiple partitions are generated and all partitions are merged into one common partition. Chen et al. [34] presented the diversity-embedded depth matrix decomposition for multi-view clustering, which uses diversity loss for the depth matrix decomposition and reduces redundant features. Fu et al. [35] used tensor to obtain high-order information and fuse multiple subspaces over the Grassmann manifold and additionally applied the rank constraint on the consensus affinity matrix to gain clustering results directly in a unified subspace.

3. TUDMPC and Its Preparation

The details of TUDMPC are described in this section. The main notations used in the methods are introduced, the motivation of the developed method is briefly presented, and the method is finally described in detail.

3.1. Notations

In the following, italic letters represent scalars, boldface lowercase letters represent vectors, and boldface capital letters represent matrices. Furthermore, boldface script letters represent third-order tensors, $||\mathbf{A}||_{2,1} = \sum_j ||\mathbf{A}(:,j)||_2$ denotes the $L_{2,1}$-norm of the matrix $\mathbf{A}$ and $||\mathbf{A}||_F$ represents the Frobenius norm of the matrix $\mathbf{A}$. Additional notations are provided in Table 1.

Table 1. Additional notations.

Notations	Descriptions
c, n and V	The number of clusters, samples and views, respectively,
m_v	Projection dimension in view v
d_v	The number of features in view v
$\mathbf{X}^{(v)} \in R^{d_v \times n}$	Data matrix of view v
$\mathbf{Z}^{(v)} \in R^{d_v \times m_v}$	Projection matrix of view v
$\mathbf{S}^{(v)} \in R^{n \times n}$	Similarity matrix in view v
$\mathbf{F} \in R^{n \times c}$	Clustering indicator matrix
$\mathbf{1}, \mathbf{I}$ and $\mathbf{0}$	Matrix of all 1 s, the identity matrix and matrix of all 0 s

3.2. Motivation

Most of the collected data in real life are high-dimensional and involve plenty of noise and redundant information due to the acquisition equipment and other factors. Therefore, poor clustering results may be obtained if the affinity map is generated directly from these raw data [22]. Although the various views provide consistent and complementary information [2], many multi-view clustering methods only generate consistent structural graphs by considering only consistent information but ignoring the complementary information. Additionally, multi-view clustering using the projection matrix for dimensionality reduction ignores the high-order correlation, thus making the generated similarity matrix less accurate and affecting the clustering performance. Therefore, the proposed TUDMPC takes the information complementarity and high-order correlation between views into full consideration in dimensionality reduction and noise removal and ensures that the affinity graph has a discrete clustering structure by introducing the Laplacian matrix rank constraint, and directly obtaining the clustering results in a unified framework without subsequent processing.

3.3. The TUDMPC Method

3.3.1. MVGC

Let $\mathbf{X}^{(1)},\ldots,\mathbf{X}^{(V)}$ denote the multi-view data containing V views and $\mathbf{X}^{(v)} = [\mathbf{x}_1^{(v)},\ldots,\mathbf{x}_n^{(v)}] \in R^{d_v \times n}$, $\mathbf{x}_i^{(v)} \in R^{d_v \times 1}$ represent data point i in view $vs.$, and d_v represent the number of features. MVGC usually first constructs a similarity graph based the on original data, followed by k-means clustering or spectral clustering [22]. Therefore, the goodness of the affinity matrix constructed for use as an input to subsequent spectral clustering influences the final performance. To resolve this issue, Wang et al. [36] preserved the local manifold structure in the following way:

$$\begin{aligned} &\min_{\mathbf{S}^{(v)}} \sum_{v=1}^{V} \sum_{i,j=1}^{n} \left\| \mathbf{x}_i^{(v)} - \mathbf{x}_j^{(v)} \right\|_2^2 s_{ij}^{(v)} + \gamma \left\| \mathbf{S}^{(v)} \right\|_F^2, \\ &s.t. \;\; s_{ii}^{(v)} = 0,\ \mathbf{0}_n \le \mathbf{S}^{(v)} \le \mathbf{1}_n,\ \mathbf{S}^{(v)}\mathbf{1} = 1 \end{aligned} \tag{1}$$

where $\mathbf{S}^{(v)} \in R^{n \times n}$ is the affinity matrix, and $s_{ij}^{(v)}$ represents the element of its row i column j.

3.3.2. Projection Learning

The purpose of using the projection matrix is to reduce the data dimension and to effectively improve the computational time complexity [37]. Based on the projection matrix, a $L_{2,1}$-norm constraint is used for feature selection and noise removal [22] to maintain compactness. The following model is used to construct the projection matrix:

$$\begin{aligned} &\min_{\mathbf{S}^{(v)},\mathbf{Z}^{(v)}} \sum_{v=1}^{V} \sum_{i,j=1}^{n} \left\| (\mathbf{Z}^{(v)})^T \mathbf{x}_i^{(v)} - (\mathbf{Z}^{(v)})^T \mathbf{x}_j^{(v)} \right\|_2^2 s_{ij}^{(v)} + \alpha \left\| \mathbf{Z}^{(v)} \right\|_{2,1} + \gamma \left\| \mathbf{S}^{(v)} \right\|_F^2, \\ &s.t. \;\; \mathbf{S}^{(v)}\mathbf{1} = 1,\ s_{ii}^{(v)} = 0,\ \mathbf{0}_n \le \mathbf{S}^{(v)} \le \mathbf{1}_n,\ (\mathbf{Z}^{(v)})^T \mathbf{X}^{(v)} (\mathbf{X}^{(v)})^T \mathbf{Z}^{(v)} = \mathbf{I} \end{aligned} \tag{2}$$

where α and γ are the parameters, and $\mathbf{Z}^{(v)} \in R^{d_v \times m_v}$ with $m_v \le d_v$.

3.3.3. Tensor Kernel Norm

Given a third order tensor $\mathcal{C} \in R^{n1 \times n2 \times n3}$, let $\mathcal{C}^{(i)}$ denote the frontal slice i of $\mathcal{C}$, and $\overline{\mathcal{C}}$ denote the discrete fast Fourier transform (FFT) of $\mathcal{C}$ along the three dimensions, i.e., $\overline{\mathcal{C}} = \text{fft}(\mathcal{C}, [\,], 3)$. Thus, $\mathcal{C} = \text{fft}(\overline{\mathcal{C}}, [\,], 3)$.

Definition 1 (tensor Kernel Norm [38]). *Given $\mathcal{C} \in R^{n1 \times n2 \times n3}$, its nuclear norm is given by*

$$\|\mathcal{C}\|_* = \sum_{i=1}^{n3} \left\| \overline{\mathcal{C}^{(i)}} \right\|_* = \sum_{i=1}^{n3} \sum_{j=1}^{\min(n1,n2)} \sigma_j(\overline{\mathcal{C}^{(i)}}). \tag{3}$$

The tensor kernel norm enables efficient acquisition of higher-order correlation information.

3.3.4. Rank Constraint

Multi-view clustering methods that use Laplace rank constraints to directly obtain clustering results can avoid the problems of being trapped in locally optimal solutions associated with the subsequent use of clustering methods such as K-means or spectral clustering. The direct implementation of multi-view clustering through the Laplace rank constraints essentially embeds the clustering step into the optimization process of representation learning, rather than treating it as an independent post-processing step. This approach outperforms the step-by-step strategy in both theoretical consistency and stability of results and is especially suitable for clustering complex multi-view data.

Lemma 1 ([39]). *The connective part of a matrix* $\mathbf{S}$ *has the same number of zero eigenvalues as its Laplacian matrix* $\mathbf{L}_s$*, where* $\mathbf{L}_s = \mathbf{D} - (\mathbf{S} + \mathbf{S}^T)/2$*,* $\mathbf{D}$ *is a diagonal matrix whose elements* $\mathbf{D}_{ii}$ *are given by* $\sum_{j=1}^{n} (s_{ij} + s_{ij}^T)/2$*, and* s_{ij} *is the element of* $\mathbf{S}$ *in row i and column j.*

Lemma 1 shows that the Laplacian matrix $\mathbf{L}_s$ with zero eigenvalues has c weights, and has rank$(\mathbf{L}_s) = n - c$. Because rank$(\mathbf{L}_s)$ is difficult to compute, the condition is relaxed based on the work of Hao et al. [36] to obtain the following:

$$\text{rank}(\mathbf{L}_s) = n - c = \sum_{i=1}^{c} \sigma_i(\mathbf{L}_s), \tag{4}$$

where $\sigma_i(\mathbf{L}_s)$ is the ith smallest eigenvalue of matrix $\mathbf{L}_s$.

Theorem 1 ([40]). *If* $\mathbf{H} \in R^{n\times n}$ *is a real symmetric matrix, then:*

$$\begin{aligned} \min_{\mathbf{f}_i^T\mathbf{f}_j=\left\{\begin{smallmatrix}1,i=j\\0,i\neq j\end{smallmatrix}\right.} \sum_{i=1}^{c} \mathbf{f}_l^T\mathbf{H}\mathbf{f}_l &= \min_{\mathbf{F}^T\mathbf{F}=\mathbf{I}} \text{tr}(\mathbf{F}^T\mathbf{H}\mathbf{F}) \\ &= \lambda_1 + \dots + \lambda_c \\ &= \sum_{l=1}^{c} \mathbf{a}_l^T\mathbf{H}\mathbf{a}_l \\ &= \text{tr}(\mathbf{\Theta}^T\mathbf{H}\mathbf{\Theta}) \end{aligned}, \tag{5}$$

where $\mathbf{\Theta} = [\mathbf{a}_1, \mathbf{a}_2 \dots, \mathbf{a}_c]$ *and* $\lambda_1 \leq \dots \leq \lambda_n$ *are the n orthonormal eigenvectors and n eigenvalues of* $\mathbf{H}$*, respectively.*

According to Theorem 1, the following can be obtained:

$$\sum_{j=1}^{c} \sigma_j(\mathbf{L}_s) = \min_{\mathbf{F}^T\mathbf{F}=\mathbf{I}} \text{tr}(\mathbf{F}^T\mathbf{L}_s\mathbf{F}), \tag{6}$$

where $\mathbf{F} = [\mathbf{f}_1, \dots, \mathbf{f}_c] \in R^{n\times c}$.

Therefore, combining the tensor kernel norm, and (1), (2), (3) and (6), the TUDMPC model is stated as follows:

$$\begin{aligned} \min_{\mathbf{S}^{(v)},\mathbf{Z}^{(v)},\mathbf{F}} & \sum_{v=1}^{V}\sum_{i,j=1}^{n} \left\|(\mathbf{Z}^{(v)})^T\mathbf{x}_i^{(v)} - (\mathbf{Z}^{(v)})^T\mathbf{x}_j^{(v)}\right\|_2^2 s_{ij}^{(v)} + \alpha\left\|\mathbf{Z}^{(v)}\right\|_{2,1} + \|\boldsymbol{\mathcal{S}}\|_* \\ & + \gamma\left\|\mathbf{S}^{(v)}\right\|_F^2 + \beta\,\text{tr}(\mathbf{F}^T\mathbf{L}_s\mathbf{F}) \\ s.t. \quad & s_{ii}^{(v)} = 0,\ \mathbf{0}_n \leq \mathbf{S}^{(v)} \leq \mathbf{1}_n,\ \mathbf{S}^{(v)}\mathbf{1} = 1,\ (\mathbf{Z}^{(v)})^T\mathbf{X}^{(v)}(\mathbf{X}^{(v)})^T\mathbf{Z}^{(v)} = \mathbf{I},\ \mathbf{F}^T\mathbf{F} = \mathbf{I} \end{aligned}, \tag{7}$$

with $\boldsymbol{\mathcal{S}}(:,v,:) = \mathbf{S}^{(v)}$. The TUDMPC model allows direct access to the clustering results.

4. Optimization and Complexity Analysis

4.1. Optimization

To obtain the optimal solution of (7), instead of using heuristic optimization procedures, an iterative alternating method is used to transform the constrained problem into non-constrained sub-problems. An iterative solution algorithm is developed to find exact solutions because heuristic procedures can only find quick and approximate solutions. Model (7) is modified by adding the auxiliary variable $\mathcal{G}$ to become:

$$
\begin{aligned}
L = & \sum_{v=1}^{V} \Big(\sum_{i,j=1}^{n} \left\| (\mathbf{Z}^{(v)})^T \mathbf{x}_i^{(v)} - (\mathbf{Z}^{(v)})^T \mathbf{x}_j^{(v)} \right\|_2^2 s_{ij}^{(v)} + \gamma \left\| \mathbf{S}^{(v)} \right\|_F^2 + \|\mathcal{G}\|_* + \alpha \left\| \mathbf{Z}^{(v)} \right\|_{2,1} \Big) \\
& + \beta \operatorname{tr}(\mathbf{F}^T \mathbf{L}_s \mathbf{F}) + \langle \mathcal{Y}, \mathcal{S} - \mathcal{G} \rangle + \frac{\mu}{2} \|\mathcal{S} - \mathcal{G}\|_F^2 \\
s.t.\ & s_{ii}^{(v)} = 0,\ \mathbf{0}_n \le \mathbf{S}^{(v)} \le \mathbf{1}_n,\ \mathbf{S}^{(v)}\mathbf{1} = 1,\ (\mathbf{Z}^{(v)})^T \mathbf{X}^{(v)} (\mathbf{X}^{(v)})^T \mathbf{Z}^{(v)} = \mathbf{I},\ \mathbf{F}^T\mathbf{F} = \mathbf{I}
\end{aligned} \quad (8)
$$

where $\mathcal{Y}$ is the tensor of Lagrange multipliers, and $\mu > 0$ is a penalty coefficient.

Thus, the optimization algorithm is composed of the following four modules.

4.1.1. Updating $\mathbf{Z}^{(v)}$ by Fixing $\mathbf{S}^{(v)}$, $\mathbf{F}$ and $\mathcal{G}$

When $\mathbf{Z}^{(v)}$ is updated, the other variables are fixed:

$$
\begin{aligned}
\min\ & \sum_{v=1}^{V} \Big(\sum_{i,j=1}^{n} \left\| (\mathbf{Z}^{(v)})^T \mathbf{x}_i^{(v)} - (\mathbf{Z}^{(v)})^T \mathbf{x}_j^{(v)} \right\|_2^2 s_{ij}^{(v)} + \alpha \left\| \mathbf{Z}^{(v)} \right\|_{2,1} \Big). \\
s.t.\ & (\mathbf{Z}^{(v)})^T \mathbf{X}^{(v)} (\mathbf{X}^{(v)})^T \mathbf{Z}^{(v)} = \mathbf{I}
\end{aligned} \quad (9)
$$

This process is discussed for only one of the views as each is independent:

$$
\begin{aligned}
\min\ & \sum_{i,j=1}^{n} \left\| (\mathbf{Z}^{(v)})^T \mathbf{x}_i^{(v)} - (\mathbf{Z}^{(v)})^T \mathbf{x}_j^{(v)} \right\|_2^2 s_{ij}^{(v)} + \alpha \left\| \mathbf{Z}^{(v)} \right\|_{2,1}, \\
s.t.\ & (\mathbf{Z}^{(v)})^T \mathbf{X}^{(v)} (\mathbf{X}^{(v)})^T \mathbf{Z}^{(v)} = \mathbf{I}
\end{aligned} \quad (10)
$$

where $\left\| \mathbf{Z}^{(v)} \right\|_{2,1} = 2\mathrm{Tr}\,((\mathbf{Z}^{(v)})^T \mathbf{W}^{(v)} \mathbf{Z}^{(\mathrm{v})})$, and $w_{ii}^{(v)}$ is the value of the diagonal element of $\mathbf{W}^{(v)}$ with $w_{ii}^{(v)} = 1/2 \left\| \mathbf{Z}^{(v)}(i,:) \right\|_2$. Thus, (10) can be written as the following:

$$
\begin{aligned}
\min\ & \sum_{i,j=1}^{n} \left\| (\mathbf{Z}^{(v)})^T \mathbf{x}_i^{(v)} - (\mathbf{Z}^{(v)})^T \mathbf{x}_j^{(v)} \right\|_2^2 s_{ij}^{(v)} + \alpha \mathrm{Tr}\,((\mathbf{Z}^{(v)})^T \mathbf{W}^{(v)} \mathbf{Z}^{(\mathrm{v})}). \\
s.t.\ & (\mathbf{Z}^{(v)})^T \mathbf{X}^{(v)} (\mathbf{X}^{(v)})^T \mathbf{Z}^{(v)} = \mathbf{I}
\end{aligned} \quad (11)
$$

Model (11) is solved by the Lagrange multiplier method with the Lagrangian as shown in (12) as follows:

$$
L = \mathrm{Tr}\,((\mathbf{Z}^{(v)})^T \mathbf{X}^{(v)} \mathbf{L}_s^{(v)} (\mathbf{X}^{(v)})^T \mathbf{Z}^{(v)}) + \alpha \mathrm{Tr}\,((\mathbf{Z}^{(v)})^T \mathbf{W}^{(v)} \mathbf{Z}^{(\mathrm{v})}) - \mathrm{Tr}\,(\boldsymbol{\psi}((\mathbf{Z}^{(v)})^T \mathbf{X}^{(v)} (\mathbf{X}^{(v)})^T \mathbf{Z}^{(v)} - \mathbf{I})), \quad (12)
$$

where $\boldsymbol{\psi}$ is a diagonal matrix of the Lagrange multipliers.

The solution approach of Sang et al. [22] can be used to find a solution of (12).

4.1.2. Updating $\mathbf{S}^{(v)}$ by Fixing $\mathbf{Z}^{(v)}$, $\mathbf{F}$ and $\mathcal{G}$

The sub-problem with $\mathbf{S}^{(v)}$ as the variables can be written as:

$$
\begin{aligned}
\min_{\mathbf{S}^{(v)}}\ & \sum_{v=1}^{V} \Big(\sum_{i,j=1}^{n} \left\| (\mathbf{Z}^{(v)})^T \mathbf{x}_i^{(v)} - (\mathbf{Z}^{(v)})^T \mathbf{x}_j^{(v)} \right\|_2^2 s_{ij}^{(v)} + \gamma \left\| \mathbf{S}^{(v)} \right\|_F^2 \Big) \\
& + \beta \operatorname{tr}(\mathbf{F}^T \mathbf{L}_s \mathbf{F}) + \langle \mathcal{Y}, \mathcal{S} - \mathcal{G} \rangle + \frac{\mu}{2} \|\mathcal{S} - \mathcal{G}\|_F^2 \quad . \\
s.t.\ & s_{ii}^{(v)} = 0,\ \mathbf{0}_n \le \mathbf{S}^{(v)} \le \mathbf{1}_n,\ \mathbf{S}^{(v)}\mathbf{1} = 1
\end{aligned} \quad (13)
$$

The problem (13) can be rewritten as:

$$\begin{aligned}&\min_{\mathbf{S}^{(v)}} \sum_{v=1}^{V}\Big(\sum_{i,j=1}^{n}\left\|(\mathbf{Z}^{(v)})^T\mathbf{x}_i^{(v)}-(\mathbf{Z}^{(v)})^T\mathbf{x}_j^{(v)}\right\|_2^2 s_{ij}^{(v)}+\gamma\left\|\mathbf{S}^{(v)}\right\|_F^2\Big)\\&\quad+\beta\,\mathrm{tr}(\mathbf{F}^T\mathbf{L}_s\mathbf{F})+\frac{\mu}{2}\left\|\mathbf{S}^{(v)}-\mathbf{G}^{(v)}+\frac{\mathbf{Y}^{(v)}}{\mu}\right\|_F^2\\&s.t.\quad s_{ii}^{(v)}=0,\ \mathbf{0}_n\le\mathbf{S}^{(v)}\le\mathbf{1}_n,\ \mathbf{S}^{(v)}\mathbf{1}=1\end{aligned} \tag{14}$$

With $d_{ij}^v=\left\|(\mathbf{Z}^{(v)})^T\mathbf{x}_i^{(v)}-(\mathbf{Z}^{(v)})^T\mathbf{x}_j^{(v)}\right\|_2^2$, $f_{ij}^v=\frac{\beta}{V}\|\mathbf{f}_i-\mathbf{f}_j\|_2^2$ and $\mathbf{E}^{(v)}=\mathbf{G}^{(v)}-\frac{1}{\mu}\mathbf{Y}^{(v)}$, and $\mathbf{e}_i^{(v)}\in R^{1\times n}$ as the row vector of $\mathbf{E}^{(v)}$, the model in (14) for view *vs*. is transformed into (15)

$$\begin{aligned}&\min\sum_{j=1}^{n}d_{ij}^v s_{ij}^{(v)}+\gamma\left\|\mathbf{s}_i^{(v)}\right\|_2^2+f_{ij}^v s_{ij}^{(v)}+\frac{\mu}{2}\left\|\mathbf{s}_i^{(v)}-\mathbf{e}_i^{(v)}\right\|_2^2,\\&s.t.\ s_{ii}^{(v)}=0,\ \mathbf{0}_n\le\mathbf{S}^{(v)}\le\mathbf{1}_n,\ \mathbf{S}^{(v)}\mathbf{1}=1\end{aligned} \tag{15}$$

where $\mathbf{s}_i^{(v)}\in R^{1\times n}$ is the row vector of $\mathbf{S}^{(v)}$.

Let $o_{ij}^v=d_{ij}^v+f_{ij}^v$, then (15) is rewritten as

$$\begin{aligned}&\min\sum_{j=1}^{n}o_{ij}^v s_{ij}^{(v)}+\gamma\left\|\mathbf{s}_i^{(v)}\right\|_2^2+\frac{\mu}{2}\left\|\mathbf{s}_i^{(v)}-\mathbf{e}_i^{(v)}\right\|_2^2.\\&s.t.\ s_{ii}^{(v)}=0,\ \mathbf{0}_n\le\mathbf{S}^{(v)}\le\mathbf{1}_n,\ \mathbf{S}^{(v)}\mathbf{1}=1\end{aligned} \tag{16}$$

The model in (16) can be rewritten as:

$$\begin{aligned}&\min\left\|\mathbf{s}_i^{(v)}+\frac{\mathbf{o}_i^v}{2\gamma}\right\|_2^2+\frac{\mu}{2\gamma}\left\|\mathbf{s}_i^{(v)}-\mathbf{e}_i^{(v)}\right\|_2^2,\\&s.t.\ s_{ii}^{(v)}=0,\ \mathbf{0}_n\le\mathbf{S}^{(v)}\le\mathbf{1}_n,\ \mathbf{S}^{(v)}\mathbf{1}=1\end{aligned} \tag{17}$$

where $\mathbf{o}_i^v\in R^{1\times n}$ is the row vector composed of o_{ij}^v.

The Lagrangian corresponding to (17) is given as follows

$$L(\mathbf{s}_i^{(v)},\ \eta,\ \delta)=\left\|\mathbf{s}_i^{(v)}+\frac{\mathbf{o}_i^v}{2\gamma}\right\|_2^2+\frac{\mu}{2\gamma}\left\|\mathbf{s}_i^{(v)}-\mathbf{e}_i^{(v)}\right\|_2^2-\eta(\mathbf{s}_i^{(v)}\mathbf{1}-1)-\mathbf{s}_i^{(v)}\delta, \tag{18}$$

where $\eta\ge0$, $\delta\in R^{n\times1}$ and $\delta\ge\mathbf{0}$ are the Lagrange multipliers.

After deriving the partial derivatives of $L(\mathbf{s}_i^{(v)},\ \eta,\ \delta)$ in (18) with respect to $\mathbf{s}_i^{(v)}$ and setting them to 0, the following is obtained

$$2(\mathbf{s}_i^{(v)}+\frac{\mathbf{o}_i^v}{2\gamma})+\frac{\mu}{\gamma}(\mathbf{s}_i^{(v)}-\mathbf{e}_i^{(v)})-\eta\mathbf{1}^T-\delta^T=0. \tag{19}$$

By the KKT condition, $\mathbf{s}_i^{(v)}\delta_j=0$ holds. Therefore, the following updated solution for $s_{ij}^{(v)}$ is obtained:

$$s_{ij}^{(v)}=\begin{cases}\left(\frac{\mu e_{ij}^{(v)}-o_{ij}^v+\eta\gamma}{2\gamma+\mu}\right)_+, & i\ne j\\0, & i=j\end{cases}, \tag{20}$$

where $e_{ij}^{(v)}$ is element j of $\mathbf{e}_i^{(v)}$.

To simplify the calculation, the k-nearest neighbor approach [22] is employed. Sorting from the smallest to the largest gives $s_{ik}^{(v)} > 0$, and $s_{ik+1}^{(v)} = 0$, and the results in (20) become:

$$-o_{ik}^{v} + \mu e_{ik}^{(v)} + \gamma\eta > 0, \quad -o_{ik+1}^{v} + \mu e_{ik+1}^{(v)} + \gamma\eta = 0. \tag{21}$$

Given $\mathbf{s}_i^{(v)}\mathbf{1} = 1$, the following can be obtained from (20):

$$\eta = \frac{1}{k}(2 + \frac{\mu}{\gamma} + \sum_{m=1}^{k} \frac{o_{im}^{v}}{\gamma} - \sum_{m=1}^{k} \frac{\mu}{\gamma} e_{im}^{(v)}). \tag{22}$$

Combining (21) and (22), the following holds:

$$\gamma = \frac{1}{2}(ko_{ik+1}^{v} - k\mu e_{ik+1}^{(v)} - \mu - \sum_{m=1}^{k} (o_{im}^{v} - \mu e_{im}^{(v)})). \tag{23}$$

By (20) and (23), the updated solution of $s_{ij}^{(v)}$ can be rewritten as:

$$s_{ij}^{(v)} = \begin{cases} \dfrac{\mu e_{ij}^{(v)} - o_{ij}^{v} + o_{ik+1}^{v} - \mu e_{ik+1}^{(v)}}{k(o_{ik+1}^{v} - \mu e_{ik+1}^{(v)}) + \sum_{t=1}^{k} (\mu e_{it}^{(v)} - o_{it}^{v})}, & i \le k \\ 0, & i > k \end{cases}. \tag{24}$$

4.1.3. Updating $\mathcal{G}$ by Fixing $\mathbf{S}^{(v)}$, $\mathbf{F}$ and $\mathbf{Z}^{(v)}$

The update of $\mathcal{G}$ can be written as:

$$\begin{aligned} &\min \ \|\mathcal{G}\|_* + \langle \mathcal{Y}, \mathcal{S} - \mathcal{G} \rangle + \frac{\mu}{2}\|\mathcal{S} - \mathcal{G}\|_F^2 \\ &= \min \ \frac{1}{\mu}\|\mathcal{G}\|_* + \frac{1}{2}\left\|\mathcal{S} + \frac{\mathcal{Y}}{\mu} - \mathcal{G}\right\|_F^2 \end{aligned}. \tag{25}$$

Using the results of Hu et al. [41], the solution to problem (25) is

$$\mathcal{G}^* = \mathbf{U}\Gamma_e[\mathbf{\Sigma}]\mathbf{V}^T, \tag{26}$$

where $\mathbf{U\Sigma V}^T$ is the singular value decomposition of the matrix $\mathcal{G}$.

4.1.4. Updating $\mathbf{F}$ by Fixing $\mathbf{S}^{(v)}$, $\mathbf{Z}^{(v)}$ and $\mathcal{G}$

The update of $\mathbf{F}$ can be written as below:

$$\begin{aligned} &\min \ \beta \, \mathrm{tr}(\mathbf{F}^T \mathbf{L}_s \mathbf{F}) \\ &s.t. \quad \mathbf{F}^T\mathbf{F} = \mathbf{I} \end{aligned}. \tag{27}$$

The matrix $\mathbf{F}$ consists of c eigenvectors corresponding to the c smallest eigenvalues of $\mathbf{L}_s$. Then, c clusters can be identified depending on the connection of graph $\mathbf{S}$ with $\mathbf{S} = \sum(\mathbf{S}^{(v)} + (\mathbf{S}^{(v)})^T)$. Let ς denote the number of eigenvalues of the Laplacian matrix $\mathbf{L}_s$ that equals 0 in each iteration. In particular, update β to $\beta = \beta \times 2$ when $\varsigma < c$ or to $\beta = \beta/2$ when $\varsigma > c + 1$. Except for the above two conditions, the search process ends.

The steps of the iterative alternating method, i.e., the TUDMPC algorithm, is outlined in Algorithm 1.

Algorithm 1 Steps in the TUDMPC algorithm

Require: Multi-view datasets $\mathbf{X}^{(v)}$ for v= 1, 2..., V, the projection dimension m_v for v= 1, 2..., V, and the parameters α, β and k.
Ensure: Graph $\mathbf{S}$ with c-connected components.

Initialize $\mathbf{S}^{(v)}$ via (1)
Initialize $\mathbf{Z}^{(v)}$ using the approach proposed by Sang et al. [22];
Initialize $\mathcal{G}$ via (26);
while the convergence criteria are not satisfied **do**
  Update $\mathbf{S}^{(v)}$ using (24);
  Update $\mathbf{Z}^{(v)}$ by (11);
  Update $\mathcal{G}$ via (26);
  Update $\mathbf{F}$ by (27);
  $\mathcal{Y}$=$\mathcal{Y} + \mu(\mathcal{S} - \mathcal{J})$;
  $\mu = \min(\rho\mu, \mu_{\max})$;
end while
Obtain the c clusters directly from graph $\mathbf{S} = \sum_{v=1}^{V} (\mathbf{S}^{(v)} + (\mathbf{S}^{(v)})^T)$.

4.2. Complexity Analysis

Four modules, i.e., the updating of $\mathbf{S}^{(v)}$, $\mathcal{G}$, $\mathbf{Z}^{(v)}$ and $\mathbf{F}$, respectively, are included in the TUDMPC algorithm to solve (7). Specifically, the complexities of updating $\mathbf{S}^{(v)}$, $\mathbf{Z}^{(v)}$, $\mathbf{F}$ and are $O(Vnk)$, $O(Vm_v{d_v}^2)$, $O(cn^2)$ and $O(n^2 Vlogn + n^2{m_v}^2)$, respectively. Overall, the complexity of the TUDMPC algorithm is $O(t(Vnk + Vm_v{d_v}^2 + cn^2 + n^2 Vlogn + n^2{m_v}^2)) \approx O(tn^2(c + Vlogn + {m_v}^2))$, where t is the number of iterations.

5. Numerical Experiments and Analysis of Results

Six datasets are used in the experiments to test the performance of TUDMPC, and seven baseline algorithms are used for comparison. Meanwhile, five evaluation metrics are selected to assess the performance of TUDMPC and other methods. Furthermore, the convergence of the TUDMPC algorithm is examined. Finally, the sensitivity of the performance of the TUDMPC algorithm is analyzed as the parameter values change.

5.1. Experimental Setup

Datasets. The effectiveness of TUDMPC is tested on six datasets. Basic details about the datasets used are given in Table 2.

- MSRC-v1: This dataset contains 20 groups of images of objects, each with about 100 images. It is mainly used for object recognition and image segmentation tasks. The dataset is suitable for multi-view clustering and image classification, where each image symbolizes a different "perspective".
- HW2sources: This is a handwritten digital recognition dataset, which contains handwritten digital samples from multiple perspectives and comes from different writings. This dataset provides diversity and different writing styles and is suitable for testing the performance of clustering algorithms on non-uniform data.
- 100leaves: This dataset contains 100 different types of leaf images, and each leaf has multiple images, which are mainly used for plant classification. It can help evaluate the effectiveness of multi-view learning in natural image data.
- NGs: This dataset contains different levels of detail of natural images and is suitable for exploring fine-grained object classification. Multi-view provides more information and is suitable for testing the performance of multi-view clustering algorithms in different details.

- Hdigit: Similar to HW2sources, this dataset is also about handwritten numbers but comes from different recording methods or devices. It provides more sample variability for handwritten digital recognition and can test the stability of clustering algorithms.
- ORL: The ORL dataset contains 400 face images of 40 different people, which includes relevant information in expressions, facial ornaments and minute gestures, and is often used in face recognition studies. The different features of the face images in the ORL dataset are extracted by using four feature extraction methods including Generalized Search Tree (GIST), Local Binary Pattern (LBP), Histogram of Orientation Gradients (HOG) and Gradient Energy Norm Tensor (CENT), which are considered as four views. The obtained feature dimensions of the four views are 512, 59, 864, and 254, respectively.

Baseline methods. The performance of the TUDMPC is compared with those of the following seven baseline methods: SC [42], Co-regMSC [3], MVGL [43], MCGC [44], AWP [45], GMC [20] and SFMC [46].

Evaluation metrics. The evaluation metrics used to measure the performance of the clustering methods include accuracy (ACC), purity, normalized mutual information (NMI), recall and F-score. The value of each of these five evaluation metrics is in the interval of [0, 1], and the larger the value of each metric, the better the clustering results. To reduce the effect of randomness, each method is run on each dataset 20 times independently, and the mean and standard deviation are calculated and reported for each method. The results are reported in the following tables and are also visualized in the following figures. The best mean value for each assessment metric is highlighted, and the next best mean value is italicized for each dataset.

Parameter setting. Some parameters must be specified beforehand. Specifically, $k = 10$ is used for the baseline methods using the KNN method. In addition, the affinity graph of SFMC is a bipartite graph, so the anchor point scale is set to 0.5 as described in Li et al. [46] where SFMC was originally proposed. For all baseline methods used in the experiments, the parameter settings proposed in the original articles publishing the corresponding methods are used.

Table 2. Basic information of the different databases.

Datasets	Instances (n)	Views (V)	Clusters (c)	Dimensions
MSRC-v1 [47]	210	5	7	24/576/512/256/254
HW2sources [36]	2000	2	10	784/256
100leaves [1]	1600	3	100	64/64/64
NGs [2]	500	3	5	2000/2000/2000
Hdigit [3]	10,000	2	10	784/256
ORL [48]	400	4	40	512/59/864/254

[1] https://archive.ics.uci.edu/dataset/241/one+hundred+plant+species+leaves+data+set, accessed on 12 May 2023; [2] http://lig-membres.imag.fr/grimal/data.html, accessed on 12 May 2023; [3] https://cs.nyu.edu/home/people/in_memoriam/roweis/data.html, accessed on 12 May 2023.

5.2. Analyses of Experimental Results

The clustering results measured in the five evaluation metrics for all methods are reported in Tables 3–8. The findings below are drawn from these results.

For the MRSC_v1 dataset, as shown in Table 3, TUDMPC has the best performance of all the methods. For example, the mean ACC of TUDMPC is 28.09%, 12.07%, 17.62%, 17.14%, 18.09%, 17.62%, and 14.28% higher, and the mean NMI of TUDMPC is 28.82%, 12.78%, 9.45%, 12.49%, 18.24%, 7.68% and 5.94% higher, than those of SC, Co-regMSC, MVGL, AWP, MCGC,

GMC and SFMC, respectively. The results of the HW2sources, 100leaves and Hdigit datasets are presented in Tables 4, 7 and 8 and have very similar patterns.

The results for the high-dimensional NGs dataset, as presented in Table 5, illustrate that TUDMPC also obtained better clustering results than the baseline methods. The main reason is that the proposed TUDMPC reduced the dimensions by using the projection matrix and using the $L_{2,1}$-norm for feature learning to remove noise and redundant information when learning the similarity matrix on clean and low-dimensional data, while the baseline methods learned the initial affinity map directly from the original data.

As the results of the ORL dataset in Table 6 illustrate, TUDMPC achieved the optimal result for the ACC, NMI, F-score and recall indicators, although it did not achieve the best results in purity. Overall, TUDMPC has better performance than the baseline method.

One of the main reasons for the proposed TUDMPC to outperform the SC method on all the datasets is that the proposed TUDMPC uses tensor to take into account the complementary information and preserves the local manifold structure. This result shows the success of the proposed approach in enhancing the functionality of MVC.

These results provide evidence to validate the performance and effectiveness of TUDMPC. Two main reasons contribute to the good performance of TUDMPC. (1) Projection learning is utilized to map high-dimensional data to a space of lower dimension to reduce method complexity, prevent dimensional curses, and lessen the effects of noise and redundancy. (2) The high-order correlations and complementarities included in the various views are effectively utilized by the application of the tensor kernel norm.

To visualize this effect, the affinity matrices are visualized for the datasets MRSC_v1, NGs and 100leaves in Figure 2–4, respectively. The number of diagonal blocks in the figure is the number of clusters obtained by running the corresponding algorithm, and the rest of the surrounding blue highlights are unclassified data points. As shown in these figures, MCGL can obtain the block diagonal structure, which is not clear and the number of obtained diagonal blocks is not equal to the total number of clusters. Although MVGL, GMC and SFMC can obtain the right number of diagonal blocks, like MCGC, many data points are clustered around these blocks resulting from noisy and redundant information. By contrast, TUDMPC not only obtained the correct diagonal blocks but also fully captured the complementary information between views using the tensor kernel norm, thereby making the clustering structure clearer.

The t-distribution random neighborhood embedding (t-SNE) [49] is also used to visualize the diagonal block distribution of affinity matrices to assess the clustering performance. As examples, the affinity matrices of the HW2sources and MSRCv1 datasets, with 10 and 7 clusters, respectively, are shown in Figures 5 and 6, where each number in the legend represents a cluster. Both SC and Co-regMSC use Gaussian functions to construct view-specific similarity maps [22]. As shown in these figures, SC cannot obtain a clear cluster structure because it does not leverage the complementary information. Compared to the baseline methods, the similarity matrices obtained by TUDMPC can reveal clearer cluster structures with fewer incorrectly clustered data points.

Table 3. Clustering results for the MRSC_v1 dataset.

Methods	ACC	NMI	Purity	R	F
SC	0.6429 ± 0.0000	0.5595 ± 0.0003	0.6905 ± 0.0000	0.5141 ± 0.0009	0.5306 ± 0.0005
Co-regMSC	0.8031 ± 0.0066	0.7199 ± 0.0095	0.8031 ± 0.0066	0.6821 ± 0.0069	0.6931 ± 0.0081
MVGL	0.7476 ± 0.0000	0.7532 ± 0.0000	0.8810 ± 0.0000	0.5860 ± 0.0000	0.6736 ± 0.0000
AWP	0.7524 ± 0.0000	0.7228 ± 0.0000	0.8810 ± 0.0000	0.6029 ± 0.0000	0.6867 ± 0.0000
MCGC	0.7429 ± 0.0000	0.6653 ± 0.0000	0.8286 ± 0.0000	0.5453 ± 0.0000	0.6191 ± 0.0000
GMC	0.7476 ± 0.0000	0.7709 ± 0.0000	0.7905 ± 0.0000	0.8089 ± 0.0000	0.6968 ± 0.0000
SFMC	0.7810 ± 0.0000	0.7883 ± 0.0000	0.8095 ± 0.0000	0.8138 ± 0.0000	0.7404 ± 0.0000
TUDMPC	**0.9238 ± 0.0000**	**0.8477 ± 0.0000**	**0.9238 ± 0.0000**	**0.8548 ± 0.0000**	**0.8505 ± 0.0000**

Bold indicates the best value and the next best value is shown in underline.

Table 4. Clustering results for the HW2sources dataset.

Methods	ACC	NMI	Purity	R	F
SC	0.6156 ± 0.0002	0.6356 ± 0.0003	0.6831 ± 0.0002	0.5193 ± 0.0002	0.5406 ± 0.0002
Co-regMSC	0.8284 ± 0.0057	0.8787 ± 0.0087	0.9152 ± 0.0097	0.7781 ± 0.0039	0.8233 ± 0.0064
MVGL	0.4326 ± 0.0059	0.4997 ± 0.0030	0.5395 ± 0.0055	0.3363 ± 0.0040	0.3737 ± 0.0037
AWP	0.7510 ± 0.0000	0.7752 ± 0.0000	0.8390 ± 0.0000	0.6575 ± 0.0000	0.7047 ± 0.0000
MCGC	0.6158 ± 0.0004	0.6359 ± 0.0006	0.6833 ± 0.0004	0.5197 ± 0.0005	0.5410 ± 0.0005
GMC	0.9940 ± 0.0000	0.9853 ± 0.0000	0.9940 ± 0.0000	0.9881 ± 0.0000	0.9880 ± 0.0000
SFMC	0.9765 ± 0.0000	0.9440 ± 0.0000	0.9765 ± 0.0000	0.9540 ± 0.0000	0.9537 ± 0.0000
TUDMPC	**0.9955 ± 0.0000**	**0.9897 ± 0.0000**	**0.9955 ± 0.0000**	**0.9911 ± 0.0000**	**0.9910 ± 0.0000**

Bold indicates the best value and the next best value is shown in underline.

Table 5. Clustering results for the NGs dataset.

Methods	ACC	NMI	Purity	R	F
SC	0.5260 ± 0.0000	0.2950 ± 0.0000	0.6040 ± 0.0000	0.3726 ± 0.0000	0.4130 ± 0.0000
Co-regMSC	0.9462 ± 0.0009	0.8458 ± 0.0027	0.9462 ± 0.0009	0.8939 ± 0.0017	0.8951 ± 0.0017
MVGL	0.9560 ± 0.0000	0.8779 ± 0.0000	0.9560 ± 0.0000	0.9119 ± 0.0000	0.9137 ± 0.0000
AWP	0.6980 ± 0.0000	0.7131 ± 0.0000	0.8940 ± 0.0000	0.6138 ± 0.0000	0.7009 ± 0.0000
MCGC	0.5340 ± 0.0000	0.5402 ± 0.0000	0.9320 ± 0.0000	0.3619 ± 0.0000	0.5131 ± 0.0000
GMC	**0.9820 ± 0.0000**	0.9392 ± 0.0000	**0.9820 ± 0.0000**	**0.9643 ± 0.0000**	**0.9643 ± 0.0000**
SFMC	0.2040 ± 0.0000	0.0160 ± 0.0000	0.2080 ± 0.0000	0.9802 ± 0.0000	0.3300 ± 0.0000
TUDMPC	**0.9820 ± 0.0000**	**0.9408 ± 0.0000**	**0.9820 ± 0.0000**	**0.9643 ± 0.0000**	0.9641 ± 0.0000

Bold indicates the best value and the next best value is shown in underline.

Table 6. Clustering results for the ORL dataset.

Methods	ACC	NMI	Purity	R	F
SC	0.5438 ± 0.0069	0.7533 ± 0.0023	0.5768 ± 0.0056	0.3783 ± 0.0067	0.3951 ± 0.0059
Co-regMSC	0.8462 ± 0.0124	0.9339 ± 0.0035	**0.8978 ± 0.0075**	0.7564 ± 0.0169	0.7953 ± 0.0130
MVGL	0.6769 ± 0.0000	0.8529 ± 0.0000	0.8563 ± 0.0000	0.1448 ± 0.0000	0.2442 ± 0.0000
AWP	0.7706 ± 0.0000	0.8936 ± 0.0000	0.8381 ± 0.0000	0.6339 ± 0.0000	0.6884 ± 0.0000
MCGC	0.6206 ± 0.0000	0.7659 ± 0.0000	0.8156 ± 0.0000	0.5760 ± 0.0000	0.1067 ± 0.0000
GMC	0.8375 ± 0.0000	0.9388 ± 0.0000	0.8675 ± 0.0000	0.8728 ± 0.0000	0.7692 ± 0.0000
SFMC	0.7500 ± 0.0000	0.9176 ± 0.0000	0.7925 ± 0.0000	0.8650 ± 0.0000	0.6565 ± 0.0000
TUDMPC	**0.8650 ± 0.0000**	**0.9516 ± 0.0000**	0.8900 ± 0.0000	**0.8956 ± 0.0000**	**0.8086 ± 0.0000**

Bold indicates the best value and the next best value is shown in underline.

Table 7. Clustering results for the 100leaves dataset.

Methods	ACC	NMI	Purity	R	F
SC	0.5417 ± 0.0075	0.7529 ± 0.0026	0.5782 ± 0.0050	0.3748 ± 0.0056	0.3939 ± 0.0049
Co-regMSC	<u>0.8474 ± 0.0087</u>	<u>0.9344 ± 0.0025</u>	<u>0.8992 ± 0.0059</u>	0.7599 ± 0.0101	<u>0.7978 ± 0.0077</u>
MVGL	0.6769 ± 0.0000	0.8529 ± 0.0000	0.8563 ± 0.0000	0.1448 ± 0.0000	0.2442 ± 0.0000
AWP	0.7706 ± 0.0000	0.8936 ± 0.0000	0.8381 ± 0.0000	0.6339 ± 0.0000	0.6884 ± 0.0000
MCGC	0.6206 ± 0.0000	0.7659 ± 0.0000	0.8156 ± 0.0000	0.0576 ± 0.0000	0.1067 ± 0.0000
GMC	0.8238 ± 0.0000	0.9292 ± 0.0000	0.8506 ± 0.0000	<u>0.8874 ± 0.0000</u>	0.5042 ± 0.0000
SFMC	0.7088 ± 0.0000	0.8633 ± 0.0000	0.7275 ± 0.0000	0.7682 ± 0.0000	0.3548 ± 0.0000
TUDMPC	**0.9325 ± 0.0000**	**0.9705 ± 0.0000**	**0.9431 ± 0.0000**	**0.9322 ± 0.0000**	**0.8690 ± 0.0000**

Bold indicates the best value and the next best value is shown in underline.

Table 8. Clustering results for the Hdigit dataset.

Methods	ACC	NMI	Purity	R	F
SC	0.6810 ± 0.0127	0.7183 ± 0.0055	0.7582 ± 0.0128	0.5917 ± 0.0104	0.6280 ± 0.0116
Co-regMSC	0.9921 ± 0.0000	0.9789 ± 0.0000	0.9921 ± 0.0000	0.9843 ± 0.0000	0.9844 ± 0.0000
MVGL	0.9965 ± 0.0000	0.9885 ± 0.0000	0.9965 ± 0.0000	0.9930 ± 0.0000	0.9930 ± 0.0000
AWP	0.7534 ± 0.0000	0.8052 ± 0.0000	0.8475 ± 0.0000	0.6817 ± 0.0000	0.7270 ± 0.0000
MCGC	0.1002 ± 0.0000	0.0018 ± 0.0000	**0.9991 ± 0.0000**	0.0999 ± 0.0000	0.1816 ± 0.0000
GMC	<u>0.9981 ± 0.0000</u>	<u>0.9939 ± 0.0000</u>	0.9981 ± 0.0000	<u>0.9962 ± 0.0000</u>	<u>0.9962 ± 0.0000</u>
SFMC	0.9924 ± 0.0000	0.9763 ± 0.0000	0.9924 ± 0.0000	0.9849 ± 0.0000	0.9849 ± 0.0000
TUDMPC	**0.9987 ± 0.0000**	**0.9957 ± 0.0000**	<u>0.9987 ± 0.0000</u>	**0.9974 ± 0.0000**	**0.9974 ± 0.0000**

Bold indicates the best value and the next best value is shown in underline.

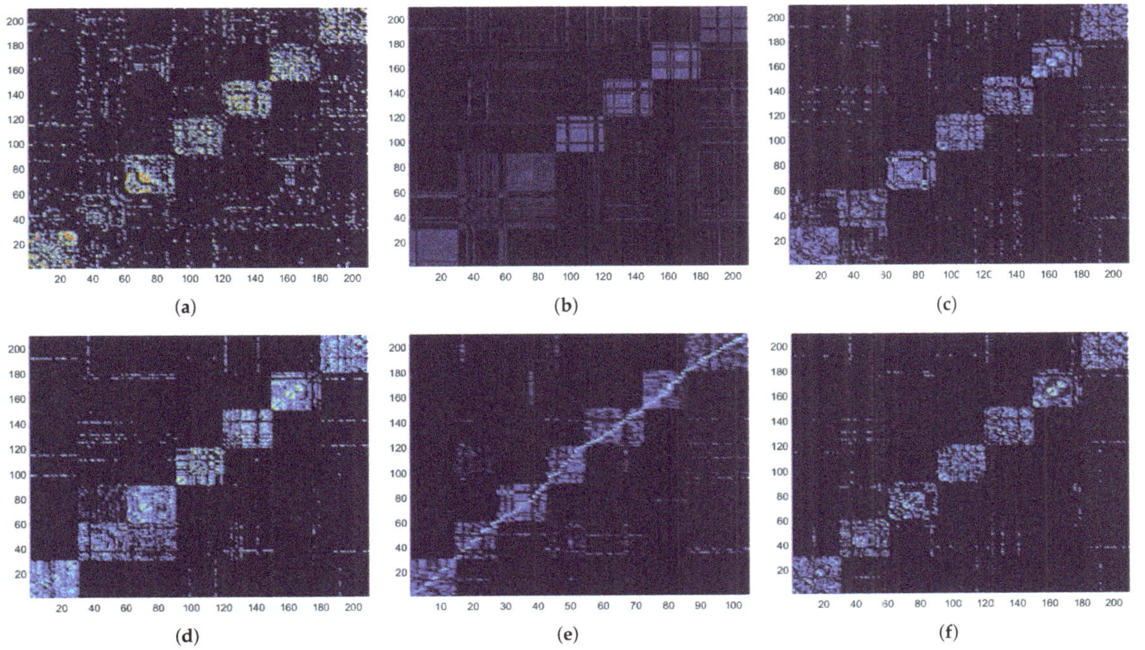

Figure 2. Visualization of the affinity matrices of the MSRC_v1 dataset. (**a**) SC. (**b**) MCGC. (**c**) MVGL. (**d**) GMC. (**e**) SFMC. (**f**) TUDMPC.

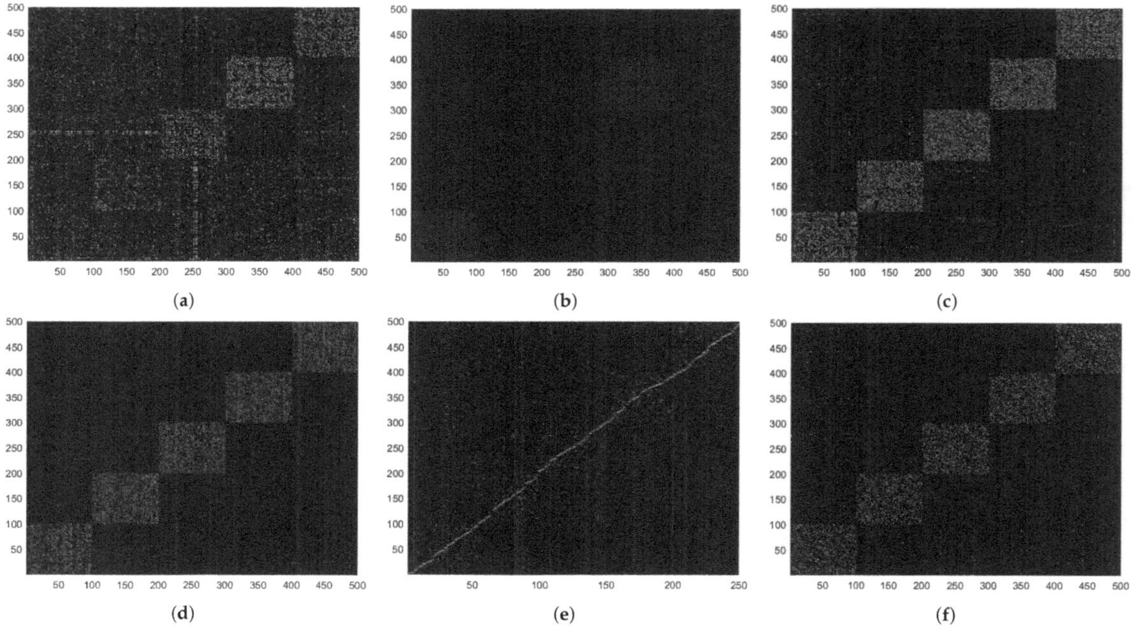

Figure 3. Visualization of the affinity matrices of the NGs dataset. (**a**) SC. (**b**) MCGC. (**c**) MVGL. (**d**) GMC. (**e**) SFMC. (**f**) TUDMPC.

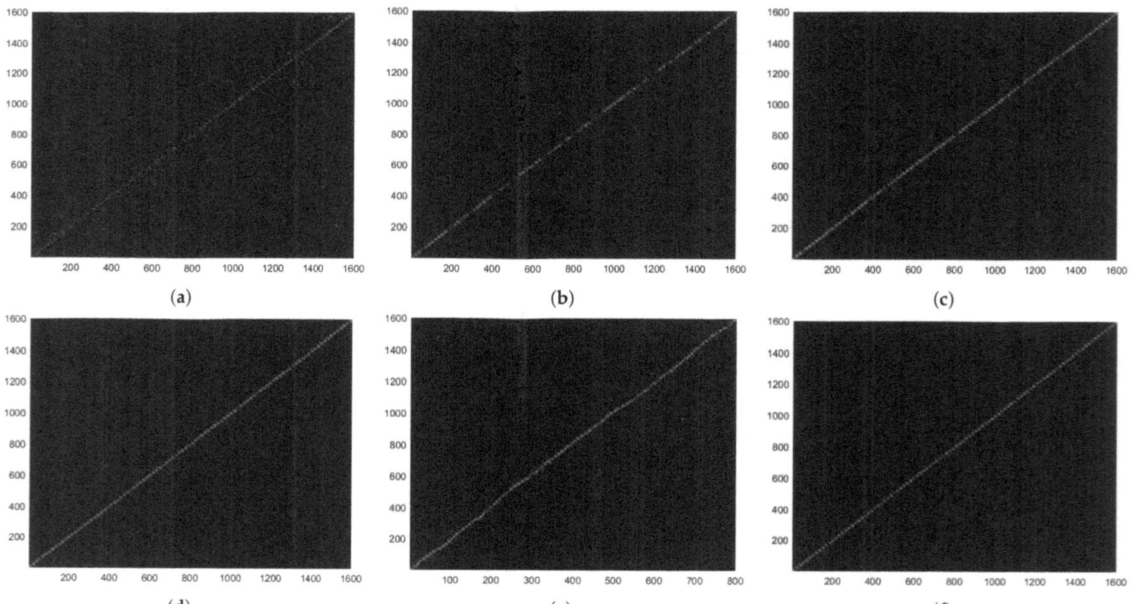

Figure 4. Visualization of the affinity matrices of the 100leaves dataset. (**a**) SC. (**b**) MCGC. (**c**) MVGL. (**d**) GMC. (**e**) SFMC. (**f**) TUDMPC.

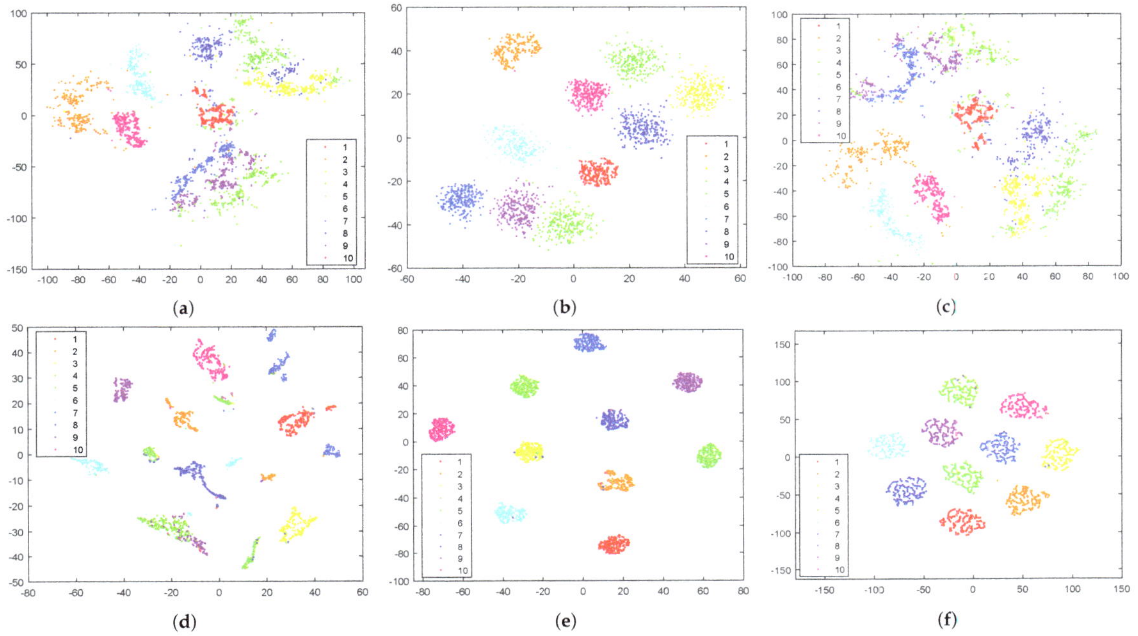

Figure 5. Visualization of the HW2sources dataset. (**a**) SC. (**b**) Co-regMSC. (**c**) AWP. (**d**) MCGC. (**e**) MVGL. (**f**) TUDMPC.

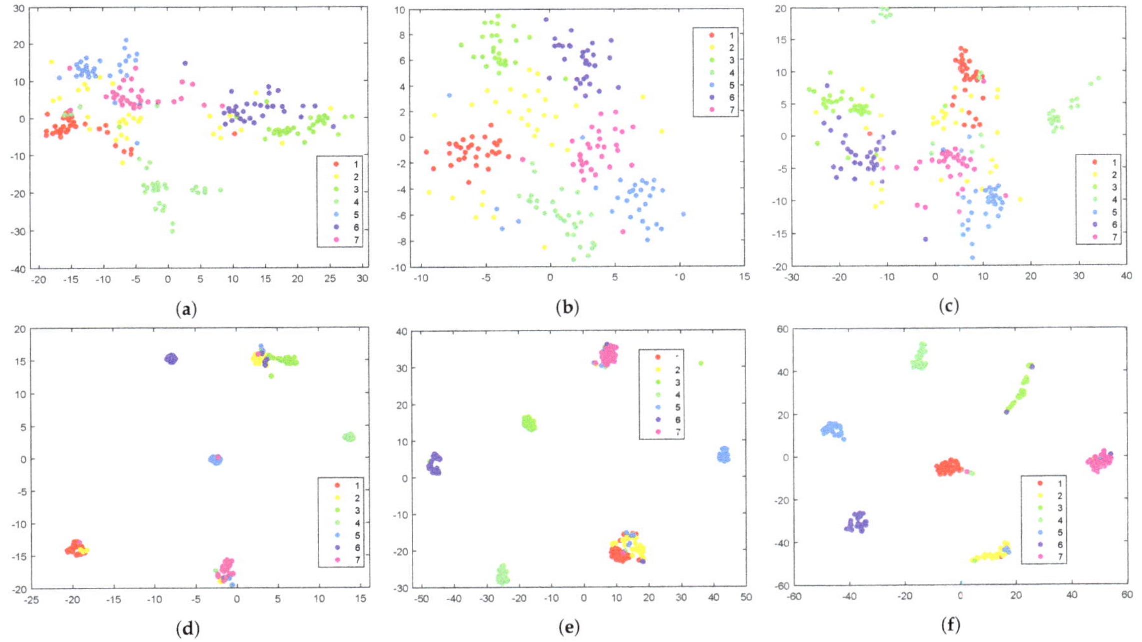

Figure 6. Visualization of the MSRC_v1 dataset. (**a**) SC. (**b**) Co-regMSC. (**c**) AWP. (**d**) MCGC. (**e**) MVGL. (**f**) TUDMPC.

5.3. More Applications

Section 5.2 demonstrated the clustering performance of TUDMPC using five metrics as compared with seven baseline methods using six real datasets. To prove the usefulness of TUDMPC, the clustering results of TUDMPC on two more real datasets are reported in this subsection. The ORL face image dataset, as used above, and the HW handwritten digital image dataset are used to verify the effectiveness of TUDMPC on real image data.

5.3.1. Datasets

The HW dataset contains handwritten digital images of the numbers 0 to 9, which are taken from a map of Dutch utilities available in the UCI Repository [50]. There are 200 samples for each digit for a total of 2000 handwritten patterns. In this work, the original image features are presented in six feature views, including 76-dimensional character shapes, 216-dimensional contour-dependent Fourier coefficients, 64-dimensional Karhunen-Love coefficients, 47-dimensional Zernike moments, 240-dimensional pixel averages in a 2×3 window, and 6-dimensional morphology features, i.e., feature dimensions for the six views are 76, 216, 64, 47, 240 and 6, respectively.

The ORL dataset is described in Section 5.1. Some of the actual images of the above two datasets are shown in Figures 7 and 8.

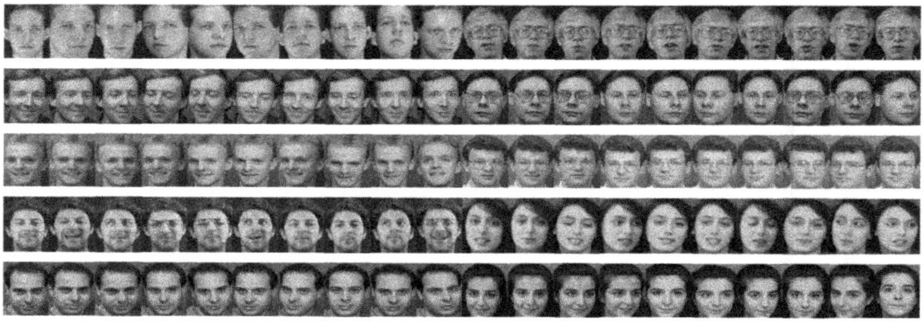

Figure 7. Some face images from the ORL dataset (10×10).

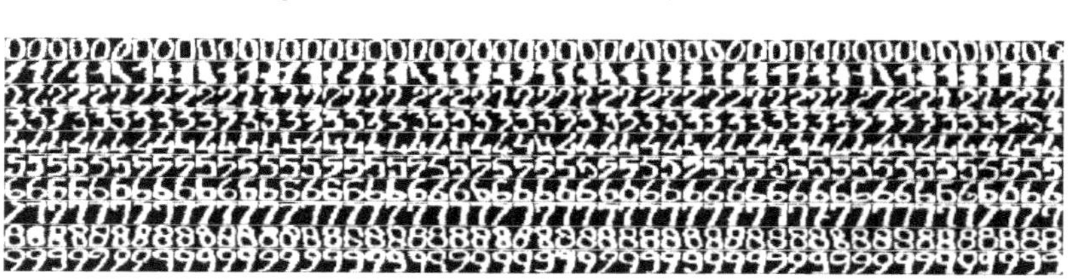

Figure 8. Some handwritten digital images from the HW dataset (10×50).

5.3.2. Analysis of the Application Results

The visual recognition results of TUDMPC for the first 100 face images of the ORL dataset are presented in Figure 9, where images in the same cluster are identified by the same color. As Figure 9 shows, TUDMPC misclassified only two groups of face images, i.e., images 12 and 20 of the first row and images 1, 4, 5, 7 and 9 of the fourth row, out of the 10 groups of face images presented, and classified the rest of the groups correctly. Thus, the face image recognition performance of TUDMPC is satisfactory.

The visual recognition results of TUDMPC for the 500 handwritten digital images from the HW dataset are presented in Figure 10, where the images in the same cluster are identified by the same color. From Figure 10, TUDMPC misclassified 28 out of the presented 500 handwritten digital images and classified the remaining 472 handwritten digital images correctly. Thus, TUDMPC has excellent performance in digital image recognition.

Figure 9. Some face image recognition results of TUDMPC on the ORL dataset (10 × 10).

Figure 10. Some handwritten digital image recognition results of TUDMPC on the HW dataset (10 × 50).

5.4. Ablation Experiments

The ablation experiments are used to verify the validity of the projection matrix and tensor. Specifically, the projection matrix $\mathbf{Z}^{(v)}$ is removed from the original model and obtained as TUDMPC1, and the tensor is removed from the original model and obtained method is designed as TUDMPC2. TUDMPC1 and TUDMPC2 are shown in (28) and (29) below:

$$\begin{aligned} &\min_{\mathbf{S}^{(v)},\mathbf{F}} \sum_{v=1}^{V}\sum_{i,j=1}^{n} \left\|\mathbf{x}_i^{(v)} - \mathbf{x}_j^{(v)}\right\|_2^2 s_{ij}^{(v)} + \|\boldsymbol{\mathcal{S}}\|_* + \gamma\left\|\mathbf{S}^{(v)}\right\|_F^2 + \beta\,\mathrm{tr}(\mathbf{F}^T\mathbf{L}_s\mathbf{F}) \\ &s.t.\ \ s_{ii}^{(v)} = 0,\ \mathbf{0}_n \le \mathbf{S}^{(v)} \le \mathbf{1}_n,\ \mathbf{S}^{(v)}\mathbf{1} = 1,\ \mathbf{F}^T\mathbf{F} = \mathbf{I} \end{aligned} \tag{28}$$

$$\begin{aligned} &\min_{\mathbf{S}^{(v)},\mathbf{Z}^{(v)},\mathbf{F}} \sum_{v=1}^{V}\sum_{i,j=1}^{n} \left\|(\mathbf{Z}^{(v)})^T\mathbf{x}_i^{(v)} - (\mathbf{Z}^{(v)})^T\mathbf{x}_j^{(v)}\right\|_2^2 s_{ij}^{(v)} + \alpha\left\|\mathbf{Z}^{(v)}\right\|_{2,1} + \gamma\left\|\mathbf{S}^{(v)}\right\|_F^2 + \beta\,\mathrm{tr}(\mathbf{F}^T\mathbf{L}_s\mathbf{F}) \\ &s.t.\ \ s_{ii}^{(v)} = 0,\ \mathbf{0}_n \le \mathbf{S}^{(v)} \le \mathbf{1}_n,\ \mathbf{S}^{(v)}\mathbf{1} = 1,\ (\mathbf{Z}^{(v)})^T\mathbf{X}^{(v)}(\mathbf{X}^{(v)})^T\mathbf{Z}^{(v)} = \mathbf{I},\ \mathbf{F}^T\mathbf{F} = \mathbf{I} \end{aligned} \tag{29}$$

The performances measured in ACC and NMI of the TUDMPC, TUDMPC1 and TUDMPC2 on the 100leaves dataset are given in Figure 11. From the figure, the projection learning and the tensor learning can be seen to facilitate MVC. Especially, projection learning can significantly enhance the clustering performance by capturing the structure of the data in a low-dimensional space free of noise and redundant data.

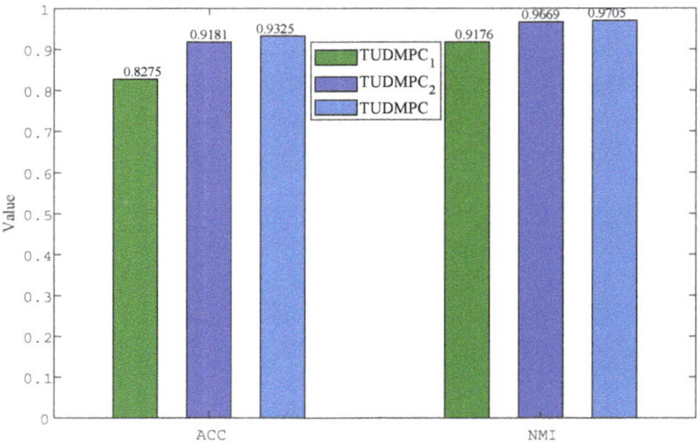

Figure 11. Results of the ablation experiments on the 100leaves dataset.

5.5. Convergence Analysis

To show the convergence more clearly and to verify the theoretical results, the convergences of TUDMPC on the MRSC_v1, HW2sources, ORL and 100leaves datasets are depicted in Figure 12. The objective function value gradually declines with the increase in the number of iterations and can stabilize after about 20 iterations. Therefore, TUDMPC has excellent convergence.

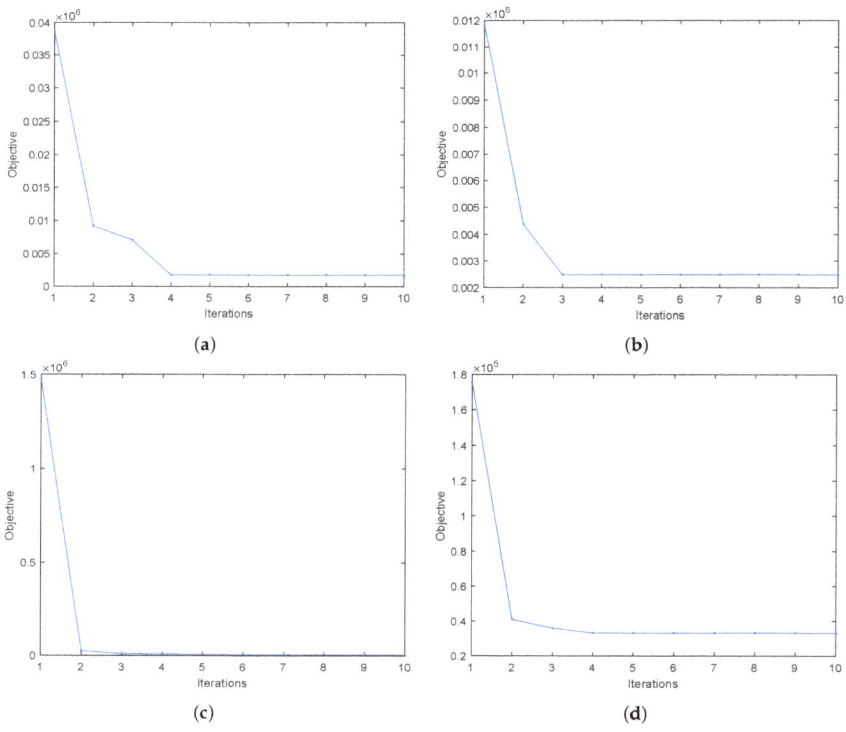

Figure 12. Convergence on some datasets. (**a**) MRSC_v1. (**b**) HW2source. (**c**) ORL. (**d**) 100leaves.

5.6. Sensitivity Analyses

The objective function (7) of the TUDMPC has three parameters, i.e., α, γ and m_v, that need to be determined. According to (23), the search for an optimal value of γ is transformed to the search for the optimal value of k. Therefore, the sensitivity of the clustering performance of TUDMPC when γ changes can be analyzed when k changes. The value of k is empirically chosen from the interval [5,30]. It is challenging for the clustering method to find the best values for α for all datasets because different datasets have distinct properties. Therefore, this study uses grid search to find the best values of the regularization parameter α from the set $\left\{10^{-2}, 10^{-1}, 1, 10, 10^{2}, 10^{3}, 10^{4}, 10^{5}\right\}$. Simultaneously, according to Sang et al. [22], the value of m_v is set according to (30) in the following,

$$m_v = \begin{cases} \frac{c}{2} - 1, & \text{if} d_v < n \\ c - 1 + d_v - n, & \text{otherwise} \end{cases}. \quad (30)$$

The obtained clustering results with different parameter values are shown in Figure 13 for the evaluation metric ACC. As shown in the figure, ACC is relatively stable as α and k change and is insensitive to the values of α and k on the ORL, NGs, and HW2sources datasets. On the MSRC_v1 and 100leaves datasets, clustering performance remains stable as the value of α changes and varies with the value of k, and as can be seen in Figure 13, the best clustering performance is achieved on the MSRC_v1 dataset when $k = 25$, and on the 100 datasets when $k = 15$, when the clustering performance is optimal.

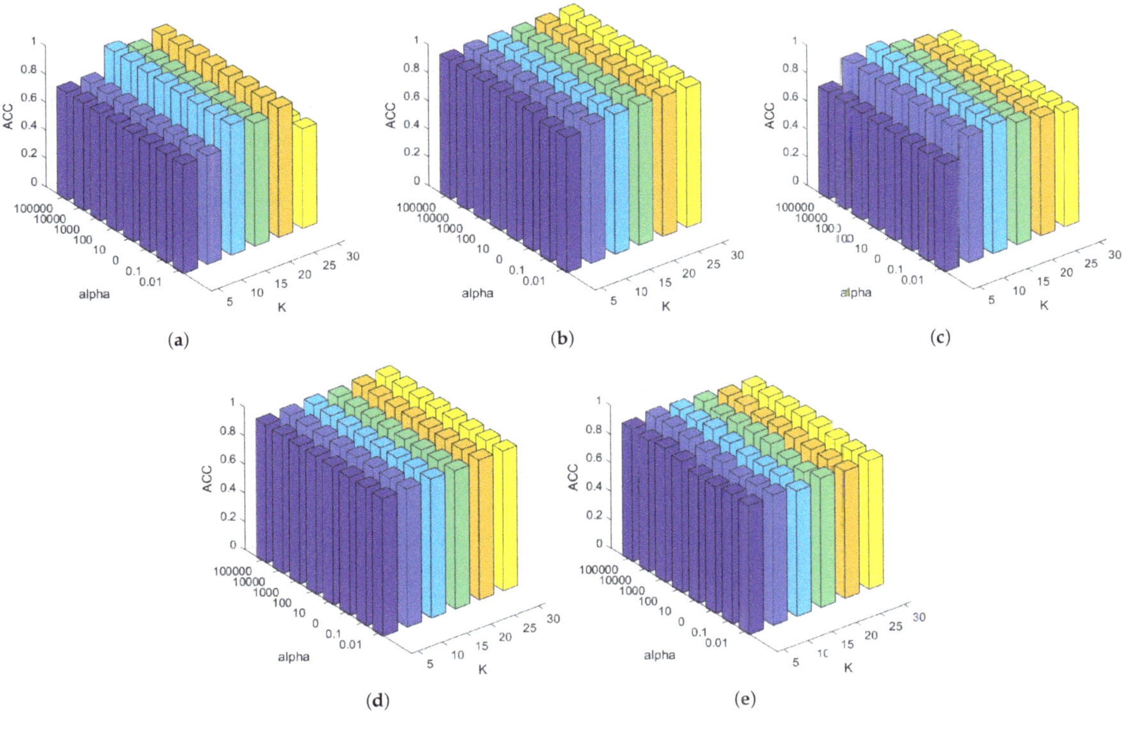

Figure 13. Sensitivity analysis on different datasets as parameters α and k change. (**a**) MSRC_v1. (**b**) HW2sources. (**c**) 100leaves. (**d**) NGs. (**e**) ORL.

5.7. Statistical Tests

The Friedman test is a non-parametric statistical test that is mainly used to determine if there are statistically significant differences among multiple related populations. In this section, the Friedman test is used to compare the clustering effects of the SC, Co-regMSC, MVGL, MCGC, AWP, GMC, SFMC and TUDMPC algorithms to determine if there are any significant differences among them to further demonstrate in more depth that TUDMPC outperforms these baseline methods. Statistical tests were carried out using the ACC, NMI and purity values. The Friedman test showed significant differences in the performance among these methods at a significance level of 0.05, and the results are reported in Table 9.

Table 9. Results of the Friedman test.

Metrics	χ^2	df	p-Value
ACC	24.97	7	0.0008
NMI	25.89	7	0.0005
Purity	18.92	7	0.0084

As the results in the table show, the p-values are all much smaller than the significance level of 0.05. Therefore, it is proved that there are significant differences in the performance among these clustering algorithms. The Nemenyi test is used to further determine the significant differences in the performance of each pair of algorithms. The test statistic CD is calculated using (31) as follows:

$$CD = q_a\sqrt{\frac{M(M+1)}{6N}}, \tag{31}$$

where q_a, N and M are the number of datasets, number of algorithms, and the threshold of the Tukey distribution, respectively. Since eight algorithms are used in this work, the conventional settings are $M = 8$, $N = 5$ and $q_a = 2.359$. Hence, $CD = 3.6545$ is obtained by using (31). Figure 14 illustrates the results of the Nemenyi test for the eight algorithms at a significance level of 0.05.

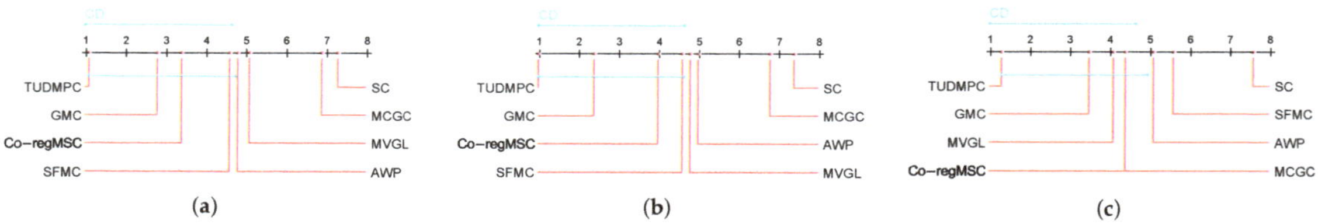

Figure 14. Results of the Nemenyi Test. (**a**) ACC. (**b**) NMI. (**c**) Purity.

From the results in Figure 14, the performance of TUDMPC is statistically different from those of SC, MVGL, MCGC and AWP in ACC and NMI, and statistically different from those of SC, SFMC and AWP in purity. The above statistical test results show that TUDMPC outperforms the baseline methods.

6. Conclusions

A novel tensor-based unified and discrete multi-view projection clustering method (TUDMPC) is proposed. This approach uses the projection matrix to extend the high-dimensional information and store the information in a low-dimensional space, thus reducing the time processing complexity. Additionally, TUDMPC uses feature selection to lessen the impact of noise and redundancy. More accurate affinity matrices can be learned adaptively in the low-dimensional space. Meanwhile, the tensor kernel norm is used to better exploit the complementarity and the high-order correlation of the views. In addition, the rank constraint is applied to keep the affinity matrices with a discrete cluster structure, and the clustering results are directly obtained in a unified framework. According to numerical experimental results, TUDMPC is more effective than the other cutting-edge methods.

However, as described in Section 5.6, TUDMPC is a little sensitive to the parameter settings. Subsequent studies will focus on parameter-free clustering approaches. Meanwhile, deep learning can further capture the underlying data structure of the original data. Therefore, in the future, deep learning will be introduced into TUDMPC for further research.

Author Contributions: Conceptualization, L.M.; methodology, L.M.; validation, X.L. and H.L.; formal analysis, H.L.; investigation, W.Z.; writing—original draft preparation, L.M.; writing—review and editing, L.M., X.L., M.S. and W.Z.; visualization, H.L.; supervision, W.Z. All authors have read and agreed to the published version of the manuscript.

Funding: This research received no external funding.

Data Availability Statement: Data are contained within the article.

Conflicts of Interest: The authors declare no conflicts of interest.

References

1. Jiang, T.; Gao, Q. Fast multiple graphs learning for multi-view clustering. *Neural Netw.* **2022**, *155*, 348–359. [CrossRef] [PubMed]
2. Si, X.; Yin, Q.; Zhao, X.; Yao, L. Consistent and diverse multi-View subspace clustering with structure constraint. *Pattern Recognit.* **2022**, *121*, 108196. [CrossRef]
3. Kumar, A.; Rai, P.; Daumé, H. Co-regularized multi-view spectral clustering. In Proceedings of the 24th International Conference on Neural Information Processing Systems, Granada, Spain, 12–14 December 2011; pp. 1413–1421.
4. Nie, F.; Li, J.; Li, X. Parameter-Free Auto-Weighted Multiple Graph Learning: A Framework for Multiview Clustering and Semi-Supervised Classification. *Int. Jt. Conf. Artif. Intell.* **2016**, *9*, 1881–1887.
5. Jing, P.; Su, Y.; Li, Z.; Nie, L. Learning robust affinity graph representation for multi-view clustering. *Inf. Sci.* **2021**, *544*, 155–167. [CrossRef]
6. Liao, S.; Gao, Q.; Yang, Z.; Chen, F.; Nie, F.; Han, J. Discriminant Analysis via Joint Euler Transform and $L_{2,1}$-norm. *IEEE Trans Image Process.* **2018**, *27*, 5668–5682. [CrossRef]
7. Xie, D.; Zhang, X.; Gao, Q.; Han, J.; Xiao, S.; Gao, X. Multiview Clustering by Joint Latent Representation and Similarity Learning. *IEEE Trans. Cybern.* **2020**, *50*, 4848–4854. [CrossRef]
8. Gao, Q.; Wan, Z.; Liang, Y.; Wang, Q.; Liu, Y.; Shao, L. Multi-view projected clustering with graph learning. *Neural Netw.* **2020**, *126*, 335–346. [CrossRef]
9. Yuan, H.; Li, J.; Liang, Y.; Tang, Y. Multi-view unsupervised feature selection with tensor low-rank minimization. *Neurocomputing* **2022**, *487*, 75–85. [CrossRef]
10. Fu, L.; Yang, J.; Chen, C.; Zhang, C. Low-rank tensor approximation with local structure for multi-view intrinsic subspace clustering. *Inf. Sci.* **2022**, *606*, 877–891. [CrossRef]
11. Ma, S.; Liu, Y.; Liu, G.; Zheng, Q.; Zhang, C. Orthogonal multi-view tensor-based learning for clustering. *Neurocomputing* **2022**, *500*, 592–603. [CrossRef]
12. Li, Z.; Tang, C.; Liu, X.; Zheng, X.; Zhang, W.; Zhu, E. Tensor-Based Multi-View Block-Diagonal Structure Diffusion for Clustering Incomplete Multi-View Data. In Proceedings of the 2021 IEEE International Conference on Multimedia and Expo (ICME), Shenzhen, China, 5–9 July 2021; pp. 1–6. [CrossRef]
13. Liu, Z.; Song, P. Deep low-rank tensor embedding for multi-view subspace clustering. *Expert Syst. Appl.* **2024**, *237*, 121518. [CrossRef]
14. Liu, Z.; Chen, Z.; Li, Y.; Zhao, L.; Yang, T.; Farahbakhsh, R.; Crespi, N.; Huang, X. IMC-NLT: Incomplete multi-view clustering by NMF and low-rank tensor. *Expert Syst. Appl.* **2023**, *221*, 119742. [CrossRef]
15. Wu, J.; Xie, X.; Nie, L.; Lin, Z.; Zha, H. Unified Graph and Low-Rank Tensor Learning for Multi-View Clustering. *Proc. AAAI Conf. Artif. Intell.* **2020**, *34*, 6388–6395. [CrossRef]
16. Dong, X.; Wu, D.; Nie, F.; Wang, R.; Li, X. Multi-view clustering with adaptive procrustes on Grassmann manifold. *Inf. Sci.* **2022**, *609*, 855–875. [CrossRef]

17. Yao, J.; Lin, R.; Lin, Z.; Wang, S. Multi-view clustering with graph regularized optimal transport. *Inf. Sci.* **2022**, *612*, 563–575. [CrossRef]
18. Ren, Z.; Li, X.; Mukherjee, M.; Huang, Y.; Sun, Q.; Huang, Z. Robust multi-view graph clustering in latent energy-preserving embedding space. *Inf. Sci.* **2021**, *569*, 582–595. [CrossRef]
19. Li, L.; He, H. Bipartite Graph based Multi-view Clustering. *IEEE Trans. Knowl. Data Eng.* **2020**, *34*, 3111–3125. [CrossRef]
20. Wang, H.; Yang, Y.; Liu, B. GMC: Graph-Based Multi-View Clustering. *IEEE Trans. Knowl. Data Eng.* **2020**, *32*, 1116–1129. [CrossRef]
21. Wei, X.; Sen, W.; Ming, Y.; Quan, X.; Jun, G.; Xin, B. Multi-view graph embedding clustering network: Joint self-supervision and block diagonal representation. *Neural Netw.* **2022**, *145*, 1–9. [CrossRef]
22. Sang, X.; Lu, J.; Lu, H. Consensus graph learning for auto-weighted multi-view projection clustering. *Inf. Sci.* **2022**, *609*, 816–837. [CrossRef]
23. Zhao, J.; Kang, F.; Zou, Q.; Wang, X. Multi-view clustering with orthogonal mapping and binary graph. *Expert Syst. Appl.* **2023**, *213*, 118911. [CrossRef]
24. Du, Y.; Lu, G.; Ji, G. Robust and optimal neighborhood graph learning for multi-view clustering. *Inf. Sci.* **2023**, *631*, 429–448. [CrossRef]
25. Nie, F.; Li, J.; Li, X. Self-weighted Multiview Clustering with Multiple Graphs. In Proceedings of the Twenty-Sixth International Joint Conference on Artificial Intelligence, Melbourne, Australia, 19–25 August 2017. [CrossRef]
26. Jiao, W.; Bin, W.; Zhen, W.; Hong, Y.; Yun, H. Multi-scale deep multi-view subspace clustering with self-weighting fusion and structure preserving. *Expert Syst. Appl.* **2023**, *213*, 119031. [CrossRef]
27. Huang, S.; Tsang, I.; Xu, Z.; Lv, J. Measuring Diversity in Graph Learning: A Unified Framework for Structured Multi-View Clustering. *IEEE Trans. Knowl. Data Eng.* **2022**, *34*, 5869–5883. [CrossRef]
28. Jun, C.; Zhao, K.; Bo, Y.; Lu, P.; Zeng, L. Multi-view subspace clustering via partition fusion. *Inf. Sci.* **2021**, *560*, 410–423. [CrossRef]
29. Jin, H.; Jian, Y. Robust subspace segmentation via low-rank representation. *IEEE Trans. Cybern.* **2014**, *44*, 1432–1445. [CrossRef]
30. Yang, B.; Wu, J.; Zhang, X.; Zheng, X.; Nie, F.; Chen, B. Discrete correntropy-based multi-view anchor-graph clustering. *Inf. Fusion* **2022**, *103*, 102097. [CrossRef]
31. Deng, P.; Li, T.; Wang, D.; Wang, H.; Peng, H.; Horng, S.-J. Multi-view clustering guided by unconstrained non-negative matrix factorization. *Knowl.-Based Syst.* **2023**, *266*, 110425. [CrossRef]
32. Liu, J.; Wang, C.; Gao, J.; Han, J. Multi-View Clustering via Joint Nonnegative Matrix Factorization. In Proceedings of the SIAM International Conference on DATA MININGs, Austin, TX, USA, 2–4 May 2013; pp. 252–260. [CrossRef]
33. Shi, S.; Nie, F.; Wang, R.; Li, X. Multi-View Clustering via Nonnegative and Orthogonal Graph Reconstruction. *IEEE Trans. Neural Netw. Learn. Syst.* **2023**, *34*, 201–214. [CrossRef]
34. Chen, Z.; Lin, P.; Chen, Z.; Ye, D.; Wang, S. Diversity embedding deep matrix factorization for multi-view clustering. *Inf. Sci.* **2022**, *610*, 114–125. [CrossRef]
35. Fu, L.; Li, J.; Chen, C. Consistent affinity representation learning with dual low-rank constraints for multi-view subspace clustering. *Neurocomputing* **2022**, *514*, 113–126. [CrossRef]
36. Wang, H.; Yang, Y.; Liu, B.; Hamido, F. A study of graph-based system for multi-view clustering. *Knowl.-Based Syst.* **2019**, *163*, 1009–1019. [CrossRef]
37. Wang, B.; Xiao, Y.; Li, Z.; Wang, X.; Chen, X.; Fang, D. Robust Self-Weighted Multi-View Projection Clustering. *Proc. AAAI Conf. Artif. Intell.* **2020**, *34*, 6110–6117. [CrossRef]
38. Misha, E.K.; Carla, D.M. Factorization strategies for third-order tensors. *Linear Algebra Its Appl.* **2011**, *435*, 641–658. [CrossRef]
39. Fan, K. On a theorem of weyl concerning eigenvalues of linear transformation. *Proc. Natl. Acad. Sci. USA* **1949**, *35*, 652–655. [CrossRef]
40. Jeribi, A. Spectral Graph Theory. In *Spectral Theory and Applications of Linear Operators and Block Operator Matrices*; Springer: Cham, Switzerland, 2015. [CrossRef]
41. Hu, W.; Tao, D.; Zhang, W.; Xie, Y.; Yang, Y. The Twist Tensor Nuclear Norm for Video Completion. *IEEE Trans. Neural Netw. Learn. Syst.* **2017**, *28*, 2961–2973. [CrossRef]
42. Ng, A.; Jordan, M.; Weiss, Y. On Spectral Clustering: Analysis and an algorithm. *Neural Inf. Process. Syst.* **2001**, *14*, 849–856.
43. Zhan, K.; Zhang, C.; Guan, J.; Wang, J. Graph Learning for Multiview Clustering. *IEEE Trans. Cybern.* **2018**, *48*, 2887–2895. [CrossRef]
44. Zhan, K.; Nie, F.; Wang, J.; Yang, Y. Multiview Consensus Graph Clustering. *IEEE Trans. Image Process.* **2019**, *28*, 1261–1270. [CrossRef]
45. Nie, F.; Tian, L.; Li, X. Multiview Clustering via Adaptively Weighted Procrustes. In Proceedings of the 24th ACM SIGKDD International Conference on Knowledge Discovery & Data Mining, London, UK, 19–23 August 2018. [CrossRef]
46. Li, X.; Zhang, H.; Wang, R.; Nie, F. Multiview Clustering: A Scalable and Parameter-Free Bipartite Graph Fusion Method. *IEEE Trans. Pattern Anal. Mach. Intell.* **2022**, *44*, 330–344. [CrossRef]

47. Winn, J.; Jojic, N. LOCUS: Learning object classes with unsupervised segmentation. In Proceedings of the Tenth IEEE International Conference on Computer Vision (ICCV'05), Washington, DC, USA, 17–21 October 2005; pp. 756–763. [CrossRef]
48. Chen, M.; Huang, L.; Wang, C.; Huang, D.; Lai, J. Relaxed multi-view clustering in latent embedding space. *Inf. Fusion* **2021**, *68*, 8–21. [CrossRef]
49. Maaten, L.; Hinton, G. Visualizing Data using t-SNE. *J. Mach. Learn. Res.* **2008**, *9*, 2579–2605.
50. Kelly, M.; Longjohn, R.; Nottingham, K. The UCI Machine Learning Repository. Available online: https://archive.ics.uci.edu (accessed on 15 November 2024).

Disclaimer/Publisher's Note: The statements, opinions and data contained in all publications are solely those of the individual author(s) and contributor(s) and not of MDPI and/or the editor(s). MDPI and/or the editor(s) disclaim responsibility for any injury to people or property resulting from any ideas, methods, instructions or products referred to in the content.

MDPI AG
Grosspeteranlage 5
4052 Basel
Switzerland
Tel.: +41 61 683 77 34

Electronics Editorial Office
E-mail: electronics@mdpi.com
www.mdpi.com/journal/electronics

Disclaimer/Publisher's Note: The title and front matter of this reprint are at the discretion of the Guest Editors. The publisher is not responsible for their content or any associated concerns. The statements, opinions and data contained in all individual articles are solely those of the individual Editors and contributors and not of MDPI. MDPI disclaims responsibility for any injury to people or property resulting from any ideas, methods, instructions or products referred to in the content.

www.ingramcontent.com/pod-product-compliance
Lightning Source LLC
Chambersburg PA
CBHW061508210926
51850CB00008B/1854
9783725868582